GREENBERG'S GUIDE TO LIONEL-FUNDIMENSIONS TRAINS: 1970-1985

By Roland LaVoie

With the assistance of **Glenn Halverson**

and **Berndt Bokelmann, Cliff Lang, Lou Caponi,**

Dan Johns, William Meyer, Donna Price,

Thomas Rollo, Glenn Salamone, Philip Smith,

Emil C. Vatter, Emil C. Vatter Jr.,

and **Charles Weber.**

D1453712

Photographs from the collections of Glenn and

Dave Halverson and **Auggie Conto.**

Photography by George Stern.

Copyright 1985

Greenberg Publishing Company
7543 Main Street
Sykesville, MD 21784
(301) 795-7447

First Edition

Manufactured in the United States of America

Greenberg Publishing Company offers the world's largest selection of Lionel, American Flyer and other toy train publications as well as a selection of books on model and prototype railroading. To receive our current catalogue, send a stamped, self-addressed envelope marked "catalogue".

Greenberg Publishing Company sponsors the world's largest public model railroad shows. The shows feature extravagant operating model railroads for N, H0, 0, Standard and 1 Gauges as well as a huge marketplace for buying and selling nearly all model railroad equipment. The shows feature, as well, a large selection of dollhouse miniatures.

Shows are currently offered in New York, Philadelphia, Pittsburgh, Baltimore, Washington, D.C., Williamsburg and Boston. To receive our current show listing, please send a self-addressed stamped envelope marked "Train Show Schedule".

Library of Congress Cataloging-in-Publication Data

La Voie, Roland, 1943-
    Greenberg's guide to Lionel-Fundimensions trains, 1970-1985.

    Includes index.
    1. Railroads--Models. 2. Lionel Corporation.
3. Fundimensions Corporation. I. Halverson, Glenn.
II. Greenberg Publishing Company. III. Title.
TF197.L22 1985   625.1'9   85-27165
ISBN 0-89778-022-1

TABLE OF CONTENTS

ACKNOWLEDGMENTS

The Greenberg Guide to Lionel-Fundimensions Trains is not just an updating of the old listings from the last combined edition; it is, quite literally, a completely new book. When we began this project over a year and a half ago, we had no idea of the hidden information about Fundimensions waiting to be discovered. What I viewed as the simplest of the three Lionel Trains Guides became the most complex of them all. That complexity came from the generosity of the toy train community as a whole — scholars, operators, collectors and dealers alike.

George Stern, our staff photographer spent two very long twelve hour days photographing the Halversons' collection. He has also printed some of the black and white photographs and assisted with a number of helpful suggestions. His skill, energy and "can do" approach were very important to this project. Francis Stem lent his beautiful 8061 engine for the cover.

Just as obviously, this book is a collaborative effort achieved by nearly a hundred people, if I count everyone who has given me a "hot tip" or who has corrected some wild-eyed misapprehension on my part. That collaboration is, in fact, what makes all of the Greenberg Guides the superior products they are. In effect, they are written by train enthusiasts for themselves!

From my vantage point, the many contributors to this book break down into several easily defined categories; many people crossed over from one area into another, but I have tried to place them into the areas where they have had the most influence. First of all, there are **friends and philosophers**, those people who keep the writer on the main line and help him avoid steaming relentlessly towards the "dead track". Foremost among these are my wife, **Jimmie**, and my son, **Tom**, the best "fan club" anyone could hope for. Their encouragement was crucial during those moments of agony when I was not sure I would ever reach the end of the job. In the toy train world, once again I drew from the inexhaustible philosophical resources of **Joe Gordon** and **Joe Bratspis** at the Toy Train Station in Feasterville, Pennsylvania. Their extensive stocks of trains meant more accurate descriptions, but it was the human contact and atmosphere of the place which enriched me. In particular, I owe thanks to the "Friday Night Irregulars" at the store — **Carl, Lew, Joe, Gray, Cal, Gary, Tom, Mitch, Jim, Fred, Joe & Kathy** and even the "Flyer Guys", **Frank** and **Terry**. Amid the wisecracks, I got some pretty good advice from these people.

A second category is the **researchers**, and here we were particularly fortunate. You will be hearing a great deal more from a young collector, **Glenn Halverson**, who became the primary researcher for this book. Glenn, a communications student at Michigan State University, reshaped the entire accessory section, unearthed a great deal of information about the Parker Brothers marketing efforts and uncatalogued sets, co-wrote other articles with me and supplied most of the trains used in the color separations in this book. Glenn's enthusiasm makes Pete Rose look catatonic! His willingness to track down unanswered questions, even to visiting the Fundimensions plant at Mount Clemens on several occasions, kept our psychic batteries charged. **Glenn** and **Dave Halverson** and **Auggie Conto** brought over 1,000 pieces of Fundimensions equipment

to our Sykesville Studio from upstate New York to photograph! **Jeff Wilson, Glenn Salamone** and a highly expert collector who has been of great service to us in the past, **Ron Niedhammer** supplied the remaining Fundimensions pieces to photograph. In addition, we owe a great debt to **Dan Johns**, the Director of Consumer Services for Fundimensions and **Fran Mauti**, the Customer Relations Director for Parker Brothers of Canada, for their great assistance to Glenn and to us.

But Glenn was not the only researcher assisting with this book. Two experienced collectors, **Cliff Lang** and **Chris Rohlfing**, checked their own collections, corrected hundreds of color descriptions and read the manuscripts for accuracy. These two assiduous workers eliminated untold mistakes, and the total accuracy of this volume speaks for their work. Just look at the number of references to "C. Lang and C. Rohlfing comments", and you will see the extent of their work.

Another category of assistance came to us through some splendid work done by our **article writers**. **Tom Rollo**, a Milwaukee collector and operator, wrote a perceptive, highly detailed article about the unusual Fundimensions 2156 Station Platform. **William Meyer**, whose work has graced the pages of our other Guides, has contributed a fine article on the 9090 Mini-Max boxcar and, along with **Pastor Phillip Smith**, another frequent contributor, has given us a guide to the new Fundimensions iron ore cars. **Berndt Bokelmann**, a collector from Rio de Janeiro, Brazil, wrote us a delightful letter about the thrill of finding a desirable Lionel train; this letter, which is virtually unedited, captures for all of us the joy of discovery so central to the enjoyment of the toy train hobby. **Emil Vatter** and **Emil Vatter, Jr.** gave us a much-needed survey of the Fundimensions Service Station Special sets. **Dr. Charles Weber** contributed a succinct letter explaining clearly why so many collectors are interested in the apparently arcane topic of boxcar variations. It is an important addition to the introduction to that chapter. Finally **Lou Caponi** of Nicholas Smith Trains in Broomall, Pennsylvania gave the author remarkable insights into the world of the toy train dealer. His comments will appear in the next edition of this book. **Glenn Salamone**, an authority on Fundimensions paper provided a virtually complete listing of Fundimensions catalogues and other paper. This report will also appear in the next edition of this book.

Once the information is gathered and assembled, it must pass the test of validation placed upon it by our **readers**, who subject it to the most exacting scrutiny. I must admit that they have saved me from many an egregious and stupid error! Of these people, **I. D. Smith** and **Phil Catalano** keep this writer on an even keel by reminding us what this hobby is all about. **Al Rudman** of Trackside Hobbies in Leonardtown, Maryland and **Lou Caponi** of Nicholas Smith Trains spent hours assisting the editors in checking numbers and production dates on Fundimensions equipment. Their expertise was indispensable to our study. We are also indebted to **Chris Rohlfing** and **Cliff Lang**, mentioned before, and **Al Passman, Stan Goodman, Richard Signurdson, Brad Smith, Peter Atonna, Mike Stella** and **Robert Greca** for performing this vital function. Not many errors can survive that kind of attention!

Other people made some remarkable individual contributions. **Tom Hawley** sent us an article which led us to change our Bettendorf truck designation to Symington-Wayne trucks, an important contribution if there ever was one. **Richard Vagner**, a faithful contributor to many volumes, straightened out a number of errors and misconceptions about the 9200, 9400 and 9700 boxcars. **R. DuBeau** sent us some fascinating pictures of the probable prototype for the Autolite boxcar. **Robert Raber** sent us a complete description of the very scarce Nibco uncatalogued set and Nibco boxcar. **Richard Shanfeld** cleared up a production mystery concerning the Wabash Fairbanks-Morse locomotive and gave us a description of the Toys 'R Us "Geoffrey" giraffe car. **Robert Maxwell Caplan** gave us a great wealth of information about his rare factory error and prototype boxcars. **Jerry LaVoie** (no relation to the editor) showed us a startling tuscan 9700 Southern boxcar previously unknown. Finally, **Fred Fisher** showed us the heretofore unseen Pep-O-Mint decal from the cancelled Pep-O-Mint tank car of 1980, providing us with a fascinating story revealed here for the first time.

Other collectors and operators sent us important contributions, too. We are grateful to the following people for sharing their information with us: **J. Aleshire, P. Ambrose, C. Anderson, D. Anderson, H. Azzinaro, W. Barnes, R. Bonney, J. Breslin, G. Cole, F. Cordone, J. Cusumano, C. Darasko and D. Dayle.**

Also: **R. Forst, R. Grandison, D. B. Griggs, R. Haffen, J. Harding, H. Kaim, R. Kaiser, G. Kline, L. Kositsky, T. Ladny, L. Lefebvre and R. Loveless.**

Also: **W. Meisel, D. Newman, A. Otten, G. Parsons, G. Rogers, W. Runft, F. Stem, W. Thomas, W. Triezenberg, J. Vega, G. Wilson and J. Zylstra.**

I certainly hope I haven't forgotten anyone, or that I haven't somehow misrepresented a name. If I have done so, the responsibility is mine, and I hope readers will write to me and let me know any corrections for the next edition. In addition, we know that this book is a great start, but it is not the whole Fundimensions story. There are more uncatalogued sets, examples of paper and new variations out there, and we hope you will be as generous to us with your knowledge as you have been in the past. In particular, we welcome any new collectors/operators to our endeavors. Write to us with any questions or observations you may have, and we will try our best to answer you as quickly as possible.

At the Greenberg office, tremendous work was done in preparing this volume for publication. **Donna Price** and **Brenda Patterson** compiled a complete list of Fundimensions catalogued sets for this book. **Cindy Floyd** with the assistance of **Brenda Patterson** organized the work flow for this very large project among the editorial, typesetting and paste-up staff. Cindy's managing of a project of this magnitude was crucial to its successful completion. **Donna Price**, our copy editor and artist in residence, wears many indispensable hats. Not only does she read and reread copy, but she organizes the text and photographs or illustrations for presentation on each page. Her concern with visual presentation and making sure that information is easy to understand are most appreciated by us all.

Finally, let me express my gratitude to **Bruce and Linda Greenberg** for their encouragement, assistance and, above all, tolerance. Who but the most tolerant of people would put up with a mad combination of English teacher, trained proofreader and Lionel train freak? I hope the results of this book justify their faith in me.

As I close this book, I have two thoughts. First, I often wonder what makes me do all these strange things with trains: chasing at meets after that elusive tank car, crawling under a layout to wire an accessory to a bus bar and shuffling index cards full of variations for a book. More than anything else, for me these trains represent America and Americans at their best — committing themselves to quality manufacturing and scholarship in a time when expediency rather than excellence is too often the rule of life.

Secondly, I am struck with an overwhelming awareness that this job will never truly be finished. The words were said best for me by an eminent historian, Barbara W. Tuchman, in her introduction to her magnificent work, **The Proud Tower**: "I realize that what follows offers no over-all conclusion. . .I also know that what follows is far from the whole picture. It is not false modesty which prompts me to say so but simply an acute awareness of what I have not included. The faces and voices of all that I have left out crowd around me as I reach the end."

Roland E. LaVoie
Cherry Hill, New Jersey
October 1985

INTRODUCTION

Greenberg's Price Guide for Lionel-Fundimension Trains, 1970-1985, is our most comprehensive report on the Fundimension toy train marketplace. The contents of this book were previously published combined with material concerned with 1945-1969 Lionel trains. Its separate publication reflects the substantial increase in our information about Lionel-Fundimension trains and the growing collector interest in this area. This edition records a very uneven pattern of price changes. At the present time, however, in the fall of 1985, prices are stable.

PURPOSE

The purpose of this book is to provide a comprehensive listing with current prices for Lionel Fundimension locomotives, rolling stock and accessories, in 0 and 0-27 Gauges, produced from 1970 through 1985. We include those variations which have been authenticated. In a few cases we ask our readers for further information where information is missing or doubtful. Values are reported for each item where there have been reported sales.

DETERMINING VALUES

Toy train values vary for a number of reasons. First, consider the **relative knowledge** of the buyer and seller. A seller may be unaware that he has a rare variation and sell it for the price of a common piece. Another source of price variation is **short-term fluctuation** which depends on what is being offered at a given train meet on a given day. If four 773s are for sale at a small meet, we would expect that supply would outpace demand and lead to a reduction in price. A related source of variation is the **season** of the year. The train market is slower in the summer and sellers may at this time be more inclined to reduce prices if they really want to move an item. Another important source of price variation is the relative strength of the seller's **desire to sell** and the buyer's **eagerness to buy**. Clearly a seller in economic distress will be more eager to strike a bargain. A final source of variation is the **personalities** of the seller and buyer. Some sellers like to quickly turn over items and, therefore, price their items to move; others seek a higher price and will bring an item to meet after meet until they find a willing buyer.

Train values in this book are based on OBTAINED prices, rather than asking prices, along the East Coast during the summer of 1985. We have chosen East Coast prices since the greatest dollar volume in transactions appears there. The prices reported here represent a "ready sale", or a price perceived as a good value by the buyer. They may sometimes appear lower than those seen on trains at meets for two reasons. First, items that sell often sell in the first hour of a train meet and, therefore, are no longer visible. (We have observed that a good portion of the action at most meets occurs in the first hour.) The items that do not sell in the first hour have a higher price tag and this price, although not representing the sales price, is the price observed. A related source of discrepancy is the willingness of some sellers to bargain over price.

Another factor which may affect prices is reconditioning done by the dealer. Some dealers take great pains to clean and service their pieces so that they look their best and operate properly. Others sell the items just as they have received them, dust and all. Naturally, the more effort the dealer expends in preparing his pieces for sale, the more he can expect to charge for them. This factor may account for significant price differences among dealers selling the same equipment.

From our studies of train prices, it appears that mail order prices for used trains are generally higher than those obtained at eastern train meets. This is appropriate considering the costs and efforts of producing and distributing a price list and packing and shipping items. Mail order items do sell at prices above those listed in this book. A final source of difference between observed prices and reported prices is region. Prices are clearly higher in the South and West where trains are less plentiful than along the East Coast.

CONDITION

For each item, we provide four categories: **Good, Very Good, Excellent and Mint.** The Train Collectors Association (TCA) defines conditions as:

GOOD - Scratches, small dents, dirty

VERY GOOD - Few scratches, exceptionally clean, no dents or rust.

EXCELLENT - Minute scratches or nicks, no dents or rust

MINT - Brand new, absolutely unmarred, all original and unused, in original box.

In the toy train field there is a great deal of concern with exterior appearance and less concern with operation. If operation is important to you, then ask the seller whether the train runs. If the seller indicates that he does not know whether the equipment operates, you should test it. Most train meets have test tracks provided for that purpose.

We include MINT in this edition because of the important trade in post-1970 mint items. However there is substantial confusion in the minds of both sellers and buyers as to what constitutes "mint" condition. How do we define mint? Among very experienced train enthusiasts, a mint piece means that it is brand new, in its original box, never run, and extremely bright and clean (and the box is, too). An item may have been removed from the box and replaced in it but it should show no evidence of handling. A piece is not mint if it shows any scratches, fingerprints or evidence of discoloration. It is the nature of a market for the seller to see his item in a very positive light and to seek to obtain a mint price for an excellent piece. In contrast, a buyer will see the same item in a less favorable light and will attempt to buy a mint piece for the price of one in excellent condition. It is our responsibility to point out this difference in perspective **and** the difference in value implicit in each perspective, and to then let the buyer and seller settle or negotiate their different perspectives.

We do not show values for Fair or Restored. **Fair** items are valued substantially below Good. We have not included **Restored** because such items are not a significant portion of the market for postwar trains.

As we indicated, prices in this book were derived from large train meets or shows. If you have trains to sell and you sell them to a person planning to resell them, you will not obtain the prices reported in this book. Rather, you should expect to achieve about fifty percent of these prices. Basically, for your items to be of interest to a buyer who plans to resell them, he must purchase them for considerably less than the prices listed here.

We receive many inquiries as to whether or not a particular piece is a "good value". This book will help answer that question; but, there is NO substitute for experience in the marketplace. WE STRONGLY RECOMMEND THAT NOVICES DO NOT MAKE MAJOR PURCHASES WITHOUT THE ASSISTANCE OF FRIENDS WHO HAVE EXPERIENCE IN BUYING AND SELLING TRAINS. If you are buying a train and do not know whom to ask about its value, look for the people running the meet or show and discuss with them your need for assistance. Usually they can refer you to an experienced collector who will be willing to examine the piece and offer his opinion.

COLLECTING FUNDIMENSIONS TOY TRAINS: A PRIMER FOR BEGINNERS

Welcome to one of the most challenging, historically enriching and rewarding hobbies on the face of this earth — collecting toy trains! If you are just rekindling an old childhood acquaintance with the playthings of your youth, or if you are discovering this activity for the first time, you are engaging yourself in an activity of great pleasure. The hours you spend perusing locomotives, boxcars and cabooses will enhance your appreciation of a worldwide occupation — some would go so far as to say that you are involved with the finest examples of machine art known to man.

It is also fair to say that you are also becoming involved with a hobby which is beset by misinformation, confusion and bewilderment. Right from the start you will be faced with some extremely important choices: how much can you spend? What kind of trains should you collect? Will you want to collect them, operate them or both? Where can these trains be found? How do you know you have gotten the best train value for your dollar?

If you happen to overhear conversations among experienced train collectors at a dealer's table in a train show or at your local hobby shop, your confusion may daunt you to the point where you will question your own wisdom. You may hear comments like these:

..."Six hundred eighty-five dollars for that Union Pacific Overland Limited set? Those Fundimensions guys can't be serious!"

..."Did you see that orange-mold 9737 on the shelf? I'd get it before somebody else does. It's the Type IX body, too."

..."He's got a lot of nerve trying to sell that 6464-525 as mint. I saw track marks on the wheels."

..."That Fundimensions stuff is a bunch of junk. All they're trying to do is rip off collectors. The colors are wrong and the workmanship is cheap compared to postwar."

..."What do you mean, cheap? The current stuff runs just fine. You can't be serious; the postwar production had its fair share of junk, too. Just look at that space and missile stuff!"

Confused? One could scarcely be blamed for failure to understand the puzzling technical vocabulary of the modern toy train collector; today's collectors speak a highly specific language which must be mastered by anyone hoping to understand the hobby. For the beginning collector, the question becomes one of sorting out the confusion and avoiding costly mistakes in selecting these trains. That is the purpose of this article.

I must say that the conclusions presented in this article are my own, since other collectors and operators of toy trains may differ in opinion, as with any other hobby. However, I believe that the information presented here represents a broadly held consensus about starting within the train collecting hobby. As you develop experience, you will arrive at your own conclusions, if only for the reason that tastes differ among collectors.

WHY FUNDIMENSIONS TRAINS?

People collect toy trains for many different reasons. They may wish to recapture memories of a childhood when they played with these toys, thereby "escaping" to a much more simple, uncluttered world for a while. Some people view toy trains as an art form and collect them for the aesthetic value alone. Others, like scale modelers, want to operate these toys by creating a complex toy train layout which represents a world in miniature controlled completely by the operator. Still others collect toy trains as good long-term investments for their spare money. Finally, whatever the personal reasons for collecting toy trains, all collectors enjoy the hobby as a social activity and a chance to make new friends.

The toy train collector has a tremendous variety of trains at hand. He can choose prewar (1901-1942) Lionel, postwar (1945-1969) Lionel, American Flyer, Ives, Marklin or any of a great variety of brand names. So why collect **Fundimensions** trains, the Lionel trains made beginning in 1970 to the current day? Despite the appeal of other eras and types of toy trains, there are four significant advantages for the beginner in choosing the most recent of the Lionel trains, those made under license by the Fundimensions subsidiary of General Mills.

192 Control Tower.

The first of these advantages is **Availability**. In order for toy trains to be collected, they must be readily available to the collector. Since the number of Fundimensions collectors is much smaller than the number of postwar Lionel collectors, Fundimensions products tend to be plentiful and relatively inexpensive. To gain experience in the hobby it is important that the beginning collector make his first purchases over a wide range of rolling stock, locomotives and accessories. Fundimensions trains offer that opportunity. Additionally, even the scarcest of these trains will show up in the toy train marketplace because many scarce pieces remain "undiscovered" by the rank and file of collectors. You may, for example, search for years before you find an original postwar 192 Control Tower in excellent condition, but the Fundimensions re-issue of this accessory, the 2318 Control Tower, is still available at a reasonable price, brand new in its box. Yet **fewer** Fundimensions pieces were made than the original postwar version!

9826 P&LE Boxcar.

The second advantage to Fundimensions toy trains is their tremendous **Diversity**. In addition to reissuing its versions of all the old collector favorites of the postwar years, Fundimensions has manufactured many new products of its own which have no parallel. A good example of this is the new Bunk Car series, an issue of modified refrigerator car bodies modeled after the cars used for temporary living quarters for track gangs on the real railroads. Not only are there new types of rolling stock, but also extensive uses of older models far beyond anything postwar Lionel ever issued. There were only two cars made by postwar Lionel from its refrigerator car body, but Fundimensions has made close to 80 from the same body in its 9800 Refrigerator Car series. In addition, the colors and graphics used by Fundimensions go well beyond anything used in the postwar era. Within the selection of Fundimensions rolling stock, there is something for nearly every taste and interest.

A third advantage has to do with **Operations**. Despite some exceptions, Fundimensions trains are well made, and they are compatible with postwar trains in every respect. To be sure, some operators feel that the bronze gears of the postwar motors are superior to the nylon gears Fundimensions uses, but it can also be argued that the nylon gears are easier to replace and considerably quieter. Fundimensions has made excellent use of modern technology to improve the operation of its trains. From the beginning, the company has equipped its rolling stock with "fast-angle" wheels and low-friction trucks which enable its locomotives to haul many more cars at lower voltage. (This editor's 8157 Santa Fe Fairbanks-Morse twin-motored locomotive absolutely ran away with a 48-car train at a recent Greenberg public train show!) Electronic innovations such as the great "Sound Of Steam", new steam whistles and diesel horns sound a great deal better than their predecessors. Fundimensions has introduced a fully electronic reversing switch and a new can-type motor which never needs lubrication and runs on AC or DC current. Finally, you would not be concerned with running "antiques" into the ground if you were running Fundimensions equipment. This discussion is not meant to belittle postwar equipment, because the fine workmanship of the classic Lionel trains of the 1950s cannot be duplicated today except at ruinous cost. My point is that Fundimensions equipment works very well and is appropriate for today's train world.

The final consideration for selecting Fundimensions toy trains involves **Condition** and **Price**. You would have to hunt for a long time to find postwar equipment in mint (never-run) condition in its original box, and when you do find it, expect to empty your wallet rapidly. On the other hand, mint Fundimensions equipment, even the older stock from the early 1970s, remains readily available. In the long run, condition is the most important determinant of a train's value. It is possible to buy many unused cars at real bargains, and even the most

common Fundimensions pieces will always be more desirable in excellent or mint condition. For example, it is still possible to buy 9700 Series boxcars, even those made ten years ago, brand new in their boxes for about $12 apiece — a real bargain in today's train world. Note that such equipment represents top-of-the-line Lionel. Even some cars with the outstanding die-cast Standard 0 Trucks can be bought for $15 or so. The trucks alone cost $10 per pair! There are still great values in Fundimensions pieces, for those who look for them. In addition, many pieces were made in very small quantities but are still priced very low; these are known as "sleepers", and they inevitably will attract attention some day. One example is the 8464-65 Rio Grande F-3 AA pair of Diesels. These were made for a Service Station Special set, and only about 3,000 of them exist. Yet they were not popular, and they still can be bought new for an extremely reasonable price for such a fine engine. Other examples include the early Fundimensions accessories made between 1970 and 1972. Recently I was able to buy a 2494 Rotating Beacon, brand new in its box, at a bargain price; the value of this piece should climb once collectors sense how scarce it is. Few collectors are even aware of the existence of the 2125 Whistle Shack made only in 1971, but it is "out there" for those who look. The piece can be bought for as little as $20, but it is extremely hard to find.

2125 Whistle Shack.

WHERE CAN FUNDIMENSIONS TRAINS BE FOUND?

With the foregoing factors in mind, one must proceed to the next logical step: **where** can these trains be found? Actually, there are four major sources for Fundimensions trains, each with specific advantages and disadvantages.

The first source, though not nearly as productive as it once was, is **garage sales, flea markets** and **private sales**. Ten years ago or so, it was possible to place an ad in the local paper soliciting old toy trains and many such trains would emerge at low prices. Since the toy train hobby has experienced explosive growth in the last few years, people have suddenly assumed that "trains are valuable", even when they are not. Once in a while, you may run into a train set priced at a real bargain. However, even when such a set is available, it will seldom be a Fundimensions set. Note that this source requires that you know what is valuable and what is not to a greater degree than most other sources.

A much better source for Fundimensions trains is **public** and **private train meets** and **shows**. These shows feature a huge variety of trains at highly competitive prices, since most of the major train dealers and many smaller train merchants rent tables at such shows to sell their stock. These shows often feature elaborate operating layouts and test tracks for your equipment and frequently they are a Mecca for the train collecting fraternity. Along the East Coast, the Greenberg Great Train, Dollhouse and Toy Shows are the largest public train shows in the United States. These shows are held in

Philadelphia, Long Island, Boston, Hartford, Pittsburgh, Baltimore, Washington, Rochester and Williamsburg, with the Philadelphia show being the largest. In Midwestern and Western cities, the Great American Train Shows operate in a similar fashion. Many smaller public shows are held in all regions of the country. The largest train show in the world, however, is a private one for members only — the twice-yearly meet sponsored by the Train Collectors' Association in York, Pa. This show is so big that six halls of the York County Fairgrounds are needed to house all the dealers and collectors with trains to sell! The Lionel Collectors' Club of America, the Toy Train Operating Society and the Lionel Operating Train Society hold smaller members-only shows on a regular basis. The only real risk of buying trains at these shows is your relative ignorance of the dealer's reputation. In the case of rarities, frauds and faked pieces turn up — although the people running these shows police them very thoroughly on the whole.

A third source for Fundimensions trains — indeed, a highly competitive one — is **mail order firms.** The larger dealers in the country advertise their wares in magazines such as **Model Railroader** and **Railroad Model Craftsman.** Most of these firms have their own set of policies and offer good service. However, purchasing trains by mail order poses real risks for the collector. Many times, you are asked to purchase trains "sight unseen" — always a risk. Some firms do not give refunds when an item is out of stock; instead, they give a voucher slip good for future purchases. In the case of limited edition trains, this happens all too often. Defective merchandise must be mailed back — always an expense and a hassle. Still, the lure of low price is hard to resist and the best of these firms give reliable, fast service. Read the terms of shipping before you order and you should be able to stay out of trouble. Train club members offer their sale or trade items in many club bulletins — another mail order source.

If you are fortunate enough to have one near you, a great source of trains would be a **good local hobby shop.** Despite the fact that the owner of a hobby shop may have to charge a slightly higher price for his trains to pay for his overhead (but not always), there are significant advantages to purchasing Fundimensions trains at such a shop. For one thing, the shopowner's reputation rests upon his expertise and his sense of fair pricing. He will be able to answer questions, supply parts and give you the benefits of his long experience with these trains. This editor is deeply indebted to a real gentleman, Frank D'Olonzo, who ran a small hobby shop until his retirement and taught me the basics of Lionel train collecting and operating during those first crucial years of my involvement with the hobby. Most of these shops also offer good repair services for your trains as well. Perhaps most importantly, every shop has a crowd of "regulars" who swap information, jokes and expertise. The camaraderie of this group of people can be a compelling reason for frequent visits to a good shop. This editor is a proud "regular" Friday nights at the Toy Train Station in Feasterville, Pennsylvania. Many times, one of the "regulars" will teach newcomers operating and collecting tips and, thanks to the friendly atmosphere of the shop, everyone enjoys a pleasant evening with a great hobby.

Whatever the source, there is always the possibility of the unexpected — and that is what can make this hobby so much fun. Not very long ago, I was idly looking at a number of inexpensive train sets for sale. Something in one of the sets caught my eye. The particular set was an inexpensive beginner's set made in the early 1950s; it had a small steam

locomotive, tender, gondola, boxcar and caboose. The locomotive didn't seem quite right to me for some reason; at the time, I wasn't sure why. However, the set was in excellent shape, so I bought it for $50. Later on, I discovered that the locomotive was the very scarce die-cast 1130, a locomotive which was supposed to be plastic but was issued in a few sets as die-cast because Lionel had some leftover 2034 boiler castings! The locomotive is worth much more than I paid for the whole set.

WHAT TRAINS SHOULD THE BEGINNING COLLECTOR ACQUIRE?

Now that you know where the trains can be found, what kind of trains should you look for once you get there? The answer to this question is necessarily personal, since tastes and preferences differ among train collectors so much. In addition, there are philosophical and financial considerations which deserve a detailed look at this point.

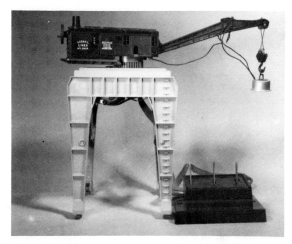

282 Gantry Crane.

First of all, are you buying these trains to collect them, to operate them or both? The toy train enthusiast who is a collector does not, as a rule, care about the way the trains run; he is only concerned with condition and future appreciation in value. He is content to let the train sit on a shelf and look attractive. At times, such an attitude can lead to situations which are difficult for some Lionel enthusiasts to understand. In his excellent biography of Joshua Lionel Cowen, **All Aboard!,** Ron Hollander tells the story of one collector who had a postwar 282 Gantry Crane new in a factory sealed box. Rather than open the box, he had X-Ray pictures taken to prove that there was really a crane inside, and he displayed these pictures when he put the crane up for sale! In this way, he added to the value of the crane considerably, and in fact the crane was sold several times without ever emerging from its box!

On the other hand, many train collectors (this editor included) believe that Lionel trains should be used for their original purpose regardless of sacrifices in value. For such people, it makes no sense to have a beautiful Norfolk and Western streamlined steam locomotive unless one can see it run, hear its whistle and watch it smoke and chug down the tracks. Therefore, such collectors care about whether the whistle or horn works and how the train tends to run. For them, much of the fun of collecting the trains is to build layouts and watch them in action. Some collectors have a stock of trains which they collect and a group of trains which they run

— even to the point that they have a mint duplicate of the train they run! Note that there is no right or wrong to this issue — only one's preference.

Another consideration you might ponder is your personal sense of aesthetics; that is, what looks good to you and what you like. There are so many varieties of trains available that one type of locomotive or rolling stock is bound to appeal to you more than other types. For example, Fundimensions has recently released three rather high-priced but attractive Berkshire steam locomotives modeled after the 726 and 736 locomotives made famous in the postwar era. These big 2-8-4 wheeled steamers command a great deal of attention, but the three are rather different in character. One is a two-tone gray Union Pacific locomotive with smoke deflectors. Another is a Chessie Steam Special locomotive done in bright yellow, orange and vermilion trim. The third is a traditional black Nickel Plate Road locomotive with gold lettering. I know people who think that the Chessie Berkshire is the most beautiful locomotive ever made by Lionel; I believe it to be over-decorated because my taste in steamers runs to traditional decorating schemes. I prefer the black Nickel Plate locomotive. Who can say what is "right"? In 1977 Fundimensions released the Mickey Mouse set featuring colorful Disney graphics on hi-cube boxcars. Some collectors go crazy over this set, but I believe it to be cheap-looking. The obvious answer is to collect what appeals to you regardless of its price, rarity or current value.

There are two ways to decide what appeals to you, and both of them have to do with exposure to all the choices. Again, a well-stocked hobby shop or a big train show can expose you to a wide variety of trains. With accessories, experienced operators can show you how each accessory works; in many big train shows, some layout operators give demonstrations for this purpose. Since the shows are periodic and a hobby shop is not always convenient, there is a second way to find out what you like. Secure as many of the Lionel Fundimensions catalogues as you can from 1970 to date and look through them. These catalogues are relatively common and inexpensive, so it won't take you long to build up a good collection. Both methods will help you decide whether you should become a boxcar collector, a Diesel locomotive enthusiast, an accessory operator or anything else. Most collectors eventually specialize in preferred areas.

INVESTING IN FUNDIMENSIONS TRAINS

It is quite possible that the idea of "quick money" has crossed the mind of many a collector. Fundimensions trains are, after all, collectibles, and if one buys and sells at the right time, one can make a great deal of money — in theory. Unfortunately, that theory seldom becomes fact! The investment value of Fundimensions trains lies in their long-term appreciation rather than in quick turnover. That is the way postwar trains have worked, and there is no reason to believe that Fundimensions trains will work any differently despite some frantic manipulation of the toy train marketplace in recent years. If you have any really serious money to invest, it should be placed into certificates of deposit rather than into trains.

This is not to say that Fundimensions trains are not worth the investment — quite the contrary. Very few toys retain their value and appreciate better than do toy trains. (It is, after all, wise to remember that you are collecting something designed as a **toy**.) You will never lose the investment value you place

into these trains. People who do not know the hobby tend to scoff at those who "play with toy trains" until they learn about the serious dollar investment made by collectors. There's an added advantage, too — these toys **do** something; they don't have to sit on a shelf and look pretty, as do Hummel figurines. Toy trains are as fine a collectible as anything else; if people can collect comic books and beer cans, you need never apologize for investing your money into a hobby you enjoy.

One of the critical factors for investing in these trains is condition, which determines the value more than any other factor. A piece which has never run on rails will always be more valuable monetarily than a piece which has been used. Each collector will have to decide for himself whether to operate his shiny new locomotive. For many, the pleasure of seeing these trains run as they were intended to do outweighs any loss in value. Whatever your views, it is wise to take care of your trains so that they will retain their mint or excellent condition.

Investing in Fundimensions trains has been complicated in recent years by a strange marketplace which manipulates supply and demand perhaps more than it should. Fundimensions has made a practice of making some items in very limited quantities. Sometimes a dealer will "sit" on these items until the demand gets so acute that he can charge a higher price for them — perfectly legal, but frustrating for collectors of such pieces. The only defense against such practices is to establish a good account with a major dealer and reserve your preferred items before they are actually produced. This is especially true of the higher-priced limited edition items.

Another factor to consider for investment is how much discretionary money you actually can invest. Most collectors do not own private oil wells; in fact, the majority of train collectors are middle-income people in their late thirties or early forties. Not too long ago, a gentleman came into the hobby shop I patronize and spent over four thousand dollars on trains in a single evening! It takes me four or five **years** to spend that much! My collection reminds me of what Daniel Webster once said about Rhode Island: "Sir, it may be a very small thing indeed, but there are those who love it." Even if your discretionary funds are limited, you can still find good investment values on a smaller scale. Patience and research are good answers for your investment problems.

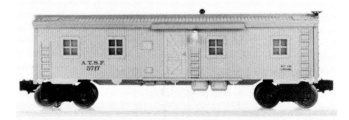

5717 Santa Fe Bunk Car.

Actually, for the collector on a budget, it makes a great deal of sense to seek the best **percentage** of return, not the best dollar figure. To understand that idea, it is best to observe a low-priced and a high-priced example. In 1981 the Chicago and Alton passenger set could be purchased new for about $300. The same set is now bringing nearly $400. That's a dollar appreciation of $100 and a percentage appreciation of 30 percent or so — not bad! Now consider the 5717 Santa Fe Bunk Car. When this car came out in 1983, it could be bought initially for $18. It now commands a price of at least $40

10

because far fewer of them were made than had been anticipated. That's only a gain of $22 in dollar appreciation, but it's a whopping 130 percent gain on the initial investment! The trick with the bunk car was to get it when it first came out. Now you should be able to see the importance of researching the toy train marketplace!

9090 Mini-Max Railcar.

Especially in the case of Fundimensions trains, the best investments are made with "sleepers" which have not been discovered by collectors — yet! Remember that a "sleeper" by definition is a piece which was made in limited quantities (either deliberately or because of a low audience for the product) but has not yet stimulated collector interest. The early years of Fundimensions production are replete with such "sleepers"; I have already mentioned several of them. The best bets for "sleepers" are in the years 1970-75, when the toy train market had not experienced its recent rapid growth and Fundimensions was struggling to rebuild interest in its products. The early small steamers, the early Hudson locomotives, certain accessories and a few pieces of rolling stock like the odd 9090 General Mills "Mini-Max" boxcar fit the category of "sleepers". Many are astonishingly low-priced and show unusual potential for appreciation. Learn what they are, seek them out and secure them before too many people read this article!

STRATEGIES FOR COLLECTION AND OPERATION

There are a few other specific strategies which should be stressed for a beginning collector/operator of Fundimensions trains. While they are not meant to be a comprehensive guide to all the cautions and tactics to use, they will be of immense help to the beginner because they are based upon the common experiences of most collectors. Bear in mind that your particular situation may necessitate adjustments as appropriate.

1. RESEARCH AND READ! There is no substitute for knowledge in the toy train field. Aside from personal experience, the best way to become familiar with the hobby is to read the accounts of those who have gone before you. Fortunately, some great toy train literature is readily available. At the end of this introduction, you will find an annotated bibliography of some of the most popular books about toy train collection and operation. Make use of it!

2. SPECIALIZE! Aside from the type of toy trains which most interests you, there are significant differences in the **way** to collect these trains. It is both wasteful and inefficient to merely "collect everything" within a toy train area, unless your knowledge is so broad that you are able to do so. Most collectors, especially beginners, are **type** collectors. These people will try to acquire one representative sample of

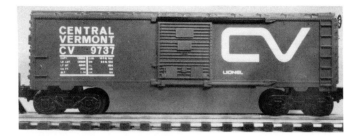

9737 Central Vermont Boxcar.

everything put out by Fundimensions; they will possess one Hudson steamer, one Berkshire, one GP-9 Diesel, etc. Another method used by type collectors is the acquisition of one example of each item in a series. For instance, I have tried to get one of each boxcar from the 9700 Series. Other collectors are **variation** collectors. They will make a study of all the variations of a piece which have come from the factory; then they will look for these variations. They are sometimes derisively called "rivet-counters", but they are smart because a small variation may make a great difference in value. For these collectors, the discovery of a new and previously unreported variation is a big thrill. Such a collector may, for example, show you a dozen 9200 Illinois Central boxcars which all look identical to the untrained eye. Each boxcar will be different, depending on the type of trucks, the shade of painting, the color of the plastic mold used for the body and door or some other factor. Still other collectors specialize in **factory errors**. These are production samples which have emerged from the factory with a defect of some kind or an omission from the usual variety. Of course, such examples can be very rare and desirable. For example, the 6905 Nickel Plate Road extended vision caboose has a gray strip with the script lettering "Nickel Plate High Speed Service". In some examples, this script is omitted from the gray stripe altogether; in others, it is either partially omitted or wrong. The erroneous examples are all factory errors and, of course, are far more scarce than the correct version. Whatever type of collector you become, it is important that you choose an area and try to specialize within it because you will be able to acquire a reasonably complete collection within the area. You are also setting a goal for yourself; therefore, you will be able to concentrate your financial and intellectual resources so that you can spend your money wisely.

3. AT THE OUTSET, BUILD A QUANTITY FIRST: THEN CONCENTRATE UPON QUALITY. Try to acquire a large number of relatively inexpensive pieces at first so that you can learn the toy train marketplace. After you have some experience with this stage, you can buy fewer pieces of higher quality with confidence. The reasons for this are based upon common sense. If you are going to make mistakes, they will most likely occur during the beginning months of your collection of these trains. Novices are much more likely to spend too much money for a piece at first because they do not fully understand the true value of the piece. It is painful to spend $450 for the Erie Lackawanna Limited set when, with further experience, you could have bought the same set for $350 elsewhere by "shopping around". It is a great deal less painful to spend only $5.00 too much for a collector series boxcar in plentiful supply. Stay with the lower end of the market until you are familiar with the financial workings of the toy train marketplace. It may be some consolation to learn that even veteran collectors get "stung" from time to time! When

in doubt about a purchase, always ask an experienced collector. Most people will be happy to assist you — that's one of the unexpected pleasures of this hobby. And don't forget that it really pays to shop around. In a recent mail order ad, a 9700 Southern boxcar is advertised "new" for $75. The same car is available from most sources for about $12 to $15!

4. KEEP AN INVENTORY. This is more than a matter of common sense; it's also a matter of prudence. Most homeowners' or renters' insurance policies do not cover special collections such as toy trains unless you specify a "fine arts rider" which can cover your collection for a small premium. It is important to check the provisions of your policy. In the event of loss due to fire or theft, an inventory, updated periodically, is absolutely essential to establish the replacement value of your collection. In addition, there are several special policies sponsored by the major train collecting organizations which are well worth their modest cost. The format of your inventory is up to you, of course.

A good inventory will describe the number, road name and variation of the piece, the year of purchase, its purchase price, its book price and its condition. Update your inventory at periodic intervals. If you have a home computer, this task is made much easier; in fact, "spread-sheet" programs are available for just this purpose. The keeping of an inventory will help you avoid duplication as your collection grows. You can't always trust your memory! A good friend of mine recently went train shopping with me. We ran into a brown 6059 Minneapolis and Saint Louis caboose, a fairly common postwar piece which was also made in bright red. Because of my inventory, I knew that I had the red version, but not the brown one. My friend could not remember which one he had. Take your inventory with you whenever you shop for trains.

5. STORE YOUR COLLECTION CAREFULLY! In order for your collection to retain its value, it must be kept away from any environment which would harm it, especially extremes of heat, cold and humidity. Find a place in your home which is clean and dry. Closed metal or wooden cabinets or chests are excellent storage places for your trains. You can secure anti-moisture material for these chests as further protection. Open shelving is also acceptable. If your trains are displayed on shelves with track, dust them as often as practical. If you operate your trains, make sure that the locomotives get periodic servicing. Beyond any question, the best storage containers for these trains are their original boxes. There are two reasons for this. The first reason is that the boxes were made specifically for the trains' protection. The second is that a piece will be more valuable if the original box is present. I try to secure empty original Lionel boxes whenever I can. When I buy a piece without the box, I then have a box which I can use for its storage. If the original box is battered, by all means use another box for storage, but **never** throw out the original box no matter how beaten up it may be! One word of caution is needed with the locomotive boxes used by Fundimensions. These boxes use foam plastic inserts. In some cases, the paint on a locomotive may be marred by these inserts. It is wise to place the locomotive in a plastic bag before placing it into the liner. However, make sure you use bags from teflon, polyethylene or polypropyline, not PVC or polystyrene ones. These can stick to paint over a long period of time!

6. DON'T RUSH YOUR PURCHASING DECISIONS! One of the most exasperating things about this hobby is the emotional response one makes when a new line of trains is introduced. It's only human to want everything in a new catalogue — but one of the worst mistakes one can make is to throw caution to the winds and go on a sudden spending spree. Even worse, when a collector finds a piece which he has sought for a long time, he is tempted to get it even if it is abysmally overpriced. This is one hobby where patience is a virtue! Especially with Fundimensions trains, don't rush your purchases! Nearly all of Fundimensions' production is reasonably available **somewhere!** As an example, one collector sought high and low for a 9209 Burlington Northern boxcar with two metal door guides, one of three such variations of that particular car. He passed one car up about a year ago because it was overpriced by about $8.00, feeling that he might find it at a better price later. That was a wise decision, because in a local hobby shop **two** of them suddenly turned up! Do not try to collect everything at once. Take your time, seek the advice of experienced collectors and hold out for a fair price. There **are** exceptions to this rule, especially with some expensive limited production items. However, for the majority of Fundimensions trains, it pays to be patient. In time, the piece you want will cross your path at a reasonable price — however hard that may be to believe at times!

7. DON'T GET GREEDY! What looks like a super "find" may not be so super at all! Face it — all of us have a little larceny in our hearts. When we find an item which seems spectacularly underpriced, there is usually a good reason for it. I have been the victim of mild greed myself on a few occasions, fortunately without getting "stung". Once, I found a 9869 Santa Fe refrigerator car in a shop. This car only came in a Service Station Set in 1976 and is seldom seen. Naturally, I snapped up the car at its low price of $12. Only later did I learn that the car originally came with the premium Standard 0 die-cast sprung trucks. My car had normal plastic trucks because someone had switched them! Since I will have to spend another $10 for the correct trucks, I will end up paying the true value of the car. On another occasion, I bought a royal blue 9135 Norfolk and Western hopper car at a show. I had read somewhere about such a car being made as a special car for Glen Uhl, a noted dealer. Since the Glen Uhl Special is worth about $125, I figured that I had stolen the car for $15. No such luck! The Glen Uhl Special was identical to the car I had bought — except that it was numbered 6446-25, not 9135! I got a good, relatively scarce car for my money, but my education was quite a come-down! I was able to avoid really costly errors, but you may not be able to do so because some unscrupulous collectors are selling out-and-out frauds at high prices. For example, if someone offers to sell you a gold 9447 Pullman Standard boxcar (the regular issue is silver), don't touch it; the car's color has been changed by a chemical process! Such oddities and rarities are dangerous ground for all but the most experienced collectors. Train collector organizations are making good efforts to police their ranks; several people have been prosecuted. However, only the most naive think that the train hobby is totally honest. **Most** of the dealers and collectors **are** honest people, to be sure, but there is always the possibility of being "taken". When in doubt, ask! Do not be so quick to surrender to your own possessiveness!

8. INVOLVE THE WHOLE FAMILY IF POSSIBLE. One of the real joys of this hobby is its potential for bringing families together. Layouts can be planned and built together, and purchasing decisions can be made **en famille**. Such cooperation avoids the strain of financing the trains, since people may have differing ideas about what money is discretionary within a family. Joe and Kathy Coffey, a married couple living in the

Philadelphia area, began to collect trains together a few years ago. They exhibit a large layout in the Greenberg show in Philadelphia; Joe designs the trackwork and operations, while Kathy specializes in Plasticville houses and makes the scenic decisions. They have obviously prospered from their shared interest and so can you. It wasn't too long ago that the world of toy trains was a rather exclusive male preserve. That's changing rapidly as Fundimensions is making a real effort to create train schemes which are aesthetically attractive to women as well as men. It will not be long before many women emerge as experienced collectors of toy trains. Another reason for involving the family is that the children of today can become the collectors of tomorrow. Toy trains have a special appeal for the young, even in this day of advanced electronics and video games. No matter how clever a video game may be, your youngster is still using someone else's creativity, not his own. When a youngster builds a train layout, it is his (or her) world from scratch. The practical knowledge of craftsmanship, electricity and mechanics can be priceless to a child. If your child sees you buying trains and asks why you bought a particular piece, you have a terrific opportunity to teach your child how to make wise purchasing decisions. The educational value of toy trains is excellent.

The foregoing discussion of the toy train world is not meant to be the last word on the subject. However, many of the basic tenets of the hobby have been discussed. For further reading, several books should be perused and studied. Therefore, I close this discussion with a listing of some of the books available to you, with the hope that you will read further and enjoy this hobby as much as I have.

FOR FURTHER READING: AN ANNOTATED BIBLIOGRAPHY

Godel, Howard. **Antique Toy Trains**. Hicksville, NY: Exposition Press, 1976. 215 pp., bibliography, photos.

This book has been out of print for a while now and that's a pity, because it is an extremely well-written and comprehensive survey of the toy train world since its beginning around the turn of the century. While Godel does not discuss Fundimensions trains directly, his descriptions of the toy train market and his assessment of the hobby are excellent for the beginner. You will be fascinated by the incredible variety of trains made as toys over the years. Check your local library or ask to borrow a friend's copy; this book is worth anyone's time.

Greenberg, Bruce C. **Greenberg's Guide to Lionel Trains, 1945-1969**. Sykesville, MD: Greenberg Publishing Company, 1984. 216pp., photos, index.

This comprehensive guide to postwar production, similar in format and content to this volume, is recognized as the standard of the toy train hobby for its description of variations and current prices. Its value to the Fundimensions collector lies in its description of the predecessors of Fundimensions trains, many of which have been modeled upon postwar production. Many excellent scholarly articles can be found in this book as well. The color plates are a great help in identifying particular pieces.

Greenberg, Bruce C. **Greenberg's Repair and Operating Manual for Lionel Trains**. Sykesville, MD: Greenberg Publishing Company, 1981. 736 pp., layout and equipment diagrams, table of contents numerically arranged.

If you are an operator of Fundimensions or postwar trains, this book is absolutely indispensable. Repair costs are high, and this book can save you money by showing you how to repair locomotives, accessories and rolling stock yourself. Most of this book's pages are carefully culled from the original Lionel Service Manuals, which were justly famous for their clarity and completeness. All parts are named and listed by number in each of the exploded diagrams. In addition, the book has a number of challenging and creative layout diagrams from Lionel catalogues of the past. This should be the first book purchased by operators; it will pay for itself many times over.

Greenberg, Bruce C. **Model Railroading: A Family Guide**. Englewood Cliffs, NJ: Prentice-Hall, Inc., 1979. 167 pp., photos, diagrams, index, glossary, supply source listings.

Very limited supply available now; a revised and expanded version may be available in 1986. In clear, simple language, the book explains the basics of the tinplate hobby for those just beginning with it. Some highlights of the book include a terrific discussion of the toy train marketplace and a great chapter on cab control wiring. Layout construction is covered in great detail, including scenery tips which can be extremely helpful. Repair techniques take several chapters and feature step-by-step instructions for the basic maintenance every train operator must master. Either in its original form or its revision, I cannot think of a better overall guide for the beginning tinplater. Many of my first layouts were based upon concepts found in this book; I recommend it very highly.

Hollander, Ron. **All Aboard! The Story of Joshua Lionel Cowen & His Lionel Train Company**. New York: Workman Publishing Company, 1981. 253 pp., photos, index.

This is the definitive biography of the founder of Lionel Trains, Joshua Lionel Cowen, a prototypical American entrepreneur if there ever was one. In a highly entertaining style, Hollander tells of the early years of the Lionel Manufacturing Company through the glory years until the final demise of the company in the 1960s. Hollander's achievement is that he has made this story a real slice of American history; his grasp of "the time and the place" is positively astonishing. Lavishly illustrated and enthusiastically written, this book is an absolute joy to read. (Sample sentence: "There was no way to control the speed of the gondola. Like Cowen himself, the "Electric Express" only operated at full speed.") Hollander has given the book a marvelous personal touch out of his own childhood experiences, too. This book is thoroughly entertaining, highly enjoyable and strongly recommended.

McComas, Tom and Tuohy, James. **Lionel: A Collector's Guide and History, Volume IV: 1970-1980**. Wilmette, IL: TM Productions, 1980. 136 pp., photos, inventory list.

This book is valuable for its story of the takeover of Lionel Trains from the original Lionel Corporation by General Mills in 1969. In addition, it is a sensible discussion of the kinds of trains Fundimensions issued in its first ten years. The production is compared with its postwar predecessors and assessed for relative scarcity. The photo sections are very good, with the archives section in particular quite fascinating. This is one of six volumes in a very valuable set. The other titles: Volume I: prewar O Gauge; Volume II: postwar O Gauge; Volume III: Standard Gauge; Volume V: The Archives and Volume VI: Advertising and Art. These volumes form a comprehensive study of the Lionel production from nearly the beginning.

On The Right Track: The History of Lionel Trains. Mount Clemens, MI: Fundimensions Division of General Mills Fun Group, Inc., 1975, Part No. 2961. 49 pp., photos.

This little book was published as part of Lionel's 75th Anniversary celebration; it is sometimes inaccurate or incomplete, but it offers a point of view worth consideration, and some of the photos in the book do not show up anywhere else. It is a collectible in its own right, of course, since it is factory production in the same way as the catalogues. As an example of an "in-house" publication, it is an interesting document worth securing for your paper collection.

Shantar, Stan. **Greenberg's Operating and Repair Manual, Lionel-Fundimensions Trains, 1970-1978.** Sykesville, MD: Greenberg Publishing Company, 1978. 124 pp., photos, diagrams, table of contents.

Although this book gives some useful repair tips and operating suggestions for Fundimensions trains, one of its most valuable features is its year-by-year catalogue discussion of Fundimensions production. Shantar assesses the significance of each year's production extremely well, and his discussions of the company's intentions are right on target. He also gives consumer reactions to the products; this information is valuable to the collector in estimating products which are desirable for a collection. There is also a good discussion of cab control wiring.

Smith, Philip K. and Shantar, Stan. **Greenberg's Enjoying Lionel Fundimensions Trains.** Sykesville, MD: Greenberg Publishing Company, 1982. 98 pp., layout diagrams, photos.

This book is a continuation of Stan Shantar's initial Fundimensions repair and operating manual. Philip Smith expertly assesses the significance of the newer products, giving practical instructions for their care and maintenance. He also mentions the possible uses of DC power for Fundimensions trains of the future. Especially noteworthy are Smith's maintenance tips based upon personal experience with the real products, not just a schematic diagram in a repair manual. The book is eminently readable and worth adding to your library.

THE NEW LIONEL TRAIN
By Berndt Bokelmann

EDITOR'S NOTE: The author of this article lives in Rio de Janeiro, Brazil, where one might expect Lionel trains to be hard to find. We often talk of the joy of discovering these trains, but few people have captured the emotions of such discoveries as well as Mr. Bokelmann does here. To preserve his original style, this letter has not been edited very much. Its wit and charm must be allowed to speak for themselves. We are happy to share his experience with you, in the hope that you too may feel the same joy at some time in your pursuit of this hobby.

Enjoying recently a mood of moderately avid collecting instinct (it comes and goes, like malaria), it was with pleasant anticipation that I made a call to a prospective seller of a Lionel train. It was five days after I had acquired a most engaging Hornby 0 passenger train (an English tinplate product — ed.), the locomotive being a nice green 4-4-0 Eton with, unfortunately, a bum right side with disintegrating wheels and a crushed cabin. The left side, however, is very good, and this is the side now exposed through the glass panel of the cupboard in my house's living room, some uninteresting china items of my wife having before been necessarily packed away.

So, it was with a buoyant confidence of being in a good season that I breezed into the train seller's house. There are good seasons and bad seasons for anyone collecting trains in Rio de Janeiro because, you see, the hunting grounds around

here are quite peculiar, with a limited supply of undiscovered old hardware and a fierce competition for it, with the same bunch of nice, dear, good old friends always showing up at the most undesirable times and places.

Anyway, here I was, and here came the Lionel train. At the first glance, I was aware of a difference. Missing were the usual soiled paper bags with machinery sticking out through the cobwebs; instead, there was a good-looking cardboard box, clean and trim, all sides with drawings of grinning toothy lions donning machinist caps. One side had the inscription "LIONEL SUPER-0 2291W". It was the first indication that possibly this was an outfit in almost mint condition, although I didn't realize it, never having seen such a presentation.

The seller opened the big box and began taking out the smaller ones with the locomotive and cars. It was a Rio Grande F-3 AB locomotive with a set of automated cars, all of which I didn't have.

The deal was duly closed after careful consideration of a number of factors, including Dr. Greenberg's **Price Guide** and the fact that a mechanical engineer's salary in these latitudes is not anymore what it used to be (this drove the price down). I felt my emotions going like a carnival ride. The seller was acting for a third party and couldn't allow for any personal sympathy towards me, although I was certainly fully deserving of it (up!). The seller was a nice guy and listened respectfully together with his much nicer young wife to my dissertation about the joys of collecting trains (up!). Or perhaps he wasn't so nice because he wouldn't hear about my proposal of consequently accepting my very good surplus 2046 steam locomotive and assorted cars as part of the payment (down!). In addition, my wife was outside waiting in the car because she couldn't see any more good money being wasted on the acquisition of more old train stuff, her house already being full of it (down!). And so on.

About economic limitations to the aforementioned joys of collecting trains, much more could be said. For instance, there was a time when I lost a well-restored 700E (the classic Lionel Scale Hudson — ed.) because of a little difference about setting a fitting value on it. But that's another story which will be written on another night, my sleep nevermore being the same after that particular incident.

By this time, to my dismay, my good old wife came storming in, flagrantly disrupting negotiations, but this proved to be a bonus because the paling seller now saw I wasn't at all kidding about her. He quickly settled at acceptable terms.

Unexpectedly, the ladies made friends at once, and we were shown around the house and invited to have a snack. We had about two hours worth of conversation, so I was a bit anxious to get out of there and play with my new train. I hope nobody noticed, what with me sitting there tightly with one foot firmly stamped over the other to control myself. Of course, it wouldn't be considerate to dive into the intimacies of my new acquisition there in front of everybody.

But the time eventually passed, we got home and, it being already late and everybody sleeping, I settled into the living room for a detailed inspection of my new equipment which, according to Mr. Simpson's **Guide to Catalogued Sets**, was indeed a complete outfit.

This train had been run. It showed on the slight wear of the pickup rollers on the locomotive. But the condition of all the train's components was brand new. It was clear that extreme care had been lavished on it since it left the store's shelf. Even the individual cardboard boxes for all cars were carefully preserved. One of them was mended in the small side, with a glue different from the original glue (yes, I am this kind of an observer).

The night wore on and, the big locomotive and cars being already known, I began to notice other kinds of details. The instruction manual was there, and also the instructions for all the individual automatic cars. All the rails, connectors and controllers were there. The transformer, a TW type, was in a separate box. It was perfect. I plugged the power in, and the clear green light shone. A very little inaudible vibration could be sensed by my hand. My new train was ready to run.

An eerie feeling came to me, late in that night. I have older objects in my collection, with much more historical value, but they are isolated and impersonal, broken and mended. The sets are composed by me in a kind of archeological study involving painstaking restorations. This particular train, however, was bridging a time gap of more than a quarter of a century without showing any signs of it, and I felt a sense of unreality, as if someone had gone out with a time machine and brought me my train from almost 30 years ago.

Some very careful boy preserved it for me. Many of the values of his time are as broken as most of the sorrily wrecked old toys we see around the flea markets. His train is not broken. Probably, it's our longing for some of these old values that makes us collect old memories and old trains. After all, there aren't any steam locomotives anymore.

But there is my new Lionel train. I glance again at the big box, and I see another inscription: "An Investment In Happiness". Yes, I believe it was true then, and I believe it still is true now.

FUNDIMENSIONS: THE TRANSITION YEARS
By Glenn Halverson

When Fundimensions took over the assets and facilities of the old Lionel Corporation train operation, the new firm not only inherited the meticulously made tools and dies, but also a huge inventory of postwar parts as well. To maximize profits in those perilous first years when every penny counted as a plus on the balance sheet and when the doubting Thomases of the General Mills parent company watched in the distance, Fundimensions made every effort to use the inventory of parts and shelf stock. That's exactly what any efficient business would do.

However, efficient business practices made for rather inefficient collecting. As time went by, the origins of these early pieces became lost, and only later have train scholars tried to put together the pieces of the immense jigsaw puzzle posed for them by Fundimensions. The period of time when these leftover pieces were utilized is best called the Transition Period, when Lionel Trains were neither fish nor fowl in many respects.

The best way to define this Transition Period is to place it between the years 1969 and 1973. The year 1969 was, of course, the last year of authentic postwar production, before the takeover by Fundimensions. Therefore, only postwar parts existed. The picture changed in the first year of Fundimensions operation. In 1970 the chief characteristic of the transition is the mixture of postwar Lionel and Fundimensions parts, seen to best advantage on the earliest accessories. In addition, complete postwar pieces were packaged and marketed in Fundimensions boxes. The chief transitional characteristic of

the year 1971 was the continuance of this practice. Not until the year 1973 did collectors and operators observe a line of trains produced completely by Fundimensions.

There are many examples of transition pieces, some of them spectacular. In 1970 Fundimensions made two cars as a special production for Glen Uhl, a noteworthy Ohio train dealer with a long history of sales of Lionel products. The first of these specials was a 6464-500 Timken boxcar produced in both yellow and orange. This car was a postwar product in every way except for one telling clue on the sides: "BLT 1-71 BY LIONEL MPC". The second example wasn't produced specifically for Uhl, but he eventually was its possessor. To test the dies, Fundimensions made a Norfolk and Western large quad hopper car in royal blue with the number 6446-25, its postwar number. The bodies of these cars showed many more lap marks in the plastic than usual, indicating the inexperience of the Fundimensions people in making this car. The run of 450 bodies was to be scrapped, but Uhl bought the entire run, fitted them with trucks and sold them.

Other transitional examples soon followed in 1971. A 6560 Bucyrus-Erie crane car, almost (but not quite) identical to the Hagerstown edition of 1968, was packaged in Type I Fundimensions boxes and sold that year. The firm also produced a strange 2125 whistle shack with a mad conglomeration of postwar and Fundimensions parts. (See the individual articles on both these pieces.) The strange, mis-bulbed 2156 station platform used everything but the paper clips in the steno pool — early postwar pieces, Fundimensions roof supports and even real prewar light bulbs over thirty years old! (See the article on this piece in the Accessory chapter.)

154 Flashing Signal in a Fundimensions box. R. LaVoie Collection, G. Stern photograph.

Many of the earliest Fundimensions accessories are, in fact, old wine in new bottles. A 2195 searchlight tower identical in every way to its 195 predecessor shows up in a Fundimensions Type I box. So do many examples of the 154 flashing signal, the 252 crossing gate and several other signal devices. Curiously, postwar items are pictured in the 1970 and 1971 catalogues as examples of the accessories to be made when there was no time to photograph a prototype. Many times, these pieces bear little, if any, relationship to what is actually found. For example, in the 1971 catalogue the 2125 whistle shack is represented by a postwar 125 piece with a light gray base and a red roof. The real 2125 has a dark brown base and a green roof! The 9121 flatcar with dozer kit is shown in the 1970 catalogue by a postwar 6816 in red, but the 9121 is actually dark brown. In one outrageous example, the 1971 catalogue shows an alleged 2154 flashing signal in an impossible amalgamation — a pole, crossbuck and light standard from the 2162 crossing gate and signal rammed into a tan 2163 block target signal base! This piece, of course, does not exist except in the minds of some extremely creative kitbashers!

Several problems in nomenclature exist because of the corporate changes Fundimensions experienced in its first few years. Postwar collectors, of course, seek out these early Fundimensions pieces because they have postwar numbers in some cases. However, for the first three years of its existence, Fundimensions was attached to the Model Products Corporation, commonly abbreviated as MPC, and that is what many collectors call these pieces. (In this book, we use the Fundimensions name generically to avoid confusion; it means anything produced since 1970.) Perhaps a good dividing line for these transitional pieces would be to search for anything which has the MPC logo on it; after 1973, when the manufacture of these trains became its own subsidiary under the name of Fundimensions, the MPC logo was removed from all pieces.

There is another problem, too: how does the collector place a value on the postwar pieces distributed in early Fundimensions boxes? Clearly, the piece itself could be worth no more than its postwar equivalent without the box — but does that mean the collector must pay a stiff premium for the box alone? Perhaps that is true of the Fundimensions production of the 6560 crane car, but collectors would be very reluctant to pay extra when a piece is postwar all the way except for its box. The factory is not much help in distinguishing the earlier pieces because records are woefully incomplete. Misinformation and rumors abound as a result. The trouble is that many of the earliest trains made by Fundimensions are really scarce items which compete, unfortunately, with far more plentiful postwar production identical to it. There is no remedy for this state of affairs.

Still, many early Fundimensions pieces, especially some of the accessories, can be told from their postwar counterparts, and since production was limited (the toy train market being small at the time), these pieces are worth pursuing. In fact, postwar collectors often find themselves in stiff competition with Fundimensions collectors for the overlapping transitional pieces. More train enthusiasts chasing fewer available trains is a sure formula for scarcity in the future.

Chapter I
DIESELS, ELECTRICS AND MOTORIZED UNITS

8030

8030

Nostalgia is a wonderful and powerful force which attracts many people to toy trains. Rare is the individual who does not cherish a memory of the prototype for a Lionel steam or diesel engine. In the case of the steamers, the "over 40" generation may well have seen the real-life original to the Jersey Central's Blue Comet and recalled a pleasant memory as the Fundimensions Blue Comet Hudson flashes by on a layout.

The only trouble with nostalgia as a motivating force is that it is pleasant for consumers, but not necessarily for producers of toy trains. As Fundimensions took over production of trains from the Lionel Corporation in 1970, its managers realized that a whole new generation awaited the production and rediscovery of these trains. The firm realized that this new generation did not necessarily share the nostalgia of their elders. Therefore, Fundimensions decided to market its locomotives not just to those with actual memories of steam locomotives, but also to those who would look for imitations of the contemporary world around them. That meant diesel engines, not steamers. The rapid proliferation of diesel engines made economic sense in the early years of Fundimensions, even if it might have been at the expense of the steamers, because a new market for toy trains had to be developed.

There was another highly significant economic advantage to the rapid marketing of many types of diesels. Fundimensions could take advantage of new decorating processes much more easily on the flat plastic surfaces of the diesel cabs than it could on the rounded boilers of the steam locomotives. The postwar decorating techniques were limited to decals, heat stamping and rubber stamping. Fundimensions, as a subsidiary of General Mills, had access to people knowledgeable in the new and versatile decorating tactics known as electrocal and tampa. (For an excellent technical discussion of these techniques, refer to Volume IV of the McComas-Tuohy Collectors' Guides.) Thus, colorful contemporary railroad paint schemes could be applied to Fundimensions' diesels — and color sells trains to the public.

Right from the start Fundimensions made their policy apparent. In the 1970 catalogue only a couple of 2-4-2 Columbia steamers actually saw production. However, the catalogue featured an exceptionally colorful orange and white Illinois Central GP-9, a bright blue Santa Fe NW-2 switcher and an Alco AA pair of Santa Fe locomotives in the famous "war bonnet" paint scheme. The GP-9 was particularly attractive; at first, it had huge handrails made from old log car stakes which looked ungainly, but this handrail soon gave way to a more realistic — and fragile — plastic and wire handrail.

As the years went by, Fundimensions issued many different styles of diesels; it is perhaps best to discuss them by type rather than by year produced.

8031

8359

8250

THE GP-7 AND GP-9 ROAD SWITCHERS

The only difference between Fundimensions' GP-7 and GP-9 models was the presence of a snap-on fan shroud atop the roof of the GP-9 model. The real GP-9 locomotives, it should be noted, came both ways. These diesels were very good models, even if they lacked the separate motor and power trucks of the Lionel originals. They also lacked the horns and did not have magnetraction. The first models off the assembly lines used hollow pickup rollers which proved an embarrassment for the company. These rollers would not bridge the switches, so Fundimensions dug up a stock of good leftover pickup assemblies and installed them on the engines until the firm perfected solid roller snap-in assemblies for the power trucks, which performed reliably.

One of the GP-7 locomotives became a landmark for Fundimensions because it proved that there was a sizable collector's market for Lionel trains. In 1973 Fundimensions issued a special model of the locomotive which commemorated

the 50th anniversary of the Electromotive Division of General Motors, the makers of the prototypes. This engine was done in gold with dark blue Chessie and General Motors markings, and it was sold out very rapidly. From that point on, Fundimensions has capitalized upon a collector's market which eagerly awaits each limited production item.

Over the years Fundimensions has issued many GP-7 and GP-9 diesels. Some of them have been entirely original in design, while others have been direct re-issues of famous GP-7 and GP-9 locomotives issued by the Lionel Corporation in the 1950s. Most of these engines are common and available at good prices for the beginning collector. On the whole, they are reliable runners which pull a medium-sized train well and give little trouble. A few of these engines made in the mid-1970s used a fiber worm gear instead of a brass or nylon one; these fiber gears strip easily under a heavy load. The rubber traction tires used on these locomotives do not slip if the operator cements them in place with rubber cement. With normal use and maintenance, they endure operations quite well.

18

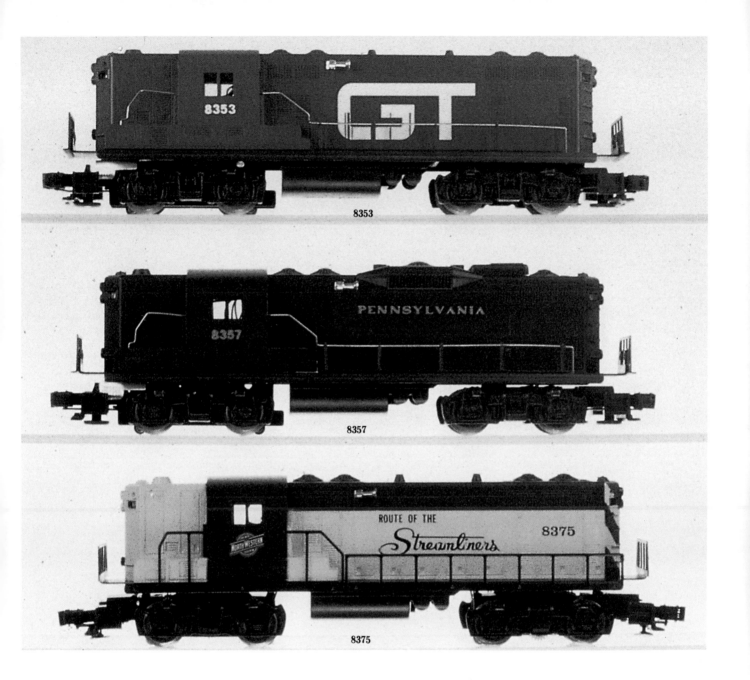

8353

8357

8375

Recently the GP series has seen two Fundimensions innovations. One is the use of an AC/DC can motor mounted right into the power truck. This arrangement is very close to the one found on the prototype. The first locomotive with this motor, the 8263 Santa Fe GP-7 of 1982, was not entirely successful. The engine is too light, and it has cheaper sliding contact shoes instead of the good roller pickups. For those reasons, it has not met with great success. Fundimensions did a much better job with the next locomotive built in this way, the 8375 Chicago & Northwestern GP-7 included in the Northern Freight Flyer of 1983. This locomotive is weighted and has two can motors, one on each power truck. It also has a fully electronic reversing switch and runs on very low voltage. This twin-motored engine has excellent hauling capacity; it is also easier to maintain because the motor never needs lubrication (though the gears do). The better roller pickups are a part of this engine as well. The twin-motored engine is far better than the single-motored locomotive.

The other innovation in the "Geep" series has just been released. It is a handsome New York Central GP-9 with extra detailing such as hand-inserted grab-irons on the front and rear. The motor in this engine is the preferable separate motor and power truck, as compared with the integral unit found in most Geeps. It also has twin-axle magnetraction, lighted number-boards and an electronic horn. The locomotive is painted in very realistic black, gray and white New York Central colors which should be met with collector enthusiasm. It already shows signs of being a highly desirable collector's locomotive.

THE GP-20 ROAD SWITCHER

In 1973 one of the mold and die experts at Fundimensions came up with a clever die insert for the GP-7 and GP-9 molds. By placing this insert into the die, Fundimensions came up with a new model, the GP-20, which had Union Pacific prototypes

8454

8550

8576

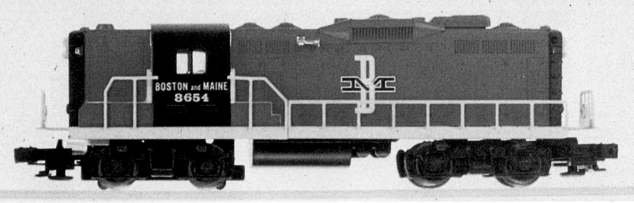

8654

8666

8750

8757

8759

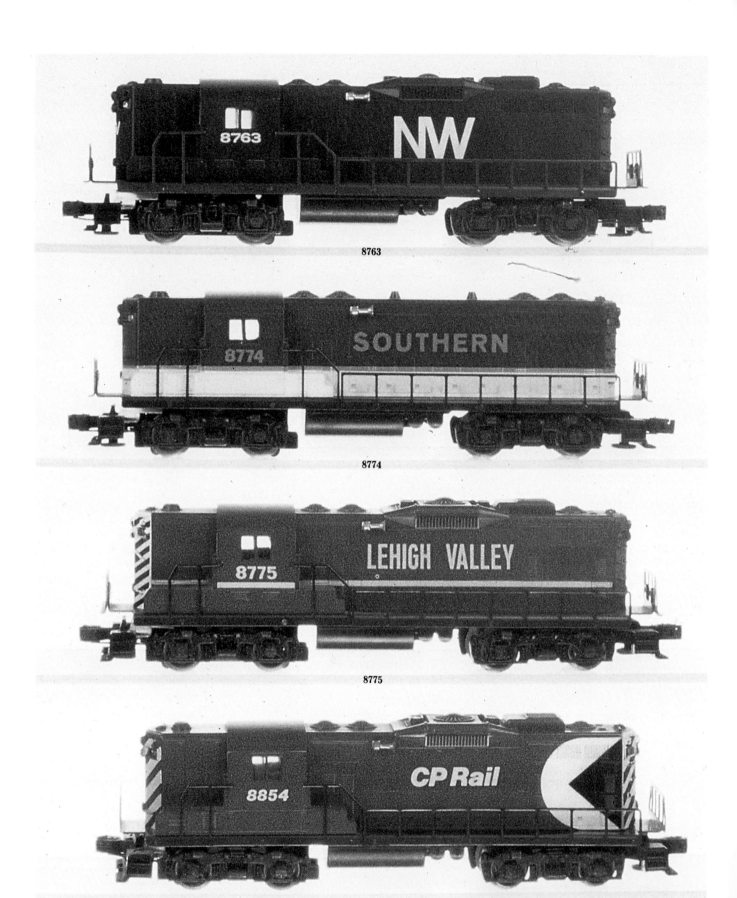

8763

8774

8775

8854

8866

8064

with fan shrouds and New York Central prototypes without the fan shrouds. This locomotive has not been issued in the quantities used for the GP-7 and GP-9, but it is the locomotive responsible for the introduction of a Fundimensions innovation — the electronic diesel horn.

Unfortunately for Fundimensions, the horn used the same troublesome controller issued with the steam engine whistles. This controller had a tendency to get stuck in the closed position and burn out the diode which changed part of the AC transformer current into DC for the horn. Therefore, it was made in very limited quantities, and any GP-20 dummy unit which has the electronic horn is quite scarce. It is a shame that the controller didn't work properly, because the horn sound itself was excellent. Some operators actually prefer it to the new electronic horns because it has a muffled sound like a real diesel heard from a distance. Some horns were used in the Union Pacific U36B dummy locomotive, and the rest were split up between the Santa Fe, Long Island and Missouri Pacific GP-20 locomotives produced in 1973 and 1974. The electronic horn was revived successfully in 1981 in the 8157 Santa Fe Fairbanks-Morse locomotive.

In 1983 an 8369 Erie-Lackawanna GP-20 with twin can motors was offered for separate sale. Like its GP-7 partners, it runs extremely well compared to its single-motored stablemates. My own example of this locomotive nearly tore the bumper off my test track when I ran it for the first time because I did not expect it to run so efficiently at such low voltage! It will pull a train at eight volts, giving the transformers an easy job to handle.

F-3 COVERED WAGON DIESELS

In the late 1930s the Electro-Motive Division of General Motors startled the real train world with its FT diesel demonstrator engines. These streamlined locomotives piled up mile after maintenance-free mile, and they routinely pulled trains of six thousand tons when the biggest steam engines could only handle half that much. Following the Second World War, these freight diesels and their sister passenger units, the E series, rapidly replaced steam engines all over the country. In 1947 General Motors introduced the F-3 series, the first truly successful freight diesels. (This story is eloquently told in Robert Carper's book **American Railroads In Transition: The Passing of the Steam Engines**).

Despite some personal doubts on the part of Joshua Lionel Cowen, a die-hard steam fan, the Lionel Corporation was quick to take notice of these streamlined beauties. In 1948, just one year after the real locomotives emerged, Lionel produced its Santa Fe and New York Central F-3 locomotives. The Santa Fe model became the best-selling locomotive in Lionel's history because of its dependable twin-motor performance and its spectacular Santa Fe "war bonnet" paint scheme of red, silver, yellow and black.

Fundimensions did not wait very long to recall this legend of the tinplate rails. In 1973 a special brochure announced the return of the F-3 diesel in Baltimore and Ohio markings. By 1978 Fundimensions had reissued many of the scarcest Lionel models; indeed, some of them, like the Canadian Pacific and Southern F-3 diesels, would become just as scarce as their forebears. In 1976 Fundimensions even reissued the Santa Fe model, expecting slow sales because of the presence of so many

8260

of the older locomotives within collections. However, Fundimensions did so good a job with the paint scheme that the firm could not make the Santa Fe locomotives fast enough, and today it is harder to find than any of its predecessors!

All of the F-3 models produced until 1978 were single-motor locomotives without magnetraction, horns and some of the intricate trim of the Lionel pieces. The F-3 disappeared from the catalogue in 1978, but not for long. Another special bulletin announced a twin-motored F-3 in New Haven markings for late 1978. It was followed the next year by a Brunswick green Pennsylvania twin-motored pair, and on this pair the deluxe trim was at last restored to the F-3. Collector pressure made Lionel issue a pair of Pennsylvania locomotives in tuscan as well, in order that the F-3 pair would match the Congressional Limited passenger cars of that year. Since that time, all F-3 locomotives have been twin-motored pairs, and several new models have appeared, such as the Southern Pacific and Union Pacific pairs. A Burlington "Texas Zephyr" has been issued in chromed plastic, and the New York Central F-3 has been revived. "B" units have been available for nearly all of the F-3 locomotives produced.

The Fundimensions F-3 diesels are excellent runners either as single or double-motored units, thanks to Fundimensions' use of a separate motor and power truck instead of the integral motor and power truck used on the GP series. They are usually brisk sellers which command a good price premium. Strangely enough, the older Lionel F-3 locomotives have also increased in value, even though they have been reproduced. The probable reason for this is the strong appeal of this locomotive both as an operating unit and a historic locomotive.

THE ALCO UNITS

One of the first diesel locomotives revived by Fundimensions was the little Alco streamlined diesel. The first of these locomotives was a Santa Fe "A-A" pair in 1970; a "B" unit was soon available. The prototype of this locomotive is considered by diesel enthusiasts to be one of the most beautiful diesels ever made, especially in its PA passenger configuration. Unfortunately, Lionel's model is not to true scale and is not nearly as impressive as the F-3 diesel. Still, the least expensive sets of the early Fundimensions era were headed by many an Alco; most of the early ones had two-position reversing units and were somewhat cheaply made.

In 1975 and 1976 Fundimensions tested the waters to see what reception a deluxe version of the Alco might engender. The firm issued a triple Alco A-B-A set in one box in Southern Pacific Daylight colors. Unlike their stablemates, these Alcos had die-cast trucks and three-position reversing units. In 1976 Fundimensions issued three Canadian National units, this time for separate sale. These locomotives came in the brilliant orange, black and white zebra-stripes of the prototype. Sales of these triple units were disappointing, so Fundimensions proceeded no further along these marketing lines. Since that time, the Alco has been limited to the lower end of the market; the most recent use of the Alco has been a Texas and Pacific pair for the Quicksilver Express passenger set.

The Fundimensions Alco is a great piece for a beginning locomotive collector to explore. Most of the Alcos are very low priced and readily available. Exceptions are the deluxe Alcos mentioned above and an 8022 A-A pair made especially for J.

U36B

8155

8470

8564

8573

8571

8650

8669

8755

8771

8857

8955

8962

27

8050

8061

8930

C. Penney in 1970. A reasonably complete assembly of Fundimensions Alcos can be acquired in a short time without exorbitant expense.

THE U36B AND U36C "U-BOATS"

The first diesel locomotive which was a new Fundimensions model not patterned after any postwar product was the U-36B, issued in 1974. Except for its non-scale length, Fundimensions' "U-boat" was a very good model of the rugged General Electric prototype. The first models were the aptly-numbered 1776 Seaboard Bicentennial locomotive and the 8470 Chessie System at the head of Fundimensions' "Grand National" top-of-the-line freight set. Both these locomotives became very popular, and in rapid succession Fundimensions issued Union Pacific, Great Northern, Frisco, Burlington Northern, Southern and Northern Pacific models.

One U36B deserves particular mention because it is one of the most valuable of all Fundimensions products. In 1977 Fundimensions began its Walt Disney series of hi-cube

boxcars, and the 8773 Mickey Mouse U36B was chosen to head it. Because collectors of Disneyana compete with train collectors for it, this locomotive increased in value explosively by 1980. Another U36B is somewhat difficult to find, but it has not attracted collector attention yet. This is the Lionel 75th Anniversary locomotive, which headed a string of freight cars with historic Lionel logos. Many collectors shy away from this set because they feel it is unattractive, but the silver and red colors of the locomotive itself have admirers. This U36B is an excellent "sleeper" candidate; it is not very common, but is still reasonably priced.

In 1979 the U36 locomotive was issued with Fundimensions' new six-wheel locomotive trucks, which were first seen on the 1978 Milwaukee SD-18. Thus, the U36 became a U36C; since that time, most U-boats have been issued with these six-wheel trucks. The exception is 1979's 8962 Reading U36B.

As a class, the U-boats offer more detailing than their GP counterparts and are slightly higher priced. Dummy units are available for many of these locomotives, including one very

Lionel made a special set with a 8182 NW-2 for Nibco

scarce Union Pacific with an electronic horn. Their massive appearance has made them favorites of some Fundimensions collectors.

THE NW-2 SWITCHERS

From Day One, Fundimensions has called its switchers SW-1 models instead of the NW-2 diesels they really are. The firm is perpetuating a Lionel mistake in nomenclature which dates back to 1950! Whatever they are called, Fundimensions' switcher engines have never really been popular with collectors, even though some of them have become quite scarce and collectible. This series began in 1970 with the 8010 Santa Fe switcher in blue and yellow colors; most of the early switchers followed the line of the cheaper Lionel models. In 1973 Fundimensions revived the Erie black switcher with its 8354; this locomotive had better features such as a three-position reversing switch. Subsequent issues included Pennsylvania, Chessie, CP Rail, Grand Trunk and Burlington models.

Fundimensions has limited its use of NW-2 switchers to the bottom of the line sets in recent years, and only a few of these locomotives are truly scarce. These include the Erie, Coca-Cola and Pennsylvania models and a special promotional switcher for

Nibco Faucet Products in 1981. Operationally, the switchers have a tendency to jump the track when they encounter a turnout next to a curved track, unless they are run cab end first. Recently, the NW-2 has used the new Fundimensions AC-DC can motor in Burlington Northern and U. S. Marines markings. Like the Alcos, the NW-2 switchers are relatively easy to acquire at good prices and are a great specialization area for the beginning collector.

SOME SIX-WHEELED DIESELS

Typically, when Fundimensions introduces a new feature, it uses the feature over a wide range of its line to help amortize the cost of the tooling. That is certainly true of the handsome six-wheeled trucks in current use on many of its diesels. In 1978 Fundimensions placed the six-wheel trucks under a Milwaukee GP-20 cab, added a fan shroud and changed the model to the SD-18. Santa Fe and Ontario Northland models were quick to follow, this time in both powered and dummy units. With a change in the cab roof from a rounded roof to a flat roof, the model became a "chop-nosed" SD-28. This version was produced in Burlington and Lionel Lines colors.

Nor were the high-nosed GP-7 and GP-9 models neglected in

8063

8071

8162

8855

the use of the new six-wheel trucks. In 1980 Fundimensions produced a round-roofed Seaboard SD-9 to head its Mid-Atlantic Limited collector set; the next year, a high-nosed Geep with a flat roof, the SD-24, was made in attractive Canadian Pacific markings for the Maple Leaf Limited. This particular

locomotive had an electronic horn, as did a Norfolk and Western SD-24 at the head end of the Continental Limited set.

The early models of the six-wheeled diesels had a peculiar operating problem. The blind center wheels of these locomotives were made a little too large, causing the drive

8950

8951

8056

wheels to skid under heavy loads. The problem was soon corrected, and the usual answer to the early problem is to file down the blind wheels carefully. The later six-wheelers have traction tires on the blind wheels as well, effectively curing the trouble. Although these locomotives will run on 027 track, they are far better runners on the wider-radius 0 gauge trackage, and their long wheelbase shows to better advantage.

THE FAIRBANKS-MORSE TRAINMASTERS

It isn't easy to reproduce a legendary locomotive, so when news came in 1979 that Fundimensions was about to revive the scale-length Fairbanks-Morse Trainmaster, collectors were anxious to see if Fundimensions would do the locomotive justice. Indeed, the firm did — the Fundimensions Fairbanks-Morse is an exact duplicate of the Lionel model, right down to the die-cast trucks, air tanks and battery box. The first models of this magnificent twin-motored diesel were a revival of the Virginian blue and yellow-striped locomotive and a stunning Southern Pacific "black widow" locomotive which had only

existed as a Lionel prototype. Both locomotives sold extremely well and are still in great demand, especially the Southern Pacific.

Three more Fairbanks-Morse locomotives followed in quick succession. A Chicago and Northwestern green and yellow locomotive in 1980 met with only a lukewarm reception, possibly because the paint scheme resembled the Virginian in style a little too much. The next year, Fundimensions produced a beautiful Santa Fe in blue and yellow freight colors, and the firm added the icing on the cake — the electronic diesel horn. Finally, Fundimensions issued a special production for J. C. Penney in 1983 which has become nearly impossible to obtain. This was the Wabash Fairbanks-Morse in gray and blue "bluebird" colors.

All of the Fundimensions Fairbanks-Morse locomotives are desirable pieces. Operationally, they can only be outpulled by the die-cast GG-1 electrics. The Wabash and Southern Pacific locomotives are very hard to find. The Virginian and Santa Fe locomotives rank a notch below these in scarcity, and the

8157

8378

Chicago and Northwestern seems to be the easiest piece to acquire. It should be noted that these locomotives can be retro-fitted with the electronic horn, and many Fairbanks-Morse owners have indeed done just that.

THE BUDD CARS

In 1977 Fundimensions introduced a Service Station Special set which was really different from its predecessors. The firm revived the handsome Budd diesel railcars in Baltimore and Ohio markings. The set had a powered baggage car and two dummy passenger coaches. Soon afterward, Fundimensions issued a powered passenger coach and a dummy baggage car. In 1978 another set was issued, this time in colorful Amtrak markings.

The Budd railcars are very attractive, and they run well because of the separate motor and power truck. The silver paint on the Fundimensions cars is brighter than that of the Lionel originals, and it should have better wear characteristics.

THE SD-40 DIESELS

In 1982 Fundimensions introduced a spectacular new modern diesel, a model of the brutish but attractive SD-40 so popular with railroads today. Fundimensions' model of this locomotive is scale length and has been considered one of the finest diesel models ever produced in tinplate. Scale 0 Gauge model railroaders have even purchased the body shell and trucks to adapt to their own operational requirements. It was first produced in bright Santa Fe blue and yellow freight colors; since then, each year has seen this locomotive issued in a new paint scheme. In 1983 a yellow, red and green Union Pacific was made. Both of these locomotives were produced in single-motor configuration; many collectors found this hard to understand, since the locomotive was so large it would easily accommodate the extra motor.

The SD-40 produced in 1984 corrected the oversight. This time the locomotive was a beautiful gray, maroon and yellow Erie-Lackawanna, and it had twin motors. Like the Union

8872

8152

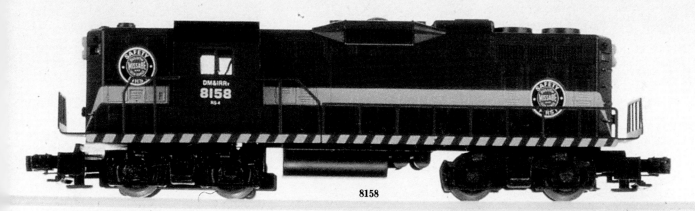

8158

8265

8376

8551

8762

8558

Pacific, it headed a limited production collector set. Scheduled for 1985 is an SD-40 in Burlington Northern Cascade green and black colors. This locomotive will head a unit train of five matching Burlington Northern Standard "0" boxcars and an extended vision caboose.

The SD-40 has been greeted with considerable acclaim by collectors because of its massive size and attractive design. It is a little too soon to tell which of these locomotives will become scarcer than others, but the twin-motor units should command a premium.

THE ELECTRICS

Fundimensions took quite some time to reissue the famous electric locomotives of the postwar era, but when they did, they produced some good locomotives indeed. The first of the electrics to emerge from the miniature erecting shops of Fundimensions was the EP-5 rectifier electric in 1975. Fundimensions has always called this engine a "Little Joe", but that is an error; the real "Little Joe" was a quite different locomotive purchased by the Milwaukee Road and the Chicago,

8659

8859

8754

South Shore and South Bend Railroad. The name came about because these South Shore locomotives were originally intended for Russian export during World War II; hence the name "Little Joe" after Josef Stalin. The EP-5 was an electric made for the New Haven by General Electric; it was famous for its rapid acceleration and thus earned the nickname "The Jet". Except for its length and its four-wheel trucks instead of the six-wheel types used on the real thing, Fundimensions' model of the EP-5 was very good.

The first EP-5 was issued in Pennsylvania tuscan with gold striping and lettering. The next year, it was followed by a Milwaukee locomotive in orange and black; in 1977 an attractive Great Northern EP-5 was made in dark green and orange. Finally, a special locomotive was made for J. C. Penney in 1982. This EP-5 had Pennsylvania markings like its 8551 predecessor, but the nose and sides of the locomotive were in bright gold with tuscan lettering.

The EP-5 is a fine runner which looks good with either freight or passenger consists. The first two EP-5s issued are the most common, with the Great Northern somewhat harder to find and the Penney locomotive the hardest of all to acquire due to its limited production.

In 1976 Fundimensions resurrected the ungainly and brutish Virginian rectifier of postwar fame. Despite its boxy look, the

8753

8850

8150

locomotive was welcomed by collectors because its glossy blue and yellow colors looked good. It was followed by a New Haven model in 1977; this locomotive was done in bright orange with white striping, a black roof and frame and the famous McGinnis "NH" logo. Finally in 1978 a blue and white Conrail rectifier was produced. No other locomotives of this type have been made since. These locomotives, still reasonably priced, are excellent runners worth attention.

Despite these good electrics, collectors were really waiting for the "creme de la creme" of all the electrics, the famous Pennsylvania GG-1. The prototype, an amazing locomotive, had a service life of nearly 50 years, and even today its Raymond Loewy-designed lines look fresh and contemporary. Three of these locomotives, including the original No. 4800, are preserved at the Railroad Museum of Pennsylvania in Strasburg, Pennsylvania. (For the full story of this locomotive,

8264   8368

8459   8379

see Karl Zimmerman's series, **The Remarkable GG-1.**)

Finally, in 1977, patience had its reward. Fundimensions put out a tuscan 8753 GG-1 which had the original die-cast body, two motors and, for the first time in a Fundimensions locomotive, magnetraction. The job was good overall, but a few minor flaws needed correcting. Collectors claimed that the nylon gearing did not hold up very well in this locomotive, and the body casting was rougher than it should have been. In 1978 Fundimensions issued an all-black GG-1 in Penn Central markings. This locomotive was an operational and cosmetic improvement over its predecessor, but collectors did not like its paint scheme and the locomotive was a slow seller. In 1981 another GG-1 was produced, this time in gloss Brunswick green with gold striping. This time the quality was right; the striping was the best ever applied to a GG-1 and the finish was very attractive.

The first and last GG-1 locomotives produced by Fundimensions are highly prized and sought by collectors and operators alike. These locomotives will outpull any other locomotive (except perhaps the Fairbanks-Morse Trainmaster) because all twelve wheels are drivers. Even the Penn Central GG-1 is beginning to attract attention, though it is not as highly valued as the other two. In fact, a case could be made that the Penn Central locomotive is a good bargain, as GG-1s go.

THE MOTORIZED UNITS

One of the most attractive areas of production in the postwar era was the little specialty units which buzzed around layouts of the mid-1950s. These motorized units were delightful to watch in action, and they are eagerly sought after by collectors. It was only natural that collectors would get curious about any possible reissues of these items.

Perhaps because of the complicated gearing in some of these units, Fundimensions did not begin to revive them until 1982, when the company issued an attractive snowplow locomotive in Canadian National maroon and gray markings. Since then, each year has seen the emergence of more of these little locomotives. In 1983 a Vulcan 0-4-0 switcher engine was produced in blue and yellow Alaska markings. In 1984 the rotary snowplow came out in black and yellow Rio Grande

markings. (This time, the "a" in "Rio Grande" was stamped correctly! Most of the postwar Rio Grande snowplows had the "a" backwards!) In the same year a Pennsylvania "fire car" was also produced, complete with its hose reels and rotating fireman, just like the original. Scheduled for 1985 is a New York Central ballast tamper unit in yellow and black. This interesting unit works by track trips; when it encounters one, it slows down, and miniature pile drivers "tamp" stone ballast between the rails and ties.

It will be interesting to see what items Fundimensions produces in the next few years in this area. Rumors have surfaced that the little Birney trolley may make an appearance in blue and red colors; this was always a popular item. Many more items could be reproduced; all should meet favor with collectors.

The diesels, electrics and motorized units have been produced in great numbers and variety by Fundimensions. Most are easily affordable, colorful and certainly varied enough to appeal to anyone's preferences. As on the real railroads, these locomotives are the mainstays of the Fundimensions line, no matter how attractive the steamers may have become.

DIESELS, ELECTRICS AND MOTORIZED UNITS

The introduction analyzes the following diesel bodies: GM Yard Switcher, F-3 Unit, Alco, GP-7 and GP-9, U36B and GP-20. It also discusses GP and U36B motors and diesel railing types.

ALCO BODY TYPES

Type I
1. Open slot on front pilot for coupler.
2. Closed slot number-board.
3. "LIONEL MPC" builder's plate at lower rear.

Type II
1. Open slot on front pilot for coupler.
2. Open slot number-board.
3. "LIONEL MPC" builder's plate behind cab door.

Type III
1. Open slot on front pilot for coupler.
2. Closed slot number-board.
3. No builder's plate.

1776

1776

Type IV

1. Closed slot on front pilot, no coupler.
2. Open slot number-board.
3. "LIONEL MPC" builder's plate behind cab door.

Type V

1. Open slot on front pilot, no strut.
2. Open slot number-board.
3. "LIONEL" only on builder's plate behind cab door.

Type VI

1. Closed slot on front pilot.
2. Open slot number-board.
3. "LIONEL" only on builder's plate behind door.

GP-7 and GP-9 Body Types

The difference between a Lionel GP-7 and a GP-9 is the addition of a snap-on plastic dynamic brake casting. The GP-7 and GP-9 bodies show a progression not unlike those of the F-3s, Alcos and Yard Switchers. Fundimensions made changes in body design to solve decorating problems or to coordinate body design with other production changes. We have identified five basic bodies:

Body Type I: 8030, 8031

(A) One piece inserted in the body to form two headlight lenses, two marker light lenses and two number-boards with actual numbers.
(B) Hinges on side door panels beneath the road name.
(C) Builder's plate carries the LIONEL and MPC logo.
(D) No indentations for stamped-steel handrails since wire handrails used.
(E) Louvers on hatch panels beneath the numerals 8030.
(F) Two steps from the cab to the frame.

Body Type II: 8250 Santa Fe, same as Type I, but:

(A) No numbers on number-boards.
(B) No hinges on side door panels near the road name.

Body Type III: Early 1976, 8576 Penn Central, same as II, but:

(A) Builder's plate carries only the LIONEL name.
(B) Indentations in the cab side (addition of Type IV railings), since stamped-steel handrails are added.

Body Type IV: Early 1978, 8866 Minneapolis and St. Louis, same as III, but:

(A) No louvers (but numbers) on the hatch panel on the cab below the window.
(B) One step only from the cab to the frame.

Body Type V: Later 1978, 8854 C.P. Rail, same as IV, but:

(G) No indentations in the cab because Type IV railing used.

U36B Body Types

Type I: No indentations for handrails.
Type II: Indentations for handrails.

GP-20 Body Types

Type I: No indentations for handrails.
Type II: Indentations for handrails.

GP and U36B Motor Types

Type I: 8010-127 has two circular pickups as found on the old-style Scout. The pickups did not bridge the switches so Fundimensions added a pickup to the dummy truck on its later production. This pickup was similar to the old Lionel GP-style pickup.

Type II: 8250-125 has two roller pickups which are similar to those found on MPC tenders and passenger cars. The rollers are attached to a shoe that slides under a brass spring plate on the truck. Fundimensions also added a pickup to the dummy trucks on its initial motor run. All GPs and U36Bs have two operating couplers, stamped metal frames and plastic steps attached to both trucks, and powered units have three-position E-units. All GP-20s have LIONEL builder's plates, U36Bs do not have any. Early MPC, GP-7 and GP-9 production included a Lionel MPC builder's plate. On later production the MPC part of the logo was dropped.

Diesel Railing Types

Type I Stamped Metal Post: Made apparently from Lionel flatcar stakes with a handrail passing through the stakes, railing end holes in north and south cab sides, oversized but sturdy.

Type II Plastic Posts - Handrail Combination: Better scaled but fragile, railing end holes in north and south cab sides.

38

1776

1776

1776

Type III Stamped Metal Railing: Riveted to frame, with large rivets for end railings, railing is turned into cab with indentations on east and west cab sides.

Type IV Metal Railing: Railing spot-welded to frame, but not connected to cab, indentations in cab filled in and railing simply lies along cab side. The change from Type III to IV apparently occurred in mid-1978 because the 8866 is a Type IV. End railings are an integral part of its frame and were formed with the frame and not separately as in Type III. (Note: Some copies of the 8866 were apparently made with Type III railings.)

                                           Gd VG Exc Mt

530: See 8378

634 SANTA FE: Circa 1970, NW-2 Yard Switcher, rerun of 1965-66 unit, chrome-plated plastic bell and radio antenna. These are leftover postwar cabs which were given Fundimensions trim pieces. Thus, this piece can be faked by adding trim pieces to a postwar 634 cab and mounting it on an early Fundimensions chassis. R. LaVoie comment.   **30 40 55 65**

1203 BOSTON & MAINE: 1972, NW-2 switcher, cab only, no chassis, made for NETCA (New England Division, Train Collectors' Association) for 1972 convention; light blue cab, white lettering and logo, no trim pieces

supplied. C. Lang comments.   **NRS**

1776 NORFOLK & WESTERN: 1976, powered GP-9, Type II plastic railings, painted red; white and blue body with flat gold lettering, silver circle of thirteen stars; black underframe, lights, nose decal, Type II motor, no pickup on dummy truck, no MPC logo. This is actually catalogued as 8559 but is listed here for your convenience.

		Gd	VG	Exc	Mt
(A) Glossy red paint.		—	—	90	120
(B) Flat red paint.		—	—	90	120
(C) Same as (A) but no circle of stars.		—	—	140	175

39

1776 SEABOARD COAST LINE: 1976, powered G.E. U36B, stamped metal railings, red, white and blue body with blue lettering; black underframe, lights, nose decal, Type II motor, no pickup on dummy truck, no MPC logo. This locomotive was part of the Spirit of '76 set, which included thirteen boxcars representing each of the original Thirteen Colonies and a 7600 Frisco N5C caboose. Fundimensions had more ambitious plans to make boxcars for the remaining 37 states, but this was never carried out. The 7610 Virginia and the 7611 New York are the scarcest cars in the set. C. Lang and R. LaVoie comments.

(A) No lettering on frame.   —   —   **85**   **100**
(B) White "SEABOARD COAST LINE" on frame   —   —   **90**   **110**
(C) Same as 1776 (B), but with medium white "SEABOARD COAST LINE" on frame.   —   —   **85**   **110**
(D) Special for TCA with TCA logo and three TCA passenger cars.
      —   —   —   **250**

1776 BANGOR AND AROOSTOOK: 1976, catalogued as 8665, powered GP-9, "Jeremiah O'Brien", Type III railing; red, white and blue with red, white and blue lettering, catalogued and sold with a 9176 caboose; "8665" not on engine, silver truck side frames, lights, nose decal, no MPC logo, "LIONEL" builder's plate, Type III body.   —   —   **80**   **110**

4935 PENNSYLVANIA: See 8150

7500 LIONEL 75th ANNIVERSARY: 1975-76, powered G.E. U36B diesel, part of set 1505; red, silver and black body, black frame, "7500" on box. The 75th Anniversary set included 7501, 7505 and 7506 boxcars, 7502, 7503 and 7507 refrigerator cars, a 7504 covered hopper and a 7508 N5C caboose. It was a slow seller at its issuance and is still available new at a relatively low price, which qualifies the set as a "sleeper" candidate for collectors. R. LaVoie comment.   —   —   **60**   **85**

8010 AT&SF: 1970, NW-2 Yard Switcher, blue with yellow lettering.
      —   —   **25**   **40**

8020 SANTA FE: 1970-76, powered Alco FA-2 A unit, red and silver body, lights, comes with 8021 or 8020 dummy.
(A) Powered 8020, Type I body.   —   —   **30**   **45**
(B) 1970-71, SANTA FE, dummy Alco FA-2 A unit, red and silver body.
      —   —   **20**   **25**

(C) Blue and silver body.   —   —   **30**   **45**

8021 SANTA FE: 1971-72, 1974-76, dummy Alco FA-2 B unit; red and silver body, "SANTA FE" under vents.   —   —   **20**   **25**

8022 SANTA FE: 1971, uncatalogued, powered, Alco FA-2, A unit; blue and yellow freight colors, made for J.C. Penney, lights.
(A) With nose decal.   —   —   **50**   **65**
(B) Without nose decal.   —   —   **50**   **65**
(C) Powered and dummy A unit set, numbered "8022", only fifty sets, made for J.C. Penney's Ann Arbor, Michigan, store. Catalano observation.
      NRS
(D) Black plastic cabs painted dark flat Navy blue, yellow striping and lettering, number "8" in "8022" stamped backwards. No window or headlight inserts, no ornamental horns, no Santa Fe decal on nose. Closed number-boards, open pilot front with lower bar below coupler. Samples observed came mounted on postwar Alco chassis with horn, headlight and two-axle magnetraction; the two chassis also have dummy metal couplers front and rear. The chassis may or may not have been original with these cabs; could be identical to (C) above. G. Halverson Collection.
      —   **65**   **125**   **185**

8025 CANADIAN NATIONAL: 1971, Alco FA-2 AA units, one powered, other dummy, black body, orange nose, white striping, both with same number, uncatalogued, Parker Brothers distribution in Canada, imported by U.S. dealers. Price for both units.   —   —   **60**   **75**

8010

8030 ILLINOIS CENTRAL: 1970-71, powered GP-9, white and orange body with black lettering; one pickup on power truck, pickup on dummy truck, black frame, lights; Type I motor, LIONEL/MPC builder's plate, Type I body, loop pickup may or may not supplement pickup on dummy truck.
(A) Lighter orange, Type I motor, Type I railing, nose decal, loop.

— **35 45 55**

(B) Darker orange, Type II railing, no nose decal, Type II motor.

— **35 45 55**

(C) Same as (B), but with nose decal and extra set of pickups. Rohlfing Collection.

— **35 45 55**

(D) ITT Special Limited Edition Railway Set for Marine Expo 9 at Washington, D.C., fall, 1975, registered as "ISBN 0-912276-13-4" and "LC 74-29700" with Library of Congress, "ITT Cable-Hydrospace" glossy black sticker with gold letters placed over "ILLINOIS CENTRAL" on locomotive side, no end decal. Twenty-five sets, each with an 8030 engine, 8254 dummy with the same sticker, three bright blue over-painted 9113 N&W hoppers with clear central decals with white-lettered "cable ITT car", one hopper with an orange cover, 9160 caboose with glossy black sticker with gold letters, two-engine four-car set. Catalano observation.

— — — **400**

See also Factory Errors and Prototypes.

8031 CANADIAN NATIONAL: 1970-71, powered GP-7; black and orange body, white lettering, lights, no nose decal, Type I motor, pickup on dummy, Lionel/MPC builder's plate, Type II body.
(A) Type I railing, Canadian edition. — **45 55 65**
(B) Type II railing. — **35 45 55**
(C) Same as (B), but slightly smaller and deeper-stamped 8031 on cab, metal railing ends behind cab. Instead of regular Type II railings, a one-piece black plastic insert is snapped into place along the cab side. The side railing is, therefore, black plastic instead of metal. Reader comments invited. R. LaVoie observation. — **40 50 65**

8050 DELAWARE & HUDSON: 1980, powered U36C, gray body, blue top, yellow striping and lettering, six-wheel trucks, matching 8051 dummy available separately; 8050 only. — — **85 100**

See also Factory Errors and Prototypes.

8051 DELAWARE & HUDSON: 1980, dummy U36C, matches 8050.

— — **40 45**

8054 C&S BURLINGTON: 1980, dual-motored F-3 A unit, metallic silver body with black and red markings, known as Texas Zephyr (C & S stands for Colorado and Southern, a group of railroads acquired by Burlington in 1908 and run as a division), matching dummy A unit (8055) and B unit (8062) available, 8054 A unit only. — — **125 140**

8055 C&S BURLINGTON: 1980, dummy F-3 A unit, illuminated; matches 8054. Price for 8055 only. — — **75 85**

8054 and 8055: Pair — — — **225**

8056 CHICAGO & NORTHWESTERN: 1980, dual-motored FM Train-master, magnetraction; yellow and Brunswick green body, yellow safety striping, six-wheel trucks. — — **200 225**

8057 BURLINGTON: 1980, NW-2 Yard Switcher, red and gray, lettered "Way of the Zephyrs", three-position reverse unit, disc-operating couplers. — — **65 80**

8059 PENNSYLVANIA: 1980, F-3 B unit, dummy, Brunswick green, matches 8952 and 8953 F-3 A units, clear plastic portholes.

— — — **175**

8060 PENNSYLVANIA: 1980, F-3 B unit, dummy, tuscan; matches 8970 and 8971 F-3 A units, clear plastic portholes. — — — **100**

8061 WESTERN MARYLAND: 1980, powered U36C, yellow and orange body with blue roof; dark blue lettering, bright orange-painted frame; three-position reverse unit, silver-painted six-wheel trucks; from 1070 Royal Limited set. — — **80 95**

8062 BURLINGTON: 1980, F-3 B unit, dummy; matches 8054 and 8055 F-3 A units, clear plastic portholes. — — — **100**

8063 SEABOARD: 1980, powered SD-9, black with yellow band with red trim and yellow frames, six-wheel trucks with blind center wheels and rubber tires on the three wheels on geared side, three-position reverse, disc-operating couplers with small tabs, heavy stamped-steel railing.

— — **75 90**

TYPE I Radio Wheel   Road Name Plate

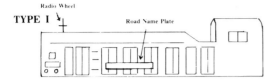

Maintenance ladders with three steps, little doors and road name plate

TYPE II

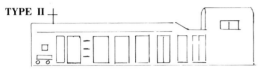

Maintenance ladder with three steps, no little doors, no road name plate

TYPE III

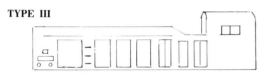

Large panel, no radio wheel, maintenance ladder with three steps

TYPE IV

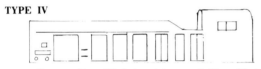

Same as Type III, but maintenance ladder with two steps

TYPE V

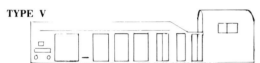

Same as Type III, but maintenance ladder with one step

TYPE I

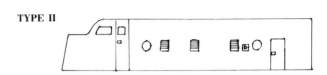

TYPE II

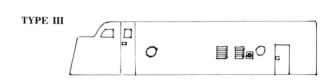

TYPE III

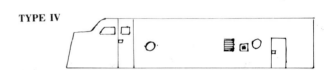

TYPE IV

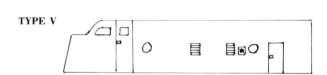

TYPE V

8064 FLORIDA EAST COAST: 1980, powered GP-9; red and yellow; catalogued with black trucks but made with silver trucks, three-position reverse unit.　　　　　— — 65 80

8065 FLORIDA EAST COAST: 1980, dummy GP-9; matches 8064.
　　　　　— — 35 45

8064 and 8065: Pair　　　— — — 125

8066 TOLEDO, PEORIA & WESTERN: 1980, powered GP-20, orange and white body, white-painted frame and railings; three-position reverse unit, catalogued with dynamic brake unit on roof, but made without brake unit; came with 1072 Cross Country Express set. Catalogue shows red color, but not produced that way. C. Lang, H. Kaim, G. Halverson and C. Rohlfing comments.
(A) Red body with white lettering. Eddins Collection. Possible prototype. Reader comments invited.　　　　**NRS**
(B) Orange body with white lettering, regular production run.
　　　　　— — 65 80

(C) Burnt orange with white lettering. G. Halverson Collection.
　　　　　— — 85 100

8067 TEXAS AND PACIFIC: 1980, powered Alco FA-2 unit, two-position reverse unit, blue and white; illustrated as part of 1051 Texas & Pacific Diesel set.　　　**Not Manufactured**

8068 THE ROCK: "1980" on locomotive cab, powered GP-20, 1980 annual LCCA convention issue; 2,700 made.　— — 125 150

8071 VIRGINIAN: 1980, powered SD-18, blue and yellow; also see 8072, six-wheel trucks, silver truck sides.
　　　　　— — 85 100

8072 VIRGINIAN: 1980, dummy SD-18, matches 8071 engine.
　　　　　— — 50 55

8071 and 8072: Pair　　　— — — 150

8111 DT&I: 1971-74, NW-2 Yard Switcher, illuminated headlight, hand reverse. Orange with black lettering.
(A) Two green marker lights.　— 20 30 35
(B) Two red marker lights.　— 20 30 35

8150 PENNSYLVANIA: 1981, dual-powered GG-1 electric, green-painted die-cast body with five gold stripes; magnetraction, three-position reverse unit.　　　　— — 300 375

8151 BURLINGTON: 1981, powered SD-28, red with gray top, white nose stripes; white frame, numbers and letters, six-wheel trucks; from 1160 Great Lakes Limited set.　　　— — 100 125

8152 CANADIAN PACIFIC: 1981, powered SD-24 flat top diesel, maroon and gray, with two yellow side stripes, three horizontal nose stripes; white frame, yellow numbers, maroon "Canadian Pacific" in script on gray background; horn, six-wheel trucks; from 1158 Maple Leaf set.
　　　　　— — 100 135

8153 READING: 1981, powered NW-2 Yard Switcher, dark green front and top; black frame, yellow sides, dark green numbers and logo; from 1154 Reading Yard King set. — — **40 55**

8154 ALASKA: 1981-82, powered, NW-2 Yard Switcher, dynamic air brake, same paint scheme as Lionel 614. — — **70 85**

8155 MONON: 1981-82, powered U36B, gold sides and ends with dark blue roof and dark blue band running along cab bottom; also see 8156. — — **60 75**

8156 MONON: 1981-82, dummy U36B, matches 8155. — — **40 50**

8155 and 8156: Pair — — **100 125**

8157 SANTA FE: 1981, dual-powered FM Trainmaster, blue with yellow trim, numbers and letters, electronic horn. — — **250 275**

8158 DULUTH MISSABE: 1981-82, powered GP-35, maroon with yellow middle side band, white numbers and letters; also see 8159. — — **60 75**

8159 DULUTH MISSABE: 1981-82, dummy GP-35; matches 8158. — — **40 50**

8160 BURGER KING: 1981-82, powered GP-20, yellow body with red top, frame, numbers and letters; from Favorite Food Freight, available only as separate sale item. — — **60 75**

8161 L.A.S.E.R.: 1981-82, Gas Turbine, bright chrome, blue lettering; part of 1150 L.A.S.E.R. Train set, a return to a late 1950s-type Lionel space set, DC powered. — — **25 30**

8162 ONTARIO NORTHLAND: 1981, powered SD-18, part of the "Fall Release Items", blue with yellow trim and lettering; also see 8163. — — **85 100**

8163 ONTARIO NORTHLAND: 1981, dummy SD-18; also see 8162. — — **50 60**

8164 PENNSYLVANIA: 1981, F-3 B unit, green body, with horn. Distributors were required to purchase nearly $800 of goods to acquire one. Matches 8952-53 AA pair. — — **— 175**

8182 NIBCO: 1982, NW-2 switcher, part of special 1264 promotional set made by Fundimensions for Nibco Plumbing Products; 2,000 made; offered as a premium for plumbers with purchase of faucet sets; set included regular production 9033 green Penn Central short hopper and 9035 blue Conrail 027-type boxcar; also had special 6482 NIBCO SP-type unlighted caboose. There were also two custom billboards, a 50-watt transformer, 027 track and a manumatic uncoupler with the set. The locomotive has a white body with blue-green "NIBCO" logo and number on the cab; green and blue ribbon runs the length of the cab; above it is blue lettering: "QUALITY PIPING PRODUCTS". Price for locomotive only. — — **125 150**

8250 SANTA FE: 1972-75, powered GP-9, Type II railing, black and yellow body with yellow lettering; black underframe, nose decal, Type II motor, pickup on dummy truck, Lionel/MPC builder's plate, Type II body. — **40 50 60**

8252 DELAWARE & HUDSON: 1972, powered Alco FA-2 unit, dark blue and silver body, two-position E-unit, Type IV body, "D & H" decal on side and nose, blank number-boards, no front coupler. — — **30 40**
See also Factory Errors and Prototypes.

8253 DELAWARE & HUDSON: 1972, dummy Alco FA-2 A unit; matches 8252.
(A) Silver with side decal. — — **20 30**
(B) Silver without side decal. — — **20 30**
See also Factory Errors and Prototypes.

8254 ILLINOIS CENTRAL: 1972, dummy GP-9, Type II railings, black lettering, orange plastic body with white stripe; no lights, nose decal, Lionel/MPC builder's plate, black frame. — — **30 40**

8255 SANTA FE: 1972, dummy GP-9; matches 8250, but not lighted. — — **30 40**

8258 CANADIAN NATIONAL: 1972, dummy GP-7, Type II railings, black and orange body with white lettering; no lights, no nose decal, Lionel/MPC builder's plate. — — **30 40**

8260 SOUTHERN PACIFIC: 1982, dual-motored F-3 A unit in distinctive red, orange, white and black "Daylight" paint scheme; three-position reverse unit, one-axle magnetraction, one operating coupler on front, fixed coupler on rear, illuminated number-boards, portholes; part of Spring Collector Series and reportedly a limited edition, comes with matching dummy 8262. Price for both units. — — **250 275**
Five matching passenger cars available as separate sales only.

8261 SOUTHERN PACIFIC: 1982, dummy F-3 B unit; matches 8260. — — **— 175**

8262: See 8260

8263 SANTA FE: 1982, powered GP-7, blue and yellow; operating couplers, electronic reverse unit, split-field motor, electronic three-position reversing unit. — — **35 50**

8264 CANADIAN PACIFIC: 1982 Vulcan 2-4-2 switcher snowplow; gray body, maroon snowplow, frame and trim; yellow lettering, non-operating headlight, gold ornamental bell; die-cast chassis, three-position reversing switch, operating die-cast coupler on rear. This unit often requires servicing before use because grease coagulates in the gear sump and the brushes arc. Remedy: flush out grease and sparingly lubricate with Lubriplate. Gears are noisy, as were original mid-1950s Lionel units. Body should be handled carefully because window struts are easily broken. R. Signurdson comment. — — **60 90**

8265 SANTA FE: 1982, powered SD-40, new cab design, blue and yellow painted body; working headlight and lighted number-boards; operating couplers at both ends, Type C six-wheel trucks, single motor with single-wound motor field for mechanical E-unit, magnetraction, electronic diesel horn; motor body housing has integral locator tab. R. Signurdson, D. Johns and C. Rohlfing comments. — — **250 300**

8266 NORFOLK AND WESTERN: 1982, SD-24, maroon body with yellow trim; three-position reverse unit, die-cast six-wheel trucks, operating couplers, illuminated number-boards, electronic diesel horn; part of 1260 Continental Limited set issued in Spring Collector Series. — — **100 125**

8268 Texas and Pacific: 1982, Quicksilver Express Set, part of 1253 in 1983. Alco body, closed front end with red number-boards, dark blue with broad silver stripe and lettering, light blue eagle and blue and silver "T&P logo on front; lighted, AC/DC can motor, solid state three-position reversing switch. To solve traction problems in the 1982 production, Lionel made available two iron weights with a piece of foam with double-sided adhesive for Service Station installation. The production of 1983 includes these weights. The set has sold exceptionally well. Price for powered A unit only. — — **50 60**

8269 Texas and Pacific: 1982-83, dummy unit, matches 8268. — — **25 30**

8272 PENNSYLVANIA: 1982, EP-5 "double-end" electric, special edition made for J. C. Penney; tuscan body, gold-painted ends and heat dissipator box atop engine, broad gold striping across sides, tuscan lettering and numbering within side striping; single motor, no magnetraction. Full price includes display board with (apparently) Gargraves piece of track and plastic display case. C. Darasko and G. Kline Collections. — — **— 220**

8350 U.S. STEEL: 1974-75, Gas Turbine, 0-4-0, maroon plastic body with silver lettering; DC motor, forward and reverse by polarity, reverse on power packs, motor will burn out if run on AC. — — **15 20**

8351 SANTA FE: 1973-74, powered Alco, FA-2 A unit, blue and silver body; Sears set. — — **35 50**

8352 SANTA FE: 1973-75, powered GP-20, plastic railings, dark blue and yellow body with yellow lettering; black underframe, no decal, Type II motor. — **35 45 60**

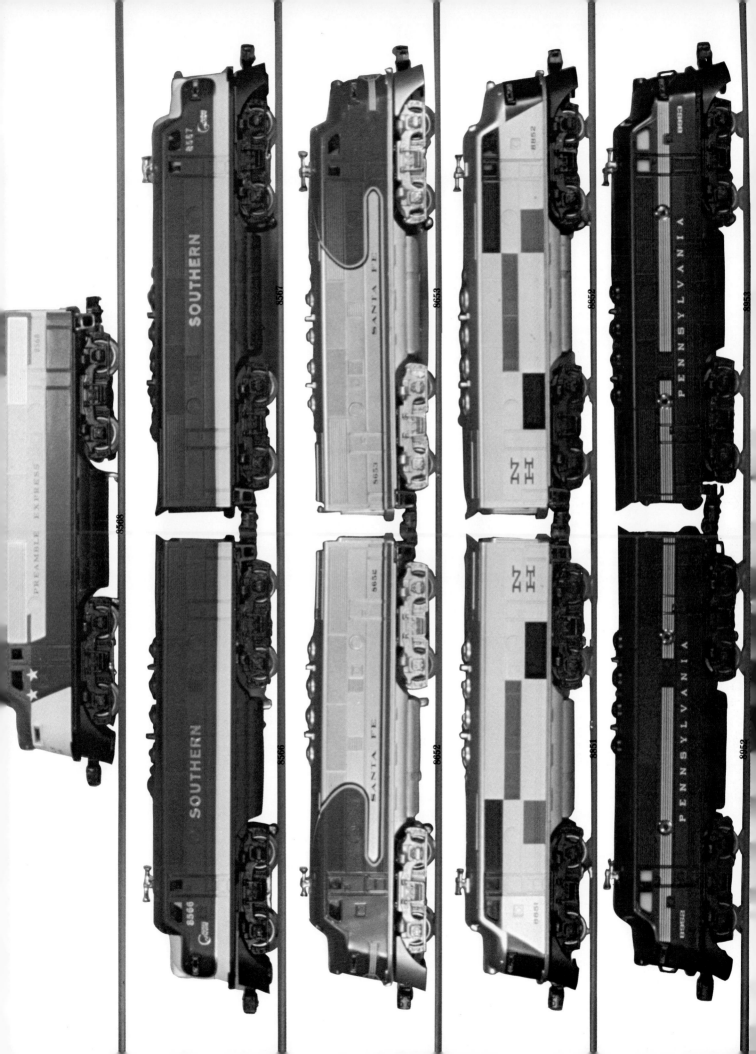

8353 GRAND TRUNK: 1974-75, powered GP-7, Type II railings, gray plastic body painted blue and orange, white lettering; lights, Type II motor, Lionel/MPC builder's plate, Type II body — 35 45 60

8354 ERIE: 1973-75, NW-2 Yard Switcher, black plastic body, heat-stamped gold lettering, lights.
(A) Type III body. — — 55 70
(B) Type IV body. — — 55 70

8355 SANTA FE: 1973-75, dummy GP-20; matches 8352, electronic diesel horn, pickup on one truck. — — 60 80

8356 GRAND TRUNK: 1974-75, dummy GP-7; matches 8353, no lights. — — 30 40

8357 PENNSYLVANIA: 1973-75, powered GP-9; Type II railings, gray plastic body painted dark green, gold lettering; lights, no nose decal, Type II motor, black frame, Lionel/MPC builder's plate, Type II body, 9,000 made. — — 75 90

8358 PENNSYLVANIA: 1973-75, dummy GP-9, matches 8357, no lights, a few units are known to have been made with horns.
(A) No horn. — — 35 50
(B) With factory installed horn. — — 60 85

8359 CHESSIE: 1973, powered GP-7, Type II railings, special gold paint for GM's 50th anniversary with blue lettering, reportedly that 9,000 made. "8359" not on locomotive, lights, nose lettering, Type II motor, black frame, Lionel/MPC builder's plate, Type II body; all blue "B & O" and "GM 50" lettering, painted nose. Mitchell Collection. — — 70 80
See also Factory Errors and Prototypes.

8360 LONG ISLAND: 1973-74, powered GP-20, Type II railings, charcoal gray-painted body with silver lettering; no nose decal, lights, Lionel/MPC builder's plate, Type II body. Shown in advance catalogue as light gray with darker roof, but not made that way.
(A) Black frame. — 35 50 60
(B) Black frame with painted red stripe. Confirmation requested; may not have been produced this way. — 45 60 70

8361 WESTERN PACIFIC: 1973-74, powered Alco, FA-2, A unit, silver and orange body; see 8362 for matching B unit, lights. — — 30 40

8362 WESTERN PACIFIC: 1973-74, dummy Alco, FA-2B unit; matches 8361. — — 25 35

8363 BALTIMORE & OHIO: 1973-75, powered F-3 A unit, dark blue plastic body painted light blue with white and gray top, yellow lettering on black stripe; Type I body, lights. See next entry for matching dummy A unit. — 65 80 100

8364 BALTIMORE & OHIO: 1973-75, dummy F-3 A unit; matches 8863. — 50 60 75

8365 CANADIAN PACIFIC: 1973, powered F-3 A unit, Type I body, reportedly only 2,500 manufactured, uncatalogued, 1973 Service Station Special; for matching dummy A unit see 8366.
(A) Gray plastic body painted brown and gray. — — 150 175
(B) Blue plastic body painted brown and gray. — — 150 175

8366 CANADIAN PACIFIC: 1973, dummy A unit.
(A) Matches 8365(A). — — 100 125
(B) Matches 8365(B). — — 100 125

8367 LONG ISLAND: 1973, dummy GP-20; matches 8360, electronic diesel horn. Sound of this horn is extremely good; horn loudspeaker faces upwards in cab where motor usually goes, and the result is a realistic "muffled" diesel horn sound. No lights, but unit easy to convert to lighted dummy. R. LaVoie comments.

(A) Plain frame. — — 60 75
(B) Red stripe on frame. Confirmation requested; may not have been made this way. — — 70 80

8368 ALASKA RAILROAD: 1983, 2-4-2, motorized unit, yellow and blue with blue lettering "ALASKA RAILROAD 8368" and eskimo logo; silver-finished bell, operating headlight, operating couplers, die-cast frame, three-position E unit; came in Type V orange and blue box. This unit often requires servicing before operation because grease coagulates in the gear sump and the brushes arc. Flush out grease and lubricate sparingly with Lubriplate. Gears are noisy, as were those on the motorized units of the 1950s. This unit intended to pull only two or three cars. The cab should be handled carefully because the window struts are easily broken. R. Signurdson comment. — — 90 120

8369 ERIE LACKAWANNA: 1983, powered GP-20, dual DC motors, operates on AC or DC, operating headlight, electronic three-position reverse, one operating coupler, only offered for separate sale in Traditional Series catalogue; shown in catalogue as blue and tuscan engine, but made in gray and tuscan Erie Lackawanna colors. Lionel also made a matching 6425 caboose. Surprisingly good runner with a medium-sized train; the AC-DC can motors used on this unit operate on much lower voltage than older motor types. The twin-motored locomotives with this motor are better than their single-motored counterparts because good pickup rollers are used rather than sliding shoes. The interior of this locomotive has a large weight to help traction. Plastic truck frames and couplers. R. LaVoie Collection. — — 60 75

8370 NEW YORK CENTRAL: 1983, powered F-3A unit, dual motors with eight-wheel magnetraction, three-position reverse unit; headlight, illuminated number boards, portholes, operating coupler at front end. Note matching 8371 and 8372 and passenger cars. In 1948-49 Lionel offered a N.Y.C. F-3 as 2333. Price for 8370 and 8372 as a pair is $300. — — 225 250

8371 NEW YORK CENTRAL: 1983, dummy F-3B unit; matches 8370 and 8372. Electronic diesel horn, portholes, not illuminated, dummy couplers. — — 60 75

8372 NEW YORK CENTRAL: 1983, dummy F-3A unit, headlight, illuminated number-boards, portholes, operating coupler at cab end; matches 8370 and 8372. — — 60 75

8374 BURLINGTON NORTHERN: 1983, DC powered NW-2 Yard Switcher, rectifier for AC or DC operation; green and black plastic body, white lettering and logo, black-enameled frame, two red indicator lights and operating headlight; two disc operating couplers, three-position electronic reversing unit; only offered for separate sale in Traditional Series Catalogue. Lionel also made a matching 6427 caboose. — — 45 55

8375 CHICAGO & NORTHWESTERN: 1983, DC powered GP-7, dual motors with rectifier for AC or DC operation, headlight, operating couplers, electronic reverse unit; yellow and green body; part of 1354 Northern Freight Flyer set. See 8369 entry for operating comments. — — 60 75

8376 UNION PACIFIC: 1983, powered SD-40, magnetraction, six-wheel die-cast metal trucks, headlight, electronic diesel horn, three-position reverse unit, operating couplers at both ends; yellow and gray body with red stripe, green hood top. Engine has a single motor with a double-wound field for the electronic E-unit. It has a drawbar pull of 10 ounces (this may vary between locomotives). The engine requires 0 Gauge track and will not pass through 027 Gauge switches. The motor body housing has a separate stamped metal locator tab mounted in it. Part of a special limited edition set, 1361 Gold Coast Limited, with 9290 barrel car, 9888 reefer, 9468 boxcar, 6114 hopper, 6357 tank and 6904 caboose. R. Signurdson and D. Johns comments. Price for locomotive only. — — 250 275

8377 US: 1983, switcher, 0-4-0, olive drab, engine does not have applied lettering as shown in the Traditional Series Catalogue. Lionel supplied a decal sheet for the operator. This locomotive is part of the low price introductory 1355 Commando Assault Train set with 6561 flat with cruise missile, 6562 flat with crates, 6564 flat with tanks, 6435 caboose, playmat, figures and supply depot kit. Set price $50.00 — — 20 25

8378 WABASH: 1983, Fairbanks-Morse Trainmaster, dual motors, magnetraction. Special production for J.C. Penney Christmas special, not listed in Lionel catalogue. "8378" does not appear on body; "530" appears on body near cab. Deep blue body, gray and white striping, Wabash flag logo on cab below window. These "Bluebird" markings are quite similar to the 2337 and 2339 Geeps made by Lionel in the 1950s, except that the blue color is darker. The carton is marked "8378-203"; it contained the engine box and a boxed display case marked "GLASS". Despite this marking, the case is plastic; it has an oak base with a piece of Gargraves Phantom track fastened to it. Two plastic bumpers are also supplied. An instruction sheet marked "LIONEL WABASH BLUEBIRD, 09-8378-250" came with the box, and a second sheet found with regular production units, 70-8157-250, was also included. A short run of about 800 was made in Mount Clemens just before the factory moved to Mexico. Thereafter, reports about production conflict. Some say that there was no more production. Others say that Mexican production did occur and can be distinguished from Mount Clemens production by an aluminized paper sticker attached to the underside of the engine which has "CPG" and "Made In Mexico" information, whereas the pieces made in Mt. Clemens have "MADE IN U.S.A" on their plates. Reportedly, there are slight color differences in the Mexican locomotive. In addition, the Wabash flags are installed at an angle, and the finish is not as sharp. The Mount Clemens pieces were made from September to December, 1983, and when it was discovered that there were substantial back orders, Mexican production began in April 1984. Back orders received the Mexican-made pieces. The total production run was supposed to be about 5,000, but it is likely that far fewer were actually made. D. Johns, P. Catalano, R. Shanfeld and R. LaVoie comments; G. Kline and R. Darasko Collections.

(A) Mount Clemens production. — — 550 600
(B) Mexican production. — — 500 550

8379 PENNSYLVANIA: 1983, motorized fire-fighting car, tuscan body with black and white bumpers and black wheels, white fire hose with gold nozzle, gray hose, reel and pump, black clad fireman with flesh-colored hands and face, yellow outriggers. Highly detailed body, gold plastic bell, illuminated red dome light atop cab which blinks after warmup; bump reverse; gold "PENNSYLVANIA" PRR Keystone and "8379" on side of body; number is divided in center by Keystone. Originally shown with "6521" number in Fall Collector Center brochure. After some use, there is a tendency for the bumper frame to loosen and slide to the neutral position. This can be alleviated by increasing the reversing slide contact spring tension. The reversing slide adjustment can also be made by bending the two tabs on the slide outward to increase friction between the shoe assembly and the car frame. The operating instructions state that the unit should not be left in the neutral position for more than five minutes. The reason for this is that the contact spring may bridge the gap between the contact rivets, which can cause the two fields to buck each other and burn out. In some cases, this unit needed adjustment prior to initial operation. R. Signurdson and D. Johns comments. — — 90 110

8380 LIONEL LINES: 1983, powered SD-28, dark blue upper body, upper cab and nose top, orange lower body, and nose; black frame, red, white and blue Lionel logo on cab side and nose; six-wheel trucks, Type IV handrails; blue number is below the logo on the cab, blue "LIONEL LINES" in modern sans-serif lettering below color division, lighted cab, chromed plastic five-horn unit atop cab, squared off cab roof; Fall Collector Center, LaVoie report. — — 110 140

8452 ERIE: 1974, powered Alco FA-2 A unit.
(A) Black plastic body painted green with yellow lettering, lights; see next entry for B unit. — 25 35 40
(B) Same as (A), but closed pilot, red number-boards and no front decal. G. Halverson Collection. NRS

8453 ERIE: 1974, dummy Alco FA-2 B unit; matches 8452 A unit (in previous entry). — 20 25 30

8454 RIO GRANDE: 1974-75, powered GP-7, Type II railings, black body with orange lettering, yellow hash marks, black frame, lights, Type II motor, Lionel/MPC builder's plate, Type II body. — 35 45 55

8455 RIO GRANDE: 1974-75, dummy GP-7; matches 8454, no lights.
— — 25 35

8458 ERIE-LACKAWANNA: 1984, SD-40, gray cab, maroon and yellow striping, yellow lettering, yellow-painted frame; two motors, electronic diesel horn, magnetraction, lights at both ends, die-cast six-wheel trucks; part of Erie-Lackawanna Limited collector set. — — 260 275

8459 RIO GRANDE: 1984, rotary snowplow, black cab, yellow cab sides with black "Rio Grande" script and number (this time the "a" in "Grande" has been inserted correctly, rather than backwards as in the Lionel unit of the 1950s). Yellow handrails and plow housing, black plow fan with yellow markings, 2-4-2 Vulcan with three-position reversing switch, one operating die-cast coupler on rear, no headlight but lens is present, gold ornamental bell. This unit runs well upon delivery, and its gears are quieter than the previous 8264, 8368 and 8379. The window struts are less likely to break because they are made with a double section. This engine intended to pull only two or three cars. Packed in Type V collector box, Mt. Clemens production. R. Signurdson and R. LaVoie comments. — — 110 125

8460 MKT: 1973-75, NW-2 Yard Switcher, gray plastic body painted red, white lettering; manual forward and reverse, Type IV body, dummy coupler. — 25 30 40

See also Factory Errors and Prototypes.

8463 CHESSIE: 1974, powered GP-20, Type II railings, blue, orange and yellow body with blue lettering; limited edition of 10,000, lights, black frame, nose decal, Type II motor, "LIONEL" logo. — — 80 95

8464 RIO GRANDE: 1974, powered F-3 A unit, yellow body with black lettering, silver roof, solid portholes, lights; only 3,000 manufactured, uncatalogued 1974 Service Station Special, Type I body. — 65 80 100

8465 RIO GRANDE: 1974, dummy F-3 A unit; matches 8464; 3,000 manufactured, lights, Type I body. — 40 50 75

8466 AMTRAK: 1974-75, powered F-3 A unit, silver body and sides, black roof and nose hood, red and blue logo; sealed portholes, lights, Type III body. — 85 110 150

8467 AMTRAK: 1974-75, dummy F-3A unit; matches 8466.
— 40 50 75

8468 BALTIMORE & OHIO: 1974, dummy F-3 B unit, blue body with white lettering, sealed portholes; matches 8363 and 8364 A units.
(A) Top edge of sides not painted. — — 50 70
(B) Top edge of sides painted. — — 50 70

8469 CANADIAN PACIFIC: 1974, dummy F-3 B unit, sealed portholes; matches 8365, 8366, top edge of side not painted maroon.
— — 75 100

8470 CHESSIE: 1974, powered G.E. U36B, stamped metal railings, blue, orange and yellow body with blue lettering; from Grand National set, black frame, lights, nose decal, Type II motor, no MPC logo. Shown in 1974 catalogue with large emblem and lettering, but not produced that way.
— — 75 90

8471 PENNSYLVANIA: 1973-74, NW-2 Yard Switcher, dark green body with yellow lettering, red Keystone on cab sides. — — 65 85

Note 8473 step variation (three versus two) to right of "Coke".

8473 COCA COLA: 1975, NW-2 Yard Switcher, red body with white lettering; two-position reverse.

(A) "Three step" variety, Type III body. — 25 35 50

(B) "Two steps", Type IV body. — 20 30 40

(C) "One step", Type V body. — 20 30 40

8474 RIO GRANDE: 1975, dummy F-3 B unit, yellow and green body, silver roof, sealed portholes; matches 8464, 8465. — — 60 75

8475 AMTRAK: 1975, dummy F-3 B unit, silver body and sides, black roof, red and blue logo, sealed portholes; matches 8466, 8467.
— — 70 85

8477 NEW YORK CENTRAL: 1984, powered GP-9, black body, large gray stripe edged by smaller white stripes on side, small "NEW YORK CENTRAL" lettering above gray stripe, gray and white striping on cab ends with New York Central logo, separate molded plastic grab-irons on front and rear; AC motor operates on either AC or DC. The power truck is similar, but not identical, to the older Lionel power trucks of the Geeps produced in the 1950s. The magnets in this truck appear to be much larger, producing stronger magnetraction. Electronic diesel horn, three-position E-type reverse unit, operating headlights, operating couplers, die-cast truck side frames, stamped-steel frame and handrails. Already in considerable demand by collectors and appreciating in price rapidly. — — 140 150

8480 UNION PACIFIC: 1984, F-3A locomotive, yellow body, red and gray striping and lettering, dark gray roof and nose, dark gray frame and trucks, lighted number-boards, Union Pacific shield-and-wing decal on nose; two motors, magnetraction. Collectors have complained that many examples do not match in color; the engine has been found in medium and darker yellow shades, and many boxes have to be examined to find matching colors. Price for powered A unit only. — — 160 175

8481 UNION PACIFIC: F-3B dummy unit, electronic diesel horn; matches 8480. — — 75 90

8482 UNION PACIFIC: F-3A dummy unit; matches 8480, lighted.
— — 90 100

8485 U.S. MARINES: 1984, NW-2 switcher, olive and black camouflage-painted cab, black frame and rails; lighted, three-position electronic reversing switch, AC/DC can motor; operating plastic couplers, plastic truck side frames, weighted, sliding shoe contacts. — — 55 60

8550 JERSEY CENTRAL: 1975, powered GP-9, Type II railings, red and white-painted body with white lettering, black frame; lights, nose decal; Type II motor, no pickup on dummy truck; "LIONEL" builder's plate.
— — 45 60

8551 PENNSYLVANIA: 1975, powered, "Little Joe" G.E. EP-5 electric, tuscan body with gold stripes on body and lettering, lights; two pantographs, can be wired for overhead operation on catenary, separate motor and power truck. — — 85 110

8552 SOUTHERN PACIFIC: 1975, powered Alco FA-2 A unit, orange body with white stripes, lights; set of three with 8553, 8554. Price for set.
— — 100 135

8553 SOUTHERN PACIFIC: 1975, dummy Alco FA-2 B unit; matches 8552. (Only B unit dummy with operating couplers at both ends, wheelbase altered to accommodate trucks.) Set price with 8552, 8554.
— — 100 135

8554 SOUTHERN PACIFIC: 1975, dummy Alco FA-2 A unit; matches 8552. Price for set. — — 100 135

8555 MILWAUKEE ROAD: 1975, uncatalogued 1975 Service Station Special, powered F-3 A unit, gray and orange body, sealed portholes, lights, Type II mold. — 75 100 125

8556

8556 CHESSIE: 1975-76, NW-2 Yard Switcher, yellow and blue, lights, Type V body. — — 50 75

See also Factory Errors and Prototypes.

8557 MILWAUKEE ROAD: 1975, dummy F-3 A unit, gray and orange body; matches 8555, Type II body. — 40 50 75

8558 MILWAUKEE ROAD: 1976, powered General Electric EP-5 electric, brown, orange and black body, lights; two silver pantographs, can be wired for catenary operation, separate motor and power truck.
— — 100 125

8559 N&W 1776: 1975, see 1776(A), (B) and (C).

8560 CHESSIE: 1975, dummy G.E. U36B, matches 8470, some reports stress this is not quite an exact match for the 8470 because the vermilion stripe at the top of the cab is slightly wider than on the powered locomotive.

(A) No lights or light pickup. G. Halverson and T. Ladny comments.
— — 40 55

(B) Lighted unit with pickup on one truck. G. Halverson comment.
— — 40 55

8561 JERSEY CENTRAL: 1975-76, dummy GP-9; matches 8550, not lighted. — — 25 35

8562 MISSOURI PACIFIC: 1975-76, powered GP-20, Type II railings, blue with white lettering, hash marks; black underframe, Type II motor.
— 35 45 60

8563 ROCK ISLAND: 1975, uncatalogued, powered Alco FA-2 A unit, red body with white letters, yellow stripe, closed pilot, available only in Sears set 1594. Details of set requested. — — 40 55

8564 UNION PACIFIC: 1975, powered G.E. U36B, Type III railing, gray and yellow body with red stripe; from North American set, black frame, lights, nose decal, Type II motor. — 55 70 85

8565 MISSOURI PACIFIC: 1975-76, dummy GP-20; matches 8562, a few with horns are known to exist.

(A) No horn. — — 25 35

(B) With horn. — — 65 80

8566 SOUTHERN: 1975-77, powered F-3 A unit, green body with gray stripes; sealed portholes, lights, Type IV body, gold lettering.
— 100 125 150

8567 SOUTHERN: 1975-77, dummy F-3 A unit. — 60 75 100

8568 PREAMBLE EXPRESS: 1975, powered F-3 A unit, red, white and blue body, sealed portholes; Spirit of '76, East Coast Clearance Engine, lights, Type IV body. No dummy unit made. — — 65 80

8569 SOO: 1975-77, NW-2, Yard Switcher, red body with white lettering; lights, dummy couplers, two-position reverse.   —   —   **30**   **40**

8570 LIBERTY SPECIAL: 1975, powered Alco FA-2, blue top, white body, with red nose and stripe, lights.   —   **30**   **40**   **50**

8571 FRISCO: 1975-76, powered G.E. U36B, Type III railing, white and red with red lettering, black frame; lights, no nose decal, Type II motor.   —   **50**   **65**   **80**

8572 FRISCO: 1975-76, dummy G. E. U36B matches 8571, lights, pickup on one truck.   —   —   **30**   **40**

8573 UNION PACIFIC: 1975, dummy G. E. U36B, stamped metal railing; matches 8564, except no lights, pickup on one truck, with horn, reportedly only 1,200 made.   —   —   **110**   **135**

8575 MILWAUKEE ROAD: Dummy F-3B unit, matches 8555.   —   —   **50**   **60**

8576 PENN CENTRAL: 1975-76, powered GP-7, Type III railings, black body with white lettering.
(A) Door outline shows through "PENN CENTRAL" lettering, black frame, lights, nose decal, Type II motor, Lionel/MPC builder's plate.   —   **40**   **55**   **65**
(B) Same as (A), but door outline painted solid, "LIONEL" builder's plate, Type III body.   —   **40**   **55**   **65**

8578 NEW YORK CENTRAL: Announced for 1985, Ballast Tamper, catalogue description: orange-yellow body, black frame and railings, black lettering, black tamper frame, silver tampers, silver headlight atop cab, silver battery box, blue man inside cab, dummy rear coupler. Track trip activates tampers and reduces speed of unit. Estimated introductory price.   —   —   —   **115**

8580 ILLINOIS CENTRAL: Set scheduled for 1985, F-3A powered diesel; separate sale item from City of New Orleans, catalogue description: medium brown body (not dark brown as shown in catalogue), orange and yellow striping, yellow lettering, lighted cab and number-boards (which may have engine numbers for the first time), clear portholes, black front grab-irons, two motors, magnetraction, black frame and trucks. Price with matching 8581 dummy F-3A unit, estimated at release.   —   —   —   **295**

8581 ILLINOIS CENTRAL: Scheduled for 1985, F-3A dummy unit, lighted; matches 8580.   —   —   —   **295**

8582 ILLINOIS CENTRAL: Scheduled for 1985, F-3B dummy unit, electronic diesel horn, matches 8580 and 8581, sold separately. Estimated introductory price.   —   —   —   **85**

8585 BURLINGTON NORTHERN: Scheduled for 1985, SD-40, catalogue description: cascade green lower body, black upper body and roof, white number, "BN" logo and safety stripes, green-painted handrails; two motors, magnetraction, electronic diesel horn, black six-wheel die-cast trucks, lighted cab and number-boards. Part of Burlington Northern Limited set. Estimated introductory price.   —   —   —   **285**

8650 BURLINGTON NORTHERN: 1976-77, powered G.E. U36B, Type III railing, black and green body with white lettering, hash marks; black frame, lights, Type II motor.   —   —   **65**   **80**

8651 BURLINGTON NORTHERN: 1976-77, dummy G.E. U36B; matches 8650, lights, pickup on one truck.   —   —   **35**   **45**

8652 SANTA FE: 1976-77, powered F-3 A unit, red and silver; lights, sealed portholes, Type V mold.   —   **75**   **100**   **125**

8653 SANTA FE: 1976-77, dummy F-3 A unit; matches 8562, Type V mold.   —   **50**   **60**   **85**

8654 BOSTON & MAINE: 1976, powered GP-9, Type III railings, blue, white and black body, white and black lettering, white frame; lights, no nose decal, "LIONEL" builder's plate, Type III body.   —   **50**   **60**   **75**

8655 BOSTON & MAINE: 1976, dummy GP-9; matches 8654, not lighted.   —   —   **30**   **40**

8656 CANADIAN NATIONAL: 1976, powered Alco FA-2 A unit, orange, black and white, lights, three-position reverse. Much harder to find than is generally realized.   —   —   **50**   **65**

8657 CANADIAN NATIONAL: 1976, dummy Alco FA-2 B unit; matches 8656. Two dummy couplers, no tank/step underbody detail. R. Young comment.   —   —   **30**   **40**

8658 CANADIAN NATIONAL: 1976 dummy Alco FA-2 A unit; matches 8656. Very hard to find.   —   —   **40**   **50**

8659 VIRGINIAN: 1976-77, G.E. EL-C rectifier electric, blue body with yellow stripe and lettering, yellow frame; can be wired for catenary, separate motor and power truck.
(A) Thin, light-colored nose decal.   —   **75**   **100**   **125**
(B) Same as (A), but with thick, light-colored nose decal.   —   **75**   **100**   **125**
(C) Same as (A), but with regular dark yellow nose decal.   —   **75**   **100**   **125**

8660 CP RAIL: 1976,77, NW-2 Yard Switcher, red body with white lettering, lights.   —   **35**   **45**   **60**

8661 SOUTHERN: Dummy F-3B unit, not lighted.   —   —   **60**   **75**

8664 AMTRAK: 1976-77, powered Alco FA-2 A unit, light, fixed rear coupler, body has black roof and nose top, silver sides and nose skirt, red nose and blue lettering. Came as part of the Lake Shore Limited set, which included 6403, 6404, 6405 and 6406 Amtrak short 027 passenger cars. A B-unit dummy engine was available separately, as were passenger cars 6410, 6411 and 6412.   —   —   **35**   **45**

8665 BANGOR AND AROOSTOOK: See 1776

8666 NORTHERN PACIFIC: 1976, uncatalogued, powered GP-9, stamped metal railings, black and gold body with red stripe, gold and red lettering; 1976 Service Station Special, gold frame, lights, no nose decal, Type II motor, no MPC logo.   —   —   **100**   **125**

8667 AMTRAK: 1976-77, dummy Alco B unit, black roof and nose top, silver sides and nose skirt, red nose, blue lettering; matches 8664, difficult to find.   —   —   **25**   **35**

8668 NORTHERN PACIFIC: 1976, dummy GP-9, matches 8666.   —   —   **45**   **55**

8669 ILLINOIS CENTRAL: 1976, powered G.E. U36B, stamped metal railings, white and orange with black lettering, from Illinois Central set, black frame, lights, Type II motor, nose decals.   —   —   **65**   **80**

8670 CHESSIE: 1976, Gas Turbine, 0-4-0, yellow body with blue trim; fixed couplers, DC motor, polarity reverse, runs only on DC, sliding shoe pickup, not lighted.   —   —   **15**   **20**

8764

8765

8868

8750 THE ROCK: 1977, powered GP-7, Type III railings, blue and white body with white and blue lettering, white frame; lights, nose decal, Type II motor, "LIONEL" builder's plate, Type III body.   —   —   **55**   **75**

8751 THE ROCK: 1977, dummy GP-7; matches 8750, no lights.   —   —   **30**   **40**

8753 PENNSYLVANIA: 1977, uncatalogued, powered GG-1 electric, wine red with gold stripes; two motors, magnetraction; 6000 produced.   —   **250**   **300**   **350**

8754 NEW HAVEN: 1977-78, powered G.E. EL-C rectifier electric, lights, black roof, orange sides, white stripes, black lettering, black frame; can be wired for catenary, separate motor and power truck.   —   **70**   **85**   **115**

8755 SANTA FE: 1977-78, powered G.E. U36B, stamped metal railing, blue and yellow body with blue and yellow lettering, silver metal truck side frame, yellow frame; lights, nose decal, Type II motor.   —   **65**   **80**

8756 SANTA FE: 1977-78, dummy G.E. U36B; matches 8755, not lighted.   —   —   **35**   **45**

8757 CONRAIL: 1977-78, powered GP-9, Type III railing, gray plastic body painted blue, white lettering; lights, nose decal, Type II motor, no pickup on dummy truck, no MPC logo.
(A) Black underframe and railings.   —   —   **60**   **75**
(B) White underframe and railings.   —   —   **60**   **75**

8758 SOUTHERN: 1978, GP-7 dummy; matches 8774, green and white. This unit is unique in that it has a lower number than does its powered unit.   —   —   **30**   **40**

8759 ERIE LACKAWANNA: 1977-79, powered GP-9, Type III railing, gray plastic body painted gray, tuscan and yellow, yellow lettering, yellow frame; lights, nose decal, Type II motor, no MPC logo.   —   —   **55**   **75**

8760 ERIE LACKAWANNA: 1977-79, dummy GP-9; matches 8759.   —   —   **30**   **40**

8761 GRAND TRUNK: 1977-78, NW-2 Yard Switcher, blue, white and orange paint; three-position E-unit, two disc-operating couplers, light.   —   —   **50**   **65**

8762 GREAT NORTHERN: 1977-78, powered G.E. EP-5 electric, gray plastic painted dark green and orange, yellow lettering and stripes, four red and white logos, two large decals on nose; two pantographs, can be wired for catenary, separate motor and power truck.   —   —   **100**   **135**

8763 NORFOLK & WESTERN: 1977-78 powered GP-9, Type III railing, gray plastic painted black, white lettering, black frame; lights, nose decal, Type II motor, no MPC logo.   —   —   **50**   **65**

See also Factory Errors and Prototypes.

8764 BALTIMORE & OHIO: 1977, powered Budd RDC passenger car, gray plastic body painted silver with blue lettering, metal frame, plastic battery box hangs from frame, three-position E-unit with lever on bottom, two disc-operating couplers, rubber tread on two wheels with gears, F-3-type power trucks with plastic two-step assembly. (The plastic assembly formerly appeared on the Lionel 44 ton dummy truck.) This is a remanufacture of the Lionel 1950s version and differs from it in the following ways: the reissues have different numbers, a plastic trim horn replaces a metal trim horn, rubber tire traction replaces magnetraction and highly shiny silver paint replaces flat silver-gray paint.   —   **60**   **80**   **100**

8765 BALTIMORE & OHIO: 1977, dummy Budd RDC baggage/mail, "US Mail Railway Post Office", "Budd RDC" in blue letters pierced by red line on small decal, lights, two disc-operating couplers, gray plastic painted silver with blue lettering.   —   —   **40**   **50**

8766 BALTIMORE & OHIO: 1977, powered Budd RDC baggage/mail, gray plastic painted shiny silver with blue lettering; lights; part of 1977 Service Station Special set 1766, uncatalogued, with 8767 and 8768. Price for set.   —   —   **200**   **225**

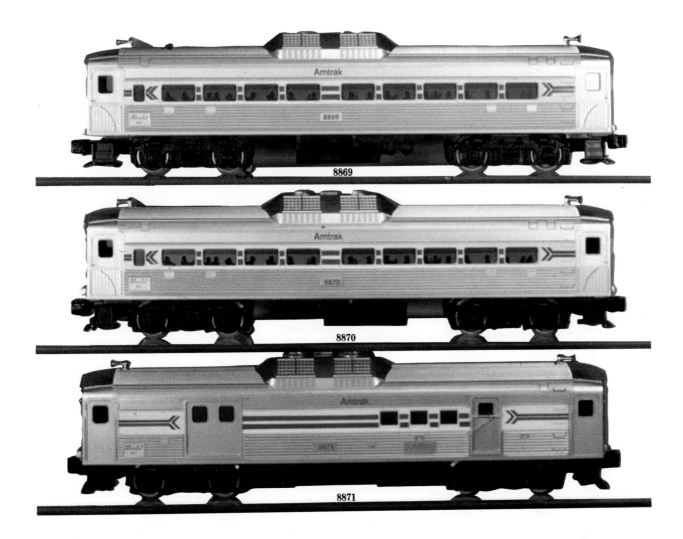

8869

8870

8871

8767 BALTIMORE & OHIO: 1977, dummy Budd RDC passenger car; matches 8766, part of set with 8766 and 8768. Price for set.

— — **200 225**

8768 BALTIMORE & OHIO: 1977, dummy Budd RDC passenger car; matches 8766, part of set with 8766 and 8767. Price for set.

— — **200 225**

8769 REPUBLIC STEEL: 1977, DC-powered, gas turbine, blue with yellow trim; fixed couplers, sliding contact pickups, for use with DC current only. — — **15 20**

8770 E.M.D.: 1977, NW-2 Yard Switcher, General Motors E.M.D. factory demonstrator paint scheme, blue and white body with white lettering, lights.
(A) Two disc-operating couplers, three-position E-unit. — **40 50 65**
(B) Fixed couplers, two-position reverse unit. — **30 40 50**

8771 GREAT NORTHERN: 1977, powered G.E. U36B, Type III railing, gray plastic painted black, white and blue with white lettering; from Rocky Mountain Special set, black frame, lights, Type II motor.

— — **70 85**

8772 GM&O: 1977, powered GP-20, Type III railing, gray plastic body painted red and white; from Heartland set, white frame, lights, nose decal, Type II motor, "LIONEL" logo. — **55 70 85**

8773 MICKEY MOUSE: 1977-78, powered G.E. U36B gray plastic body painted red and white with Mickey, Pluto and Donald. This item has shown greater appreciation than most Fundimensions engines. — — **175 200**

8774 SOUTHERN: 1977-78, powered, GP-7, small pickup rollers mounted on power truck, gray plastic body painted green and white, gold stripe and gold lettering, Southern decal at front end; black frame, Type IV railing, Type III body, Type II motor. — — **55 70**

8775 LEHIGH VALLEY: 1977-78, powered GP-9, gray plastic body painted bright red, yellow heat-stamped lettering and stripe; Type III railing, Type III cab, three-position E-unit. — — **55 70**

8776 C&NW: 1977-78, powered GP-20, gray plastic body painted yellow and very dark green, green lettering, red, white, and black decal beneath cab window; number-boards do not have numbers, black frame, Type III railing. — — **55 70**

8777 SANTA FE: 1977-78, dummy F-3 B unit; matches 8652, fixed couplers at both ends, Santa Fe decal on side, no portholes, no separate grate units. — — **45 60**

8778 LEHIGH VALLEY: 1977-78, dummy GP-9; matches 8775, not lighted. — — **30 35**

8779 C&NW: 1977-78, dummy GP-20; matches 8776, not lighted, two disc-operating couplers. — — **30 35**

8850 PENN CENTRAL: 1978-79, powered GG-1 electric, black-painted die-cast body with white "PENN CENTRAL" and Penn Central logo on side; two magnetraction motors, magnetic couplers, headlamps at both ends, operating pantographs with black insulators, shiny metal shoes on pantographs, E-unit lever goes through roof. This engine has not sold as well as the first GG-1 rerun. However, according to reliable sources, about the same number of black GG-1s were made as the 8753.

— **225 250 275**

8851 NEW HAVEN: 1978-79, powered A unit, Type VI body, three ridges run from the cab door to the rear of the side, gray plastic body painted silver-white, orange and black. "NH" in white letters on nose, the "N" has no serifs on the bottom right side - this matches the original Lionel F-3 New Haven but differs from the way NH is shown on the boxcars. Silver-painted frame, black truck side frames, disc-operating front coupler, two motors, rubber tires; came with 8852 as set. Price for set. — — **175 200**

8852 NEW HAVEN: 1978-79, dummy F-3 A unit, Type VI body; matches 8851, lights; came with 8851 as set. Price for set. — — **175 200**

8854 CP RAIL: 1978-79, GP-9, gray plastic body painted red, white and black, white lettering, white and black CP design; black truck sides, two disc-operating couplers, two geared wheels with rubber tires, Type IV railing, came with Great Plains Express set, "LIONEL" builder's plates, Type V body. — — **50 60 75**

8855 MILWAUKEE ROAD: 1978, powered SD-18, the first in the SD-18 locomotive series, it is a combination of a U36B chassis with six-wheel trucks and a GP-20 cab unit with added dynamic brake and five-unit horn cluster. In real railroad parlance, a "cab" unit is a GM F diesel or an Alco FA diesel, and a "hood" unit is a GP, "U-Boat" or SD diesel. However, in tinplate terms, when we refer to the "cab", we are talking about the plastic shell of any tinplate diesel. Because of the increased truck size, the "battery box" was redesigned and now reads "LIONEL MT. CLEMENS MICHIGAN 28045". Two disc-operating couplers, three-position reverse unit, rubber tires on end geared wheels (center wheels are blind). (For better operation note that center blind drivers are often too high and cause the rubber tire drivers to lose traction, particularly under a heavy load. Solution: hold the running engine upright and gently place a fine file against the blind driver and reduce its diameter.) Gray plastic body painted dull orange and black, black and white lettering, red and white logo underneath cab window; light, two disc-operating couplers, three-position E-unit. Sold only as part of the specially boxed Milwaukee Road set and not available for separate sale. Most sets are believed to have been sold to collectors and not run, matching dummy not available, five-horn cluster and bell, Type IV frame, Type II motor. — — **100 135**

8857 NORTHERN PACIFIC: 1978-80, powered G.E. U36B, gray plastic painted black with orange band along base, yellow cab end, yellow frame and rails, burnished truck side frames, Ying/Yang logo on cab decal; disc-operating couplers, five-unit plastic horn on hood roof, three-position E-unit, Type IV railing, Type II motor. — **50 65 80**

8858 NORTHERN PACIFIC: 1978-80, dummy G.E. U36B; matches 8857, not lighted.
(A) No horn. — — **30 40**
(B) With horn. Confirmation requested. — — **65 80**

8859 CONRAIL: 1978-80, 1982, powered G.E. EL-C rectifier electric, gray plastic body painted blue, white lettering and Conrail design, two disc-operating couplers, black truck side frames, one operating pantograph, shiny metal pantograph shoe, can be wired for catenary operation, separate motor and power truck. Though as many of this rectifier were produced as the Virginian and the New Haven examples, this version is not found quite as often. — — **90 125**

8860 ROCK: 1978-79, powered NW-2 Yard Switcher, gray plastic body painted blue, black and white lettering and logo, white-enameled frame, white nose with two pronounced red indicator lights, blue paint around headlight; two disc-operating couplers, three-position E-unit, rubber tires on two geared wheels, plastic unit suspended from frame behind E-unit, Type II motor. — — **50 60**

8861 SANTA FE: 1978-79, powered Alco FA-2 A unit, red and silver paint; light, two-position reverse, Type II motor. — **25 35 45**

8862 SANTA FE: 1978-79, dummy Alco FA-2; matches 8861.
— **20 25 30**

8864 NEW HAVEN: 1978, dummy F-3 B unit; matches 8851 and 8852, not lighted. — — **45 60**

8866 MINNEAPOLIS & ST. LOUIS: 1978, GP-9 powered Service Station Special sold by Lionel to Service Stations for their exclusive sale as part of a special set. This is the only item not specifically available for separate sale in the 1978 Service Station Special set, although in reality it was available separately when dealers broke up the sets. Gray plastic body painted red and white, blue cab roof, white and red lettering, red and white logo beneath cab windows and on hood front; two disc-operating couplers, three-position E-unit, rubber tires on two geared wheels, Type IV body, Type III railing with cab indentations. (Note that the matching 8867 dummy unit has a Type IV railing. This fact supports the belief that the railing design change occurred in 1978.) Other components of the set are the 9408 Lionel "Circus" stock car, the 9138 Sunoco three-dome tank car, the 9213 M.&St.L. covered hopper, the 9726 Erie-Lackawanna boxcar and the 9271 Minneapolis & St. Louis bay window caboose. This set, still available at a relatively inexpensive price (about $185 at press time), is a good bet as a "sleeper" and could appreciate in value because it is the last of the Service Station Special sets. The 8867 dummy unit was sold separately. LaVoie comment.
(A) Type III body and railing (see illustration). — — **75 85**
(B) Type IV body and railing. — — **75 85**

8867 MINNEAPOLIS & ST. LOUIS: 1978, dummy GP-9; matches 8866, lighted (apparently the only GP-9 dummy with lights) Type IV railing, two disc-operating couplers. — — **40 50**

8868 AMTRAK: 1978, 1980, powered Budd RDC baggage/mail unit, gray plastic body painted silver, blue lettering, white band through windows with red and blue stripes; lights, three-position reverse unit, two disc-operating couplers. Pauli Collection. — **60 80 100**

8869 AMTRAK: 1978, 1980, dummy Budd RDC passenger car, lighted, two disc-operating couplers; matches 8868. — — **45 55**

8870 AMTRAK: 1978, 1980, dummy Budd RDC passenger car, lighted; matches 8868. — — **45 55**

8871 AMTRAK: 1978, 1980, dummy Budd RDC baggage/mail; matches 8868, lighted, two disc-operating couplers. — — **45 55**

8872 SANTA FE: 1978-79, gray plastic body painted yellow and blue, blue and yellow lettering, Santa Fe decal on nose, yellow frame (see 8855 for SD-18 background); six-wheel trucks, two disc-operating couplers, Type IV handrails, one light, three-position reverse unit. — — **70 85**

8873 SANTA FE: 1978-79, dummy, lights; matches 8872. The second digit of the number of every Lionel-MPC steam, diesel or electric locomotive indicates the year of manufacture. — — **40 55**

8950 VIRGINIAN: 1978, dual-motored, magnetraction, Fairbanks-Morse Trainmaster; rerun of 1950s locomotive with new number and other modifications, not illustrated. — **225 250 275**

8951 SOUTHERN PACIFIC: 1979, dual-motored, magnetraction, Fairbanks-Morse; rerun of prototype Trainmaster shown at 1954 Toy Fair with new number and other modifications. — — **275 325**

8952 PENNSYLVANIA: 1979, F-3 A unit, Type VII body, powered; comes with matching dummy A unit 8953, gray plastic body painted Brunswick green, five gold stripes, portholes with clear plastic lenses, nose grab-irons, frosted-white cab windows; two motors, each motor has two geared wheels with rubber tires and a single pickup roller, disc-operating coupler on front, fixed coupler on rear, steps on rear, red, black and gold Keystone nose decal, five stripes merge on nose, decal, gold stripes and lettering are electrocals. (Note that the area in which the electrocal is applied has a flat finish readily visible when the train is held upon its side.) Has clear number-boards without numbers. Price includes 8953. — — **270 295**

8953 PENNSYLVANIA: 1979, F-3 A unit, dummy; matches 8952.
— — **270 295**

8955 SOUTHERN: 1979, U36B gray plastic body painted green and white with gold lettering, five-horn cluster on roof, brakewheel on hood near cab, gold stripe runs completely around cab, "SOUTHERN RAILROAD" decal on hood near cab; Type IV frame, two disc-operating couplers, geared motor wheels with rubber tires, not illustrated. — — **70 80**

8956 SOUTHERN: 1979, U36B dummy; matches 8955. — — **35 45**

8957 BURLINGTON NORTHERN: 1979, powered GP-20, black and green body, white lettering, no stripe. — — **50 65**

8958 BURLINGTON NORTHERN: 1979, GP-20 dummy, matches 8957. — — **30 35**

8960 SOUTHERN PACIFIC: 1979, G.E. U36C, powered, basically a U36B frame and cab with six-wheel trucks with added brakewheel on cab, two small marker lights near forward facing hood; Type IV frame, shortened battery box, two disc-operating couplers with tabs, bright red-orange and yellow "Daylight" colors, white lettering. Some units have been found with the railings spot-welded off center so that the frame looks as if it has been bent. — — **75 85**

8961 SOUTHERN PACIFIC: 1979, G.E. U36C dummy; matches 8960. — — **35 45**

8962 READING: 1979, U36B, powered, green and yellow body, "BEE LINE SERVICE", die-cast trucks, metal wheels and handrails, disc-operating couplers, one working headlight, illuminated number plates without numbers and three-position reverse unit, part of Quaker City Limited set. Miller observation — — **70 85**

8970 PENNSYLVANIA: 1979-80, dual-motored F-3 A unit, tuscan-painted body, five gold stripes, grab bars, clear portholes. Price includes matching 8971 dummy. — **150 195 225**

8971 PENNSYLVANIA: 1979-80, F-3 dummy; matches 8970. — **150 195 225**

Chapter II
STEAM ENGINES

No.3

3

8315

During its years of existence, Fundimensions has been very creative with its steam engines in one sense and not so creative in another. That apparent contradiction is not easy to explain, but perhaps some knowledge of the manufacturing process might be of some help in understanding the paradox.

The molds for steam engines tend to be more detailed and expensive than those for the diesel engines. In the first place, the boilers are rounded instead of square-sided, making for a more intricate mold-creating process. Additionally, the molds have to be made strong enough to withstand die-casting with metal, even though the same mold can be (and has been) used with plastic. Tooling costs can be enormous; for example, when Fundimensions issued its American Flyer passenger cars, the firm found that key pieces of the observation car molds were missing. It cost Fundimensions well over $30,000 just to supply those pieces and change the molds.

Imagine, if you will, the enormous costs of creating a steam engine mold from scratch, and you will see why Fundimensions chose not to be creative. Instead, Fundimensions nearly always used the steam engine molds it inherited from the original Lionel Corporation and modified them as needed. Now, if you want to put out a product which at least **seems** to be new, what would you do? The most cost-effective strategy would be to modify currently existing molds and to issue new paint schemes, and in that sense, Fundimensions has been extremely creative with its steam engines.

Of course, there is a price to be paid — dies and molds eventually wear out with use. We may be coming to a time when Fundimensions will have to invest in retooling with entirely new steam engine dies or freshened versions of the old ones; either way, considerable expense will be involved. As an example, consider that there are two basic molds for the

8004

8005

8410

Hudson 4-6-4 steam engine — the smaller Baldwin boiler and the larger Alco boiler. The last time the Baldwin mold was used was in 1979 for the 8900 ATSF Hudson. Since then, every Hudson made by Fundimensions has used the larger Alco boiler. The probable reason is wear and tear on the Baldwin boiler mold. Compare an 8603 or 8900 Fundimensions locomotive with an original 665 or 2065 Lionel Hudson from the 1950s and 1960s, and you will see the advance of fuzziness in detail as the die has worn.

The foregoing explanation probably accounts for the slow variation in steam engines relative to the rapid expansion of the diesel engines. In 1970 Fundimensions began its production of steamers with simple 2-4-2 Columbia locomotives in plastic. A die-cast Great Northern Hudson was pictured in the catalogue, but never made. Only in 1972 did Fundimensions issue the 8206 Hudson steamer, and it was the only large steamer made until 1976, when the 8600 and 8603 Hudsons appeared. After that, however, the story gets much more complicated, probably because Fundimensions had built its market to sufficient numbers to justify the issue of many new steamers.

The small steam engines issued by Fundimensions range from very inexpensive 0-4-0 switchers made almost entirely of plastic to die-cast 4-4-2 and plastic 2-6-4 locomotives. One of

these small locomotives, the 8141 Pennsylvania 2-4-2 Columbia of 1971, was the recipient of a significant technical innovation of the firm — the electronic Sound of Steam. An intermittent copper contact was attached to the locomotive smoke unit and geared so that the contact was made and broken with each revolution of the drive wheels. This contact led back through a wire to the rear of the locomotive, where it was clipped to a wire leading to the tender. The tender contained an electronic circuit board and a small loudspeaker which translated the contact into a realistic hissing sound simulating the chug of a steam engine. With a few refinements, this system is still in use. The real steamers chug twice per wheel revolution, while the Lionel sound system gives only one chug. Perhaps it is just as well; two chugs per wheel revolution would "blur" the sound at high speeds.

Two other smaller steamers, a die-cast 4-4-2 8204 and the 8206 Hudson, were the first recipients of a Fundimensions innovation which was not so successful — an electronic steam whistle. Though the whistle itself sounded very good, it tended to make the Sound of Steam muddy. The worst problem was contained in the controller Fundimensions issued with this whistle. The controller contained an electronic diode which rectified some of the transformer's current into a DC charge which activated the whistle. Unfortunately, the diode contacts tended to stick in the closed position, and this quickly burned out the diode. After dropping the whistle in 1973, Fundimensions revived it in 1980 with the two Berkshire locomotives of that year. This time they had solved the problem relating to the Sound of Steam, and they wisely let operators use the old Lionel transformers with DC rectifier discs to work the whistle. It's probably one of the best whistles ever put into a tinplate engine; it even has a "trill" (a falling tone when the control is released) like the real whistles had when blown by an expert engineer!

The small steamers represent excellent collecting opportunities for the new collector because they are readily available in considerable variety, and they are relatively inexpensive. The 2-4-2 Columbias have been issued in both plastic and die-cast versions, mostly for inexpensive sets. Only in the last two years have two die-cast 2-4-2 locomotives been available once again for separate sale. Little 2-4-0 and 0-4-0 locomotives have been made for many sets; some have used the old Lionel 1060 Series boiler, while others have used a new plastic boiler. One set of 0-4-0 locomotives is remarkable because even the drive rods and wheels are made of plastic!

The 4-4-2 locomotives have been made mostly in die-cast versions, beginning with the 8142 C&O. These locomotives have used a modified version of the old Lionel 637/2037 boiler, last used on 2-6-4 locomotives in the 1960s. They are good pullers, but many collectors would favor them more had they been issued with a three-position reversing switch instead of the two-position unit they used. The two-position unit has no neutral position, thus limiting the operating use of these locomotives. One of the latest 4-4-2 locomotives, the 8402 Reading, has a boiler front which many collectors consider very ugly. Most of the 4-4-2 locomotives are fairly good looking, however.

One small 0-4-0 locomotive would have been very interesting, but it was pulled from production at the last minute. The 8901 was scheduled to be the locomotive for the Radio Control Express. It would have had a battery-powered DC motor and a radio control for starting, stopping and reversing the locomotive. This arrangement reminded many collectors of the Electronic Control Sets of 1946, which were well ahead of their time. However, the Radio Control Express was an expensive set which was judged by Fundimensions to be limited in appeal. It was never mass marketed.

One of the few original small locomotive designs was a strange looking 0-4-0 dockside switcher. Delicate but whimsical, this little locomotive headed a set with a small four-wheeled tender, but as marketed for separate sale it did not have a tender. The 8209 docksider was catalogued for four years; recently, the docksider has been scheduled for use in a 1985 Santa Fe work train.

Until this year, Fundimensions has made just one deluxe switch engine modeled after the old Lionel 1600 models. This was a die-cast Pennsylvania switcher first issued in 1975. It had a slope-back tender with a working backup light (curiously, with a red lens instead of a clear one) and a three-position reverse. Fundimensions plans to revive this model for 1985 in New York Central guise; they also plan to add a smoke unit, which would be a first for a switch engine.

Except for the 773-boilered Scale Hudson, the Hudson locomotives issued by Fundimensions have come in only two boiler styles. The smaller of the two is the Baldwin boiler, which has horizontal shaded windows on its cab. The larger one is the Alco-boilered Hudson, which has square windows on the cab which are cross-hatched into four smaller windows. Lately, the Alco boiler has been used exclusively.

As mentioned before, the 4-6-4 Hudson locomotives did not show much variation until 1977, but beginning in that year, many new ones were issued, culminating in the reissue in 1984 (actually released in 1985) of the magnificent scale 773-style New York Central Hudson, the 8406. By 1977 collectors had begun to ask for revivals of their favorite Lionel postwar steamers. Fundimensions responded well, but not quite as expected. The firm put out a beautiful 8702 Southern Crescent Hudson in Southern green and gold livery; they also made five matching passenger cars, all to be sold separately, not as a set. In practice, this usually meant that there were many more sets of cars than there were locomotives. So well received was this Hudson that the next year Fundimensions revived one of the most revered names in Lionel history, the Blue Comet. This locomotive was done in two shades of glossy blue with gold trim and had a feed water heater on its boiler front. It too had its own set of matching passenger cars in a rich two-tone blue color scheme with gold lettering and a broad cream stripe. Collectors snapped up this locomotive and its cars even more eagerly than they had the Southern Crescent, even though the plain 2046W tender did not do the locomotive full justice. After issuing the last Baldwin-boilered steamer to date, the 8900 Santa Fe Hudson, Fundimensions issued another Hudson-powered passenger set, the Chicago and Alton, in 1981. This time they had a real surprise for collectors. Instead of the plastic 2046W tender, this locomotive came with a revived 224W tender not seen on a Lionel product since 1940! This tender was die-cast and magnificently detailed. It had new six-wheel trucks, a whistle and the Sound of Steam. Many collectors like the maroon, red and gold paint scheme of this set. The last regularly issued Hudson to date has been the 8210 Joshua Lionel Cowen commemorative locomotive in bronze, black and gold. Mention must also be made of a very scarce Hudson, the Atlantic Coast Line, made for J. C. Penney as a special in 1980. This engine is almost impossible to acquire and has shown substantial appreciation in value.

In recent years, Fundimensions has revived the postwar 736 2-8-4 Berkshire locomotive with three models, the 8002 Union Pacific in a two-tone gray with smoke deflectors, the 8003 Chessie Steam Special locomotive with a bright paint scheme of blue, gray, yellow and vermilion Chessie colors and a nice 8215 Nickel Plate Road locomotive in the traditional black. Only the Nickel Plate locomotive has had the 224W die-cast tender; the other two have the plastic 2046W tender. This boiler style was used for two offshoots, the 2-8-2 8309 Southern Mikado in green, tuscan and gold Southern markings with the 224W tender and the 3100 Great Northern 4-8-4 locomotive in green and tuscan with the 2046W tender. In 1981 Fundimensions revived the beautiful Norfolk and Western "J" class streamlined 4-8-4 locomotive, originally numbered 746 but numbered 611 after the prototype. This locomotive headed a matched set of maroon and black Powhatan Arrow aluminum passenger cars to form a train well over ten feet long! It had all the deluxe Lionel features, including smoke from the cylinders, a feature introduced by Marx a long time ago. (The maintenance crew at the Norfolk and Western shops in Roanoke, Virginia would have been greatly troubled by any sign of steam leaking from the cylinders because this would indicate a bad job of packing the seals!) The "J" boiler was used in 1983 for the 8307 Southern Pacific "Daylight" locomotive, a fine model of the original which could also be used to pull matching aluminum passenger cars.

Fundimensions did not neglect another old favorite, the "General" old-time 4-4-0 locomotive first made by Lionel in the late 1950s. In 1977 the Western & Atlantic No. 3 (8701) met with great success, especially after the old-time cars were issued for it. Since then, the "General" locomotive has been used in chromed Rock Island, blue and black B & O and other color schemes. One version of this locomotive became a special issue for J. C. Penney.

Finally, in 1985, Fundimensions revived one of the great favorites of all the Lionel steamers — the Pennsylvania 6-8-6 S-2 steam turbine. The original 671, 2020, 681 and 682 versions of this locomotive sold by the thousands in the postwar era. Fundimensions has issued the locomotive in a handsome gray, Brunswick green and black color scheme with its streamlined tender, whistle, Sound of Steam, smoke and even the delicate oiler linkage from the old 682. This locomotive is bound to become a collector favorite very rapidly. It even has the legendary backup lights in the tender!

If Fundimensions' options in tool and die-making have been somewhat limited, the firm has certainly gotten the most mileage out of what has been available for its steamers. Fundimensions has succeeded in carrying on the great tradition of tinplate steamers with some of the nicest and best made products imaginable — even though the cost of these locomotives has been prohibitive for many collectors. The lesser Fundimensions steamers run reasonably well, are highly collectible and, as a group, offer the chance for a fine collection. It took a while for the variety, but it was worth the wait.

Gd VG Exc Mt

STEAM LOCOMOTIVES

3 UNION PACIFIC: 1981, see 8104.

3 W.&A.R.R.: 1977, see 8701.

611: See 8100.

659: See 8101.

779: See 8215.

783: See 8406.

3100 GREAT NORTHERN: 1981, 4-8-4, Famous American Railroad Series #3; whistle, electronic Sound of Steam, magnetraction, three-position E-unit; dark green boiler, silver boiler front and smoke box, "elephant ears", tuscan cab roof, black sand and steam domes, white-edged running board; dark green streamlined tender with "GREAT NORTHERN" logo on side, superb "runner".   —   —   300   350

4449: See 8307.

4501: See 8309.

5734-85 TCA: 1985, 4-6-4 Hudson, dark green-painted die-cast, alco-style boiler which matches the TCA passenger cars of previous years. Magnetraction, smoke, white stripe and white-edged drivewheels, headlight. Came with die-cast 224 W tender with black coal pile, white circular TCA logo on sides, electronic steam whistle and Sound of Steam and die-cast six-wheel passenger trucks. Available on order to Train Collectors' Association members only.   —   —   —   300

8001 NICKEL PLATE: 1980, 2-6-4, plastic K-4 locomotive, remake of 2025/675 die-cast steamer from late 1940s. This (with 8007) is the first Lionel six-wheel driver plastic locomotive. DC-powered engine; running on AC will burn out the motor.   —   —   40   50

8002 UNION PACIFIC: 1980, 2-8-4, Berkshire, second in Fundimensions' Famous American Railroad Series (FARR); two-tone gray boiler, yellow-edged running board; electronic whistle, electronic Sound of Steam, magnetraction, smoke, three-position reverse unit; gray tender with dark gray center band, yellow-lettered "UNION PACIFIC", with FARR diamond logo. The UP prototype is actually a 4-8-4 Northern since the UP did not use a 2-8-4 Berkshire, first locomotive with smoke deflectors astride the boiler. Bohn comment.   —   300   350   375

8003 CHESSIE: 1980, 2-8-4; die-cast Berkshire. This locomotive marked an important development in Fundimensions' history, the rerun of the 2-8-4 Berkshire, Lionel's top-of-the-line postwar steam engine. Fundimensions also offered handsome matching passenger cars as separate sale items. The Chessie Steam Special engine and cars were based on a prototype Chessie train which actually toured the United States to celebrate the 150th Anniversary of American railroading. The model engine featured an electronic whistle, electronic Sound of Steam, smoke, magnetraction and a three-position reverse unit. The engine boiler is light gray (forward of the bell) and dark gray (behind the bell); it has a yellow-edged running board, yellow and red stripes beneath the cab window and "8003" under cab window. Dark gray tender with six-wheel trucks and large yellow area topped by orange band, "Chessie System" lettering on side. The engine as delivered did not run well. After adjustments it ran better, and its sound, properly synchronized, is delightful. Miller observation. Apparently the difficulties only occurred with early production; other operators have stated that this locomotive has been an excellent, trouble-free runner right from the start. C. Lang comment.   —   —   350   400

8004 ROCK ISLAND & PEORIA: 1980, 1982, 4-4-0, General chassis but modeled after an engine built by the Rock Island and Peoria Railroad in the late 1800s for the World's Fair; engine has chrome boiler, tuscan cab and steam chest, black stack and boiler bands, smoke and two-position reverse unit; tender has tuscan sides with mountain mural.   —   —   125   140

8005 ATSF: 1980, 1982, 4-4-0, General chassis, DC powered, very lightweight locomotive, red and maroon engine with gold trim; 8005T tender with gold rectangle trim with ATSF. Came as part of 1053 The James Gang set with three cars, figures and building. Price for engine and tender only.
          —   —   30   40

8006 ATLANTIC COAST LINE: 1980, 4-6-4, gunmetal-painted die-cast boiler, one-piece boiler front with "LIONEL" cast beneath the headlight and numbered "2065-15" on inside, steam chest side is decorated in white with a rectangle; inside of the rectangle is another rectangle with rounded corners. The engine, known as "The Silver Shadow", has white tires and a high gloss black paint beneath the white-painted running board edge. The New York Central-style tender has a water scoop; two-thirds of the prototype tender was a coal bunker. The line of rivets that descends from the rear of the coal bunker indicates the demarcation between coal and water in the prototype. The model tender has die-cast six-wheel trucks. This model was made for J. C. Penney as a special item and was not catalogued by Lionel. It came with a display track, probably Gargraves Phantom track, mounted on a wooden base in a clear plastic case. Only 2,200 reportedly were manufactured and these were sold out very quickly. Many collectors believe that this item has unusual appreciation potential. Degano, Lang and White observations.   —   —   450   500

8007 NEW YORK, NEW HAVEN & HARTFORD: 1980, 2-6-4, plastic K-4 locomotive with silver boiler front, a remake of 2025/675 die-cast steamer from later 1940s. This is the first time Lionel has ever made a six-driver plastic locomotive. Locomotive, with smoke, gold-striped running board edge; square-backed 8007T tender with gold "NEW YORK, NEW HAVEN & HARTFORD" stripe and mechanical Sound of Steam. The K-4 prototype appeared only on the Pennsylvania Railroad, but Fundimensions' management reportedly liked the New Haven logo. Came as part of 1050 New Englander set. DC-powered engine; running on AC will burn out the motor.   —   —   40   50

8008 CHESSIE: 1980, 4-4-2, dark blue-painted die-cast locomotive with yellow-painted running board edge, smoke, red firebox light (a feature not seen since the 226E steamer was made in 1938); dark blue 8008T tender with large yellow area topped with orange stripe, Chessie System logo and mechanical Sound of Steam. Came as part of 1052 Chesapeake Flyer set. DC-powered engine; running on AC will burn out the motor.
          —   —   50   60

8040

57

8001

3100

8002

NOTE: The 8040 has been made in several different railroad markings.
8040 NICKEL PLATE: 1970-72, 2-4-2, black plastic body, no light, manual reverse switch atop boiler.
(A) White flat lettering, "NICKEL PLATE/ROAD" on slope-back tender, came with set 1081, lowest priced set in the line. G. Halverson comment.

— 15 20 30

8040

(B) 1972, Same as (A) but white raised lettering, "NICKEL PLATE/ROAD" on short 1130T box tender, came with set 1081, the lowest priced set in the line. G. Halverson comment. — 15 20 30
8040 CANADIAN NATIONAL: 1971, 2-4-2, black plastic body, slope-back tender with white lettering "CANADIAN NATIONAL" on side in rectangular box. Manual reversing switch atop boiler. Based upon observation of the Canadian catalogue, we think this locomotive was unlighted. Tender type and coupler type unknown. Came as part of set T-1171 with maroon 9143 CN gondola and maroon 9065 CN caboose. This set was listed in both the small and the large versions of the 1971 Canadian catalogue. K. Wills comment, D. Anderson Collection. — 25 35 50

8041

8041 NEW YORK CENTRAL: 1970, 2-4-2, silver gray body, white lettering, red stripes, 1130T tender with AAR trucks, dummy coupler. C. Rohlfing comment. — 15 25 30

8042

8042 GRAND TRUNK WESTERN: 1970, 2-4-2, black, die-cast metal body, white lettering.
(A) Thin cab floor. — 15 20 30
(B) Thick cab floor. — 15 20 30

8043 NICKEL PLATE: 1970, 2-4-2, black plastic body with white lettering, slope-back tender, manufactured for Sears as part of set 1091.

— 20 25 40

8062 GREAT NORTHERN: 4-6-4 Hudson, 1970, catalogued but not manufactured. **Not Manufactured**

8100 NORFOLK & WESTERN: 1981, 4-8-4, J Class, streamlined engine, whistle, electronic Sound of Steam, three-position reverse unit, engine and tender paint match extruded aluminum Powhatan Arrow passenger cars. These cars were available only as separate sale items. This N&W was the first Lionel engine to simulate steam smoke actually issuing from its steam cylinders. (Marx introduced this feature many years before on its little 1666, and it works better!) Black die-cast boiler, black plastic "bullet" boiler front, broad maroon trim stripe edged in yellow, matching long-striped 2671W tender with die-cast six-wheel trucks. "611" appears on the side of the engine; "8100" appears on box only. — 500 525 575

8101 CHICAGO & ALTON: 1981, 4-6-4, maroon-painted die-cast boiler (color scheme based on "The Red Train"), silver smoke box and boiler front, gold striping with gold "C&A" inside rectangle under cab window, whistle, electronic Sound of Steam, three-position reverse unit, smoke; 2224W maroon die-cast tender with red frame, fully detailed riveting, steps and handrails, black coal pile, gold striping; six-wheel die-cast trucks and gold numbered "659" on side; "8101" appears only on box. Matching passenger cars available for separate sale. Tender is a remake of Lionel 2224 tender, not produced since it came with the 224 2-6-2 engine beginning in 1938. R. LaVoie comment. — 250 275 295

8003

611

659

8102 **UNION PACIFIC:** 1981-82, 4-4-2, dark gray-painted die-cast boiler with yellow-edged running board, yellow numbers and letters; electronic Sound of Steam, smoke, headlight, two-position reverse unit, traction tires and 8102T square-back tender. Part of 1151 Union Pacific Thunder Freight and 1153 Union Pacific Thunder Freight Deluxe, made for J.C. Penney sets.

— — **45 60**

8104 **UNION PACIFIC:** 1981, 4-4-0, General-type locomotive, green cab, pilot, lamp, wheel spokes and bell, black stack, chrome-finished boiler, "3" appears on side of head lamp and under cab window, green plastic "General"-style tender with arch-bar trucks and simulated wood pile. This locomotive was sold by J.C. Penney as an uncatalogued special called "The Golden Arrow"; display case for locomotive with wooden base and plastic cover. — — **195 225**

See also Factory Errors.

8140

8140 **SOUTHERN:** 1971, 2-4-0 or 0-4-0, mechanical Sound of Steam, green and black body with gold lettering on tender cab; reportedly available as part of Sears set no. 1190 in all-black body.
(A) 2-4-0. — **15 20 25**

8140

(B) 0-4-0. — **15 20 25**

8141 **PENNSYLVANIA:** 1971, 2-4-2, gray plastic body with red stripe; electronic Sound of Steam (the first locomotive to carry this feature), smoke, headlight.
(A) White lettering, from set 1183. — **15 25 30**
(B) Same as (A), except heat-stamped red lettering. This was the version separately sold. Riley Collection. — **15 25 30**

8142 **CHESAPEAKE & OHIO:** 1971, 4-4-2, black die-cast metal body, white lettering, smoke.
(A) Electronic Sound of Steam. — **25 35 45**
(B) Same as (A), but also has electronic whistle. — **35 45 65**

8142

8200 **KICKAPOO DOCKSIDE:** 1972, 0-4-0 Switcher, black plastic body, gold lettering and trim. — **20 25 35**

8203 **PENNSYLVANIA:** 1972, 2-4-2, Columbia-type, electronic Sound of Steam, smoke, charcoal black plastic body, red stripe and lettering.

— **20 30 40**

8204 **CHESAPEAKE & OHIO:** 1972, 4-4-2, black die-cast metal body, Sound of Steam, whistle, smoke, headlight. — **45 60 70**

8200

8203

8206 NEW YORK CENTRAL: 1972-74, 4-6-4, metal die-cast body, Sound of Steam, smoke, whistle, headlight, white lettering. Many of these locomotives were assembled with off-center drive wheels which cause the locomotives to wobble from side to side as they run. Typically, the die casting is very fuzzy on the shiny examples, and the whistles and Sound of Steam do not sound clear. Used examples should be tested before purchase. R. LaVoie comments.

(A) Flat charcoal black body.   —   **150**   **175**   **200**

(B) Shiny black body.   —   **150**   **175**   **200**

8206

8209 PIONEER DOCKSIDE SWITCHER: 1972, 0-4-0, same as 8200 except for number. The version with the four-wheel tender bears a very close resemblance to a logging engine once used by the Northern Pacific.

(A) With four-wheel tender, from Kickapoo Valley set.   —   **30**   **40**   **50**

(B) No tender.   —   **20**   **25**   **30**

8210 COWEN: 1982, 4-6-4, Hudson, gold and burgundy-painted die-cast engine, headlight, smoke, magnetraction, die-cast tender with six-wheel trucks, electronic whistle, electronic Sound of Steam, simulated gold "Joshua Lionel Cowen" nameplate. Note: when boxes are opened many units are reported to have broken rear trucks. Deitrich observation.

   —   —   **275**   **300**

8212 BLACK CAVE: 1982, 0-4-0, black plastic body, slope-back tender, with glow-in-the-dark decal, D C motor; part of 1254 Black Cave Flyer set.

   —   **15**   **20**   **25**

8213 RIO GRANDE: 1982-83, 2-4-2, die-cast metal body; smoke, headlight, electronic reversing unit, split-field motor, tender with mechanical Sound of Steam; part of 1252 Heavy Iron Set.   —   —   **60**   **70**

8214 PENNSYLVANIA: 1982-83, 2-4-2, die-cast metal body, headlight, smoke, electronic reverse unit, split-field motor; tender with mechanical Sound of Steam.   —   —   **60**   **75**

8215 NICKEL PLATE ROAD: 1982, 2-8-4, die-cast black painted boiler with white stripe on side, white-painted wheel rims, gold "779" on cab, magnetrction, smoke, optical headlight lens on swing-out boiler front. Die-cast 224W tender in black with gold script lettering, six-wheel die-cast trucks, operating coupler, electronic whistle and Sound of Steam. Pictured in 1982 Fall Collector Center. Excellent runner.   —   —   **350**   **400**

8209

8300 SANTA FE: 1973-75, 2-4-0, black plastic body, slope-back tender with gold "ATSF" lettering, Symington-Wayne trucks and dummy coupler. C. Rohlfing comment.   —   **15**   **20**   **25**

8302 SOUTHERN: 1973-76, 2-4-0, mechanical Sound of Steam, black plastic body painted green, plastic silver bell on top, headlight, MPC logo on both sides; from Sears set 6-1384, oil-type tender.   —   **20**   **25**   **30**

8303

8303 JERSEY CENTRAL: 1973-74, 2-4-2, electronic Sound of Steam, smoke, blue plastic body, light blue and gold lettering, dark blue trim. According to Volume IV of the McComas-Tuohy Lionel Series, this engine was once considered for a Blue Comet set!   —   **25**   **30**   **35**

NOTE: There are four different 8304 locomotives.

8304

8304 ROCK ISLAND: 1973-74, 4-4-2, black die-cast body, electronic Sound of Steam, white lettering.   —   **30**   **40**   **50**

8304

8304 BALTIMORE & OHIO: 1975, 4-4-2, black die-cast body, white lettering, electronic Sound of Steam.   —   **40**   **50**   **60**

8304

8304 CHESAPEAKE & OHIO: 1974-77, 4-4-2, black die-cast body, gold lettering, electronic Sound of Steam, smoke.   —   **30**   **40**   **50**

8304

8305

8304 PENNSYLVANIA: 1974, 4-4-2, black die-cast body, gold lettering, electronic Sound of Steam, smoke, headlight. — 30 40 50

8305 MILWAUKEE ROAD: 1973, 4-4-2, black die-cast body, red and gold stripes with gold lettering on tender, electronic Sound of Steam, electronic whistle, dummy coupler, smoke, headlight. C. Rohlfing comments.
— 40 50 60

8306 PENNSYLVANIA: 1974, 4-4-2, black plastic body, smoke, Sound of Steam. — — 25 30

8307 SOUTHERN PACIFIC: 1983, 4-8-4, "Southern Pacific Daylight", "4449" below cab window and on boiler front, vertical dual headlights, magnetraction, smoke from stack and "simulated" steam (actually smoke from generator) from cylinders, three-position E-unit, electronic Sound of Steam and whistle. Orange, white, and black paint scheme, silver boiler front. Matching passenger cars were available for separate sale.

Catalogue portrays a 2046-W coal tender, but production version has prototypical oil-burning tender and "99" unlighted number-boards halfway down the top of the boiler sides. Early reports indicate that this locomotive is an outstanding runner. However, in early production there has been a problem with chipping paint on the boiler. Fundimensions has corrected this problem quickly. — — 650 700

8308 JERSEY CENTRAL: 1973-74, 2-4-2, black plastic body, gold lettering, 1130T-type tender; made for Sears set 1392. — 20 30 40

8309 SOUTHERN: 1983, 2-8-2, gold, "4501" beneath locomotive cab window and "SOUTHERN" and "FAMOUS AMERICAN RAILROAD SERIES" on tender side. Die-cast locomotive is green with silver boiler front and red cab roof. Freight cars with special FARR 4 markings: 6104 hopper, 6306 tank, 9451 boxcar, 9887 reefer and 6431 caboose were available for separate sale. — — 300 350

8309 JERSEY CENTRAL: 1974, uncatalogued, 2-4-2, further details requested. — 20 30 40

NOTE: The following five locomotives are similiar except for their road names and paint schemes.

8310

8310 NICKEL PLATE: 2-4-0, 1973: black die-cast body, gold lettering, slope-back tender; part of Sears set 1390. — 20 30 40

8310 JERSEY CENTRAL: 2-4-0, uncatalogued, black die-cast body, gold lettering, mechanical Sound of Steam; part of Sears set 1492.
— 20 30 40

8310 NICKEL PLATE ROAD: 1974-75, 2-4-0, black die-cast body, gold lettering, slope-back tender lettered "NICKEL PLATE ROAD".
— 20 30 40

8310 JERSEY CENTRAL: 1974-75, uncatalogued, 2-4-0, black die-cast body, gold lettering, mechanical Sound of Steam. — 20 30 40

8310

8310 ATSF: 1974-75, 2-4-0, black die-cast body, gold lettering, slope-back tender lettered "ATSF," made for Sears. Haffen Collection.
— 20 30 40

8311 SOUTHERN: 1973, 0-4-0, uncatalogued, black plastic body; made for J.C. Penney set 1395. — 15 20 30

8313 SANTA FE: 1983, 0-4-0, black plastic locomotive body with gold boiler front, stack and bell, gold number "8313" under cab window and gold Santa Fe logo and A.T.&S.F. on slope-back tender. DC powered, no headlight, fixed coupler on tender. This is the same locomotive model that appeared in the Black Cave Set and is noteworthy for how few pieces of metal are used in its construction. Part of set No. 1352, Rocky Mountain Freight, shown in Traditional Series catalogue. Set value: $50.00. Loco and tender price. — — 15 20

8314 SOUTHERN STREAK: 1983, 2-4-0, dark green plastic locomotive body with headlight, DC powered, white number "8314" under cab window and white lettering "SOUTHERN STREAK" on tender sides, square back oil-type tender with hatch and mechanical Sound of Steam, fixed coupler on tender. Part of 1353 Southern Streak set shown in Traditional Series Catalogue. Set price: $60.00. Locomotive and tender price.
— — 17 20

8315 B&O: 1983, 4-4-0, "General"-style plastic locomotive with blue boiler and stack, black pilot, steam cylinders and cab and black tender. White lettering and numbering: "8315" beneath cab windows and "B&O" on tender sides. DC motor with rectifier for AC operation as well as DC operation, illustrated with non-illuminating headlight but made with operating headlight which takes a small screw-base bulb, fixed coupler on tender, electronic three-position reverse unit, part of Set 1351 Baltimore and Ohio, shown in Traditional Series Catalogue. Set price: $145.00. Loco and tender price. — 45 55 65

8402 READING: 4-4-2, 1974-75: black die-cast body, silver number on cab, solid state reversing unit, can motor, 1130T oil-type tender with mechanical Sound of Steam, silver lettering and black and silver Reading logo.
— — — 60

8403 CHESSIE SYSTEM: 4-4-2, 1974-75, part of set 1402, die-cast boiler, headlight, smoke, solid state reversing unit, can motor, 1130T oil-type tender with mechanical Sound of Steam, yellow stripe, number and logo.
— — — 60

8404 PENNSYLVANIA: 1984-85, 6-8-6 S-2 turbine, Brunswick green-painted die-cast boiler, graphite gray smoke box and boiler front; white striping, trim and "6200" on boiler cab, red and gold "6200" Keystone on boiler front, oiler linkage, white-edged drive wheels, magnetraction, electronic Sound of Steam, electronic whistle, smoke; 2671W-type tender with operating red back-up lights, Brunswick green with white "PENNSYL-VANIA" lettering high on sides, die-cast six-wheel Fundimensions passenger trucks, water scoop. There have been a few complaints about poorly operating reversing units and Sound of Steam units which do not work well in reverse, but direct observation has shown that this locomotive, essentially a dressed-up postwar 682, is an excellent runner and a strong puller which operates efficiently on as little as eight volts. R. LaVoie comment. — — 300 325

8406 NEW YORK CENTRAL: 1984, 4-6-4, 1/4" scale die-cast Hudson, 23" long, reissue of the 1964 version of the 773 without the cylinder slide valve casting but with the die-cast 2426W tender. Locomotive has detailed Baker valve gear, die-cast smoke unit with simulated steam from the smoke chests (something the proud New York Central would have not allowed, since this would indicate leaky valve packing), magnetraction, optical headlight, electronic Sound of Steam and whistle, 2426W-type tender with six-wheel Fundimensions passenger trucks, "NEW YORK CENTRAL" in small white serif lettering ("783" is the number on the boiler cab). This engine's magnetraction has been improved over its predecessor 773 because

8210

779

4449

there are more magnets and they are larger. The steps on the boiler front are missing in catalogue photographs but are included in the production run. The locomotive has won praise for its sharp boiler detail. Such is the demand for this locomotive that it is easily the most expensive single item ever produced by either the original Lionel Corporation or Fundimensions. There have been persistent reports of hoarding of this locomotive; its initial purchase price for those who pre-ordered it was about $575, but the price has nearly doubled in just a few months. Purchasers of the current model should beware of sharp fluctuations in supply and demand, especially at the time any new Hudson is produced. R. LaVoie comment.   —   —   **950 1000**

8410 REDWOOD VALLEY EXPRESS: 1984-85, 4-4-0, "General"-style locomotive with tuscan boiler, yellow cab, pilot and drive wheels, cylindrical headlight, tall thin stack instead of usual balloon stack, gold trim; DC-only motor, tender with simulated woodpile, arch-bar trucks with dummy coupler, brown "REDWOOD VALLEY EXPRESS" and logo on tender sides. Came as part of Redwood Valley Express set no. 1403; current set price $85. Price for locomotive and tender only.   —   —   **40   45**

8500

8500 PENNSYLVANIA: 1975, 2-4-0, black plastic body, gold lettering, mechanical Sound of Steam.   —   **15   20   25**

8502

8502 SANTA FE: 1975, 2-4-0, black plastic body, gold lettering, slope-back tender.   —   **15   20   25**

8506

8506 PENNSYLVANIA: 1976-77, 0-4-0, black die-cast body, gold lettering, slope-back tender with red light which lights only when locomotive is in reverse.   —   **60   80   95**

8507 ATSF: 1975, 2-4-0, black plastic cab with gold heat-stamped number, detailed cab interior, "LIONEL" on firebox door (as on postwar 1060), molded window shades, plated main rods only, manual reverse with curved reversing lever slot in boiler top behind Phillips screw, shiny ornamental bell, slope-back tender with simulated backup light, "ATSF" in gold on tender sides, Symington-Wayne trucks, dummy coupler. Part of a set sold by K-Mart in 1975; reader comments needed concerning set details. Triezenberg Collection.   **NRS**

8510 PENNSYLVANIA: 1975, not catalogued, 0-4-0, slope-back tender, made for Sears.   —   **15   20   25**

8512 SANTA FE: Announced for 1985, Dockside Switcher, 0-4-0, DC-only operation, part of Midland Freight Set in Traditional 1985 catalogue. Dark blue plastic body, yellow lettering and number, gray smoke box, stack and steam chests, yellow Santa Fe logo, short coal box behind cab instead of

4501

8702

8801

tender, one dummy coupler on rear. Estimated set price is $55.00. Price for locomotive only:

         —   —   25

8516 NEW YORK CENTRAL: Announced for 1985, 0-4-0 switcher, as part of Yard Chief set in Traditional catalogue. Die-cast postwar 1660-series switcher body, headlight, smoke (a first for any Lionel switcher), three-position electronic reversing switch, front operating coupler, slope-back tender with operating coupler on rear, Symington-Wayne trucks; white "NEW YORK CENTRAL" lettering, operating backup light with red lens. Estimated set price is $195.00. Price for locomotive only:

         —   —   95

8600

8600 NEW YORK CENTRAL: 1976, 4-6-4, black die-cast body, white lettering, electronic Sound of Steam, smoke, magnetraction, silver boiler front, shown as 646 in 1976 catalogue; part of Empire State Express set.

         —   160   195   225

8601

8601 ROCK ISLAND: 1976-77, 0-4-0, black plastic body, large white numbers on cab, slope-back tender with red "ROCK ISLAND" logo.

         —   15   20   25

8602 RIO GRANDE: 1976-78, 2-4-0, plastic body, white lettering; tender with mechanical Sound of Steam.

         —   20   25   30

8602

8603 CHESAPEAKE & OHIO: 1976-77, 4-6-4, black die-cast body, white lettering, silver boiler front, electronic Sound of Steam, headlight, smoke, rubber tires, tender lettered "CHESAPEAKE & OHIO", over 19-1/2 inches long. The earlier Baldwin disc drivers had polished steel rims, but when reports of corrosion arose, Fundimensions changed production to white-painted driver rims. The painted rims are probably more scarce. Typically, the details on the Baldwin disc drivers on these locomotives are not very sharp. As with the earlier 8206 New York Central Hudson, many examples were assembled with off-center drive wheels, causing the locomotive to wobble when it moves down the track. Used examples should be test-run. R. LaVoie comment.

8603

(A) Polished steel driver rims. LaVoie Collection.   —   150   175   200

(B) White-painted driver rims. Boehmer Collection.   —   170   200   225

8604 JERSEY CENTRAL: 1976, 2-4-2, Black plastic body, gold number on cab, smoke, headlight, two-position reversing unit.

(A) Part of Sears set 1696, 1130T oil-type tender, gold Jersey Central lettering and logo, mechanical Sound of Steam, Symington-Wayne trucks, dummy coupler. Came in set with 9020 flatcar, 9044 boxcar, 9011 hopper car and 9069 caboose. Set also included ten curved and four straight track and a pair of manual switches. D. Johns and P. Catalano comments, G. Halverson and L. Kositsky Collections.   —   20   25   35

(B) Same locomotive as (A), but slope-back tender with no lettering. G.
Halverson Collection.   — 20 25 35

8701 GENERAL: 1977-78, 4-4-0, cab numbered No. 3, rerun of Lionel 1882
General, 1959-62, black plastic boiler, and frame, red cab, gold boiler bands,
dome and bell, yellow lettering, headlight, smoke, two-position reverse,
black plastic tender with yellow-lettered "Western & Atlantic".
                                                             — 80 100 135

8702 CRESCENT LIMITED: 1977, 4-6-4, also known as Southern Crescent, green-painted die-cast boiler with silver-painted boiler front, gold
crescent and border on steam chest, crescent emblem and "8702" in gold on
cab; magnetraction, white-outlined drivers, liquid smoke. This locomotive
appears to have exactly the same castings as the 646. Originally the 8702
came in flat green; the second run was in shiny green. It appears that equal
quantities were produced. The tender is painted green with a black coal
pile, lettered "CRESCENT LIMITED" in gold with gold border, Symington-
Wayne trucks, Sound of Steam, dummy coupler.   — 225 250 300

8703

8703 WABASH: 1977, 2-4-2, black plastic body, white stripe on locomotive
and tender; electronic Sound of Steam, smoke, headlight.
                                                             — 20 25 35

8800 LIONEL LINES: 1978-81, 4-4-2, die-cast boiler, red marker lights,
battery box on pilot, similar to Lionel 2037 with the following modifications;
the marker lights, which protrude above the boiler on a 2037, were moved to
a more protected location inside the boiler front; the "Made by Lionel"
builder's plate was replaced with a Lionel/MPC logo, and the valve gear
was given a moving control rod reminiscent of the 1666. The main rod is
heavily sculptured with ridges; there is a side rod; liquid smoke unit,
two-position reversing unit; a wire connects the tender and locomotive, with
electronic Sound of Steam in the 8800T tender and a fixed rear tender
coupler. Tender base is marked "8141T-10" and has a large black "L" in
white and black box and "LIONEL LINES" in sans-serif rounded letters
across its side. (Same engine as Chesapeake Flier with one rubber tire on
locomotive.)   — 50 65 80

8801 THE BLUE COMET: 1978-79, 4-6-4, dark blue upper boiler section,
lighter blue lower boiler section, gold-outlined steam chest, "8801" in gold
on cab, decal on locomotive feed water tank reads "THE BLUE COMET";
"LIONEL" on small plate beneath headlight; drivers outlined in white, blind
center drivers, plastic trailing trucks, side frames and a modified 646 boiler.
A major modification is its feedwater tank which has a 665 boiler front with
marker lights on the boiler front door and a small nameplate beneath the

headlight. The tender's paint design is similar to that of the locomotive,
with a dark blue upper section, black coal pile, light blue lower section with
gold circle and gold-lettered "NEW JERSEY CENTRAL". The Blue Comet
brings back memories of the top-of-the-line, classic Standard and 0 Gauge
locomotives of the 1930s. The Blue Comet has met with great popularity.
As with many of the limited sets, the passenger cars made to match this
locomotive are still readily available, but the locomotive itself is very hard to
find. This lends support to the belief that many more sets of cars were
produced than were the locomotives needed to pull them as part of a
matched set. R. LaVoie comment.   — 200 275 300

8803 SANTA FE: 1979, 0-4-0, black plastic engine with silver boiler front
and red plastic drivers, two-position reverse, 8803T square-back tender with
Santa Fe logo. Part of 1860 Timberline set, 1862 Logging Empire set, 1892
Penney Logging Empire and 1893 Toys-R-Us-Logging Empire.
                                                             — 10 15

8900 A.T.S.F.: 1979, 4-6-4, black-painted die-cast boiler with silver-
painted boiler front, green marker lights, tuscan-painted cab roof,
magnetraction, same boiler as 2065 without the feed water tank; rear trailing
truck has same side frames as 2065, side configuration same as 2065 but
brighter, shinier plating; nylon gears substitute for metal gears. Tender has
"8900" in very large white numerals and a small diamond-shaped block
outlined in gold with gold-lettered "Famous American Railroad Series" with
a spike (indicates it is first in a series); water scoop pickup, Sound of Steam
inside tender (power pickup for Sound of Steam comes in part from tender
trucks and in part from wire from locomotive); fixed coupler on rear of
tender with rear number plate "2671W-6", gray wheels on tender. Our
search indicates that most if not all pre-Fundimensions 2671-W tenders did
not carry a plate with such a number. The number has been carried on the
tender plate since MPC began using this tender.   — 250 275 300

8902 ATLANTIC COAST LINE: 1979-82, 2-4-0, black plastic engine,
DC-powered, 8902T slope-back tender with "ATLANTIC COAST LINE"
logo; available as part of No. 1960 and No. 1993 Midnight Flyer sets, 1990
Mystery Glow Midnight Flyer and 1155 Cannonball Freight set.
                                                             — — 15 20

8903 RIO GRANDE: 1979, 2-4-2, black plastic engine, DC-powered, 8602T
tender with mechanical Sound of Steam; white script "Rio Grande".
Available as part of No. 1963 Black River Freight set.   — 15 20 25

8904 WABASH: 1979, 1981, 2-4-2 die-cast engine with white stripe along
running board, smoke, working headlight, two-position reverse unit, AC-
powered; 8904T oil-type tender with or without mechanical Sound of
Steam; dark-lettered "WABASH" on white stripe across tender side; from
1962 Wabash Cannonball set or 1991 Wabash Deluxe Express.
(A) With mechanical Sound of Steam, 8906T.   — 30 35 40
(B) Without mechanical Sound of Steam, 8904T.   — 25 30 35

8905 SWITCHER: 0-4-0, 1979, plastic engine, no headlight, diamond-
shaped stack, DC-powered, fixed coupler, no tender; part of 1965 Smokey
Mountain Line.   — — 10 15

783

WHAT DO YOU CALL YOUR LIONEL HUDSON?
OR
SCALING THE HEIGHTS OF
TINPLATE TERMINOLOGY

1. My nice new 8406 Fundimensions Hudson locomotive
is: (A) scale; (B) semi-scale; (C) scale-proportioned; (D)
scale-detailed; (E) none of the above.

If you were in some imaginary school for tinplate train
operators and collectors, how would you answer that question?
Shakespeare might have had a few glib answers such as
"What's in a name?" or "A rose by any other name would
smell as sweet". But he didn't collect Lionel trains, unless you
want to consider Malcolm's comment to MacDuff in

Macbeth: "Devilish MacBeth hath by many of these TRAINS sought to win me into his favor". And Shakespeare didn't have the right name for a collector, either, unlike a news reporter who covers Australia and New Zealand for NBC and has the ideal tinplate collector's name: Lionel Hudson. (Absolutely true, folks!)

This question, in fact, arouses considerable anger among those who like to be absolutely precise with definitions. True scale modelers have always insisted upon precise terminology, so they would be horrified at the thought of someone referring to the 8406 or its postwar predecessor, the 773, as a "scale" Hudson. Tinplaters are far less concerned with this question and frequently call this locomotive a "scale" Hudson in conversation. So who is right?

Actually, much depends upon the frame of reference used to define the term "scale". Strictly speaking, "scale" means that the item is reproduced in exact proportions and detail, as if one were able to take the proptotype, put it in a shrinking machine and reduce it to 1/48th its real size. That isn't always practical in the real world of miniature trains, of course. The cost of such items would be prohibitive.

It has been suggested that we refer to the 8406 as a "semi-scale" Hudson. That gets us into trouble both colloquially and realistically. The term "semi-scale" is used among tinplaters to refer to the prewar freight cars produced to match the fabled 700E Hudson steam locomotive. Some of these cars were made with trucks and couplers produced to National Model Railroad Association standards; these were called the "scale" freight cars. However, some of these cars were produced with tinplate trucks and couplers; these are the "semi-scale" cars. Realistically, "semi-scale" is a weasel word; it could mean anything which has the remotest proportions of the real thing. How "semi" is "semi-scale"? Even Marx lithographed cars are "semi-scale" to some extent!

Some light is thrown upon the matter by the terms "scale-proportioned" and "scale-detailed". The 8406 Fundi-mensions Hudson is indeed scale-proportioned; its length, width and height have been reduced to proper 0 Gauge size. However, it is not scale-detailed. That honor belongs to the prewar 700E Lionel Hudson produced in 1937; it is both scale-proportioned and scale-detailed. The term "scale-detailed" means that every detail on the real thing is there in proportion. On the 700E, even the wheel flanges are correct because Lionel made special track for this Hudson to run upon! The 773 and 8406 cannot have scale wheel flanges because they are designed to run on 0 Gauge track. In operation, if these locomotives had scale flanges, they would become airborne as soon as they hit an 0 Gauge switch — surely not the best in scale operations!

In his book **All Aboard**, Ron Hollander tells an amazing story of the exacting demands of scale modelers. It seems that Joshua Lionel Cowen stated that the tender was absolutely correct, right down to the number of rivets on the tender. A customer actually checked out this claim at the New York Central's Harmon yards by counting the number of rivets on the real tender and those on Lionel's tender. Lionel was three rivets short! Cowen hurriedly had his own staff check the situation. Sure enough, the real Hudson had 1,402 rivets and the Lionel model 1,399!

Some readers must be thinking at this point, "That's absolutely ridiculous! So what if a few details are missing? Since it's scale-proportioned, I'm still referring to the 8406 as the Scale Hudson!" Since the term is in fact colloquial among tinplaters, it is doubtful that any campaign by the terminologically pure of heart will eradicate the use of the term "scale" in reference to the Fundimensions Hudson. The truth of the matter is that scale modelers (many of whom started in tinplate) should not be condescending to their tinplate brethren, and tinplaters should show respect for the real concerns of the scale modeler, a truly knowledgeable fellow.

What do I call the Fundimensions 8406 Hudson?

How about "a darn fine-looking tinplate steam locomotive"?

Chapter III
HOPPER CARS

6104

6105   6109

6113

With all the variety shown in its freight car lines, it is somewhat odd that Fundimensions has only used two basic types of hopper cars. Perhaps this is because the company has been able to make good use of the two existing types without resorting to new dies. Some collectors, however, have expressed a desire to see new versions of this car, especially the ultra-modern cylindrical bodied center-flow hoppers such as those recently issued in O scale by the Weaver concern in Northumberland, Pennsylvania. (Just prior to press time, we learned that a new type of hopper will indeed be introduced soon.)

The first hopper issued by Fundimensions was the 9010 Great Northern short hopper car of 1970, essentially a revised version of the 6456 Lehigh Valley hopper cars so common to postwar construction.

The only difference between the Fundimensions car and the postwar car (aside from the usual change of trucks) is the presence of a molded brakewheel on one end of most of the Fundimensions cars. The Fundimensions short hopper has been used almost universally in inexpensive production since the beginning. It has been issued in Chessie, Rio Grande, D.T.&I., Canadian National and many other railroad markings.

Some of the earlier cars have color variations which are quite scarce. For example, there is a very rare 9011 Great Northern in a dark royal blue color and two T.,A.&G. color variations which are hard to find. Some cars have lettering variations, too, which mark them as scarce variations, notably another T.,A.&G. hopper with yellow lettering instead of white.

In 1981, the short hopper was modified to reproduce the operating hopper car of postwar years. It is somewhat curious that four versions of this car have been produced, but the coal ramp to make these cars work has not been reissued to date! (The postwar version is, however, readily available. The only trouble is that the coupler release at the top of the ramp will not work with a disc-operating coupler; perhaps that is what has held up the production of this accessory.) A metal plate is attached to the bottom of the car, and the square bin ports are punched out of the car. A plunger is attached to the plate which, when pulled down by an electromagnet, opens the bins and releases the coal. Fundimensions has put this car out in Great Northern, Reading, Chesapeake & Ohio and Erie markings thus far.

The second type of hopper car issued in the Fundimensions era has been the big and handsome "quad" hopper which was

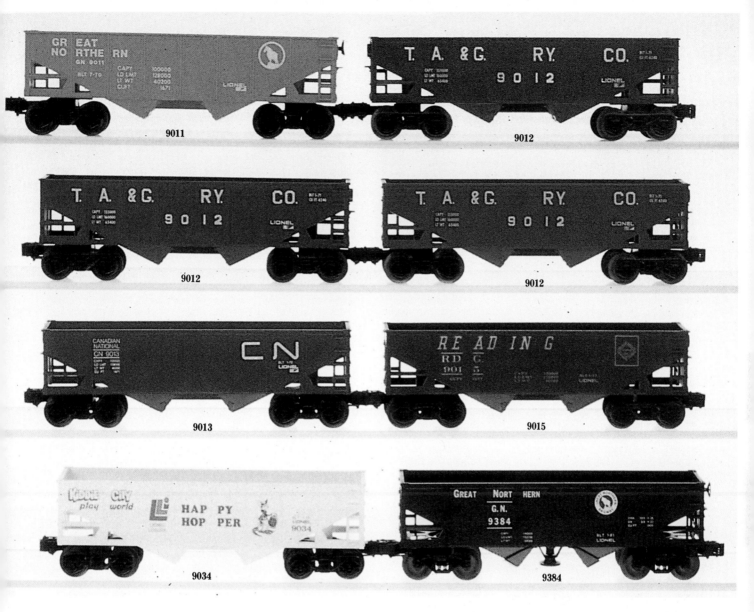

9011　　9012

9012　　9012

9013　　9015

9034　　9384

first issued in the postwar years in Lehigh Valley markings. This car has come at various times with and without hatched covers, with and (mostly) without a metal center spreader bar, and with metal or plastic plates holding the trucks to the car. Some versions have been produced with rectangular builders' plates on the car sides; others have lacked them. Some cars come both ways. Many, many versions of this car have been produced in both railroad and corporate markings, beginning with the blue uncovered 9130 B&O hopper of 1970.

Tom Rollo, the author of our 2156 Passenger Station article in this edition, has pointed out a curious construction feature of this car. If you look at the car's interior, you will see a large drum-shaped projection at the bottom center of the car where the mold mark is. From underneath, there is a deep recess with two bracket slots on each side; just adjacent to the outer edge, there are two holes which look like receptacles for screws. Mr. Rollo's conjecture is that at one time an operating mechanism was considered for this car, but it was never produced. The same construction feature shows up on the postwar cars right from the beginning. (Other collectors have arrived at this conclusion independently.) Even more fascinating is the conjecture that this opening was meant to

accommodate a radio receiver such as those designed for the Electronic Radio Control sets produced from 1946 to 1949. It should be noted that the first quad hoppers were not produced in the postwar era until 1954. We would like to hear from our readers about this bit of speculation, for which there is strong circumstantial evidence. It is even more interesting that the Fundimensions versions of these hopper cars retain this odd feature so many years later.

Another oddity about these Fundimensions hoppers is that there are frequently differences between the cars offered as part of sets and the same cars offered for separate sale. For example, the 9111 Norfolk and Western hopper in sets is an unpainted chocolate color. The same car in separate sale boxes is frequently, though not always, tuscan-painted brown plastic. The normal 9135 Norfolk and Western hopper is navy or royal blue with white lettering. In the late example included with the 1975 Spirit of America set, the lettering on the car is gray instead of white. The separate sale 9117 Alaska hopper has a black cover; reportedly, some versions included in a service station set has an orange cover (A.J. Conto Collection). There are several other examples of this phenomenon, especially in the early production of these hopper cars.

There seem to be three levels of value attached to the quad hoppers. The most common of these hoppers seem to be the ones with corporate logos, such as the Domino Sugar, Planters Peanut and Sun Maid Raisins examples. (A noteworthy exception is the Ralston Purina car, which is very hard to find). Most of the cars with railroad names are a little more desirable and scarce, such as the Pennsylvania, Virginian, Illinois Central and some of the early B & O and Norfolk and Western cars. The scarcest cars are those available as club convention cars, those available only in special sets and some variations of the earliest cars. Examples of these are the gray-lettered 9110 B&O, the LCCA Corning car, the Alcoa and the Southern cars. Most of the hopper cars are relatively easy to find, and the beginning collector can amass quite a few of them readily at reasonable prices. None of these cars can be considered as truly rare, but they add a nice look to an operating layout, especially the cars with railroad markings and full covers.

Another hopper recently introduced is worth mention because it shows that Fundimensions is indeed moving into new areas with these cars. In 1984, Fundimensions introduced two versions of a stubby little iron ore hopper car similar to those used in western sections of this country. One car came in black with white Penn Central markings, and the other was a tuscan Soo car with white lettering.

This little car is an excellent model of the real cars and looks similar to the Atlas scale O cars which have been made for a long time. The only complaint collectors have expressed about these cars is that they sit too high on their Symington-Wayne trucks.

Nonetheless, these cars have been brisk sellers for the very good reason that collectors have bought whole fleets for their unit trains. As a result, the value of these cars has doubled in less than a year's time. Fundimensions will probably market many more versions of this car in the years to come.

It is interesting to guess whether Fundimensions has other new designs of hopper cars in the works. One possibility is that the firm has molds for a scale Standard "O" version which has yet to be made. Whatever the case, the Fundimensions hoppers once more illustrate the ability of the firm to make the most of its existing resources.

Gd   VG   Exc   Mt

0784 LIONEL RAILROADER CLUB: 1985, covered hopper, white body, black lettering and cover. Special issue only available to members of Lionel Railroader Club. This and all other quad hoppers have a cavity in the mold on the bottom center which may have been suitable for mounting a coil or solenoid, as was stated in the introduction. Reader comments are invited. Rollo, Bonney and Cole comments.   **NRS**

6076 LEHIGH VALLEY: 1970, short hopper, black body with white lettering, equipped with Symington-Wayne trucks, one operating and one dummy coupler. Possible postwar carry-over equipped with Fundimensions trucks and included in an early set. Reader comments invited. C. Lang Collection.   **NRS**

6100 ONTARIO NORTHLAND: 1981-82, blue sides and cover, yellow trim, yellow "triple lightning" logo; Symington-Wayne trucks.
—   —   **17   25**

6101 BURLINGTON: 1981, 1983, green sides and cover, white lettering.
—   —   **13   15**

6102 GREAT NORTHERN: 1981, tuscan body and cover, white lettering, FARR Series 3 logo, disc-operating couplers; from Famous American Railroad Series 3, available only as separate sale item.   —   —   **15   20**

6103 CANADIAN NATIONAL: 1981, gray with maroon lettering, maroon cover, die-cast sprung trucks; part of 1158 Maple Leaf Limited set.
—   —   **20   25**

6104 SOUTHERN: 1983, dark green body with coal load, gold lettering and FARR 4 logo. Available for separate sale. L. Caponi comment.
—   —   **20   25**

6105 READING: 1982, tuscan body, white lettering and logo, operating hopper.   —   —   **30   35**

6106 NW: 1982, gray with black lettering, black cover, die-cast sprung Standard 0 trucks, disc-operating couplers; part of 1260 Continental Limited set.   —   —   **20   25**

6107 SHELL: 1982, covered hopper, yellow body and cover, black and red lettering; Symington-Wayne trucks.   —   —   **12   15**

6109 C&O: 1983, operating car with opening bins, black body; white lettering.   —   —   **30   35**

6110 MISSOURI PACIFIC: 1983, covered hopper, black body, black cover, white lettering; Symington-Wayne trucks.   —   —   **13   15**

6111 L&N: 1983, covered hopper, gray body and cover with red lettering, Symington-Wayne trucks.   —   —   **13   15**

6112 COMMONWEALTH EDISON: 1983, covered hopper, produced for LCCA convention in Rockford, Illinois; tuscan body, left third of car side painted black with Reddy Kilowatt logo, black and white lettering, black coal pile; Symington-Wayne trucks; 2,500 made. Somewhat hard to find. C. Lang and C. Rohlfing comments.   —   —   —   **75**

6113 ILLINOIS CENTRAL: 1983, short hopper, black with white lettering; sold as part of 1354 Northern Freight Flyer set.   —   —   —   **10**

6114 CNW: 1983, covered hopper, dark green body and cover, yellow lettering and logo; available only as part of 1361 Gold Coast Limited set.
—   —   **20   25**

6115 SOUTHERN: 1983, short hopper, gray with red lettering; sold as part of 1353 Southern Streak set.   —   —   —   **10**

THE FUNDIMENSIONS IRON ORE CARS
By William Meyer and Philip Smith

Editor's Note: William Meyer has contributed articles to us about the Hell Gate Bridge, the NW-2 Switcher and, in this book, the 9090 General Mills Mini-Max boxcar. Pastor Philip Smith has been a frequent contributor for our prewar books; he is also the author of **ENJOYING FUNDIMENSIONS TRAINS,** a Greenberg publication of 1982. His knowledge of prototypes comes from his devotion to the old Reading Railroad and its rich history. We have combined Mr. Meyer's article with Pastor Smith's comments to produce the essay which follows.

The 1984 Lionel Collector Series catalogue portrays two new ore cars: the 6116 Soo Line in tuscan with white lettering and the 6122 Penn Central in black with white lettering. These Lionel models are remarkably similar to the prototypes. The catalogue illustrations apparently show Atlas 0 Scale ore car bodies mounted on Fundimensions Symington-Wayne freight trucks. (Independent observations have confirmed that these ore car bodies are indeed close to the Atlas models — ed.) Atlas cars were made for trucks with flat bolsters. They supported the car near the center line of the axles. Fundimensions trucks, like those of postwar Lionel, have bolsters which curve upward. They lift the ore cars too high and make them look a bit awkward.

Ore cars look much shorter and stubbier than coal cars, for a good reason. Ore is much heavier than coal. If a coal car were fully loaded with ore, the weight would exceed its limits, working woe upon the sides, trucks and draft gear. Railroads which used coal cars in occasional ore service loaded them only about two-thirds full. Photographs of these cars show the ore well below the top of the sides.

The Soo Line is a particularly good name for Fundimensions to model, as it was a major ore carrier in the upper Michigan

Peninsula serving the ports of Superior, Ashland and Marquette. Slow-moving trains of up to 135 50-ton ore cars were commonly seen on the line headed by two 1,500 horsepower road Alcos, two F-7 diesels or two GP-9 diesels. In the days of steam, the Soo used 2-8-2 locomotives which could handle 135 ore cars easily.

While the Soo was primarily concerned with hauling ore from mines to ports, the Penn Central did not serve a rich ore-producing region. It was, however, a major ore hauler, moving about 28 million tons per year from ports to inland steel mills. It handled Lake Superior ore from its connections at Lake Erie ports and foreign ore which came primarily from Philadelphia.

Among the most renowned users of these chunky ore cars was the Duluth, Missabe & Iron Range. Mammoth Baldwin 2-8-8-4 compound steam locomotives regularly handled 19,000-ton trains — the world's heaviest. Can you imagine one steam locomotive hauling 19,000 tons?

Not only do Fundimensions' new ore carriers look good, they are also named for proper ore-carrying roads. If you can't make up a consist of 135 ore cars, remember that shorter ore trains WERE commonly seen!

6116 SOO LINE: 1984-85, iron ore car, tuscan body, white lettering; Symington-Wayne trucks, open framework on car ends. Somewhat erratic availability because many operators have bought whole fleets of these cars for unit trains. — — **18 22**

6117 ERIE: 1984-85, operating hopper, black body, white lettering, gold Erie diamond logo, Standard 0 trucks. Plunger opens bins when activated by remote track. Operating coal ramp has still not been reissued; possible reason is that Standard 0 trucks will not uncouple by remote control from top of postwar ramp. R. LaVoie comment. — — — **25**

6118 ERIE: 1984-85, covered hopper, gray body and cover, black lettering, black and white diamond Erie logo; Standard 0 trucks. From Erie-Lackawanna Limited set. — — — **25**

6122 PENN CENTRAL: 1984-85, iron ore car, black ore car body, white PC lettering and logo; Symington-Wayne trucks, open framework on car ends. Same comments as those for 6116 above. — — **18 22**

6123 PENNSYLVANIA: 1984-85, covered hopper, gray body and cover, black lettering, white and black PRR Keystone, gold FARR 5 diamond-shaped logo, Standard 0 trucks. From Famous American Railroad Set 5. Reportedly, fewer of these hoppers were produced than the other cars. — — — **25**

6124 DELAWARE & HUDSON: 1984-85, covered hopper, bright red body and cover, yellow lettering and logo; Symington-Wayne trucks. — — — **15**

6131 ILLINOIS TERMINAL: Announced for 1985, covered hopper, yellow body and cover, red lettering, Symington-Wayne trucks. Erroneously listed as Illinois Central by some dealer lists. Estimated price at introduction: — — — **16**

6150 ATSF: Announced for 1985, short hopper, blue body, yellow lettering and logo, Symington-Wayne trucks, dummy couplers. Part of Midland Freight set. — — — **10**

6446-25 N&W: 1970, covered hopper, special production by Fundimensions with postwar number for Glen Uhl, an Ohio Lionel dealer. Royal blue

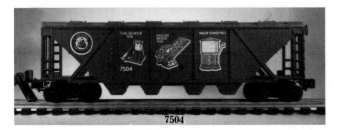

7504

body and cover, Type I unlabeled box, AAR trucks. This car has many more plastic lap lines than usual; these are formed as the styrene plastic cools in the mold. Reportedly, only 450 were made. T. Rollo and G. Halverson comments. — — **125 150**

7504 LIONEL 75th ANNIVERSARY: 1975, covered hopper, blue body, red cover, no builder's plate. — **10 15 20**

9010 GREAT NORTHERN: 1971, blue body, white lettering, plastic brakewheels, metal wheels, one manumatic coupler, one fixed coupler, MPC logo.

(A) Medium blue body, AAR trucks, "1-70". 1 2 3 5
(B) Light blue body, AAR trucks, "1-70". 1 2 3 5
(C) Medium light blue body, AAR trucks, "7-70". 1 2 3 5
(D) Light blue body, Symington-Wayne trucks, "1-70".
    1 2 3 5

See also Factory Errors and Prototypes.

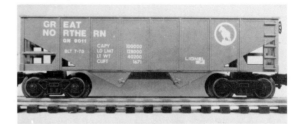

9011 GREAT NORTHERN: 1971, 1979, medium blue body, white lettering, "7-70", Symington-Wayne trucks, plastic wheels, one manumatic coupler, one fixed coupler.

(A) Externally-mounted brakewheel, MPC logo. 3 4 5 6
(B) Built-in brakewheel, MPC logo. 3 4 5 6
(C) Built-in brakewheel, no MPC logo. 3 4 5 6
(D) Same as (A), but AAR trucks. C. Rohlfing Collection. 3 4 5 6
(E) Deep royal blue mold. — — **120 165**

9012 TA&G: 1971-72, 1979, blue body, white lettering, built-in brakewheel, "1-70," Symington-Wayne trucks, plastic wheels, one manumatic coupler, one fixed coupler, MPC logo.

(A) Dark blue body (navy). 2 3 5 7
(B) Bright blue body (royal blue). — — **22 40**

9013 CANADIAN NATIONAL: 1972-74, 1979, red body, white lettering, built in brakewheel, "1-72", Symington-Wayne trucks, plastic wheels, one manumatic coupler, one fixed coupler, MPC logo.

(A) Dark red body. 2 3 4 5
(B) Medium red body. 2 3 4 5
(C) Light red body. 2 3 4 5

9015 READING: 1973-74, 1979, brown body, yellow lettering, built-in brakewheel, "1-73," Symington-Wayne trucks, metal wheels, one disc coupler, one fixed coupler, no MPC logo. Has been sought after in Middle Atlantic states for use in unit trains by operators. R. LaVoie comment.

7 10 12 15

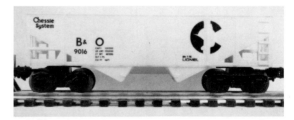

9016 CHESSIE: 1975-79, yellow body, blue lettering, built-in brakewheel, "1-75", Symington-Wayne trucks, metal wheels, one operating coupler, one fixed coupler, no MPC logo.

(A) Yellow body. 1 2 3 4
(B) Light yellow body. 1 2 3 4
(C) Same as (A), but has "LCCA 1980-81 MEET CAR" overstamp.
    C. Rohlfing comment. NRS

9018 DT&I: 1978, 1981, yellow body, black heat-stamped lettering, plastic brakewheel, "BLT 1-78," Symington-Wayne trucks, one manumatic coupler, one fixed coupler. 2 3 5 8

6100

6101

6102

6103

6107

6114

6124

6446-25

9110

9111

9113

9115

9117

9119

9130

9134

9135

9135

9213

9213

9260

9262

9263

9265

9276

9374

9322

9388

9358

9366

9371

9018

9025 **DT&I:** 1978, short hopper, came with Santa Fe Double Diesel set as an optional insert.
(A) Yellow body with black lettering. Forst Collection. — — 5 7
(B) Orange body with black lettering. Forst Collection. — — 5 7

9028 **B&O:** 1978, dark blue body, yellow lettering, Chessie emblem, plastic brakewheel, "BLT 1-78", Symington-Wayne trucks, metal wheels, one manumatic coupler, one fixed coupler. The existence of this car has been questioned. Confirmation requested. T. Ladny comment. **NRS**

9034 **LIONEL LEISURE:** Made for Kiddie City retail outlet as part of special 1790 set in 1978; white short hopper body, red, blue and orange lettering, brown, blue and orange Casey Kangaroo logo. Hard to find. G. Halverson comment and Collection. — — 25 30

9038

9038 **CHESSIE:** 1978, 1980-81, plastic trucks and wheels, blue body with yellow lettering one operating coupler, one fixed coupler.
1 2 3 4

9079

9079 **GRAND TRUNK:** 1977, deep blue body, white lettering, built-in brakewheel, "1-77", Symington-Wayne trucks, metal wheels, one disc coupler, one fixed coupler, no MPC logo. 5 7 9 12

9110 **B&O:** 1971, black body, "2-71", builder's plate, not covered, metal truck plate holders.
(A) Gray lettering, reportedly only 1,000 made. 20 30 40 50
(B) White lettering. 10 12 15 20

9111 **N&W:** 1972, not covered, builder's plate, metal plate holding trucks. Symington-Wayne trucks. Versions found in a unpainted chocolate brown body came in sets; those with painted tuscan bodies were sold separately. R. LaVoie and G. Halverson comments.
(A) Unpainted chocolate brown body, white lettering, center spreader bar. R. LaVoie Collection. 5 7 10 15
(B) Painted tuscan body, white lettering, center spreader bar, came with set 1388, the Golden State Arrow. G. Halverson Collection. 7 10 15 20
(C) Dark red body, white lettering, less than 40 reportedly produced. Probable trial run. A. Otten Collection. — — — 125
See also Factory Errors and Prototypes.

9112 **D&RGW:** Orange body, black lettering, orange cover, builder's plate, metal plate holding trucks, Symington-Wayne trucks
(A) Light orange body, deep heat-stamped lettering.
7 10 12 15

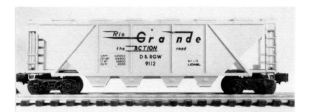

9112

(B) Light orange body, flatter heat-stamped lettering.
7 10 12 15
(C) Darker orange body, flatter heat-stamped lettering.
7 10 12 15

9113 **N&W:** 1973, uncatalogued, gray body, black lettering, from 1973 Canadian Pacific Service Station set, not covered, center spreader bar, Symington-Wayne trucks, builder's plate, metal plate holding trucks.
10 12 15 20

9114 **MORTON'S SALT:** 1975-76, navy blue body, white and yellow lettering, yellow cover, builder's plate, metal plate holding trucks.
6 8 10 12

9114

9115 **PLANTER'S PEANUTS:** 1974-76, dark blue body, yellow lettering, yellow cover, builder's plate, metal plate holding trucks.
6 8 10 12

9116

9116 **DOMINO SUGAR:** 1974-76, gray body, blue lettering, navy blue cover, builder's plate, metal plate holding trucks. 6 8 10 12

9117 **ALASKA:** 1974-76, black body, black cover, from 1974 Service Station set. Also sold separately.
(A) Orange-yellow lettering, builder's plate. 10 12 15 20
(B) Light yellow lettering, builder's plate. 10 12 15 20
(C) Light yellow lettering, no builder's plate. 10 12 15 20
(D) Orange unpainted cover instead of black; came with some of the Service Station set production. Halverson observation, A.J. Conto Collection. **NRS**

9118

9118 **CORNING:** 1974, white and mist green body, covered, LCCA 1974 Convention car; 2,000 made. — — 65 75

9119 **DETROIT & MACKINAC:** 1975, red body, white lettering, shiny red cover, "1-76", 1975 Service Station set, no builder's plate; metal plate holding trucks. Also sold separately.

(A) As described above.   **6   8   10   12**

(B) Stamped "SEASON'S GREETINGS" for the Detroit-Toledo Chapter of the TCA: green Christmas ball with gold lettering over-stamped in middle of car side. H. Azzinaro Collection.   **—   —   25   30**

9130 B&O: 1970-71, medium royal blue paint on gray plastic, white lettering, "1-70", not covered, center spreader bar; AAR trucks. Some examples came in Type I long boxes with a 9110 label which had the 9110 number crossed out in blue marker ink and the number 9130 reprinted on the label. Incredibly, the picture of the car is numbered 9130! It is also curious to note that this car was produced before the 9110, not afterward. R. LaVoie Collection.

(A) Plastic plate holding trucks.   **8   10   12   15**

(B) Metal plate holding trucks.   **10   12   15   25**

9134 VIRGINIAN: 1976-77, silver body, blue lettering, blue cover, plastic plate holding trucks, Symington-Wayne trucks.

(A) No builder's plate.   **7   9   11   15**

(B) Builder's plate.   **7   9   11   15**

9135

See also Factory Errors and Prototypes.

9135 N&W: 1971, blue or purple body, white lettering, royal blue cover; "9-70", usually Symington-Wayne trucks, metal plate holding trucks, from N&W set and sold separately.

(A) Royal blue body, no builder's plate.   **8   10   12   15**

(B) Royal blue body, builder's plate.   **8   10   12   15**

(C) Purple body, builder's plate; 3,000 manufactured.   **10   15   20   25**

(D) Light blue body, builder's plate, AAR trucks.   **8   10   12   15**

(E) Same as (D), but covers glued on by factory. Reader comments requested; this would be a most unusual manufacturing technique.   **8   10   12   15**

(F) Flat Navy blue-painted blue plastic body, glossy unpainted dark blue cover, light gray lettering instead of white, builder's plate, MPC logo, "9-70", Symington-Wayne trucks. It is possible that this particular version was issued in 1974 as part of the "Spirit of America" diesel set. Reader comments invited. Halverson comment, LaVoie and Halverson Collections.   **—   —   20   25**

9213 M&St L: 1978, red, white lettering, cover, sprung die-cast Standard 0 trucks; part of Service Station set from 1978.   **—   —   15   20**

9260 REYNOLDS ALUMINUM: 1975-78, "NAHX 9260", blue body, silver lettering, "1-75", metal plate holding trucks, silver cover with blue hatches; Symington-Wayne trucks.

(A) No builder's plate.   **6   8   10   12**

(B) Builder's plate.   **6   8   10   12**

9261

9261 SUNMAID: 1975-76, "GACX 9261", red body, yellow and white lettering, yellow cover, "Raisin Lady", "1-75", no builder's plate; metal plate holding trucks, Symington-Wayne trucks.   **6   8   10   12**

9262 RALSTON-PURINA RPFX 9262: 1975-76, white body, red and white checks, red and black lettering, "1-75", red and black covers, no builder's

plates, metal plate holding trucks, Symington-Wayne trucks. Somewhat hard to find.   **20   25   30   35**

9263 PENNSYLVANIA: 1975-77, tuscan body, white lettering, black cover, no builder's plate; Symington-Wayne trucks.

(A) Metal plate holding trucks.   **10   12   15   20**

(B) Plastic plate holding trucks.   **10   12   15   20**

NOTE: A few boxes were mislabeled Penn Central but the cars inside were labeled properly.

9264

9264 ILLINOIS CENTRAL: 1975-77, bright orange body, black lettering, black IC circular logo with white "IC", black cover; Symington-Wayne trucks

(A) Metal plate holding trucks, no builder's plate.   **8   10   15   20**

(B) Same as (A), but plastic plate holding trucks.   **8   10   15   20**

(C) Same as (A), but builder's plate.   **8   10   15   20**

(D) Plastic plate holding trucks, builder's plate.   **8   10   15   20**

(E) Same as (A), but stamped "TCA MUSEUM EXPRESS", only 108 made. C. Rohlfing Collection.   **NRS**

9265 WM: 1975-77, "Chessie System", yellow body, blue lettering, blue cover, "1-75", no builder's plate; Symington-Wayne trucks.

(A) Metal plate holding trucks.   **10   12   15   20**

(B) Plastic plate holding trucks.   **10   12   15   20**

9266

9266 SOUTHERN: 1976, gray plastic painted silver, black lettering, red cover, plastic plate holding trucks, red "BIG JOHN" script logo; Symington-Wayne trucks.

(A) Builder's plate.   **12   20   30   35**

(B) No builder's plate.   **8   15   20   25**

9267

9267 ALCOA: 1976, silver-painted gray body, blue lettering, silver cover, no builder's plate, Standard 0 trucks; from Northern Pacific Service Station set.   **12   15   20   25**

9276 PEABODY: 1978, yellow body, dark green lettering, "BLT 1-78", Standard 0 trucks, hole for center bar but no bar, part of Milwaukee Limited set.   **—   —   20   25**

9286 B&L E: Orange body, black lettering, black and white decal logo (one of the few instances where Fundimensions has used decals), black cover, builder's plate, plastic plate holding trucks.   **8   10   12   15**

9304 C&O: 1973-76, blue body, yellow lettering, coal carrier attached to cradle tilts and dumps plastic coal into bin; Symington-Wayne trucks.

        6   **8**   **10**   **12**

See also Factory Errors and Prototypes.

9306 C&O: 1974-76, same as 9304 entry, but remote track is included with car. Number on car remains 9304.   **6**   **8**   **10**   **12**

9311 UP: 1978, red body with yellow lettering, coal dump with black plastic coal, Symington-Wayne trucks, one disc coupler, one fixed coupler; load dumps when operating disc pulled down.   **6**   **8**   **10**   **12**

9330

9322 A.T.S.F.: 1979, red plastic body painted red, white lettering, black and white Santa Fe logo, diamond shaped herald "Famous American Railroad Series 1" in gold, plastic brakewheel, hole for center brace, no center brace, covers, Symington-Wayne trucks.   — — **20** **25**

9330 KICKAPOO VALLEY: 1972, four wheels.

(A) Green.	**1**	**2**	**3**	**4**
(B) Red.	**1**	**2**	**3**	**4**
(C) Yellow.	**1**	**2**	**3**	**4**

9338 PENNSYLVANIA POWER & LIGHT: 1979, tuscan body, yellow lettering, no cover, Standard 0 trucks, no spreader bar; from 1971 Quaker City Limited set, an excellent copy of the Bethlehem Steel Corporation prototype. Hard to find because operators have used large numbers of them for unit trains. C. Rohlfing and R. LaVoie comments.   — — **35** **40**

9358 SAND'S OF IOWA: 1980, LCCA 1980 National Convention car; bright powder blue and black body, powder blue cover, black lettering, Symington-Wayne trucks; 4,500 made. R. LaVoie Collection.

      — — **20** **25**

9366 U.P.: 1980, silver-painted gray body, black cover, red, white and blue UNION PACIFIC logo, gold FARR 2 diamond-shaped logo, Symington-Wayne trucks, from Famous American Railroad Series 2, only available as separate sale item.   — — **11** **15**

9371 LANTIC SUGAR (Seaboard): 1980, yellow sides and cover, Standard 0 trucks, red logo with white "Lantic Sugar" lettering, black lettering. Type IV box is labeled "SEABOARD COAST LINE COVERED HOPPER", but that lettering does not appear on the car; from 1071 Mid-Atlantic Limited set.   — — **15** **20**

9374 READING: 1980-81, black sides, white lettering, red and black Reading diamond logo, Symington-Wayne trucks; from 1072 Cross Country Express.   — — **25** **30**

9384 GREAT NORTHERN: 1981, operating hopper, dark green body, white lettering, red, black and white mountain goat logo, bins open by remote control, Standard 0 trucks; from 1160 Great Lakes Limited set.

      — — **40** **50**

Chapter IV
BOX, REFRIGERATOR AND STOCK CARS

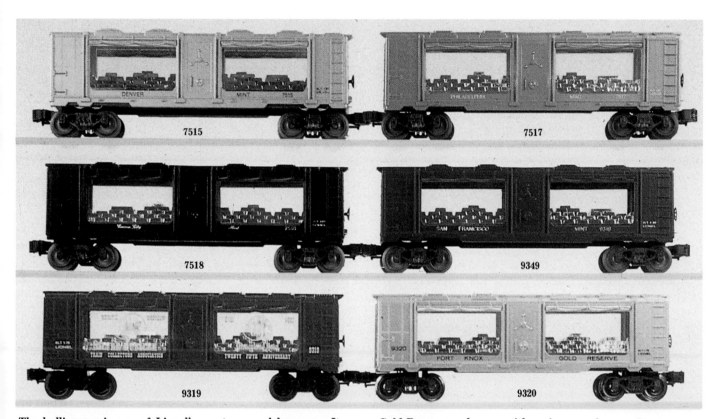

The bullion car is one of Lionel's most unusual boxcars. Its origins are the 3435 Aquarium car from 1959. This car was subsequently redesigned in 1961 as the 6445 Ft. Knox Bullion Gold Reserve and rerun with various numbers and new names by Fundimensions.

With the assistance of Dr. Charles Weber

Ask a Fundimensions collector about his specialty, and the chances are he/she will tell you about some form or class of boxcar. That really is no surprise, for box, refrigerator and stock cars are by far the most numerous and variable pieces of rolling stock issued by Fundimensions. This was also true of postwar production, and it is easy to see why. In the first place, boxcars are fixed in the public mind as the "typical" rolling stock, aside from passenger cars, which have their own stories to tell. Look at any movie dealing with railroads, and chances are you will see many different boxcars. Read some of the great railroad fiction by such luminaries of the genre as Gilbert Lathrop and E. S. Dellinger, and you will probably read of some desperate struggle against the elements by courageous brakemen trying to control a runaway train by turning brakewheels — atop the boxcars. Another reason for the popularity of collecting boxcars is more specific to tinplate production. As we have seen many times, color and graphics sell toy trains, and what better place to put your most colorful graphics than on the flat sides of a box or refrigerator car? The many types of box, refrigerator and stock cars outsell all other types of tinplate rolling stock combined. These cars are truly crucial to the success of Fundimensions as a producer of trains.

The only real trouble in collecting these cars lies in their utterly astonishing variety and vast quantity. Type collectors will have a difficult time collecting all of a particular series because of the sheer weight of numbers. When you consider that there are 80 boxcars in the 9700 Series alone, not to mention the 70 or so 9800 Series refrigerator cars, the 9200 and 9400 Series boxcars, the Wood-sided Reefers, the mint cars, the bunk cars, the Bicentennial series, the Tobacco Road and Favorite Spirits Series and the smaller box and stock cars, you would need quite a bit of shelf space for the whole production!

Variation collectors have even more problems than the type collectors, because many of these cars have seemingly endless variations in body styles and molds, frames, doors, colors and so on. It's not unusual for many of these cars — the 9748 CP Rail boxcar comes to mind — to exist in fifteen or more variations!

Therein lies considerable controversy. Why should a beginning collector bother with variations of the same car at all, if it is nearly hopeless to try to get them all? Wouldn't that make the collector into one of those detestable "rivet counters" for whom every production change, no matter how slight, is a significant variation? Some collectors believe that these variations should be neither stressed nor even mentioned in pricing and quantity studies. The answers to these questions revolve primarily around interest; you should have the opportunity to observe what you are interested in, and many collectors are very interested in the boxcar variations because they come from the same heritage as those found in the old and venerated postwar 6464 Series. One of the real pioneers in the study of boxcar variations, Dr. Charles Weber, stated the case recently in a reply to a collector who asked why these variations were important enough to report. His letter is highly significant and, with his permission, deserves quoting in full.

"In the 'early days' of collecting 6464 boxcars, we started noticing that similar cars when placed next to each other looked different. Why? Investigation showed that some were painted and some were not. Some came from different batches of paint. Then we noticed that even unpainted cars showed similar slight but recognizable differences."

"So, those of us who were nuts over these cars started to collect anything which looked different. It followed, then, that as we were studying these cars, we would also notice some differences which do not readily show — specifically, the colors of the plastic used to mold the cars. Therefore, we noted those differences for completeness."

"Very few of us seek out variations which can't be seen, such as these molds which have been painted over. But, if the price is right, we might even buy such a minor variation. In any event, whether one collects these minor variations or not, it is still interesting for many of us to learn about them. If a given collector isn't interested, that's his business, but lots of us are interested. That's why they make chocolate and vanilla!"

Dr. Weber and his fellow collectors began their studies in the mid to late 1960s. The results of those studies speak for themselves in the Greenberg Guide to Postwar Trains, 1945-1969. The pioneering efforts of Dr. Weber and others have indeed carried over into Fundimensions production, which also has its interesting variations.

What is the best advice for the beginning collector? The best place to start collecting these cars is probably the 9800 Series refrigerator cars. There are only a few cars in this series which are really hard to find, and the number of variations is not particularly awesome. In addition, these cars are rather handsome and attractively priced; some of the more common cars have recently been sold at "clearance" sales for as little as $7.00, brand new in the box! Collectors have not shown as much interest in these cars as they have in the 9200, 9700 and 9400 boxcar series, so the field is wide open for the beginner. After experience with the toy train marketplace, the collector can turn to other box and refrigerator car series where the prices are more variable and the variations more complex. Just what are the critical variables in collecting variations of these cars? Perhaps a run-down of these variables would be helpful to the collector at this juncture.

THE 9200, 9700 AND 9400 SERIES BOXCARS: CRITICAL VARIABLES

1. Body Types: There are five basic body types found in these three series of boxcars; the last one, known as the Type IX body, is by far the most common and has been used since late in 1972. Types I to IV refer to postwar production and need not concern us here. The first body type, V, features one partially complete rivet row vertically to the right of the door. The end plates are blank, and it is found with Type I or II door guides (see below). Type VI is identical, but the partially complete rivet row is absent. The Type VII body has Type I or II door guides, but this time the end plates are stamped "9200/ SERIES" at one end and "LIONEL" at the other end with the early MPC logo. The Type VIII body is the same as Type VII, but it has Type III door guides. Finally, the common Type IX body has Type III door guides and a "9700/SERIES" end plate.

Curiously, when Fundimensions changed from the 9700

9200 and 9700 BOXCAR VARIATIONS

TYPE V BODY

(A) One partially complete rivet row
(B) Blank end plates
(C) Metal or plastic door guides at top and bottom

TYPE VI BODY [also known as '70 Body]

(A) Absence of even partially complete rivet row
(B) Blank end plates
(C) Metal or plastic door guides at top and bottom

TYPE VII BODY [also known as '71 Body]

(A) Absence of even partially complete rivet row
(B) "9200" on one end plate, "LIONEL MPC" logo on other
(C) Metal or plastic door guide at top and bottom

TYPE VIII BODY

(A) Absence of even partially complete rivet row
(B) "9200" on one end plate, "LIONEL MPC" logo on other
(C) One plastic door guide at top, hooks on bottom

TYPE IX BODY [also known as '72 Body

(A) Absence of even partially complete rivet row
(B) "9700" on one end plate, "LIONEL MPC" logo on other
(C) One plastic door guide at top, hooks on bottom

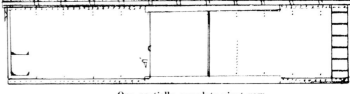

One partially complete rivet row

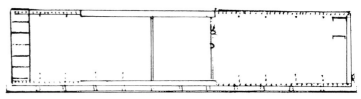

Absence of even partially complete rivet row

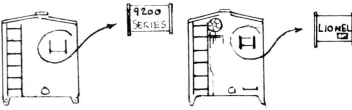

In our description we have omitted the body mold types '70, '71 and '72 as found in the last edition since these are now redundant to our new classification.

In this edition we have completely rewritten the 9200 and 9700 series box

car descriptions to conform to the general pattern of this book. Common elements are described first and varying characteristics follow under subheadings (A), (B), etc. This method focuses the reader's attention on the varying elements and makes identification easier. Drawing by Bob Fox

Series to the 9400 Series, the firm never changed the end plate; it still reads "9700/SERIES".

2. Door Guides: There are three basic types of door guides used in the 9200, 9700 and 9400 Series. The first, Type I, is a repetition of postwar practice; upper and lower door guides are both metal and are fastened by rivets. The Type II door guide is somewhat less common; it represents a brief transition period. This arrangement has two plastic door guides which simply snap into the rivet holes. The common Type III door guide has a plastic top guide, but the lower end of the car door has two plastic hook extensions which slide back and forth on a sill molded into the car body.

3. Frame Types: Since these frames are easily switched, the frame type is not a major factor in determining the car's value. The Type I stamped metal frame has a concave "bubble" on the bottom center and two holes, no doubt once intended for an operating car's wiring. In the Type II frame, the "bubble" is no longer present, but the two holes are still there. The Type III frame retains the holes, but this time there is stamped lettering present: "LIONEL 00-6464-009". This is the original 6464 part number; the body and doors also carry 6464 part numbers, reflecting the heritage of these cars.

4. Body Mold Colors: The phrase "Body Mold" refers to the color of plastic used for the body, whether it is painted or not. In the first five years of its existence, Fundimensions used plastic which came in the form of solid pellets. Since it was hard to control the color of the plastic, some odd combinations sometimes resulted. For example, a car painted brown might have been molded in orange plastic in one case and brown plastic in another. To compound matters further, the door might have been molded of an entirely different color than the body. Some time in late 1975 or early 1976, Fundimensions switched to a liquid plastic compound which was much easier to color-control. As a result, boxcars made after 1975 show far fewer variations in body mold and paint. To determine the body mold color, open the car door and look inside the car; the inside surfaces are unpainted. Be mindful that in some cases, the body itself is unpainted plastic. Sometimes the body is found both ways! A typical entry might read: "Tuscan-painted orange body, tuscan-painted gray doors."

THE 9800 REFRIGERATOR CARS: CRITICAL VARIABLES

Body Types: The 9800 Series refrigerator car is an all-plastic car with the roof and ends made of one piece and the bottom and sides made of another. The two pieces attach at the ends by screws. The oldest body type is more of a carry-over from postwar production than its successors, which had more and more detail eliminated in an attempt to simplify construction. The Type I body features two metal door guides and a metal channel which runs the length of the car bottom and is attached by a single screw to the car body. In turn, the trucks are attached to the channel. The little metal control door of postwar production is missing, but three ice hatches are molded into the roof, and machinery doors underneath the ladders on each side of the body are wider than the ladders. The Type II body is similar, but there are only two ice hatches at diagonal corners of the roof. Machinery doors are the same width as the ladders on the sides. The Type III body, the most recent and the most common, retains the two ice hatches and the Type II machinery doors, but the door guides become snap-in plastic pieces and the metal channel under the car is eliminated. Instead of the channel, the trucks are secured directly to the car

body by a plastic or metal rivet. It should be noted that the 7600 Bicentennial cars and the 7700 Tobacco Road cars are constructed quite similarly, except that the doors are sliding boxcar-style instead of refrigerator plug-door style.

Now that the critical variables have been established for some of the boxcar series, a brief history of the boxcar varieties will help the collector sort out the many types available on the toy train market.

THE 9200 BOXCARS

The 9200 Series boxcars were first out of the block when Fundimensions began its production of Lionel trains in 1970. They featured the same construction characteristics as their illustrious 6464 predecessors, along with Fundimensions improvements such as the Delrin plastic trucks and fast angle wheels. They were advertised as part of a "Famous Name Collector Series", so it seems evident that Fundimensions had an adult audience in mind for these cars, at least in part. These cars were produced until 1972, when they were superceded by the 9700 Series.

The type collector will have a comparatively easy time acquiring a representative sample of these cars, because strictly speaking there are only 15 cars in the series: numbers 9200 through 9211, 9214, 9215 and 9230. But oh, the variations in these cars! The 9200 Illinois Central, probably the most common of these cars, has at least a dozen variations, with more yet to be catalogued! The series makes use of all five body types (yes, there are 9200 cars with 9700 end boards!), all three door attachment types and all three frame types. Sometimes all the body types and all the door types can be found on different samples of the same car number! To make matters worse, some cars, such as the 9210 B&O automobile double-door boxcar, have had different colors of doors added outside the factory. These are not, of course, regarded as legitimate factory pieces, but some collectors are still interested in them.

Most of the 9200 Series boxcars come in Type I boxes, but a few of the later ones come in the earliest of the Type II red and white boxes. These are worth looking for, since they represent late production and often indicate a 9200 car with 9700 features. The 9206, 9214 and 9230 are known to come in Type II boxes, and no doubt many others do as well.

Only a few of the 9200 boxcars are truly rare; specific examples are the 9202 Santa Fe in orange with black lettering and the pre-production 9207 Soo Line in 9700 white and black colors. The orange and black 9202 has a particularly fascinating story which is well told by McComas and Tuohy in Volume IV of their Collector's Guide series. The assembly line workers had to clear a small quantity of orange plastic from the molds before they began production of the red 9202. Enough plastic remained to make about 65 "shots", as these trial moldings are called. Normally, these "shots" are discarded, but this time some of the workers added detail to them. Eventually, these cars made their way into the collector mainstream, becoming the single most rare Fundimensions boxcar to date. The same thing happened to the two dozen or so preproduction samples of the 9207 Soo Line cars. Fundimensions has been very careful not to let "odd" production slip past the assembly line for the most part, but now and then odd lots such as these will emerge.

Some of the 9200 cars are harder to find than others, of course, but good stocks of new cars with their boxes can be found rather easily. As the first of the new Fundimensions

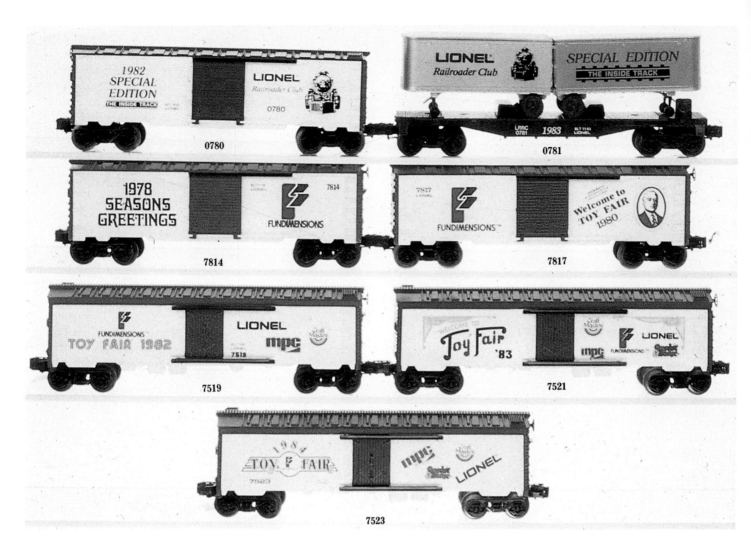

line, these cars are eminently collectible.

THE 9700 SERIES BOXCARS

The 9700 Series of boxcars began with the production of the 9700 Southern car in 1972 and ended in 1978, with two "stragglers" made in 1979 and 1982. By the time the series yielded to the 9400 Series, 80 different numbers had been issued; every number from 9700 to 9789 was used except 9720-22, 9736, 9741, 9746, 9756 and 9765-66. The challenge for the collector, therefore, is one of both types and varieties. It is possible to build up a very good type collection because only a few of the 9700 Series are really hard to find. For the most part, these consist of special issues for Toy Fairs, Season's Greetings and various collectors' clubs.

Beginning with the cars first produced in 1976, the number of variations drops off sharply. This occurs because Fundimensions re-designed its injection molders for liquid plastic instead of pelletized plastic. The color of the liquid plastic can be made to match the paint on the cars much more closely with liquid plastic. Between 1972 and 1975, or from numbers 9700 to about 9758, large numbers of variations abound; these have been well documented by collectors ever since the series was first produced. For instance, we have identified 19 variations of the 9748 CP Rail and 14 variations of the 9739 Rio Grande alone! A complete collection of variations would entail the acquisition of hundreds of boxcars, and more varieties turn up all the time!

It was with the 9700 Series that Fundimensions began to resurrect old favorites from the 6464 Series produced in postwar years. The first of these cars was the 9707 MKT stock car in its original red and yellow colors; its predecessor is the scarcest of all the postwar stock cars. The next car in the series was a duplication of the red, white and blue Post Office car. Many others followed. Unfortunately for collectors, some of the cars were considerably more difficult to acquire than others, thanks to Fundimensions' practice of including some cars with year-end special dealer promotions. In these packages dealers were required to purchase specified amounts of merchandise as a package and a number of the special 9700 boxcars were included free. The dealer could then charge whatever he wanted for the special car. This made some collector favorites like the 9757 Central of Georgia quite difficult to obtain, while regular-issue favorites like the 9754 New York Central Pacemaker were readily available.

Another marketing ploy by Fundimensions was rather novel and fairly successful in building interest in new lines. Special coupons were included in some of the first runs of the 9800 Series refrigerator cars and some of the 9100 Series covered hopper cars. Two of these coupons with five dollars enabled the customer to acquire a special 9700 Series boxcar available nowhere else. The 9719 New Haven double-door boxcar and the 9742 Minneapolis and St. Louis cars were marketed in this way. Both of these cars had been favorites in the postwar 6464 Series, so the demand for the limited supply was brisk.

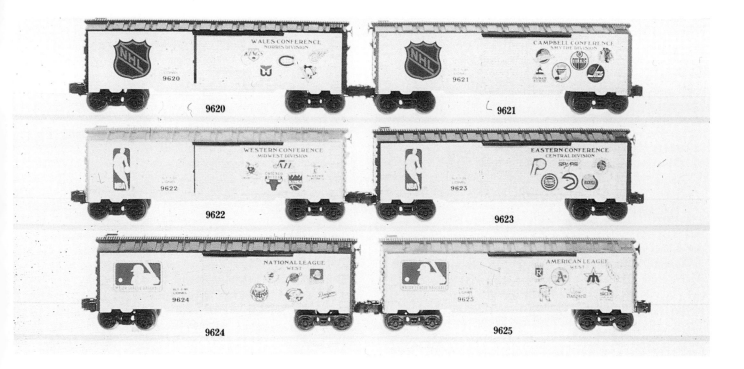

The Sport Series came in both the larger cars as well as the smaller boxcars.

Strangely enough, both of these cars can be found at reasonable cost on the open market today. Fundimensions also marketed a 9511 "Minneapolis" passenger car in this manner.

One of the 9700 boxcars produced for the Lionel Collectors' Club of America was a strange anomaly which has not been repeated. The 9733 Airco boxcar was really two cars in one. When the collector took the boxcar body off the frame, he found a single-dome tank car included within the boxcar body! Many collectors have put the tank car body on its own frame and added trim pieces to form a second Airco car, which is numbered 97330. If you find this highly desirable car, make sure that both car bodies are included if the car's full price is demanded.

There are, more or less, three tiers of scarcity for the 9700 Series boxcars. The most common cars are those which were catalogued as regular issues, though a few of the catalogued cars are somewhat harder to find than others. These cars, such as the 9781 Delaware and Hudson, the 9737 Central Vermont and the 9768 Boston and Maine, are still readily available at this writing. The second tier includes some scarcer regularly catalogued cars such as the 9710 Rutland, some cars included only in sets such as the 9772 Great Northern and some of the more common collector organization cars such as the 9728 LCCA stock car. The third and most scarce tier includes cars which are catalogued but very scarce, such as the 9703 CP Rail, the Season's Greetings and Toy Fair cars and the more scarce collector organization cars such as the 9727 T.A.&G. You can expect the value of these cars to rise proportionately as time passes.

The 9700 Series boxcars are colorful, well made and astonishingly diverse, thanks to Fundimensions' excellent use of both nostalgia and modern graphics. They are still widely available at good prices, and collectors are only now beginning

to appreciate their collectibility. Therefore, these cars offer excellent collecting opportunities for the beginner who is willing to research and look in odd corners of dealers' stocks.

THE 9400 SERIES BOXCARS

Perhaps it is fitting that Fundimensions began the 9400 Series in 1978 with a tuscan 9400 Conrail boxcar, a car which existed only in prototype on the real railroad (Conrail's boxcars are painted blue). The 9400 Series is identical in construction techniques to its 9700 predecessors, even to the extent that all the 9400 Series cars still have 9700 Series end plates! However, there are two very important differences between the 9400 Series and the 9700 Series, one of which makes it very difficult to collect the whole series.

One major difference between the 9400s and the 9700s is the presence of many color schemes of short-line railroads, as opposed to the almost exclusive modeling of Class I railroads within the 9700 Series. In the 9400 Series, the collector will find cars modeled after the Minneapolis, Northfield and Southern, the New Hope and Ivyland, the Chattahoochee Industrial Railroad and the Napierville Junction Railroad — all of which are short-line, localized railroads. This represents the real world rather well because of the increased number of these railroads in recent years. Many of the paint schemes are very colorful and attractive to operators as well.

The other difference is much more significant to collectors. Many more of the 9400 Series boxcars are special issues which can only be found in collector sets or as special package issues produced in extremely limited quantities. For this reason, many of the 9400 Series cars command high prices, and this makes the series less of a good bet for a beginning collector than the 9700 Series would be. It is also significant that far fewer variations of these cars have turned up; essentially, this means that Fundimensions has standardized its plastics and paints much more than in the early 9700 boxcars. It also means that many of the 9400 Series boxcars have had only one production run. A look at the catalogues tends to confirm this supposition. In the earlier Fundimensions years, a 9700 boxcar might run through three years in the catalogues. Now, the 9400 cars (if they are catalogued at all) can only be found for one year. Therefore, we are seeing more variety with less production — almost a guarantee of future scarcity. With some of the cars, the future is now! It is not unusual for a 9400 Series boxcar out of a collector set to double or even triple in value before it even hits the toy train marketplace! That makes collecting the 9400 Series a difficult proposition for all but the most experienced collectors. Some marketing ploys between series have annoyed collectors quite a bit. For example, in 1978 Fundimensions produced its Great Plains Express with a 9729 CP Rail boxcar available only in that set. Since it was not sold separately, the collector of 9700 boxcars had to purchase the set to get the boxcar. In the next year, Fundimensions marketed the set again, but this time it had a 9417 CP Rail boxcar identical to its 9729 predecessor except for the number and gold lettering! The collector who wanted complete numbers for both series had to buy the Great Plains Express set all over again to get the 9417 boxcar! Fundimensions has not made this mistake since, but the severe restriction of the 9400 Series to limited sets has continued to anger many collectors who feel that Fundimensions is manipulating the collector market without justification.

At this writing, the 9400 Series has almost run its full course; the 1985 catalogue pictures the 9484 Lionel 85th Anniversary Car as the highest 9400 number scheduled for production. It is somewhat early to predict the relative scarcity of the whole series, but the extensive use of special issues would indicate that these will get collector attention at the expense of the regular issues.

THE 9800 REFRIGERATOR CAR SERIES

It is hard to imagine why the 9800 Series of refrigerator cars has not commanded more attention among collectors than it has. These cars represent the creativity of Fundimensions at its best. Longer than their boxcar counterparts, these cars are made entirely of stout plastic pieces which are extremely well detailed with wood-sided scribing on the sides and interior floors. The bottoms of the cars have realistic air tank details, and the plug doors open and close (though with peril to the plastic door guides of the later cars).

Most importantly, the 9800 Series gave Fundimensions a chance to show off its capabilities with graphics. Colorful electrocals grace the sides of these cars, advertising just about every conceivable product in food and drink. These include some strange choices for refrigeration — Bazooka bubble gum, Cheerios and Old Dutch cleanser among them! Meat packing plants, juice companies and breweries have advertised their wares on these cars. The situation is reminiscent of the late 19th Century on American railroads, where for quite some time American companies would hire out space on railroad boxcars to advertise their wares. It wasn't unusual for a boxcar on a New York Central train of those years to advertise Lydia Pinkham's Patented Vegetable Elixir while carrying machine tools!

The numbering system of these cars has been a little odd, too. The 9800 refrigerator cars were introduced in 1973 at the same time the 9800 Standard "0" Series was produced. Since the Standard "0" Series began with the 9801 Baltimore and Ohio, the refrigerator cars started with the 9850 Budweiser. In recent years, the 9800 refrigerator cars have begun to use numbers in the lower half of the numbering system, most recently with the Favorite Spirits cars, which are numbered in the 9840s and complete the series. About 70 cars have been produced altogether.

Collectors have been attracted to many sub-series within the 9800 Series. Most prominent are the collectors of the beer cars and the Favorite Spirit whiskey cars. There are about ten beer cars and (so far) a dozen spirits cars to collect, and some of these cars command slightly higher prices than other issues. Some collectors, on the other hand, like the soda pop and juices cars, such as the 9861 Tropicana Orange Juice car and the 9831 Pepsi-Cola car. For the real high-brow collectors, there is the 9814 Perrier Spring Water car. Still others like the candy cars, such as the 9816 Brach's, the 9854 Baby Ruth and the 9858 Butterfinger cars. Finally, railroad realists like to stick to cars modeled after real prototypes, such as the 9863 Railway Express car, the 9819 Great Northern Fruit Express car and the 9869 Santa Fe. There's something for everybody in this series!

There is a terrific collector story behind the production of the 9853 Cracker Jack car in 1973 and 1974. The first cars produced were a dark caramel color, as portrayed in the 1973 catalogue. However, a few cars came out at the end of the production run with white sides, and collectors scrambled to acquire them. In 1974 these collectors were surprised to see the car pictured in white in the catalogue, and soon a flood of white 9853 cars hit the market! The expected situation became completely reversed; the caramel car is now regarded as the scarce car, while the white car is readily available. This is a graphic example of the unpredictability of the collector marketplace, though with current marketing policies it does not appear that such a reversal will ever happen again.

These colorful cars represent a fine opportunity for the beginning collector because most of them are readily available, some at real bargain prices. Only a few of the 9800 Series refrigerator cars are scarce, mostly those in collector sets. These cars look great when they are placed in a long string behind a modern set of diesels. They add color to a collection and offer many chances for specialization.

THE STANDARD "0" SERIES

In 1973, Fundimensions introduced a line of full scale box and refrigerator cars known as the Standard "0" Series. These cars, reportedly based upon Pola designs made by the firm of Rivarossi in Europe, were also the cars first equipped with the excellent Standard "0" sprung trucks. Although the cars were extremely well made, they did not meet the sales expectations of Fundimensions and did not persist for very long. Recently, the genre has been revived for rolling stock to match the 8406 Scale Hudson and as part of an interesting Burlington Northern unit train. This would seem to indicate that the reason the cars did not sell well in the 1973-1975 period was that Fundimensions had not produced true scale locomotives and cabooses to match them in an operating train. With the reissue of the Hudson and the creation of the scale SD-40 diesel and the extended vision scale cabooses, that situation has changed. It is possible that these cars will undergo a rebirth of popularity and the original issues will increase in value. Flatcars and gondolas have also been produced in scale; it would not be too much of a surprise to see hopper cars in the future.

The availability of the Standard "0" cars varies considerably. Common cars such as the 9803 Johnson's Wax and the 9809

Clark are easy to acquire at good prices. On the other hand, some cars such as the 9807 Stroh's and the 9806 Rock Island are very hard to find. Behind the right engine, these cars make a very impressive train on a large layout. Their construction details are excellent as well. The beginning collector may have a difficult time acquiring some of these cars, but a few representative samples of these cars would be good additions to anyone's collection.

THE 5700 TURN OF THE CENTURY REEFERS

In 1980, Fundimensions tried something it had never tried before — a realistic "weathered" paint job. The firm issued eight cars which it called its "Turn of the Century" refrigerator cars. These cars were modeled after wood-sided prototypes which were common on American railroads around 1910. The cars used 9800 Series roof and end pieces, but the pieces which formed the sides and bottoms were new; they used horizontal wood scribing, extremely realistic riveting and a scribed undercarriage. The cars also had true-to-life markings and a special weatherbeaten treatment for the paint which is readily visible when the doors are opened to reveal the real color of the paint and plastic. These cars were also equipped with Standard "0" trucks; they represented Fundimensions construction practices at their best.

Probably because the weathered look was so dramatically non-Lionel, the cars did not sell very well, and after only eight cars were produced, the series was discontinued in favor of the Wood-sided Reefer Series, which sold much better. These cars are still readily available, making them highly desirable items if the collector favors their realistic look. The Oppenheimer, Budweiser and Lindsay Brothers cars command a slight premium over the other five cars, but none are really scarce. These eight cars look great in a train pulled by a postwar 675 or 2025 Pennsylvania K-4 steam locomotive and followed by an all-metal postwar 2457 Pennsylvania N5 caboose. They make a fine, high-quality set for the beginner's collection, and in later years they may appreciate in value because of their realistic appearance.

THE 5700 WOOD-SIDED REEFER SERIES

In 1982 Fundimensions tried again to introduce a new series of refrigerator cars based upon an old-time theme, and this time the firm was much more successful with sales. The Wood-sided Reefers began with the 5708 Armour car and to date, four new cars in the series have been produced each year (three in 1985). These cars used the same highly detailed side and bottom pieces used on the Turn of the Century reefers, but without the weathering process. The roof and end pieces are entirely new. The ends are scribed vertically and the roof is scribed across its width. Four ice hatches are present in the corners of the roof, and the wood scribing has been given a skillfully grained look. The brakewheel is atop the roof end rather than on the end itself. Although true to the prototype, this feature can be annoying when the collector puts the car back in its box because the brakewheel always catches on the box divider. The cars are equipped with the less expensive but realistic plastic arch bar trucks.

The Wood-sided Reefers have sold very well as a class, and most are readily available to the beginning collector. The 5709 Railway Express is a little harder to find than most of the others, but only one of these reefers is truly rare — the 5712 Lionel Lines Wood-sided Reefer of 1983. This car ballooned in value almost overnight and is nearly impossible to acquire.

Operationally, the Wood-sided Reefers can look very good when pulled behind any old-style steam engine — even the "General" engines. The new center-cab transfer cabooses have just the right old-fashioned look for a set of these cars. Most have been produced in prototypical orange, yellow and tuscan colors, so a train of these cars provides a realistic look lacking in the 9800 Series and matched only by the Turn of the Century Reefers.

THE BUNK CARS

In 1983 Fundimensions produced a real surprise for collectors in the form of a totally new piece of rolling stock — the bunk car. In the real world of railroading, these cars were used to house overnight the track gangs working on long-term repair jobs out on the road. Usually, the bunk car was converted from a boxcar, and Fundimensions has followed the prototype extremely well.

The Fundimensions bunk car uses the ends, roof and trucks of the Wood-sided Reefer series, but the sides and bottom show Fundimensions' continued ingenuity in combining parts from existing series. The side and bottom pieces are unmistakably 9800 Series refrigerator car parts which have been heavily modified. The bottom retains the air tanks of the 9800 Series, and the wooden scribing on the sides is vertical instead of horizontal, as on the Wood-sided Reefers. Four windows per side have been added which are divided into four smaller panes. A new insert has been added to the door openings so that the sides are one piece with a much smaller entrance door instead of the plug door of the 9800s. Small square holes cut out of the sides accommodate white marker lamps next to the doors, while another hole in the roof is provided for a short smokestack. The result of these modifications is a car which is remarkably faithful to its prototype.

So far, five bunk cars have been produced or announced. They are the 5717 Santa Fe in gray, the 5724 Pennsylvania in yellow, the 5726 Southern in dark green, the 5727 U.S. Marines in olive-drab camouflage paint and the 6127 New York Central in gray. All but the U.S. Marines car are lighted; the Marines car partially compensates for its unlighted status by including a sheet of decals for owner "customizing". Each of the lighted cars has a small plastic envelope in its box which contains the detachable smokestack and two clear marker lights for the car sides.

Of the five bunk cars, the first one, the 5717 Santa Fe, seems to be the hardest to find because far fewer of them were produced than had been planned. These cars are very recent, so it is somewhat difficult to predict their order of scarcity. However most collectors feel that the 5726 Southern will be a relatively scarce car, while the 5724 Pennsylvania will be fairly common. The 5727 U.S. Marines car is probably the easiest to obtain. The New York Central car has not been produced up to the time of this writing, but it is expected to be in heavy demand because it is part of a highly desirable New York Central work train scheduled for 1985 production.

The bunk cars are good additions to a beginner's set, if only because they represent a very creative approach to rolling stock on the part of Fundimensions. These unusual cars will probably show good appreciation in value.

THE MINT CARS

In 1979 Fundimensions included a revival of the postwar Fort Knox mint car in its Southern Pacific collector set. This fanciful

5700   5701

5702   5703

5704   5705

5706   5707

5708   5709

5710   5711

car, rather silly in terms of any real railroad, always had a whimsical charm to it, and its inclusion was one of the reasons why this set sold out so quickly. The car uses the body first developed in the postwar years for the operating aquarium car. The sides of the boxcar each have two large clear plastic panels. These are "revealed" by imitation fold-up curtains molded into the car body atop the clear panels. Each pair of clear panels is separated by a door resembling a safe with a combination lock. Inside the car, a gold or silver plastic insert simulates stacks of bullion. The roof has a coin slot and the ends of the car have circular ventilation grates.

All of the Fundimensions mint cars are equipped with Standard "O" trucks; and seven have been issued since 1979.

Aside from the Fort Knox car and a special mint car issued for the Train Collectors Association, one car has been issued for each of the real mints of the United States, past and present: San Francisco, Denver, Philadelphia, Carson City and New Orleans. With the issue of the New Orleans car this series as such should end, unless Fundimensions decides to issue cars named after famous banking houses. (The mind boggles a bit at the thought of a Chase-Manhattan mint car or a Crocker National Bank mint car!) Many collectors consider these cars a little silly, but they are so impossibly whimsical that they have an appeal of their own. By combining them with a postwar 3535 Security Car, a Marines searchlight car and an appropriate locomotive, the Lionel operator could run one of the more unusual trains in his/her collection! The Carson City, New Orleans and Denver cars seem to be the easiest of these cars to find, but the New Orleans car is too new to predict as to relative scarcity. The Fort Knox and the TCA Special are the hardest to find.

THE 9600 HI-CUBE BOXCARS

In 1976 Fundimensions added another completely new boxcar to its growing variety reflecting modern prototype practices. This was the all-plastic Hi-Cube boxcar, derived from a 40-foot boxcar which is built 12 to 18 inches higher than the norm. Like their prototypes, Fundimensions' Hi-Cubes had no catwalks on the roof; they also featured extensive riveting detail along the car sides, going against the trend towards eliminating rivet detailing. The Hi-Cubes featured large sliding doors fastened in place by hooks at both top and bottom. In addition, an all-new plastic frame was created for them.

Instantly, the Hi-Cubes diverged into two distinct series. One featured real railroad names. There were ten of these numbered from 9600 to 9609 and also 9610 Frisco Hi-Cube which was only available as part of the 1977 Rocky Mountain Set. A 9611 TCA "Flying Yankee" Hi-Cube was made for that association's 1978 national convention in Boston. (See entry 1018-1979 for a good story about the conversion of this car to the TCA Mortgage Burning Ceremony Car.) The other was the Mickey Mouse Hi-Cube Series, a colorful issue of these cars with Disney logos and characters. These cars ran from numbers 9660 to 9672, with the last number issued as the extremely scarce Mickey Mouse 50th Birthday Car in 1978. After that year the cars were phased out, only to reappear in 1982 in numbers 9626-29 with slightly simplified paint schemes which repeated previous prototype road name issues. They were again deleted after 1984. One other Hi-Cube was produced for the Toy Train Operating Society's 1978 convention in Hollywood.

Most of the common issue Hi-Cubes are not in great demand; only the 9600 Chessie, the 9610 Frisco and the special convention issues have aroused any real interest. Of the Disney cars, which are in considerably greater demand, the Pinocchio, Snow White and Pluto cars are very hard to find, and the 50th Birthday Car is a true rarity.

Although the Hi-Cubes are colorful and contemporary, many operators complain that the rolling characteristics of these cars are poor. Because of their plastic frames and high center of gravity, they have a tendency to tip over unless they are weighted. Despite this problem, these cars show real effort by Fundimensions to add a contemporary flair to tinplate railroading.

THE OPERATING BOXCARS

In 1972, amid much fanfare, Fundimensions began the production of a car which has defied obsolescence; it didn't vanish from the catalogues until 1985. This is the 9301 Operating Post Office Car, in which the press of a button opens the car door and activates a little man who tosses a mail sack out the door. This car had no company until as late as 1982, when the 9218 Monon Mail Delivery Car joined it in the Fundimensions lineup. Since that year, other operating boxcars modeled after the old postwar 3454-64-74-84 cars have been revived.

By this time, most of the old favorites in operating boxcars have been resurrected by Fundimensions. These cars include the horse car, in which two horses bob heads out of side ports in a small stock car; the operating giraffe car in two versions;

the cop and hobo car; the icing station refrigerator car and a few others.

Nor have the larger operating box and stock cars been neglected. In the last few years, Fundimensions has released the fanciful Poultry Dispatch Car, known irreverently as the "Chicken Sweeper" car, in which the press of a button opens the car door and releases a man with a broom suspended on a hairspring; he appears to be sweeping feathers out of the car door. The deluxe Borden operating milk car, an old favorite, has been a brisk seller and the operating Churchill Downs horse car and corral will probably be another item in heavy demand.

The operating boxcars have been welcome additions to the Fundimensions line because they add animation to an operator's layout. Many of these cars are still priced very reasonably, and no collection is really complete without a few of them.

THE 027 SHORT BOXCARS

Like its postwar predecessors, Fundimensions has made shorter inexpensive boxcars for its Traditional sets from the beginning. These little cars, sometimes erroneously referred to as "plug door" boxcars, are probably the most neglected of all the boxcars because they lack the glamor of their larger cousins. Yet some of these cars are extremely hard to find; they represent a real opportunity for the beginning collector to get a scarce car at a reasonable price. Although most of these cars came in sets an occasional straggler will be found for separate sale, usually in a Type II box.

By far, the scarcest of these cars are the special ones made up for department stores such as J.C. Penney, True Value Hardware, Toys 'R Us and Kiddie City. There are, in fact, at least five different Toys 'R Us cars, each with variations!

The 027 boxcars are very much like their 6014 postwar predecessors, but they have a new molded plastic bottom piece in place of the metal frame used on the 6014 Series. Most have one operating and one dummy coupler. Some have railroad markings, such as the Conrail, Erie-Lackawanna and Santa Fe cars, while others have corporate markings such as Wheaties, Ford Motorcraft and Hershey's Chocolate.

Since very few collectors pay attention to these cars, the small 027 boxcars are a wide-open field for the beginning collector. They are even available as throw-ins in collections of assorted junk! These cars deserve far more attention than they have gotten to date.

SOME ODDS AND ENDS

Mention should be made of a few more series of boxcars which do not fit conveniently into any category. The 7600 Series Bicentennial long boxcars were produced from 1974 to 1976; they feature colorful markings for each of the 13 original states, and many have variations. The Virginia and New York cars are highly prized in this set, but most of the rest are quite readily available in their Bicentennial boxes.

The 7800 Soda Pop Road Series should have been a very popular set when it was first introduced in 1977, but only six cars were produced overall. Of these cars, which use 9700-style bodies with colorful corporate logos, the Pepsi car is in a little more demand than the other five. Cars with Sprite, Tab and Fanta logos were included as part of a Coca-Cola set, but they are part of the 9700 Series. The 7700 Tobacco Road Series was produced from 1976 to 1978. These long boxcars featured some of the biggest names in the tobacco industry and were obviously aimed at an adult audience. Nine of them were eventually produced, with the El Producto and Mail Pouch cars

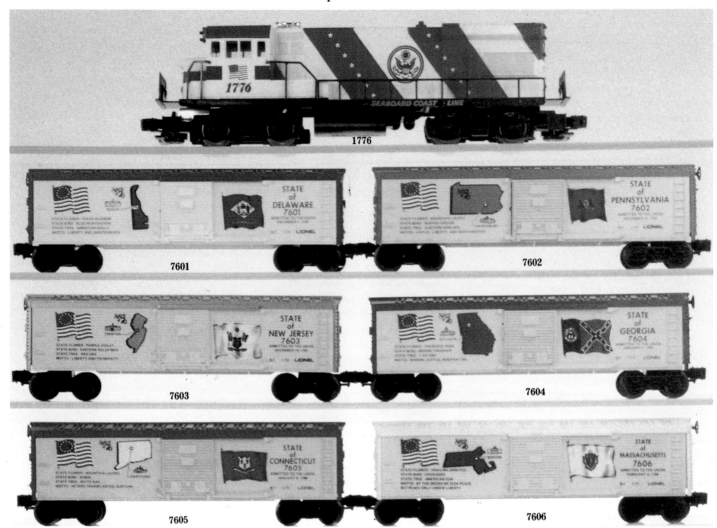

being a little harder to find than the rest of the series, which is very common and readily available.   Finally, mention must be made of the strange little 9090 Mini-Max boxcar, although William Meyer's article (see listings) covers its particulars thoroughly. This odd little car was made in 1971 only. It had all-door sides which swung open to reveal a scribed floor and three little pallet containers which could be loaded and unloaded. This car is quite hard to find today, especially in a separate sale Type I box and in a light blue color.

If variety is the spice of tinplate life, Fundimensions has certainly added it with its incredibly well-varied and extensive line of box, refrigerator and stock cars. It can truly be said that these cars range from the realistic to the whimsical and that there is a boxcar in the Fundimensions product line for everyone.

	Gd	VG	Exc	Mt
0512 TOY FAIR: 1981, reefer. Details needed.	—	—	75	110

0780 LIONEL RAILROADER CLUB BOX CAR: 1982, white-painted white body, red-painted white doors, red roof and ends, Type IX body, Symington-Wayne trucks; black electrocal of steam locomotive front end at right of door; red "1982" and black "SPECIAL EDITION THE INSIDE TRACK" to left of door; red "LIONEL" and "0780" and black "RAILROADER CLUB" to right of door. This car was only available to members of the Lionel Railroader Club, a Fundimensions sponsored organization. F. Stem Collection.   — — — **35**

1018-1979 TCA MORTGAGE BURNING CEREMONY CAR: 1979, light tan-painted gray plastic body, light yellow-painted white door, Hi-Cube boxcar; orange, black and red rectangular mortgage burning logo at left, orange Toy Train Museum logo and black lettering at right. There is an intriguing story behind the making of this car. In 1978 the TCA held its convention in Boston. The 9611 "Flying Yankee" hi-cube boxcar was produced for this convention in official Boston and Maine sky blue and black (see 9611-1978 entry). Large anticipated sales of the Flying Yankee car never materialized, and at convention's end the TCA found itself in possession of a considerable backlog of unsold cars. In the next year, the organization was to finish paying the mortgage on its museum in Strasburg, Pennsylvania. Rather than order a special car, the TCA shipped its entire backlog of 9611 Flying Yankee cars to the Pleasant Valley Process Company of Cogan Station, Pennsylvania. There, the Flying Yankee cars were repainted into the Mortgage Burning Ceremony car. Faint traces of the original black paint show through the light tan paint on the ends and roof. Bratspis observation.   — — — **125**

3764 KAHN: 1981, refrigerator car, convention car of the Lionel Operating Train Society. Dark tan body, brown roof and ends, Symington-Wayne trucks. C. Lang Collection.   — — — **25**

5700 OPPENHEIMER SAUSAGE CASINGS: 1981, dark blue-green "weathered" paint; black lettering, red and black logo, Standard 0 sprung trucks, the first in the "Turn of the Century" series. C. Lang and C. Rohlfing comments.   — — **14 18**

5701 DAIRYMEN'S LEAGUE: 1981, milk reefer, off-white "weathered" paint, black roof and ends; blue lettering and logo, Standard 0 sprung trucks. C. Rohlfing comment.   — — **11 14**

Spirit of '76 Cars.

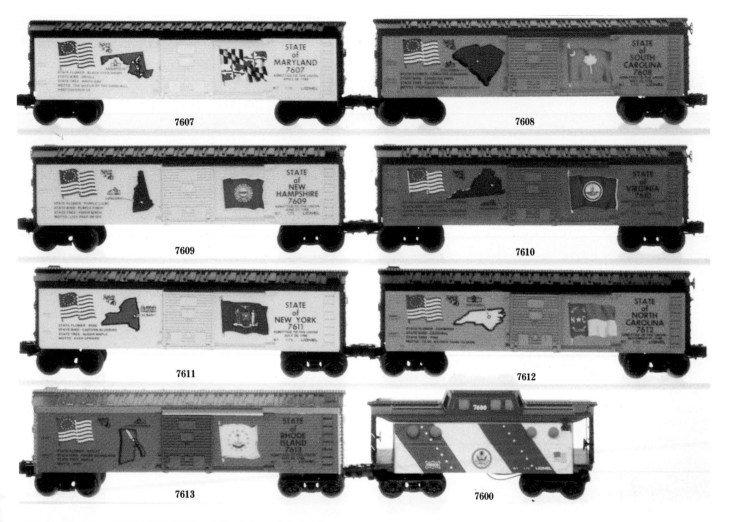

7607   7608

7609   7610

7611   7612

7613   7600

5702 NATIONAL DAIRY DESPATCH: 1981, Universal Carloading & Distributing Co., silver-gray body, red and silver "weathered" paint, dark red roof and ends; black lettering, Standard 0 sprung trucks. C. Lang and C. Rohlfing comments.   —   —   **11**   **14**

5703 NORTH AMERICAN DESPATCH: 1981, "FRIGICAR", weathered light yellow and dark brown roof and ends; black lettering, Standard 0 sprung trucks. C. Rohlfing comment.   —   —   **11**   **14**

5704 BUDWEISER: 1981, dark green "weathered" paint; white lettering, Standard 0 sprung trucks. This car is a little scarcer than the others in this group because of interest from beer car collectors. C. Rohlfing comment.   —   —   **14**   **18**

5705 BALL GLASS JARS: 1981, yellow "weathered" paint, brown roof and ends; blue lettering, Standard 0 sprung trucks. C. Rohlfing comment.   —   —   **11**   **14**

5706 LINDSAY BROS. BINDER & TWINE: 1981, tuscan-maroon "weathered" paint; brown and yellow lettering, Standard 0 sprung trucks. C. Rohlfing comment.   —   —   **14**   **18**

5707 AMERICAN REFRIGERATOR TRANSIT CO.: 1981, yellow "weathered" paint, brown roof and ends; black lettering, Standard 0 sprung trucks. C. Rohlfing comment.   —   —   **11**   **14**

5708 ARMOUR: 1982-83, wood-sheathed reefer, yellow sides, tuscan roof and ends, blue lettering, arch bar trucks. C. Rohlfing comment.   —   —   **12**   **15**

5709 REA (Railway Express Agency): 1982-83, wood-sheathed reefer, medium green-painted body; white lettering, red and white diamond electrocal, arch bar trucks. Somewhat scarcer than the other early wood-sided reefers. C. Lang, C. Rohlfing and R. LaVoie comments.   —   —   **20**   **25**

5710 CANADIAN PACIFIC: 1982-83, wood-sheathed reefer, tuscan body; white lettering, arch bar trucks. C. Rohlfing comment.   —   —   **12**   **15**

5711 COMMERCIAL EXPRESS: 1982-83, wood-sheathed reefer, light caramel body, brown roof and ends; black lettering, arch bar trucks. C. Rohlfing comment.   —   —   **12**   **15**

5712 LIONEL ELECTRIC TRAINS: 1983, wood-sheathed reefer, bright orange body, bright blue roof and ends; blue and white "LIONEL" electrocal, blue lettering, arch bar trucks. Very hard to find; the price of this car has increased dramatically since it was first introduced. C. Lang, C. Rohlfing and R. LaVoie comments.   —   —   **125**   **150**

5713 COTTON BELT: 1983, St. Louis Southwestern, wood-sheathed reefer, yellow sides, brown roof and ends; black "COTTON BELT" logo to right of door, arch bar trucks. C. Lang and C. Rohlfing comments.   —   —   **11**   **15**

5714 MICHIGAN CENTRAL: 1983, wood-sheathed reefer, white sides, brown roof and ends; black lettering, arch bar trucks. C. Lang and C. Rohlfing comments.   —   —   **11**   **15**

5715 SANTA FE: 1983, wood-sheathed reefer, orange sides, brown roof and ends (shown as dark blue in catalogue, but not produced that way); black lettering, black and white Santa Fe cross logo to left of door, arch bar trucks. C. Rohlfing comment, R. LaVoie Collection.   —   —   **11**   **15**

5716 VERMONT CENTRAL: 1983, wood-sheathed reefer, silver-gray sides, black roof and ends, black and green lettering, arch bar trucks. C. Rohlfing comment.   —   —   **11**   **15**

5717 A.T.S.F.: 1983, bunk car. This was the first in a series of cars original to the Fundimensions line. Basically, it features a heavily modified 9800 Series reefer sides and bottom combined with a 5700 Series reefer roof and ends. The original door opening is made narrower and a smaller, non-opening door is made as part of the car side. Four square windows per side are present, each of them cross-hatched into four smaller sections. There are holes in the sides for clear plastic marker lights and a hole in the roof for a short black chimney stack; these pieces come in a little plastic packet included with the car. Opaque plastic window pieces are fitted into the windows from the inside in lighted versions of the car. The first production pieces of this car were found with parts missing, broken or haphazardly assembled, but the problem was soon corrected. Fewer of the Santa Fe cars were produced than expected, making it somewhat scarce. R. LaVoie comment and Collection.   — — 40 45

5718: See 9849

5719 CANADIAN NATIONAL: 1984, wood-sheathed reefer, gray body; dark red lettering and maple leaf logo, arch bar trucks. — — 11 15

5720 GREAT NORTHERN: 1984, wood-sheathed reefer, dark green body; gold lettering, red, white and black Great Northern logo, arch bar trucks.   — — 11 15

5721 SOO LINE: 1984, wood-sheathed reefer, orange sides, brown roof and ends; black lettering, black and white Soo Line logo, arch bar trucks.   — — 11 15

5722 NICKEL PLATE ROAD: 1984, wood-sheathed reefer, yellow sides, brown roof and ends, black lettering, arch bar trucks. — — 11 15

5724 PENNSYLVANIA: 1984, bunk car, see 5717 for construction details. Light yellow-painted gray body; black "PRR/5724" and black and yellow Keystone logo, arch bar trucks, illuminated. R. LaVoie Collection.   — — 18 22

5726 SOUTHERN: 1983-84, bunk car, see 5717 for construction details. Dark green-painted gray body; white "S.S.R.R./5726" below left pair of windows, arch bar trucks, illuminated. Becoming hard to find. R. LaVoie Collection.   — — 30 35

5727 U.S. MARINES: 1984-85, bunk car, camouflage-painted olive and yellow gray plastic body; black lettering, no window inserts, unlighted, arch bar trucks. Came with sheet of decals with U. S. Army and U. S. Marines markings to be applied to car by purchaser. — — 11 14

5730 STRASBURG RAIL ROAD: Announced for 1985, wood-sheathed reefer, tuscan body, roof and ends; yellow-gold lettering and numbering, arch bar trucks.   — — — 15

5731 LOUISVILLE & NASHVILLE: Announced for 1985, wood-sheathed reefer, tuscan body, roof and ends; white lettering and numbering, arch bar trucks.   — — — 15

5732 CENTRAL RAILROAD OF NEW JERSEY: Announced for 1985, wood-sheathed reefer, tuscan body, roof and ends; white lettering, red and white bull's eye logo, arch bar trucks. — — — 15

6014-900 FRISCO: 1975, 027-style short boxcar, uncatalogued; white Type III body, black lettering, numbered 6014 on side as were postwar examples, AAR trucks, came in a Type I Fundimensions box labeled "6014-900/LCCA 75-76" on its side. This car was previously reported as version 6014(I) in the postwar volume by C. Rohlfing. We need further details of the distribution and manufacturing of this car, since there are no marks on the car different from later postwar production. D. Dayle Collection.   **NRS**

6127 NEW YORK CENTRAL: Announced for 1985, bunk car, gray body, black lettering and oval New York Central logo, illuminated, arch bar trucks. Part of Yard Chief set in Traditional catalogue. — — — 20

6234 BURLINGTON NORTHERN: Announced for 1985, Standard 0 boxcar, part of Burlington Northern Limited set: Cascade green body and doors, white lettering and large BN logo, black roof and catwalk, Standard 0 trucks.   — — — 20

6235 BURLINGTON NORTHERN: Standard 0 boxcar, matches 6234.   — — — 20

6236 BURLINGTON NORTHERN: Standard 0 boxcar, matches 6234.   — — — 20

6237 BURLINGTON NORTHERN: Standard 0 boxcar, matches 6234.   — — — 20

6238 BURLINGTON NORTHERN: Standard 0 boxcar, matches 6234.   — — — 20

6464-1 WESTERN PACIFIC: See Factory Errors and Prototypes.
6464-500 TIMKEN: 1970, Fundimensions product with postwar number;

identifiable by "BLT. 1970/BY LIONEL MPC" to right of doors; metal door guides.
(A) Type V body, light yellow body and doors, black lettering, orange, black and white Timken decal logo, postwar bar-end metal trucks. Rare; approximately 500 made. G. Halverson comment. — — — 100
(B) Same as (A), but light yellow body and door paint. — — — 200
(C) Type VI orange-painted body and doors, AAR trucks; approximately 1,300 made. G. Halverson comment. — — 80 100
(D) Same as (C), but postwar bar-end metal trucks. — — 80 100
(E) Same as (C), but Type VII body with 9200 number-board. Extremely rare; only about 50 produced. G. Halverson comment.
                     — — — 450

6464-1970 TCA SPECIAL: 1970, uncatalogued TCA Chicago convention car for 1970; Type V yellow-painted lighter yellow body, red door, no decals, white heat-stamped lettering; about 1,100 made.
(A) Unpainted red door.   — — 100 125
(B) Red-painted red door.   — — 100 125

6464-1971 TCA SPECIAL: 1971, uncatalogued TCA Disneyland national convention boxcar. White-painted white body, roof and ends; dark orange-yellow-painted yellow doors; metal door guides, postwar bar-end metal trucks; red, white and blue heat-stamped Disneyland logos. NOTE: other colors of this car have been seen with gold heat-stamped markings. Reportedly, those colors were produced outside the factory. Only the white-painted white car is known to be genuine. — — 175 225

See also Factory Errors and Prototypes.

6700 PACIFIC FRUIT EXPRESS: 1982, refrigerator car, modified 6464 boxcar body; orange body, dark brown doors, metal door guides, UP and SP logos, Standard 0 trucks, operating hatch and bin cut into roof. Made for 2306 Icing Station; price for car only. — — 50 60

7301 N&W: 1982, cattle car, brown and white lettering, Standard 0 trucks; from Continental Limited set. — — 35 45

7302 T&P: 1983, short-body cattle car, brown with white lettering.
                     — — — 10

7303 ERIE: 1984-85, stock car, dull slate blue body, white lettering and Erie logo, Standard 0 trucks; from Erie-Lackawanna Limited set.
                     — — — 25

7304 SOUTHERN: 1983, stock car, dark green body, tuscan roof and ends, tuscan double-tier doors; white "SOUTHERN" and "7304" to right of doors, circular white Southern logo to left of doors, gold Famous American Railroads 4 diamond-shaped logo, Standard 0 trucks. Extra car meant to accompany Southern set but offered in year-end package for separate sale; hard to find.   — — — 45

7309 SOUTHERN: 1984, short stock car, tuscan body, white lettering, Symington-Wayne trucks.   — — — 10

7401 CHESSIE SYSTEM: 1984-85, short stock car, red body; white lettering, Symington-Wayne trucks, one operating and one dummy coupler; part of 1402 Chessie System set in Traditional catalogue. C. Lang comment.   — — — 10

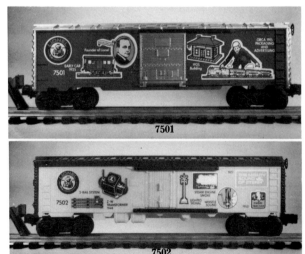

7501

7502

7509 7510

Pizza Hut 7511 Arthur Treacher's SEAFOOD 7512

Bonanza International, Inc. BONANZA STEAKHOUSE 7513 TACO BELL 7514

7501 LIONEL 75th ANNIVERSARY: 1975, Cowen picture, blue body, silver roof and ends, 9700-type boxcar. — 7 10 14

7502 LIONEL 75th ANNIVERSARY: 1975, reefer, innovations, yellow body, blue roof and ends. — 7 10 14

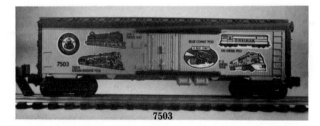

7503

7503 LIONEL 75th ANNIVERSARY: 1975, reefer, famous engines, orange body, brown roof and ends. — 7 10 14

7505

7505 LIONEL 75th ANNIVERSARY: 1975, 9700 series boxcar, accessories, silver body, red roof and ends. — 7 10 14

7506

7506 LIONEL 75th ANNIVERSARY: 1975, 9700 series boxcar, famous catalogues, green body, gold roof and ends. — 7 10 14

7507

7507 LIONEL 75th ANNIVERSARY: 1975, reefer logos, white body, blue roof and ends. — 7 10 14

7509 KENTUCKY FRIED CHICKEN: 1981-82, reefer, dark brown-red sides, tuscan roof and ends, white lettering, Colonel Sanders electrocal, Symington-Wayne trucks; from Favorite Food Freight, available only as separate sale. C. Rohlfing comment. — — 10 14

7510 RED LOBSTER: 1981-82, reefer with white sides, black roof and ends; red lettering, lobster electrocal, Symington-Wayne trucks; from Favorite Food Freight, available only as separate sale. — — 20 25

7511 PIZZA HUT: 1981-82, reefer with white sides, red roof and ends; red lettering, hut electrocal, Symington-Wayne trucks; from Favorite Food Freight, available only as separate sale. — — 10 14

7512 ARTHUR TREACHER'S SEAFOOD: 1982, 9800-type reefer, yellow sides, green roof and ends; green lettering, Symington-Wayne trucks; part of Favorite Food series, sold separately. C. Lang comment. — — 11 14

7513 BONANZA: 1982, 9800-type reefer, white sides, red roof and ends; red and black lettering, Bonanza electrocal to right of door, Symington-Wayne trucks; part of Favorite Food series, sold separately. C. Lang comment. — — 11 14

7514 TACO BELL: 1982, 9800-type reefer, white sides, brown roof and ends, brown lettering, multicolor Taco Bell electrocal to right of door; part of Favorite Food series, sold separately. C. Lang comment. — — 11 14

7515 DENVER MINT: 1981, light gold paint on clear plastic, stack of silver ingots inside car, Standard O trucks. See introduction for construction details. Other mint cars produced, 7517, 7518, 7522, 9319, 9320 and 9349. C. Lang comment. — — 35 45

7517 PHILADELPHIA MINT: 1982, clear plastic body painted burnished bronze, coin slot, circular grates at each end, silver bullion inside, Standard

0 trucks, disc-operating couplers; from Spring '82 Collector Center.

— — 25 30

7518 CARSON CITY MINT: 1983, clear plastic body painted black, silver bullion inside car. Plastic appears to be thinner and less crisply cast than other mint cars. Standard 0 trucks. — — 20 25

7519 TOY FAIR: Boxcar; details needed. NRS

7520 NIBCO: 1982, boxcar, special promotion for Nibco Plumbing Products offered as a premium to plumbers; reportedly only 500 made. 9700-type boxcar with Type IX body and Type III frame, white body, green doors; green and blue ribbon running across car on both sides of door, blue lettering, gold NIBCO emblem on upper left side, blue "NIBCO/EXPRESS" and "QUALITY PIPING PRODUCTS" to right of door. This car was offered independently of the NIBCO 1264 train set; see 8182 diesel engine entry in Chapter I for set details. Very hard to find. — — — 200

7521 TOY FAIR: 1983, boxcar; details needed. NRS

7522 NEW ORLEANS MINT: 1984-85, dark gloss blue body, clear plastic windows on sides, silver ingots stacked inside car, circular grates on each end, fake "safe" door between windows on both sides, Standard 0 trucks,

— — — 25

7523 TOY FAIR: 1984, refrigerator car, "1984" and "TOY FAIR" logos to left of door, current General Mills toy division logos to right of door. Color descriptions needed. NRS

7524 TOY FAIR: 1985, refrigerator car, light brown sides, dark brown roof and ends; brown lettering, varied red and blue Fundimensions logos.

— — — 80

SPIRIT OF 76 SERIES CARS

The Spirit of '76 Boxcars were numbered 7601 through 7613 for the first thirteen states admitted to the Union. Each state's car names the state capital and portrays its flag, admission date, state flower, bird, tree and motto. At one time, Fundimensions may have had an ambitious plan to produce these colorful cars for the remaining 37 states, but this never happened. C. Lang comment.

TYPE I AND TYPE II BODIES

Type I: Black metal strip runs car length and is used to attach trucks. Underneath the strip at each end are square holes. Black metal strip is attached to the bottom of the car by one screw, the trucks then attach to the black strip.

Type II: No strip version with a round hole at each end on the bottom. Round hole is for the screw that holds the one-piece roof and ends to the car sides.

7601 DELAWARE: 1975-76.
(A) Type I light yellow body and door painted light yellow, blue roof painted blue; blue lettering, gold diamond in flag. C. Lang comment and Mitarotonda Collection. — 10 12 15
(B) Type I cream-white body and door painted light yellow, blue roof painted blue; blue lettering. — 10 12 15
(C) Type II light yellow body and door painted light yellow, blue roof painted blue; light gold diamond in flag; blue lettering. Mitarotonda Collection. — 10 12 15

7602 PENNSYLVANIA: 1975-76, light blue plastic body painted light blue, orange plastic roof painted orange; black or blue lettering.
(A) Type I body, light blue plastic door painted light blue; black lettering.
— 10 12 15
(B) Type II body, cream-white plastic door painted light blue.
— 10 12 15

7603 NEW JERSEY: 1975-76.
(A) Type I light green plastic body and door painted light green, gray roof painted gold; medium gold flag. Mitarotonda Collection.
— 10 12 15
(B) Same as (A), but Type II body. — 10 12 15
(C) Type II light green body and door painted light green, clear-white roof painted gold; light gold flag. Mitarotonda Collection. — 10 12 15

7604 GEORGIA: 1975-76, blue lettering.
(A) Type I light blue body painted light blue, clear-white door painted light blue, clear-white roof painted red; red flag, yellow-gold bars and stripes border. Mitarotonda Collection. — 10 12 15
(B) Type I cream-white plastic body and door painted light blue, red roof

painted flat red. Eddins Collection. — 10 12 15
(C) Type II light blue body and door painted light blue, red roof painted dark red; dark red flag, lighter gold bars and stripes border. Mitarotonda Collection. — 10 12 15
(D) Type II light blue plastic body and door painted light blue, glossy red roof painted glossy deep red. Eddins Collection — 10 12 15

7605 CONNECTICUT: 1975-76, black lettering.
(A) Type I body, cream-white plastic body and door painted medium pale blue, blue roof painted medium pale blue. — 10 12 15
(B) Type II body, medium pale blue plastic body and door painted medium pale blue, dark blue roof painted dark blue. — 10 12 15
(C) Same as (A), but white roof painted dark blue. Mitarotonda Collection.
— 10 12 15

7606 MASSACHUSETTS: 1975-76, black lettering.
(A) Type 1 body, cream-white plastic body and door painted light yellow, cream-white roof painted white. — 10 12 15
(B) Type I body, cream-white plastic body and door painted medium yellow, cream-white roof painted white. — 10 12 15
(C) Type I body, shiny white plastic body and door painted dark yellow, cream-white roof painted white, flag is bordered in dark gold, purple crest, light purple shadowing. Mitarotonda Collection. — 10 12 15
(D) Type II body, shiny white plastic body and door painted very dark yellow, cream white roof painted white, flag is bordered in yellow gold, dark blue crest, light blue shadowing. Mitarotonda Collection.
— 10 12 15

7607 MARYLAND: 1975-76, black lettering.
(A) Type I body, white plastic body and door painted light yellow, white roof painted black; checkered quadrants of the flag are alternating gold and black sqaures, gold flagstaff is topped by a dark gold eagle. Mitarotonda Collection. — 10 12 15
(B) Type II body, light yellow body and door painted light yellow; yellow and black checkered flag quadrants, light gold cross tops flagstaff, black roof painted black. Mitarotonda Collection. — 10 12 15
(C) Type II body, cream-white plastic body and door painted mustard, cream-white roof painted black. — 10 12 15
(D) Type I body, cream-white plastic body and door painted dark yellow, cream-white roof painted black. — 10 12 15
(E) Type II light yellow body and door painted light yellow, black roof painted black; black and yellow alternating flag quadrant squares, white quadrants slightly shadowed, yellow-gold cross tops yellow-gold flagstaff. Mitarotonda Collection. — 10 12 15

7608 SOUTH CAROLINA: 1975-76, black lettering.
(A) Type I body, dark yellow body and door painted mustard, brown roof painted chocolate brown. Mitchell and Mitarotonda Collections.
— 10 12 15
(B) Same as (A), but white door painted darker mustard. Mitarotonda Collection. — 10 12 15
(C) Type II body, dark mustard plastic body and medium mustard door painted dark mustard, mustard roof painted chocolate brown; medium blue flag . — 10 12 15

7609 NEW HAMPSHIRE: 1975-76, black lettering. Harder to find than most of the series.
(A) Type I body, dark yellow plastic body and door painted dark yellow, light green roof painted dark green. — 30 35 45
(B) Type II body, dark yellow plastic body painted dark yellow, dark yellow door painted dark yellow, green roof painted dark green; dark blue flag bordered in light gold with light gold leaves and printing on the flag. Mitarotonda Collection. — 30 35 45
(C) Same as (A), but Type II body and white border around right side of map, half moon on map by star. — 30 35 45
(D) Type I body, dark yellow plastic body painted dark yellow, white door painted dark yellow, white roof painted dark green, purple flag bordered in gold, gold leaves and printing on flag. Mitarotonda Collection.
— 30 35 45

7610 VIRGINIA: 1975-76, black lettering. Rarest of the series, though nobody seems to know why fewer of these cars were produced. C. Lang comment.
(A) Type I body, cream-white plastic body and door painted orange, cream-white roof painted dark blue. 25 50 100 125

(B) Type I body, orange plastic body and door painted orange, blue roof painted blue; quarter moon on map. 25 50 100 125

(C) Same as (B), but Type II body. 25 50 100 125

(D) Type I body, cream-white body painted orange, orange door painted orange, dark blue roof painted dark blue. Mitarotonda Collection. 25 50 100 125

7611 NEW YORK: 1975-76, black lettering. Harder to find than most other cars in the series.

(A) Type I cream-white plastic body and medium yellow door painted light yellow, dark blue roof painted dark blue. — 40 50 60

(B) Type II cream plastic body and medium yellow door painted dark yellow; near perfect flag, dark blue roof painted dark blue. — 40 50 60

(C) Type II cream plastic body and medium yellow door painted dark yellow; flag with red border, dark blue roof painted dark blue. — 40 50 60

(D) Type II dark cream plastic body and medium yellow door painted dark yellow; flag with red and white border, dark blue roof painted dark blue. — 40 50 60

(E) Type II cream plastic body and white door painted medium yellow; flag with white border, dark blue roof painted dark blue. — 40 50 60

(F) Type I pale yellow body and medium yellow door painted dark yellow (door darker than body) clear-white roof painted dark blue. Mitarotonda Collection. — 40 50 60

(G) Type I medium yellow body and medium yellow doors painted dark yellow (doors darker than body) clear-white roof painted dark blue. Mitarotonda Collection. — 40 50 60

7612 NORTH CAROLINA: 1975-76, black lettering.

(A) Type I cream plastic body painted dark mustard, yellow door painted medium mustard, slight contrast between door and darker body, cream-white roof painted black; flag heavily shadowed in blue tint, yellow letters and banners subsequently show green tint. Mitarotonda Collection. — 12 15 20

(B) Type I white plastic body and cream door painted light mustard, cream-white roof painted black. — 12 15 20

(C) Type II mustard body and door painted dark mustard, no contrast between door and body, black roof painted black; flag in light shadow, blue portion is dark blue. Mitarotonda Collection. — 12 15 20

(D) Type II dark yellow body painted light mustard, yellow door painted dark mustard, large contrast between darker door and body, black roof painted black; flag in medium shadow, red portion is light red. Mitarotonda Collection. — 12 15 20

7613 RHODE ISLAND: 1975-76, black lettering.

(A) Type I body, aqua-blue plastic body and door painted green, gray roof painted gold. — 12 15 20

(B) Type II body, green plastic body and door painted green, white roof painted gold. — 12 15 20

(C) Type I body, aqua-blue body painted dark green, dark green door painted dark green, green roof painted gold. Mitarotonda Collection. **NRS**

7700 UNCLE SAM: 1976, white-painted body and door, red-painted roof, plastic top door guides with molded hook on bottom, white and black lettering.

(A) Opaque-white plastic body and door. 30 40 60 75

(B) Translucent-white plastic body. 30 40 60 75

7701 CAMEL: 1976-77, brown, black and silver lettering, plastic top door guides with molded hook on bottom, dark brown roof and ends.

(A) Opaque-white plastic body and doors painted medium yellow. — 4 6 9

(B) Same as (A), but medium dark yellow body and light yellow doors. — 4 6 9

(C) Same as (A), but dark yellow body and doors. — 4 6 9

(D) Translucent-white plastic body painted light yellow, dark yellow doors. — 4 6 9

7702 PRINCE ALBERT: 1976-77, red plastic body painted red and yellow, door painted yellow, black roof; yellow, black and white lettering, black and white oval electrocal to right of door, plastic top door guides with molded hook on bottom. C. Lang comment. — 4 6 9

7703 BEECH-NUT: 1976-77, opaque-white plastic body painted white, red roof and ends, blue doors painted blue; blue and red lettering, plastic top door guides with molded hook on bottom, Beech-Nut electrocal to right of door. C. Lang comment. — 4 6 9

7704 WELCOME TOY FAIR: 1976 (U S Toy Fair), opaque-white plastic body painted white, red roof and ends, translucent-white doors painted red; blue and red lettering, plastic top door guides with molded hook on bottom, American flag logo to right of door. C. Lang comment. — 100 125 150

7705 TOY FAIR: 1976 (Canadian Toy Fair), opaque-white plastic body painted white, red roof and ends, translucent-white door painted red; red lettering in English and French to left of door, red Maple Leaf logo and numbers to right of door, plastic top on door guides with molded hook on bottom. — — 250 350

7706 SIR WALTER RALEIGH: 1977-78, opaque-white plastic body painted orange, blue roof, translucent-white door painted gold; white and gold lettering, black and gold electrocals on each side of door, plastic top on door guides with molded hook on bottom. C. Lang comment. — 4 6 9

7707 WHITE OWL: 1977-78, opaque-white plastic body painted white, brown roof, translucent-white door painted gold; brown lettering, brown and white square electrocal to right of door, plastic top door guides with molded bottom hook. C. Lang comment. — 4 6 9

7708 WINSTON: 1977-78, red plastic body painted red, gold roof, translucent-white door painted gold; white and red lettering, red and white oblong electrocal to right of door, plastic top door guides with molded bottom hook. C. Lang comment. — 4 6 9

7709 SALEM: 1978, green-painted sides, gold roof, ends and doors, electrocals on both sides of doors. C. Lang comment. — 4 6 9

7710 MAIL POUCH: 1978, white painted sides, tuscan roof and door, red, brown and black Mail Pouch electrocal to left of door. — 10 12 15

7711 EL PRODUCTO: 1978, white sides, gold door, dark red roof and ends. — 10 12 15

7712 ATSF: 1979, yellow sides, silver roof; black "SHIP AND TRAVEL SANTA FE ALL THE WAY"; gold FARR 1 diamond-shaped logo; part of Famous American Railroad Series No. 1, but sold separately. — 15 20 25

7800 PEPSI: 1977, white plastic body painted white, red roof and ends, blue doors painted blue; red and blue lettering, Type IX body, Type III door guides, Symington-Wayne trucks, Type III frame, "LIONEL" on right side. — 10 12 15

7801 A&W: 1977, white plastic body painted yellow, orange roof and ends; brown lettering, white doors painted brown, Type IX body, Type III door guides, Symington-Wayne trucks, Type III frame, "LIONEL" on right side. — 8 10 12

7802 CANADA DRY: 1977, green plastic body painted green, gold roof and ends, cream door painted gold; white and gold lettering, Type IX body, Type III door guides, Symington-Wayne trucks, Type III frame, "LIONEL" on left side. — 8 10 12

7803 TRAINS 'N TRUCKING, 1978, white body, gold roof; green and gold lettering. 10 15 20 25

7806 SEASONS GREETINGS: 1976, silver-painted body, green door; white lettering, Type IX body. — 80 100 125

7807 TOY FAIR: 1977, green body, gold-painted doors, roof and ends; red and green lettering, "TRAINS 'N TRUCKIN' " on right side of door in capitals with apostrophes, white locomotive and truck logos, Type IX body. C. Lang comment. — 100 125 150

7808 NORTHERN PACIFIC: 1978, stock car, brown with silver roof, black door; silver lettering, "The Pig Palace" electrocal on white plastic board glued to slats at right of doors. Part of 1764 Heartland Express. C. Lang comment. 20 25 35 45

7809 VERNORS: 1978, yellow-painted sides, black roof and door; green lettering and logos. — 8 10 12

7810 CRUSH: 1978, orange-painted sides, green roof, ends and door; green, orange and silver logos. — 8 10 12

7811 DR. PEPPER: 1978, dark orange-painted roof, dark brown body; white lettering. — 8 10 12

7812-1977 TCA: 1977, Convention Stock Car, brown cattle car body, brown-yellow plastic plaque inserted in place of double doors, center metal door guide removed; yellow lettering on car body, "23rd NATIONAL CONVENTION/HOUSTON/ TEXAS/JUNE 1977", brown lettering and logos on plaque, Symington-Wayne trucks. — — 30 35

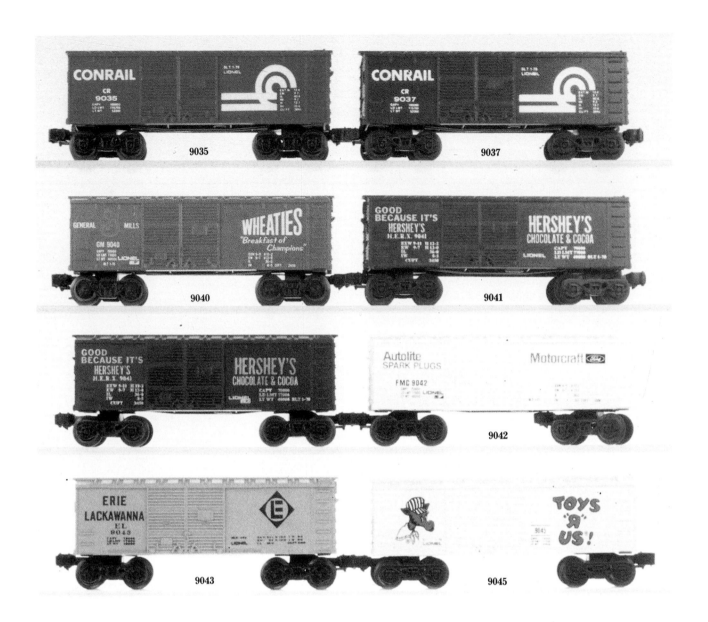

9035   9037

9040   9041

9042

9043   9045

7813 SEASONS GREETINGS FROM LIONEL: 1977, 9700-type boxcar, white body, gold roof and ends, unpainted red doors; red and dark green lettering to left of door, red and dark green toy logos to right of door. C. Lang comment.   —   —   **100   125**

7814 SEASONS GREETINGS: 1978, 9700-style boxcar, white body, dark blue roof and ends, royal blue doors; red "1978 SEASON'S GREETINGS" to left of door, Fundimensions "F" logo in red and blue to right of door. C. Lang comment.   —   —   **100   125**

7815 TOY FAIR: 1978, 9700-style boxcar, silver body, white doors, red roof and ends; black lettering, "BIG TRAINS/FOR SMALL/HANDS" and boy with locomotive electrocals to right of door in black. C. Lang comment.   —   —   **100   125**

7816 TOY FAIR: 1979, 9700-type boxcar, white body, gold roof and ends, dull gold doors; red and blue lettering and train electrocal to right of door, blue and red Fundimensions "F" to left of door. C. Lang comment.   —   —   **100   125**

7900 OUTLAW CAR: 1982-83, orange stock car with outlaw and sheriff who move in and out of car windows as car moves, mechanism like Horse Transport Car.   —   —   **11   14**

7901 LIONEL LINES: 1982-83, cop and hobo car, "HYDRAULIC PLAT-FORM MAINTENANCE CAR", one figure moves from car platform to overhead trestle while other figure moves from trestle to car platform.   —   —   **20   25**

SMALL SHORT 027 BOXCARS: The short 027 boxcars produced by Fundimensions had Symington-Wayne trucks and one operating and one

dummy coupler, with few exceptions. C. Lang comment.

7902 A.T.S.F.: 1982-83, red plastic plug door, white lettering; from 1353 Southern Streak set (1983).   —   —   **6   8**

7903 ROCK: 1983, blue plastic plug door boxcar; white lettering, one fixed coupler, one disc-operating coupler, metal wheels. Caponi comment.
  —   —   **6   8**

7904 SAN DIEGO ZOO: 1983, dark red plastic car with all-yellow giraffe; white lettering "SAN DIEGO ZOO/BLT 1983/LIONEL", Symington-Wayne trucks, one operating and one dummy coupler, rerun of 3376 and 3386 from 1960s. With tell-tale and cam device. Catalogue shows car numbered "7903" in error. C. Rohlfing comment, R. LaVoie Collection.
  —   —   **25   30**

7909 LOUISVILLE & NASHVILLE: 1983, blue plastic, short 027 boxcar, yellow lettering, Symington-Wayne trucks, two dummy couplers, plastic trucks, part of 1352 Rocky Mountain Freight set.   —   —   —   **10**

7910 CHESSIE SYSTEM: 1984-85, boxcar, 6454-mold boxcar with dark blue body; yellow lettering, yellow Chessie cat logo, Symington-Wayne trucks, one operating and one dummy coupler, metal door guides with opening doors. The reintroduction of the 6454 mold marks the first time Fundimensions has used this boxcar style, which has not been produced since 1953. The rivet detail has been fully restored, and the boxcar's lettering has been rubber-stamped right over it. The body fastens to the frame with two Phillips screws instead of the single screw and slot system used on other boxcars. The frame is the same one used on the Sheriff and Outlaw and Horse Transport Cars produced by Fundimensions; the large

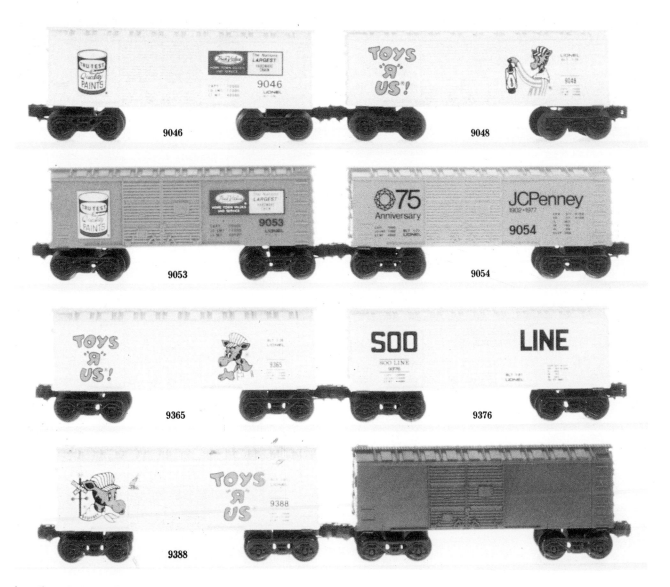

9046   9048

9053   9054

9365   9376

9388

hole where the **swinging mechanism would be is closed** by a plastic plug. Actually, **the special 7912 Toys 'R Us "Geoffrey Car" was the first car to use this mold (see entry below). This is a highly significant development,** since it means that Fundimensions can produce a line of high-quality boxcars at a very reasonable price. R. LaVoie comment and Collection.

— — — 10

7912 GEOFFREY CAR: 1982-83, operating giraffe car, special production for Toys 'R Us retail toy stores. White 6454-mold body, orange "TOYS 'R US" logo to left of door, yellow and black "STAR CAR" logo to right of door, sliding doors with metal guides, orange giraffe with brown spots. This giraffe figure is far more elaborate than the one used in regular production. It has a larger nose and a nape on its neck. Car has Symington-Wayne trucks, one operating and one dummy coupler. The instruction sheet for the car is labeled "GEOFFREY CAR" instead of "GIRAFFE CAR". This car came as part of a "Heavy Iron" special set with a die-cast 8213 Rio Grande 2-4-2 steam locomotive, a short yellow flatcar with stakes, a 9013 Nickel Plate Road short gondola with two gray canisters and an orange Rio Grande unlighted SP-type caboose. Price for 7912 car only. R. Shanfeld Collection.

— — — 100

7913 TURTLE BACK ZOO: Announced for 1985, operating giraffe car, green short stock car body, yellow giraffe and cam follower piece, white lettering and logo, Symington-Wayne trucks, one operating and one dummy coupler. Comes with cam, mounting plate and black pole with white telltales. — — — 20

9035 CONRAIL: 1978-82, blue Type V body, white lettering.

— — 4 5

9037 CONRAIL: 1978-81, brown or blue Type V body, white lettering, plastic trucks and wheels.
(A) Brown   — — 4 5
(B) Blue   — — 4 5

9040 WHEATIES: 1970, orange body, white and blue lettering, MPC logo. Some came as separate sale items in Type I boxes.
(A) Type V body, AAR trucks, one operating coupler, one fixed coupler, plastic wheels.   — 4 5 6
(B) Type IV body, Symington-Wayne trucks, one operating coupler, one fixed coupler, plastic wheels.   — 4 5 6
(C) Type V body, Symington-Wayne trucks, one operating coupler, one fixed coupler, plastic wheels.   — 4 5 6
(D) Type V body, Symington-Wayne trucks, one operating coupler, one manumatic coupler, metal wheels.   — 4 5 6

9041 HERSHEY'S: 1971, silver lettering, metal wheels, one operating coupler, one fixed coupler, MPC logo. Some came in Type II boxes for separate sale.
(A) Type IV chocolate body, AAR trucks, plastic wheels, silk-screened lettering. Askenas Collection.   — 4 5 6
(B) Type V dark chocolate body, Symington-Wayne trucks, plastic wheels.
                                                             — 4 5 6
(C) Type V maroon body, Symington-Wayne trucks, two fixed couplers.
                                                             — 4 5 6
(D) Same as (C), but one disc coupler, one fixed coupler. Askenas Collection.   — 4 5 6
(E) Type IV chocolate body, Symington-Wayne trucks. Rohlfing Collection.
                                                             — 4 5 6

9042 AUTOLITE: 1972, 027 short boxcar, Type V white body embossed with Part 100-4-3 on the inside; black and orange lettering, Symington-Wayne trucks, one operating coupler, one fixed coupler, metal wheels, MPC logo on car end. Apparently, this car was only included in one set, the 1284 Allegheny, although it also came in a Type I box as a separate sale item. The catalogue illustration shows the car with a Ford logo on the upper right on page 7, but with the logo overprinted in black on the separate sale car on page 12. The example observed has the Ford logo. Reader comments are invited as to a possible tie-in sale with the Ford Motor Company, especially in view of the fact that the prototype for this car has been discovered. See entry MX-9145 in the Factory Errors and Prototype section. R. DuBeau coment.
            —   4   5   6

9043 ERIE LACKAWANNA: 1973-74, gray body, wine lettering, Type V body, Symington-Wayne trucks, one operating coupler, one manumatic fixed coupler, plastic wheels, no MPC logo. Some versions packaged in Type II boxes for separate sale.
            —   4   5   6

9044 D&RGW: 1975, 1979, orange body, black lettering, Type V body, Symington-Wayne trucks, one operating coupler, one manumatic fixed coupler, no MPC logo.
            3   4   6   8

9045 TOYS"R"US: On special order, Fundimensions has made 027 short boxcars for national retail stores such as Toys 'R Us, True Value Hardware, Sears and J.C. Penney. These cars, like the regular issues, have Symington-Wayne trucks, one operating and one dummy coupler; white body, orange and black lettering; Type V body, plastic wheels, no MPC logo. C. Lang comment.
         20   30   40   50

9046 TRUE VALUE, 1976, white body, red and black lettering, Type V body, Symington-Wayne trucks, one operating coupler, one fixed coupler, metal wheels, no MPC logo. Part of special set 1698 with 8601 steam locomotive, 9020 flatcar, 9078 caboose, four straight and eight curved 027 track pieces. D. Johns and G. Halverson comments.   **20   30   40   50**

9047 TOYS"R"US: White body, orange and black lettering, Type V body, Symington-Wayne trucks, one operating coupler, one manumatic dummy coupler, plastic wheels, no MPC logo.   —   **20   25   35**

9048 TOYS"R"US: White body, orange and black lettering, Symington-Wayne trucks, one operating coupler, one manumatic coupler, plastic wheels.   —   **20   25   35**

(9049) TOYS"R"US: 1979, white body, orange and black-lettered "GEOFFREY POWER", number does not appear on car; part of uncatalogued set 1971. G. Halverson Collection.   —   —   **35   50**

9052 TOYS"R"US: White body, orange and black lettering, Symington-Wayne trucks, one operating coupler, one manumatic coupler, plastic wheels.   —   **20   25   35**

9053 TRUE VALUE: 1977, green short 027 boxcar with True Value yellow, black and red decals, red number on car. Originally came in specially marked Tru-Value bag within set; mint condition must include this bag. Came as part of special set 1792, identical to set 1698 except for special car, (see 9046 for set contents). D. Johns comments, G. Halverson Collection.   —   —   **35   50**

9054 JC PENNEY: Orange body, black lettering, "75th Anniversary".
           —   —   **35   50**

THE GENERAL MILLS MINI-MAX RAIL CAR
By William Meyer

Editor's Note: Mr. Meyer, a charter member of the Lionel Operating Train Society, is a frequent correspondent and contributor to our Guides. His last essay, about the General Motors NW-2 Switcher, appears in the 1985 edition of Greenberg's Guide to Lionel Trains, 1945-1969.

In 1971 Lionel produced the 9090 General Mills 027 boxcar. It was seven inches long and had only four wheels. The entire side of the car could be raised. It came in the Yardmaster Set and was also available separately. The 9090 was not, as some have suggested, a Fundimensions concept, but in actuality was modeled after the two-axle Mini-Max rail car introduced in 1969 by General Mills and the United States Railway Equipment Company. It was designed for lightweight loading of low density food products. The prototype for the 9090 is an all-door car with a weight of only 50,000 pounds. The doors are fabricated of aluminum extrusions with reinforced fiberglass skin, and the car is forty feet, seven and one-half inches in length. Except for bobber cabooses, two-axle rail cars have not been common in the United States until recently, although they are in Europe, and this is an unusual car in the consist of any freight.

Lionel's model of the Mini-Max railcar is quite accurate and well detailed, and its construction is not like any other car. The flatcar base is scribed on both bottom and top, and two non-operating but self-centering couplers are riveted to it. The roof and ends are cast in one piece, and the flatcar base snaps onto this piece. The base, roof and sides are in medium or dark blue; the lighter shade is a little harder to find. The lettering on the doors is blue as well, while the doors themselves are white. Like the prototype, the model has doors which swing outward along the whole side of the car. Inside, some versions of the car have six rather fragile floor-to-roof support struts. A sheet of paper found in the separate-sale boxes explains that these struts were molded into the car for protection during shipping; they were not meant to be part of the car's design and could be removed by the purchaser. In some versions, the General Mills logo is found on the fourth panel from the right, as on the prototype, while on other versions the logo starts in the fourth panel from the left. When it is sold separately, the car comes in a small Type I box with "9090/ Mini Max" stamped in black or purple on the ends. The car includes a few small pallet loads with black undersides and yellow or green square cases. The tag board on the car's end reads "9090/Series", which would seem to suggest that more cars were planned. However, this car is unique in the Fundimensions inventory.

With General Mills as the parent for Fundimensions, one might have expected more General Mills product line cars, but the Mini-Max is one of the few that carry the logo of the parent company. There are actually more Fundimensions cars for beer than for General Mills products!

9090 MINI MAX: 1971, blue body, white door; blue lettering, four metal wheels. Dark blue versions have roof brackets and palletainer loads; light blue versions do not have roof brackets and loads. Palletainers have black bases, but color of square plastic top pieces can vary from yellow to light green. Separate sale cars came in Type I boxes. Light blue versions are harder to find. G. Halverson and R. LaVoie comments.
(A) Three roof brackets, "G" is in fourth panel from right.

10	12	15	20

(B) Same as (A), but without three roof brackets.

15	20	25	30

(C) Same as (A), but without three roof brackets and USLX 9090 lettering on lower left side.

—	—	30	40

(D) Three roof brackets, "G" is in fourth panel from left.

10	12	15	20

MX 9145 AUTOLITE: 1972, See Factory Errors and Prototypes.

9200 SERIES BOXCARS

9200 ILLINOIS CENTRAL: Several body types, black and white lettering.
(A) Orange-painted Type V orange body and doors, IC spread, deep heat-stamped lettering, metal door guides, open AAR trucks with bar inset into uncoupler discs, MPC logo to left of fourth bottom rivet. G. Halverson Collection.

10	15	20	25

(B) Same as (A), but Type VI body, IC close. G. Halverson Collection.

8	10	12	15

(C) Type VI body, metal door guides, flat orange-painted orange body and doors, AAR trucks, Type I frame, IC spread.

8	10	12	15

(D) Dull orange-painted Type VI body, orange-painted orange doors (brighter than body paint), IC spread, metal door guides, Symington-Wayne trucks, wheel axles blackened. G. Halverson Collection.

8	10	12	15

(E) Orange-painted orange plastic Type VI body and doors, IC spread, two

plastic door guides, MPC logo atop fourth bottom rivet, Symington-Wayne trucks with black uncoupler discs. G. Halverson and R. LaVoie Collections.

10	15	20	25

(F) Type VII body, metal door guides, glossy orange-painted orange body and doors, AAR trucks, Type I frame, IC close.

8	10	12	15

(G) Same as (E), but plastic door guides.

8	10	12	15

(H) Same as (E), but plastic door guides, Symington-Wayne trucks, IC spread.

8	10	12	15

(I) Same as (E), but dull dark orange-painted orange body, IC spread.

10	12	15	20

(J) Type VIII body, flat orange-painted gray body and doors, Symington-Wayne trucks, Type II frame, IC spread.

8	10	12	15

(K) Same as (I), but Type IX body.

8	10	12	15

(L) Type IX body, glossy orange-painted orange body, flat orange-painted gray doors, Symington-Wayne trucks, Type II frame, IC spread.

10	12	15	20

See also Factory Errors and Prototypes.

9201 PENN CENTRAL: Type VI body, metal door guides, white lettering, AAR trucks, Type I frame.
(A) Jade green-painted jade green plastic body and door.

12	15	20	25

(B) Dark green-painted dark green plastic body and door.

12	15	20	25

9202 SANTA FE: Type VI body, metal door guides, AAR trucks, Type I frame, all have red-painted red bodies and white lettering.
(A) Silver-painted gray door.

12	17	25	35

(B) Same as (A), but only two dots on left side of door.

12	17	25	35

(C) Gray-painted gray door.

12	17	25	35

See also Factory Errors and Prototypes.

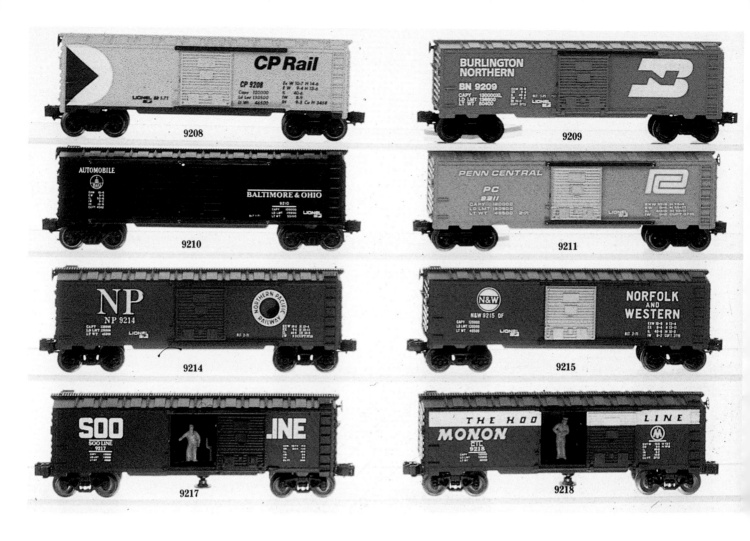

9208   9209

9210   9211

9214   9215

9217   9218

9203 UNION PACIFIC: Type V body, metal door guides, yellow-painted yellow doors; blue lettering, red, blue and white-striped UP shield to right of door, AAR trucks, Type I frame. C. Lang comment.

(A) Yellow-painted yellow body.   15   20   30   35

(B) Light yellow-painted light yellow body.   15   20   30   35

9204 NORTHERN PACIFIC: White and black-outlined letters, Type I frame, AAR trucks except as noted.

(A) Type VI body, dark green-painted dark green body and shiny green door, metal door guides, dark red logo insert, built date.
   10   22   30   35

(B) Green-painted Type VI green body, bright lime green unpainted doors, metal door guides, open AAR trucks with bar in uncoupler discs. G. Halverson Collection.   10   22   30   35

(C) Same as (A), but light red logo insert.   10   22   30   35

(D) Type VII body, apple green-painted apple green body and door, no built date, metal door guides.   10   17   28   35

(E) Same as (D), but plastic door guides and Symington-Wayne trucks.
   10   17   28   35

(F) Same as (C), but body is painted same green color as 9209 Burlington Northern boxcar. C. Lang Collection.   10   22   30   35

9205 NORFOLK & WESTERN: Type VI body, metal door guides, white lettering, AAR trucks except as noted, Type I frame.

(A) Dark blue-painted dark blue body and navy blue door.
   8   10   12   15

(B) Same as (A), but Symington-Wayne trucks.   8   10   12   15

(C) Medium blue-painted medium blue body and navy blue door.
   8   10   12   15

(D) Royal blue (reddish-blue)-painted royal blue body and door. G. Halverson and R. LaVoie Collections.   10   12   15   20

9206 GREAT NORTHERN: White lettering, metal door guides, AAR trucks except as noted, Type I frame.

(A) Type VI body, light blue-painted body and door.   8   10   12   15

(B) Type VII body, paler blue-painted paler blue body and light blue door.
   8   10   12   15

(C) Type VII body, palest blue-painted palest blue body and light blue door, Symington-Wayne trucks, Type II box.   8   10   12   15

9207 SOO: Type VII body, Type I frame.

(A) Red-painted red body and red door; white lettering, AAR trucks, metal door guides.   8   10   12   15

(B) Flat red-painted red body and door; white lettering, Symington-Wayne trucks, metal door guides.   8   10   12   15

(C) Shiny red-painted red body and door; white lettering, Symington-Wayne trucks, plastic door guides.   8   10   12   15

See also Factory Errors and Prototypes.

9208 CP RAIL: Type VII body, black lettering, Type I frame. One sample observed came in Type I box dated 2/71. T. Rollo comment.

(A) Medium yellow-painted medium yellow body and door; metal door guides, Symington-Wayne trucks.   8   10   12   15

(B) Light yellow-painted light yellow body and door, metal door guides, Symington-Wayne trucks.   8   10   12   15

(C) Light yellow-painted light yellow body, light yellow-painted medium yellow door, plastic door guides, AAR trucks.   8   10   12   15

(D) Dark yellow-painted dark yellow body, dark yellow-painted medium yellow door, AAR trucks, plastic door guide.   8   10   12   15

(E) Same as (D), but Symington-Wayne trucks, Type II frame. C. Rohlfing comment.   8   10   12   15

9209 BURLINGTON NORTHERN: Type I frame, white lettering.

(A) Type VII body, apple green-painted apple green body and dark green-painted dark green door, AAR trucks, metal door guides.
   8   10   12   15

(B) Type VII body, dark green-painted dark green body and doors, metal door guides, Symington-Wayne trucks.   8   10   12   15

(C) Same as (B), but Type VIII body.   **8   10   12   15**

(D) Same as (B), but Type IX body and Type III door guides, Type II box.
    10   12   15   20

(E) Same as (B), but plastic door guides.   **8   10   12   15**

(F) Same as (A), but Type VII body and plastic door guides. Knopf Collection.   **8   10   12   15**

9210 B&O: Double-door automobile car, 6468-type body, metal door guides, Type I frame; white lettering, all doors with different colors added outside the factory (only the black door is authentic factory production, but the other varieties are listed here because there is considerable collector interest in them), all Symington-Wayne trucks except (A).

(A) Black-painted black body and doors, AAR trucks.
    10   12   15   20

(B) Same as (A), but dark 9771 N&W navy blue-painted blue doors. C. Lang Collection.   **8   10   12   15**

(C) Same as (A), but Penn Central jade green-painted green doors. C. Lang Collection.   **8   10   12   15**

(D) Same as (A), but 9200 IC orange-painted orange doors. C. Lang Collection.   **8   10   12   15**

(E) Same as (A), but 9703 CP Rail burnt-orange-painted orange doors. C. Lang Collection.   **8   10   12   15**

(F) Same as (A), but turquoise-painted turquoise doors.
    8   10   12   15

9211 PENN CENTRAL: Type VII body, except for (A), silver-painted gray doors, white lettering, Type I frame.

(A) Jade green-painted Type VI jade green body, AAR trucks, 1000 made, no end imprints, metal door guides.   **15   20   30   35**

(B) Jade green-painted jade green body, Symington-Wayne trucks, metal door guides.   **12   15   20   25**

(C) Pale green-painted pale green body, AAR trucks, metal door guides.
    12   15   20   25

(D) Medium green-painted medium green body, AAR trucks, metal door guides.   **12   15   20   25**

(E) Same as (D), but plastic door guides.   **12   15   20   25**

(F) Same as (D), but Symington-Wayne trucks.   **12   15   20   25**

(G) Dark green-painted dark green body, Symington-Wayne trucks, plastic door guides.   **12   15   20   25**

9212: Assigned to Lionel Collector's Club of America, 1976 Flatcar.

9213: Not assigned.

9214 NORTHERN PACIFIC: Type VII maroon plastic body except for (D), white and black-outlined lettering, Type I frame, metal door guides, red oxide-painted maroon doors.

(A) Flat red oxide-painted body, Symington-Wayne trucks.
    5   7   10   12

(B) Red oxide-painted body, AAR trucks.   **5   7   10   12**

(C) Red oxide-painted Type VII body and doors, two plastic door guides, Symington-Wayne trucks, black uncoupler discs. G. Halverson Collection.
    10   12   15   20.

(D) Red oxide-painted Type IX tuscan body, tuscan-painted tuscan door, Symington-Wayne trucks, Type II frame, Type II box. R. LaVoie Collection.
    8   10   12   15

9215 NORFOLK & WESTERN: Type VII body, silver-painted gray doors, white lettering, Type I frame.

(A) Royal blue-painted royal blue Type VI plastic body, plastic door guides, AAR trucks; 1000 manufactured.   **15   20   30   35**

(B) Dark blue-painted dark blue body, metal door guides, Symington-Wayne trucks.   **8   10   12   15**

(C) Same as (B), except plastic door guides.   **8   10   12   15**

(D) Same as (B), except plastic door guides and AAR trucks.
    8   10   12   15

9217 SOO: 1982, operating box, plunger opens door, worker moves towards door, brownish-maroon-painted body, white lettering, Standard 0 trucks. C. Rohlfing comment.   **—   —   15   18**

9218 MONON: 1981-82, operating mail delivery boxcar, plunger opens door, worker tosses mail sack out of door. Tuscan body, white stripe across top of car with deep red lettering, white reporting marks, Standard 0 trucks. C. Rohlfing and C. Lang comments, R. LaVoie Collection.
    —   —   12   15

9219 MISSOURI PACIFIC: 1983, operating car with plunger mechanism, door opens, worker moves toward door, blue sides with gray stripe and gray ends and roof, Standard 0 trucks. Reissue of 3494-150 M.P. from 1956. Reader comments on the specific differences and similarities of these cars would be appreciated.   **—   —   25   30**

9220 BORDEN: 1983, operating milk car, white body, brown roof and ends; black lettering, yellow and black "ELSIE" cow logo to right of door. Came with gray and white milk can platform and plastic milk cans. Car has postwar bar-end metal trucks because sliding shoe is needed to operate car. C. Lang comment.   **—   —   —   75**

9221 POULTRY DISPATCH: 1983, sometimes known as the "Chicken Sweeper" car, reissue of 3434 from 1959-60. Dull brown-painted stock car body, white lettering, unpainted gray doors, Standard 0 trucks, three celluloid rows of chickens on way to market show through car slats, two bayonet-base light bulbs inside car provide illumination. When plunger is pulled down by remote track section, door opens and gray man with broom mounted on delicate hairspring appears to be swinging back and forth, sweeping feathers out of car. R. LaVoie Collection.   **—   —   25   30**

9223 READING: 1984-85, operating boxcar, tuscan-painted body and doors; white lettering, black and white diamond-shaped "READING LINES" logo, gray man appears when plunger opens car door, Standard 0 trucks.   **—   —   —   25**

9224 LOUISVILLE: 1984-85, scheduled for late 1985 production, operating horse car and corral, reissue of 3356 postwar accessory in new colors. Car has yellow sides, doors and ends, dark brown roof and lettering, postwar bar-end metal trucks with sliding shoes for operation. Horse corral has white frame and fencing and dark green corral chute and watering trough. Nine brown horses are included. When car is on remote control track and button is pushed, car doors drop down to meet corral platform and horses move into and out of car by vibrator action in car and corral. Price for complete accessory.   **—   —   —   75**

9229 EXPRESS MAIL: 1984-85, operating boxcar, blue sides and doors, orange ends and roof; white lettering and Post Office logo, white and orange Express Mail logo, Symington-Wayne trucks, gray man tosses out mail sack when door opens by plunger action.   **—   —   —   20**

9230

9230 MONON: Type VII body (A-D) and Type IX body (E-F), white lettering, Symington-Wayne trucks. One sample had box dated 2/70. T. Rollo comment.

(A) Tuscan-painted maroon body, red oxide-painted maroon doors, Type I frame, metal door guides.   **4   6   8   10**

(B) Same as (A), but red oxide-painted red oxide body.
    4   6   8   10

(C) Same as (A), but Type VII postwar bar-end metal trucks which appear to be original with car. Probable early production. J. Aleshire Collection.
    NRS

(D) Flat red oxide-painted flat red oxide body, red oxide-painted maroon doors, Type I frame, plastic door guides.   **4   6   8   10**

(E) Tuscan-painted tuscan body, tuscan-painted tuscan doors, Type I frame.   **4   6   8   10**

(F) Same as (E), but Type II frame. Came in Type II box.
    6   8   10   12

9237 UNITED PARCEL SERVICE: 1984, operating boxcar, dark brown body; white UPS logo and lettering, plunger opens door and gray man advances to door opening. Pictured in 1984 Traditional catalogue, but never produced because at the last moment, after the prototypes had been made, United Parcel Service withdrew its permission to make the car.
    Not Manufactured

9360 9359

9362

9280 ATSF: 1978-80, horse transport car, short stock car body; white horses bob in and out, red with white lettering. 4 6 8 11

9301 U.S. MAIL: 1975-83, red, white and blue-painted red plastic body and door; white and black lettering, 1972-Type body mold, Symington-Wayne trucks, Type I frame, single door guides, "LIONEL" on left, man tosses mail sack when door is opened by plunger.
(A) Dark blue paint, MPC plate. 6 10 13 20
(B) Light blue paint with darker blue doors, MPC plate.
6 10 13 20
(C) Medium blue paint, no MPC plate. 6 10 13 20
(D) Light blue paint, no MPC plate. 6 10 13 20
(E) Overprinted "SACRAMENTO SIERRA" for TCA regional meet of 1976 in Sacramento, CA. C. Lang Collection. NRS

9305 SANTA FE: 1980, 1982, stock car with bobbing sheriff and outlaw figures, mechanism identical to 9280. Dark green short stock car body, gold lettering, plastic wheels, Symington-Wayne trucks, one operating and one dummy coupler; from James Gang set. C. Lang comment.
— — 10 14

9308 AQUARIUM CAR: 1981-83, reissue of 3435 from 1959-62; green-painted clear plastic body; gold lettering, die-cast 027 passenger trucks, windows with fish tanks, two bayonet base bulbs inside car for illumination, vibrator motor turns two spools with film attached which is painted with fish; turning action makes fish appear to swim through car. C. Lang and C. Rohlfing comments. — — 50 60
See also Factory Errors and Prototypes.

9319

9319 TCA SILVER JUBILEE: 1979, gloss dark blue body, silver bullion car for TCA's 25th anniversary, silver bullion, white lettering on clear sides, special coin available only at TCA's National Convention, coin sits in car slot but does not fall into car, coin lettered "TCA 25 Years", coin about size of half dollar; 6,000 made.
(A) Car only. — — 60 85
(B) Car with coin. — — 70 90
9320 FORT KNOX GOLD RESERVE: 1979, clear plastic body painted

9320

silver, coin slot, circular grates at each end, "gold reserve" bullion stacks inside car, Standard 0 trucks; from Southern Pacific Limited set.
— — 65 75

9339 GREAT NORTHERN: 1979-81, 1983, green plastic short 027 boxcar; white lettering, Symington-Wayne trucks; part of 1960 Midnight Flyer set (1980-81) and 1252 Heavy Iron set (1983). C. Lang comment.
(A) 1980-81, one operating and one dummy coupler. — 2 4 6
(B) 1983, two operating couplers. — 2 4 6
9349 SAN FRANCISCO MINT: 1980, dark maroon body, gold lettering, gold ingots stacked inside car, Standard "O" trucks. Type III box with ends marked "9349 Gold Bullion Car". — — 50 55
9359 NATIONAL BASKETBALL ASSN: 1980, short 027 boxcar, came in year-end special only, many labels provided with car so that the purchaser could decide which to place on car. — — 20 25
9360 NATIONAL HOCKEY LEAGUE: 1980, short 027 boxcar, Stanley Cup, came in year-end special, many labels provided so that car purchaser could decide which to place on car. — — 20 25
9361 Not Used: 1980, this number was for the National Football League Car. At the last minute the League withdrew permission (perhaps they wanted a fee, which Lionel did not want to pay) and production was canceled. Not Manufactured
9362 MAJOR LEAGUE BASEBALL: 1980, came in year-end special, many labels provided with car, each for a different team, purchaser to decide which to place on car. — — 20 25
9365 TOYS "R" US: 1979, part of 1993 TOYS "R" US Midnight Flyer set.
— — 30 35
9376 SOO: 1981, part of uncatalogued 1157 Wabash Cannonball set. Details needed. — — 10 15
9388 TOYS "R" US: 1981, part of 1159 TOYS "R" US Midnight Flyer set. Details needed. — — 30 35
9400 CONRAIL: 1978.
(A) Tuscan-painted tuscan plastic body and door; white lettering, Type IX body mold, Type III door guides, Symington-Wayne trucks, Type III frame, "LIONEL" on left. 5 7 10 12
(B) Same as (A), but brown-painted brown body and door.
5 7 10 12

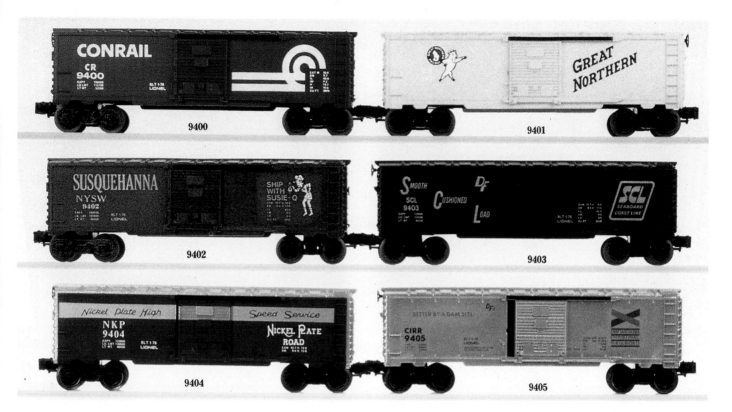

9400   9401

9402   9403

9404   9405

(C) Same as (A), but NETCA (New England Division, Train Collectors Association) overprint in gold. C. Lang Collection.   **NRS**

9401 GREAT NORTHERN: 1978, pale green-painted pale green plastic body and door; white lettering, Symington-Wayne trucks, Type IX body mold, Type III door guides, Symington-Wayne trucks, Type III frame, "LIONEL" on left.   **6   8   10   12**

9402 SUSQUEHANNA: 1978, green-painted green plastic body and door; gold lettering, red, gold and gray "SUSIE-Q" logo to right of door, "LIONEL" and built date to left of door, Type IX body mold, Type III door guides, Symington-Wayne trucks, Type III frame. C. Lang comment.   **10   12   15   20**

9403 S C L: 1978, (Seaboard Coast Line); black-painted black plastic body and door, yellow lettering, Type IX body mold, Type III guides, Symington-Wayne trucks, Type III frame, "LIONEL" on right.
(A) Yellow lettering.   **8   8   10   12**
(B) Extremely bold yellow lettering.   **10   12   15   20**
(C) Shiny white lettering, scarce.   **—   —   —   145**

9404 NICKEL PLATE: 1978, maroon and silver-painted maroon body and door; black and white lettering, Type IX body mold, Type III door guides, Symington-Wayne trucks, Type III frame, "LIONEL" on left.
   6   8   10   12

9405 CIRR: 1978, (Chattahoochie Industrial Railroad), silver-painted gray plastic body and door; orange and black lettering, Type IX body mold, Type III door guides, Symington-Wayne trucks, Type III frame, "LIONEL" on left.   **4   6   8   10**

9406 D&RGW: 1978, "Rio Grande", white and brown-painted white plastic body, brown-painted brown plastic door; black and red lettering, Type IX body mold, Type III door guides, Symington-Wayne trucks, Type III frame, "LIONEL" on right, "Cookie Box".   **3   5   7   10**

9407 UNION PACIFIC: 1978, "LIVESTOCK DISPATCH", gray and yellow-painted yellow plastic body, black-painted black doors; red lettering, Type I mold, three metal door guides, Symington-Wayne trucks, Type I frame, "LIONEL" on right.   **10   12   15   20**

9408 LIONEL LINES: 1978, "CIRCUS CAR", white and red-painted white plastic body, white-painted white plastic door; red lettering, red-painted catwalk and hatches atop roof, Type I mold, three metal door guides, Standard O trucks, Type I frame, "LIONEL" on left; part of 1868 Minneapolis & St. Louis Service Station set.   **10   12   15   20**

9411 LACKAWANNA: 1978, tuscan-painted tuscan plastic body and door; white lettering, Type IX body mold, Type III door guides, Standard 0 trucks, Type III frame, "LIONEL" on right, "The Route of Phoebe Snow" script and built date to right of door; part of Milwaukee Special set.
   10   12   15   20

9412 RICHMOND, FREDERICKSBURG & POTOMAC: 1979, blue-painted body, white lettering and map logo.   **7   9   12   15**

9413 NAPIERVILLE JUNCTION: 1979, yellow-painted sides, red-painted roof and ends, black lettering.

(A) Dark red leaf logo. R. Vagner Collection.   **4   6   8   10**
(B) Light red leaf logo. R. Vagner Collection.   **4   6   8   10**

9414 COTTON BELT: 1980, tuscan body, white lettering, blue lightning streak logo.   **4   6   8   10**

9415 PROVIDENCE & WORCESTER: 1979
(A) Red-painted body, white and black lettering.   **4   6   8   10**
(B) Same as (A), but New England Division, Train Collectors Association (NETCA) overprint for regional convention. C. Lang Collection.   **NRS**

9416 MINNESOTA, DAKOTA & WESTERN: 1979, white and green-painted body, green door.   **4   6   8   10**

9417 CP RAIL: 1979, black, white and red sides, gold letters; from No. 1860 Great Plains Express set. This car was shown in the 1979 catalogue, but it did not become part of the set until 1980, when it replaced the 9729 car identical except for number and white lettering. C. Lang comment.
   —   —   25   35

9418 FAMOUS AMERICAN RAILROAD SERIES: 1979, (FARR), railroad emblem car with markings of Southern, Santa Fe, Great Northern, Union Pacific and Pennsylvania Railroads, emblem of FARR series reads #1.   **—   —   50   60**

9420

9406   9411

9407   9408

9412   9413

9414   9415

9419 UNION PACIFIC: 1980, tuscan sides, black roof, FARR Series 2 (Famous American Railroads), sold separately . — — **20   25**

9420 B&O: 1980, Sentinel, dark blue and silver, same color scheme as 9801 Standard 0 series car, but decals on that car are done in electrocals on this car. — — **15   20**

9421 MAINE CENTRAL: 1980, yellow sides, black "MAINE CENTRAL" logo and lettering. — — **10   12**

9422 ELGIN, JOLIET & EASTERN: 1980, turquoise and orange body, black lettering, Symington-Wayne trucks. — — **10   12**

9423 NEW YORK, NEW HAVEN & HARTFORD: 1980, tuscan-painted tuscan body and doors, white New Haven script logo, Symington-Wayne trucks.

(A) As described above. — — **10   12**

(B) Same as (A), but NETCA (New England Division, Train Collectors Association) overprint for regional convention. C. Lang Collection. **NRS**

9424 TOLEDO, PEORIA & WESTERN: 1980, orange sides, silver roof and ends; white lettering "TOLEDO PEORIA & WESTERN", Symington-Wayne trucks. C. Rohlfing comment. — — **10   12**

9425 BRITISH COLUMBIA: 1980, double-door boxcar, dark green sides and roof, one light green and one dark green door per side; white lettering, yellow and white logo. — — **15   20**

9426 CHESAPEAKE & OHIO: 1980, horizontally divided blue and yellow sides, silver roof and ends; yellow and blue lettering, Symington-Wayne trucks. — — **10   12**

9427 BAY LINE: 1980

(A) Green body with yellow logo, green lettering, "THE BAY LINE" inside of broad yellow stripe; white number and technical data. — — **10   12**

(B) Similar to (A), but logo and stripe are white. — — **135**

9428 TOLEDO, PEORIA & WESTERN: 1980, distinctive light green and cream body, same colors used in lettering to contrast with sides, very different from 9424, Symington-Wayne trucks; available only with 1072 Cross Country Express set. C. Lang and C. Rohlfing comments. — — **25   30**

9429 THE EARLY YEARS: 1980, "COMMEMORATING THE 100th BIRTHDAY OF JOSHUA LIONEL COWEN" (car came in a special limited edition box as did the 9430, 9431, 9432, 9433 and 9434). Light yellow sides, red roof and ends, Standard 0 trucks. C. Rohlfing comment. — — **25   30**

9430 THE STANDARD GAUGE YEARS: 1980 "100th BIRTHDAY", matches 9429, silver sides, maroon roof and ends, Standard 0 trucks. C. Rohlfing comment. — — **25   30**

9431 THE PREWAR YEARS: 1980, matches 9429, gray sides, black roof and ends, Standard 0 trucks. C. Rohlfing comment. — — **25   30**

9432 THE POSTWAR YEARS: 1980, available only with 1070 Royal Limited set. Tan sides, green roof and ends, Standard 0 trucks. C. Rohlfing comment. — — **85   100**

9433 THE GOLDEN YEARS: 1980, matches 9429, available only with 1071 Mid-Atlantic set. Gold sides, dark blue roof and ends, Standard 0 trucks. C. Rohlfing comment. — — **75   85**

9434 JOSHUA LIONEL COWEN-THE MAN: 1980, the last car in the series; series began with 9429. Yellow sides, brown roof and ends, Standard 0 trucks. C. Rohlfing comment. — — **100   125**

9435 CENTRAL OF GEORGIA: 1981, made for LCCA Chattanooga, TE convention. Black Type IX body with large silver-painted oval on sides, silver-painted gray doors; black and white lettering, Type III frame, Symington-Wayne trucks. J. Vega Collection, C. Lang and C. Rohlfing comments. — — **25   30**

9416

9417

9418

9419

9420

9421

9422

9423

9436 BURLINGTON: 1981, red with white lettering, Standard 0 trucks, copy of postwar prototype which was never produced; came with 1160 Great Lakes Limited set.   —   —   **30**   **40**

9437 NORTHERN PACIFIC: 1981, stock car, dark green body, black doors; white lettering, Standard 0 trucks; from 1160 Great Lakes Limited set. C. Lang and C. Rohlfing comments.   —   —   **30**   **40**

9438 ONTARIO NORTHLAND: 1981, dark blue body, yellow ends; yellow lettering, "triple lightning" logo in yellow on side. Harding Collection, C. Rohlfing comment.   —   —   **15**   **20**

9439 ASHLEY, DREW & NORTHERN: 1981, green with white doors and lettering, yellow, green and white logo, Symington-Wayne trucks.   —   —   **8**   **10**

9440 READING: 1981, yellow sides, green roof and ends; green lettering, Standard 0 trucks; from 1158 Maple Leaf Limited set. C. Rohlfing comment.   —   —   **35**   **40**

9441 PENNSYLVANIA: 1981, tuscan with white stripe, white and red lettering; "MERCHANDISE SERVICE", Standard 0 trucks; from 1158 Maple Leaf Limited set.   —   —   **35**   **40**

9442 CANADIAN PACIFIC: 1981, silver-painted gray body, dark red lettering, black roof and ends, Symington-Wayne trucks. C. Lang and C. Rohlfing comments, G. Rogers Collection. .   —   —   **12**   **15**

9443 F E C: 1981, tuscan sides, silver roof and ends; white lettering, red and white striping on sides, "FLORIDA EAST COAST RAILWAY". C. Rohlfing and C. Lang comments.   —   —   **10**   **12**

9444 LOUISIANA MIDLAND: 1981, white sides, blue ends and doors; red and blue lettering, Symington-Wayne trucks. C. Rohlfing comment.
     —   —   **7**   **9**

9445 VERMONT NORTHERN: 1981, yellow sides, silver roof and ends, Symington-Wayne trucks. C. Lang and C. Rohlfing comments.
     —   —   **7**   **9**

9446 SABINE RIVER AND NORTHERN: 1981, red body and doors, silver roof and ends; white logo and lettering, Symington-Wayne trucks. C. Rohlfing comment, R. DuBeau and J. Vega Collections.   —   —   **7**   **9**

9447 PULLMAN STANDARD: 1981, "This is the 1,000,000th", Symington-Wayne trucks.

(A) Silver body, black lettering. R. LaVoie Collection.   —   —   **14**   **17**

(B) Gold body with black lettering. This and a similar silver-bodied car with gold lettering may have been faked by a chemical change. Reader comments requested. C. Lang and R. LaVoie comments.   **NRS**

9448 ATSF: 1981, double-door cattle car, brown with white lettering, black doors, Symington-Wayne trucks; from 1154 Reading Yard King set.
     —   —   **12**   **15**

9449 GREAT NORTHERN: 1981, boxcar, dark green and orange body; FARR 3 diamond logo in gold, white lettering, GREAT NORTHERN goat logo, Famous American Railroads, Series 3; car sold separately. C. Lang comment.   —   —   **15**   **20**

9450 GREAT NORTHERN: 1981, cattle car, FARR Series 3; red sides, black roof, doors and ends, Symington-Wayne trucks. Like the others in this set, this car was sold separately. C. Rohlfing comment.   —   —   **15**   **20**

9451 SOUTHERN: 1983, tuscan box car, yellow lettering, FARR Series 4, Standard 0 trucks; car sold separately.   —   —   —   **25**

9424

9425

9426

9427

9428

9429

9430

9431

9452 WESTERN PACIFIC: 1982-83, tuscan-painted body, white lettering, Symington-Wayne trucks. — — 9 12

9453 MPA: 1982-83, blue-painted body, white lettering, Symington-Wayne trucks. — — 9 12

9454 NEW HOPE & IVYLAND: 1982-83, dark green-painted body, white lettering, Symington-Wayne trucks. Shown in catalogue with circular arrow logo, but not made that way; instead, "McHUGH/BROS./LINES" is present in white. R. LaVoie comment. — — 9 12

9455 MILWAUKEE ROAD: 1982-83, yellow-painted body, black lettering, black "AMERICA'S RESOURCEFUL RAILROAD" to left of door, Symington-Wayne trucks. C. Lang comment. — — 9 12

9456 PENNSYLVANIA: 1984-85, double-door boxcar, tuscan-painted tuscan body and doors, metal door guides; white lettering, white and black PRR Keystone logo on black circle, gold diamond-shaped FARR 5 logo, Standard 0 trucks. — — — 25

9460 DETROIT, TOLEDO & SHORE LINE: 1982, double-door boxcar, made for LCCA national convention in Dearborn, MI. Blue body and doors, white lettering, metal door guides, bright maroon and white logo to right of door, "EXPRESSWAY FOR INDUSTRY" underscored in white to left of door with built date, Symington-Wayne trucks. C. Rohlfing comment, J. Vega and C. Lang Collections. — — — 25

9461 NORFOLK SOUTHERN: 1982, tuscan body, yellow doors, Standard 0 trucks; from Continental Limited set. — — 35 40

9462 SOUTHERN PACIFIC: 1983, silver-painted gray body, black-painted roof and ends, unpainted black doors, black lettering, circular black and white SP logo to right of doors. G. Rogers and R. LaVoie Collections, C. Rohlfing comment. — — 12 15

9463 TEXAS & PACIFIC: 1983, yellow sides and roof, black lettering, yellow doors, black T & P logo, Symington-Wayne trucks. C. Lang and C. Rohlfing comments. — — — 13

9464 NASHVILLE, CHATTANOOGA & ST. LOUIS: 1983, light red body, yellow-orange stripe on side; white lettering, Symington-Wayne trucks. The Type III box ends are labeled "North Carolina & St. Louis", but this is an error. C. Lang and C. Rohlfing comments. — — — 13

9465 ATSF: 1983, dark green body, yellow lettering and logo, dark green doors, Symington-Wayne trucks. Pictured as blue in catalogue, but not produced that way. C. Lang and C. Rohlfing comments. — — — 13

9466 WANAMAKER RAILWAY LINES: 1982: wine-painted plastic body with gold-painted door and gold lettering. This car commemorated the Ives special Wanamaker cars of the early 1920s. At that time, Ives produced specially lettered cars for John Wanamaker, then and now the pre-eminent department store of Philadelphia. The moving force behind this new commemorative car was Nicholas Ladd, a long-time train enthusiast and senior Wanamaker store manager. The Eagle logo is original Wanamaker art adapted by Arthur Bink. The Wanamaker Railway Lines logo was copied from the original lettering on an authentic Ives Wanamaker car. Note that the Lionel artist intentionally made the "M" look like an "N" in the script. It is not a factory error. Lionel produced 2,500 of these cars. Interested Wanamaker employees bought 1,400 of them and another 1,000 were sold over the counter at a special train fair held at Wanamaker's Philadelphia store in conjunction with the car's release. The remaining 100 cars were retained by the store. — — 75 85

9467 WORLD'S FAIR: 1982, boxcar, white-painted white body, tuscan-painted roof and ends; black lettering, white doors, red, black and white World's Fair logo to left of door, Symington-Wayne trucks. Reportedly only

9432   9433

9434   9435

9436   9437

9438   9439

2,500 made for Ak-Sar-Ben Hobby Company of Nashville. C. Darasko and J. Vega Collections.   —   —   —   **35**

9468 UNION PACIFIC: 1983, double-door boxcar, tuscan body, yellow lettering, Standard 0 trucks; available only in 1361 Gold Coast Limited set. C. Rohlfing comment.   —   —   **40**   **50**

9469 NEW YORK CENTRAL: Scheduled for 1985 release, pacemaker Standard 0 boxcar, red and gray Pacemaker paint scheme; white lettering, Standard 0 trucks, black-painted catwalk.   —   —   —   **25**

9470 CHICAGO: 1984-85, green body, gold lettering and Great Lakes logo, Symington-Wayne trucks.   —   —   —   **12**

9471 ATLANTIC COAST LINE: 1984-85, tuscan body, white lettering, circular white Atlantic Coast Line logo, Symington-Wayne trucks.
   —   —   —   **12**

9472 DETROIT & MACKINAC: 1984-85, white roof and ends, white and red half-and-half sides and doors, white and red contrasting lettering, Symington-Wayne trucks.   —   —   —   **15**

9473 LEHIGH VALLEY: 1984-85, light green body, light green doors, white lettering, red LV flag on door panels, Symington-Wayne trucks.
   —   —   —   **15**

9474 ERIE-LACKAWANNA: 1984-85, boxcar, tuscan-painted body and doors, white lettering and logo, Standard 0 trucks; from Erie-Lackawanna Limited set.   —   —   —   **25**

9475 DELAWARE & HUDSON "I LOVE NEW YORK": 1984-85, unusual blue and white paint scheme with colors on sides and doors separated diagonally from upper left to lower right; large black serif "I", red heart and "N Y", white D&H shield logo and lettering, Standard 0 trucks. May be in demand by operators for unit trains.   —   —   **25**   **30**

9476 PENNSYLVANIA: 1984-85, tuscan-painted body and doors, white lettering, white and black PRR Keystone logo, gold FARR 5 diamond-shaped logo, Standard 0 trucks.   —   —   —   **25**

9480 MINNEAPOLIS, NORTHFIELD & SOUTHERN: Announced for 1985, dark blue body and doors; white lettering, red MNS logo, red and white diamond-shaped logo, Symington-Wayne trucks.   —   —   **14**

9481 SEABOARD SYSTEM: Announced for 1985, tuscan body and doors; white lettering, white interlocked "S" logo, Symington-Wayne trucks.
   —   —   —   **14**

9482 NORFOLK SOUTHERN: Announced for 1985, gray body and doors; black lettering, black and red "NS" logo, Symington-Wayne trucks.
   —   —   —   **14**

9483 MANUFACTURERS RAILWAY COMPANY: Announced for 1985, gray sides and doors, red lower side sills, black roof and ends; black lettering, black and gold logo, Symington-Wayne trucks.
   —   —   —   **14**

9484 LIONEL 85TH ANNIVERSARY: Announced for 1985, silver-gray body, black doors, black roof and ends; gold lettering, red, white and blue circular Lionel logo, black steam engine electrocal, Symington-Wayne trucks.   —   —   —   **20**

9600 CHESSIE: 1976, hi-cube, dark blue body; yellow lettering and door.
(A) Thin door stop.   **7**   **9**   **12**   **15**
(B) Thick door stop.   **7**   **9**   **12**   **15**

9601 ILLINOIS CENTRAL: 1976-77, hi-cube, orange body; black lettering and door.   **5**   **7**   **10**   **12**

9602 ATSF: 1977, hi-cube, red body; white lettering, 2 inch high emblem, silver door.   **5**   **7**   **10**   **12**
See also Factory Errors and Prototypes.

9603 PENN CENTRAL: 1976-77, hi-cube, green body; white lettering, silver door.   **5**   **7**   **10**   **12**

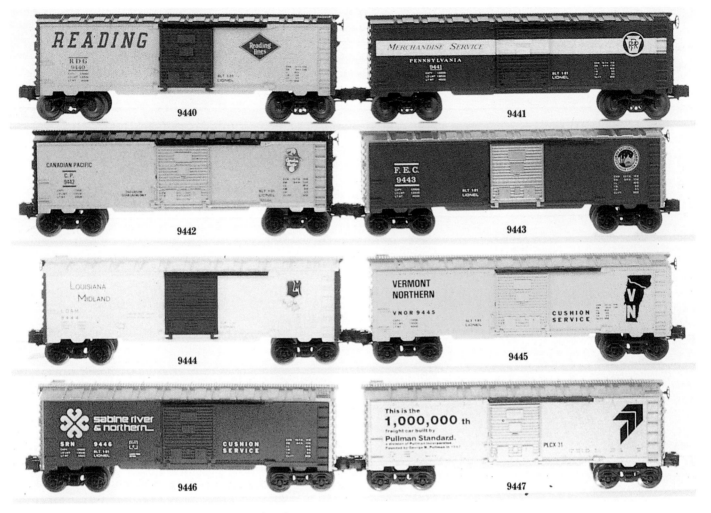

9440   9441

9442   9443

9444   9445

9446   9447

9604 NW: 1976-77, hi-cube, black body; white lettering, silver door.

            5   7   10   12

9605 NH: 1976-77, hi-cube, orange body; white lettering, black door.

            5   7   10   12

9606 UNION PACIFIC: 1976-77, hi-cube, yellow body; blue lettering, yellow door.

(A) Lighter yellow.   5   7   10   12

(B) Darker yellow.   5   7   10   12

9607 SP: 1976-77, hi-cube, red body, gray stripe arrow, gray roof, white letters.   5   8   11   13

9608 BURLINGTON NORTHERN: 1977, hi-cube, green body; white lettering.   5   7   10   12

9610 FRISCO: 1977, hi-cube, yellow body; black lettering, available only in Rocky Mountain set.   12   15   20   25

9611 TCA: 1978, "TWENTY FOURTH NATIONAL CONVENTION BOSTON MA", "Home of the Flying Yankee", light blue sides, black roof and ends, one brakewheel, white doors, white clearance boards on car ends, Symington-Wayne trucks, disc couplers with tabs. Some of these cars were repainted into the 1018-1979 Mortgage Burning Ceremony Car. See entry 1018-1979 for details of this interesting story.   —   25   30

9620 NHL WALES CONFERENCE: 1980, white car with different team symbols on each side, black doors, Symington-Wayne trucks.

            —   —   9   12

9621 NHL CAMPBELL CONFERENCE: 1980, white car with different team symbols on each side, Symington-Wayne trucks, opening doors.

            —   —   9   12

9622 NBA WESTERN CONFERENCE: 1980, white car with different team symbols on each side, Symington-Wayne trucks, opening doors.

            —   —   9   12

9623 NBA EASTERN CONFERENCE: 1980, white car with different team symbols on each side, Symington-Wayne trucks, opening doors.

            —   —   9   12

9624 NATIONAL LEAGUE: 1980, white car with different baseball team symbols on each side, Symington-Wayne trucks, opening doors.

            —   —   9   12

9625 AMERICAN LEAGUE: 1980, white car with different baseball team symbols on each side, Symington-Wayne trucks, opening doors.

            —   —   9   12

9626 ATSF: 1982-83, hi-cube, red with white lettering and door, Symington-Wayne trucks. This and the following entries differ from the earlier hi-cube boxcars mostly because they do not have the white-painted clearance warning on the car ends.   —   —   8   10

9627 UNION PACIFIC: 1982-83, hi-cube, yellow with red lettering, white door, Symington-Wayne trucks. J. Breslin Collection.   —   —   8   10

9628 BURLINGTON NORTHERN: 1982-83, hi-cube, green with white lettering and door, Symington-Wayne trucks.   —   —   8   10

9629 C&O: 1983, hi-cube, dark blue with yellow lettering and logo, Symington-Wayne trucks.   —   —   —   10

MICKEY MOUSE SET

NOTE: The Mickey Mouse set consists of cars 9660-9672 plus an 8773 U36B engine, 9183 caboose and the limited edition 9672 50th Anniversary car. Set price.   —   —   —   950

9660 MICKEY MOUSE: 1977-78, hi-cube, white body, yellow roof and ends.   8   10   12   15

9661 GOOFY: 1977-78, hi-cube, white body, red roof and ends.

            8   10   12   15

9662 DONALD DUCK: 1977-78, hi-cube, white body, green roof and ends.   8   10   12   15

8773

9183

9660

9661

9662

9663

9664

9665

9666

9667

9668

9669

9670

9671

9672

9448 | 9450
9449 | 9451
9452 | 9453
9454 | 9455

9663 DUMBO: 1978, hi-cube, white body, red roof and ends.

                                10   12   15   20

9664 CINDERELLA: 1978, hi-cube, white body, lavender roof and ends. C. Rohlfing comment.   10   12   15   20

9665 PETER PAN: 1978, hi-cube, white body, orange roof and ends.

                                10   12   15   20

9666 PINOCCHIO: 1978, hi-cube, white body, blue roof and ends.

                                35   40   50   60

9667 SNOW WHITE: 1978, hi-cube, white body, green roof and ends. By far the hardest car to find in the regularly issued series.

                    100 125 150 170

9668 PLUTO: 1978, hi-cube, white body, brown roof and ends.

                              30   45   55   65

9669 BAMBI: 1978, hi-cube, white body, lime green roof, ends and doors. C. Rohlfing comment.   10   12   15   20

9670 ALICE IN WONDERLAND: 1978, hi-cube, white body, jade green roof, ends and doors. C. Rohlfing comment. 10   12   15   20

9671 FANTASIA: 1978, hi-cube, white body, dark blue roof, ends and doors. C. Rohlfing comment.   10   12   15   20

9672 MICKEY MOUSE 50th ANNIVERSARY: 1978, hi-cube, white body, gold roof and ends, dull gold doors, limited edition. C. Rohlfing comment.   —   — 225 250

9678 TTOS: 1978, hi-cube, convention car, white plastic body painted white, red ends and roofs, red doors, lettered "Hurrah for Hollywood", symington-wayne trucks, two disc couplers with tabs, cars come with TTOS decal; convention attendees received a special decal showing Chaplin with "78" on his derby.

(A) Regular car.   —   —   30   40

(B) With Chaplin decal.   —   —   40   50

9700 SERIES BOXCARS

9700 SOUTHERN: Type IX body except for (A), red-painted red door, white lettering, Symington-Wayne trucks, Type I frame.

(A) SOO red-painted Type VI SOO red plastic body, metal door guides.   —   —   60   75

(B) Shiny red-painted shiny red body.   6   8   10   12

(C) Dark red-painted dark red body, green dot added by dealer. The prototype had green paint within the "O" of "SOUTHERN" to symbolize the railroad's motto, "Southern Gives A Green Light To Innovations". To make the car more realistic, dealers received sheets of stick-on green dots to place into the "O" of "Southern". C. Lang comment, R. LaVoie Collection.   6   8   10   12

(D) Same as (C), but no green dot.   6   8   10   12

See also Factory Errors and Prototypes.

9700-1976 TCA BICENTENNIAL CONVENTION CAR: 1976, unpainted white body, unpainted blue doors, red-painted roof and ends, Symington-Wayne trucks. Brown, black, white and gold eagle electrocal and TCA logo to left of door, TCA Philadelphia convention data to right of door.   —   —   —   45

9701 BALTIMORE & OHIO: Double-door automobile car with metal door guides, Symington-Wayne trucks. Different colored doors were added outside the factory; only the black doors are authentic factory production. However, since there is substantial collector interest in the door variations, we include them in this listing.

(A) Shiny black-painted black body, flat black-painted black doors, white lettering, Type I frame; 900 made.   30   40   60   70

(B) Same as (A), but white rubber-stamped "LCCA CONVENTION CAR". Many of these cars were faked later by rubber-stamping. R. Vagner comment.   —   —   75   85

(C) Same as (A), but only one built date. —   —   65   75

9460 9466 9467 9468 9470 9471 9473 9472

(D) Silver-painted gray plastic body, black-painted black doors, black lettering, Type II frame.   6   8   11   15

(E) Same as (D), but Type I frame.   6   8   11   15

NOTE: The following varieties have had doors installed outside the factory:

(F) Same as (D), but dark blue-painted dark blue doors.   6   8   11   15

(G) Same as (D), but medium blue-painted medium blue doors.   6   8   11   15

(H) Same as (D), but light blue-painted light blue doors, Type I frame.   6   8   11   15

(I) Same as (D), but green-painted 9209 Burlington Northern green doors, Type I frame. C. Lang Collection.   6   8   11   15

(J) Same as (D), but 9200 IC orange-painted orange doors. C. Lang Collection.   6   8   11   15

(K) Same as (D), but burnt orange-painted burnt orange doors.   6   8   11   15

(L) Same as (D), but silver-painted gray doors, Type I frame.   6   8   11   15

(M) Same as (D), but silver-painted gray doors.   6   8   11   15

(N) Same as (D), but dark Navy blue 9205 NW doors. C. Lang Collection.   6   8   11   15

(O) Same as (D), but dark red 9207 Soo doors. C. Lang Collection.   6   8   11   15

See also Factory Errors and Prototypes.

9702 SOO: White sides, black roof painted on white body, red-painted red door, black lettering, Symington-Wayne trucks

(A) Type VIII body, Type I frame.   6   8   10   12

(B) Type IX body, Type II frame.   8   10   12   15

9703 CP RAIL: Type IX body, black lettering, Symington-Wayne trucks

(A) Burnt orange-painted burnt-orange body, burnt orange-painted red doors, Type II frame.   30   40   55   65

(B) Light burnt orange-painted medium red body, medium red-painted red doors, Type I frame.   30   40   55   65

See also Factory Errors and Prototypes.

9704 NORFOLK & WESTERN: Type IX body except (A), white lettering except (C), Symington-Wayne trucks.

(A) Tuscan-painted Type VII maroon body, metal door guides, tuscan-painted maroon doors, Type I frame.   —   —   95   120

(B) Tuscan-painted tuscan body, tuscan-painted tuscan doors, Type II frame.   —   6   10   12

(C) Same as (B), but gray lettering.   —   6   10   12

(D) Same as (B), but Type I frame.   —   6   10   12

(E) Tuscan-painted gray body, tuscan-painted tuscan doors, Type I frame.   —   10   12   15

9705 DENVER & RIO GRANDE: Silver-painted gray plastic doors, black lettering, Symington-Wayne trucks.

(A) Dark orange-painted Type VIII orange plastic body, Type I frame, deep stamped lettering.   —   50   60   75

(B) Light orange-painted Type VIII orange plastic body, Type I frame.   —   10   12   15

(C) Dark orange-painted orange plastic body, Type I frame.   —   10   12   15

(D) Dark orange unpainted orange body, silver-painted gray doors; very deep stamped gloss black lettering, MPC logo, Symington-Wayne trucks, Type IX body, Type II frame, probably late production. La Voie Collection.   —   10   12   15

(E) Same as (C), but Type II frame. C. Rohlfing Collection.   —   10   12   15

9706 C&O: Type VIII body (A), Type IX body (B-C); yellow lettering, Symington-Wayne trucks.

(A) Blue-painted blue plastic body, yellow-painted yellow door, Type II frame.   —   8   10   12

9700   9701

9701   9702

9702   9703

9704   9704

R. Vagner Collection.

(B) Same as (A), but Type I frame.	6	8	10	12
(C) Same as (A), but blue-painted gray plastic body.	6	8	10	12

See also Factory Errors and Prototypes.

9707 MKT: Stock car, metal door guides, red-painted translucent plastic except (D); white lettering, Symington-Wayne trucks, 6356-19 frame.

(A) Light yellow-painted light yellow door, electrocal decoration.

     6   8   10   12

(B) Medium yellow-painted medium yellow door, rubber-stamped lettering.

     6   8   10   12

(C) Same as (B), but heat-stamped lettering.   6   8   10   12

(D) Dark red-painted red plastic, medium yellow-painted medium yellow doors. Reader confirmation requested.   **NRS**

(E) Flat red-painted red body, unpainted yellow doors, dull white rubber stamped lettering. LaVoie Collection.   8   10   12   15

(F) Same as (E), but yellow-painted yellow doors. Came as part of 1388 Golden State Arrow set. G. Halverson Collection.   8   10   12   15

9708 US MAIL: Type IX body, painted red plastic body except (J); white and black lettering, Symington-Wayne trucks, Type II frame, MPC logo on (A-D), no MPC logo on (E-J), painted red plastic door.

(A) Dark red and light blue-painted body, red-painted door.

     5   7   8   12

(B) Same as (A), but red and light blue-painted door.   5   7   8   12

(C) Dark red and medium blue-painted body, red and medium blue-painted door.   5   7   8   12

(D) Same as (C), but red and dark blue-painted door.   5   7   8   12

(E) Light red and dark blue-painted body, red and dark blue-painted doors, no MPC logo.   5   7   8   12

(F) Dark red and light blue-painted body, red and medium blue-painted door.   5   7   8   12

(G) Dark red and medium blue-painted body, red and medium blue-painted door.   5   7   8   12

(H) Dark red and medium blue-painted body, red and dark blue-painted door.   5   7   8   12

(I) Medium blue and dark red-painted gray body, red-painted door.

     —   —   —   400

(J) Gold overstamped "Toy Fair '73" in small oblong box at lower left end of each side. C. Lang Collection.   —   —   125   150

See also Factory Errors and Prototypes.

9709 BAR: 1973-74, Type VIII bodies: (A-)C; Type IX bodies: (D-H); Symington-Wayne trucks, Type II frame.

(A) Blue and dark red-painted gray body, blue and red-painted gray door; white lettering, printed one side only in white areas.   35   45   50   60

(B) Same as (A), but white and black lettering, printed white and black on both sides.   15   20   30   40

(C) Blue and dark red-painted gray body, red-painted red door, white and black lettering. Red doors added outside factory. R. Vagner comment.

     30   45   60   70

(D) Blue and dark red-painted gray body, blue and red-painted gray doors; printing on one side only in white area.   20   30   40   60

(E) Dark blue and medium red-painted blue body, blue and red-painted blue doors; white and black lettering.   15   20   30   40

(F) Medium blue and light red-painted medium blue body, dark blue and red painted red doors; white and black lettering.   15   20   30   40

(G) Blue and light red-painted gray body, blue and red-painted gray doors; white and black-painted lettering.   20   35   40   50

(H) Blue and red-painted blue body, dark blue and dark red-painted dark blue doors, Type IX body, Type II frame. C. Rohlfing Collection.

     20   35   40   50

See also Factory Errors and Prototypes.

9710 RUTLAND: 1973-74, Type VIII bodies: (A),(B) and (C); Type IX bodies: (D) to (G); yellow-painted yellow doors, green and yellow lettering, Type II frame.

(A) Medium yellow and green-painted gray body; shifted shield.

| | 12 | 15 | 20 | 25 |

(B) Light yellow and green-painted gray body; shifted shield.

| | 12 | 15 | 20 | 25 |

(C) Same as (B), but shield centered, "9710" not underscored.

| | 25 | 30 | 35 | 40 |

(D) Dark yellow and green-painted gray body; shifted shield.

| | 10 | 15 | 20 | 25 |

(E) Medium yellow and light green-painted green body; shifted shield, no "CAPY 100000".

| | 20 | 25 | 30 | 35 |

(F) Light yellow and light green-painted green body; shifted shield, "9200" on car end.

| | 20 | 25 | 30 | 35 |

(G) Dark yellow and green-painted gray body; shifted shield.

| | 10 | 15 | 20 | 25 |

9711 SOUTHERN: 1974, Type IX body, white lettering, Symington-Wayne trucks, Type II frame, "LIONEL" to the right of door, except (C).

(A) Tuscan-painted tuscan body, tuscan-painted white doors.

| | 10 | 12 | 15 | 20 |

(B) Same as (A), but tuscan-painted tuscan doors.

| | 10 | 12 | 15 | 20 |

(C) Same as (A), but tuscan-painted tuscan doors, "LIONEL" to the left of door.

| | 10 | 12 | 15 | 20 |

(D) Tuscan-painted translucent body, reported but not verified. **NRS**

9712 BALTIMORE & OHIO: 1973-74, double-door automobile car, metal door guides, blue-painted blue body, yellow-painted yellow door; yellow lettering, Symington-Wayne trucks, Type II frame. 9 12 15 20

9713 C P RAIL: 1973-74, Type IX body, green-painted green doors; black lettering, Symington-Wayne trucks, Type II frame.

(A) Green-painted green body.

| | 8 | 10 | 12 | 15 |

(B) Light green-painted green body.

| | 8 | 10 | 12 | 15 |

(C) Same as (A), but metallic gold overprinted, "SEASONS GREETINGS '74".

| | — | — | 125 | 150 |

(D) Green-painted clear body, reported but not verified. **NRS**

9714 RIO GRANDE: 1973-74, Type IX body, silver-painted, Symington-Wayne trucks, Type II frame.

(A) Silver-painted gray body, red-painted red doors; red lettering.

| | 8 | 10 | 12 | 15 |

(B) Same as (A), but silver-painted opaque body. 8 10 12 15

(C) Same as (A), but orange-painted orange doors; orange lettering.

| | — | — | — | 295 |

(D) Same as (A), but silver-painted translucent doors, dark orange lettering. — — — 280

9715 CHESAPEAKE & OHIO: 1973-74, Type IX body, Symington-Wayne trucks, Type II frame.

(A) Black-painted black body, yellow-painted yellow door.

| | 8 | 10 | 12 | 15 |

(B) Same as (A), but yellow-painted white door. 8 10 12 15

(C) Black-painted white body, light yellow-painted white door.

| | 8 | 10 | 12 | 15 |

(D) Same as (C), but dark yellow-painted white door. 8 10 12 15

9716 PENN CENTRAL: 1973-74, Type IX body, green-painted green body and green door, Symington-Wayne trucks, Type II frame.

| | 8 | 10 | 12 | 15 |

9717 UNION PACIFIC: 1973-74, Type IX body, black roof, yellow-painted yellow door; black lettering, Symington-Wayne trucks, Type II frame.

(A) Light yellow-painted yellow body. 10 12 15 20

(B) Medium yellow-painted yellow body. 10 12 15 20

9718 CANADIAN NATIONAL: 1973-74, Type IX body, white lettering, Symington-Wayne trucks, Type II frame.

(A) Tuscan-painted tuscan body, yellow-painted yellow door.

| | 8 | 10 | 12 | 15 |

(B) Tuscan-painted orange body, yellow-painted translucent door.

| | 12 | 15 | 20 | 25 |

(C) Same as (B), but yellow-painted yellow door. 12 15 20 25

(D) Tuscan red-painted tuscan red body, yellow-painted yellow door. **NRS**

9710	9711
9712	9713
9714	9714
9715	9716

(E) Tuscan red-painted gray body, yellow-painted yellow door. J. Breslin and P. Catalano comments.   —   —   —   **100**

9719 NEW HAVEN: Double-door boxcar, orange-painted orange body, black-painted black door, Symington-Wayne trucks, Type II frame, coupon car.

(A) Black and white lettering.   10   12   17   25

(B) Black overprinted on white lettering.   NRS

(C) White overprinted on black lettering.   NRS

9720 ASSORTED CASE OF CARS: NRS

9721 ASSORTED CASE OF CARS: NRS

9722: Not used

9723 WESTERN PACIFIC: 1974, Type IX plastic body, black lettering, Symington-Wayne trucks, Type II frame.

(A) Unpainted orange plastic body and doors.   15   20   25   30

(B) Same as (A), but gold overstamped "Toy Fair '74". C. Lang Collection.   50   75   100   125

(C) Fanta orange-painted orange body and orange doors.   30   35   40   45

(D) Fanta orange-painted orange body and white doors. Doors added outside factory. R. Vagner comment.   30   35   40   45

(E) Fanta orange-painted orange body, orange-painted translucent doors, Type IX body, Type II frame. C. Rohlfing Collection.   30   35   40   45

(F) Same as (A), but gold overstamp "SEASON'S GREETINGS 1974". C. Lang Collection.   —   —   125   150

9724 MISSOURI PACIFIC: 1974, Type IX plastic body, black and white lettering, Symington-Wayne trucks, Type II frame, silver-painted roof and side band.

(A) Medium blue-painted opaque-white body, yellow and silver-painted yellow doors.   25   30   35   40

(B) Same as (A), but medium blue-painted gray body.   25   30   35   40

(C) Dark blue-painted gray body, yellow and silver-painted yellow doors.   25   35   40   45

(D) Dark blue-painted navy body, yellow-painted yellow doors.   25   35   40   45

9725 MKT: 1974-75, double-door cattle car, "The Katy SERVES THE SOUTHWEST", black-painted black door, Symington-Wayne trucks, Type I frame.

(A) Light yellow-painted yellow body.   6   8   10   12

(B) Medium yellow-painted yellow body.   6   8   10   12

(C) Medium dark yellow-painted yellow body.   6   8   10   12

(D) Dark yellow-painted yellow body.   6   8   10   12

9726 ERIE LACKAWANNA: 1978, glossy blue-painted Type IX body, blue painted blue doors; white lettering, Type III frame, Standard 0 trucks, part of 1868 Minneapolis & St. Louis Service Station set.

(A) Shiny blue-painted blue body.   15   17   20   25

(B) Lighter shiny blue-painted blue body.   15   17   20   25

(C) Glossy Brunswick green-painted body and doors instead of blue. R. Vagner Collection.   NRS

9727 T.A.G.: Uncatalogued, Type IX body, white-lettered "TENNESSEE ALABAMA & GEORGIA" and "1973 LCC of A". Convention car, maroon-painted body, Symington-Wayne trucks, Type II frame.
    —   —   150   175

9728 UNION PACIFIC: Uncatalogued, stock car, yellow-painted yellow body, silver-painted roof and ends, unpainted yellow doors; red lettering, LCC of A 1978 Convention car, "LCCA" stamped on yellow rectangular plate in red which is glued to slats on right side of door, Type III box ends read "LCCA CONVENTION CAR", 6,000 made. C. Lang and R. LaVoie Collections.   —   —   25   30

9729 CP RAIL: Type IX body, Symington-Wayne trucks, black, white and red-painted black body, black-painted black door; white lettering, Type III

9717

9718

9719

9719

9723

9723

9724

9724

frame, from Great Plains set, some sets came with 9417 car identical except for number and gold lettering. C. Lang and C. Rohlfing comments.

	10	20	25	30

9730 CP RAIL: 1974-75, Type IX body, Symington-Wayne trucks, Type II frame, white-lettered (A) and (B), black-lettered (C) through (F).

White Lettering

(A) Silver-painted gray body, silver-painted gray door.	9	11	14	20
(B) Same as (A), but silver-painted white body.	9	11	14	20

Black Lettering

(C) Same as (A), but flat silver-painted white body.	11	14	20	25
(D) Same as (A), but silver-painted opaque door.	11	14	20	25
(E) Same as (A), but silver-painted white doors.	11	14	20	25
(F) Same as (A), but silver-painted yellow door.	11	14	20	25

9731 MILWAUKEE ROAD: 1974-75, Type IX body, white lettering, red door, Symington-Wayne trucks, Type II frame.

(A) Light red-painted red body.	6	8	10	12
(B) Medium red-painted red body.	6	8	10	12

(C) Red-painted red body, silver-painted roof, as shown in 1974 catalogue. Confirmation requested; doubtful this car was made this way. C. Lang comment. **NRS**

9732 SOUTHERN PACIFIC: 1979, black roof and silver sides on gray plastic Type IX body, black-painted black door, black and orange lettering, Standard 0 trucks, Type III frame, from Southern Pacific Limited set. T. Ladny comment. — — 30 40

9733 AIRCO: 1979, LCC of A National Convention car, a unique Lionel car in that inside there is a full-sized white molded unpainted tank with an orange-painted base. Blue tank lettering cannot be seen unless boxcar shell is removed from frame, leaving only the tank. The tank is secured to the boxcar frame by a screw through a crudely punched hole. This is essentially two cars in one. Tank car is numbered 97330. White boxcar and tank car bodies, light blue lettering, orange striping; 6,000 made. Reportedly, many

collectors have fitted the tank car body with a frame, trucks and trim pieces to make up a second Airco car. Reports state that a few of these cars are still available from the LCCA for its members. Price is for original configuration; add $5.00 if tank car has been fitted with trim, but be aware that these cars should not be purchased separately, though they are sometimes seen apart. C. Lang and R. LaVoie comments.

	—	—	35	40

9734 BANGOR & AROOSTOOK: Type IX body, red body, red doors, white lettering, Standard 0 trucks; from Quaker City Limited set of 1978. R. Vagner comment. 15 25 30 35

9735 GRAND TRUNK WESTERN: 1974-75, Type IX body, white lettering, Symington-Wayne trucks, Type II frame.

(A) Blue-painted blue body, blue-painted dark blue doors.

	6	8	10	12
(B) Same as (A), but blue-painted opaque body.	6	8	10	12

(C) Blue-painted opaque body, blue-painted white doors.

	6	8	10	12

9736: Not used.

9737 CENTRAL VERMONT: 1974-75, Type IX body, white lettering, Symington-Wayne trucks, Type II frame.

(A) Tuscan-painted tuscan body and tuscan doors.	6	8	10	12
(B) Same as (A), but tuscan-painted orange body and tuscan-painted white doors. Hard-to-find variation.	30	35	45	60

(C) Same as (B), but tuscan-painted tuscan body. R. LaVoie Collection..

	6	8	10	12

9738 ILLINOIS TERMINAL: 1982, Type IX body, yellow-painted sides and blue-painted roof, Standard 0 trucks; part of 1260 The Continental Limited set. — — 40 50

9739 RIO GRANDE: 1975, Type IX body, black lettering, Symington-Wayne trucks, Type II frame. Regular issues with stripe were also part of 1974 Rio Grande Service Station Special set. C. Lang comment.

9725

9726

9726

9727

9728

9729

9730

9730

(A) Dark yellow and silver-painted yellow body, silver-painted yellow doors, no stripe. Rare.   100 140 160 175

(B) Light yellow and silver-painted transparent white body, silver-painted gray doors. Rare.   100 140 160 175

(C) Medium dark yellow and silver-painted yellow body, same doors as (B), long stripe.   6 8 10 12

(D) Dark yellow and silver-painted yellow body, same doors as (B), long stripe.   6 8 10 12

(E) Medium yellow and silver-painted yellow body, same doors as (B), long stripe.   6 8 10 12

(F) Light yellow and light silver-painted yellow body, same doors as (B), long stripe.   6 8 10 12

(G) Same as (F), but silver-painted yellow doors.   6 8 10 12

(H) Dark yellow and silver-painted yellow body, same doors as (B), short stripe.   6 8 10 12

(I) Light yellow and silver-painted opaque body, silver-painted opaque doors, short stripe.   6 8 10 12

(J) Medium yellow and silver-painted opaque body, silver-painted opaque doors, long stripe.   6 8 10 12

(K) Same as (J), but silver-painted gray doors.   6 8 10 12

(L) Light yellow and light silver-painted opaque body, silver-painted opaque doors, long stripe.   6 8 10 12

(M) Medium yellow and silver-painted yellow body, silver-painted translucent doors, long stripe. R. LaVoie Collection.   6 8 10 12

(N) Similar to (H), but special edition made for 1978 L.C.C.A. Convention, long stripe, "L.C.C.A./THE LION ROARS" and heat-stamped lion logo in black to right of door. Reports conflict concerning number of cars produced. One report indicates that Fundimensions made fewer than 100 of these cars and donated them to the L.C.C.A. Breslin comment. However, another report states that many more were eventually produced. Bohn comment. Readers are asked to help resolve this conflict. Breslin Collection.   **NRS**

9740 CHESSIE: 1974-75, Type IX body, yellow-painted yellow doors, except (D) and (E), blue lettering, Symington-Wayne trucks, Type II frame

(A) Dark yellow-painted yellow body.   6 8 10 12

(B) Medium yellow-painted yellow body.   6 8 10 12

(C) Light yellow-painted yellow body.   6 8 10 12

(D) Light yellow-painted yellow body, yellow-painted white doors.   6 8 10 12

(E) Light yellow-painted opaque body, same doors as (D).   6 8 10 12

9741: Not used

9742 MINNEAPOLIS & ST LOUIS: Type IX body, metallic gold lettering, Symington-Wayne trucks, Type II frame, coupon car offered to purchasers of specially marked boxes of refrigerator or covered hopper cars. Two coupons and $5.00 would be sent to Lionel factory at Mt. Clemens. Other cars used for this marketing approach were the 9719 New Haven double-door boxcar and the 9511 Milwaukee "Minneapolis" passenger car. The cars could not be purchased on the open market. R. LaVoie comment.

(A) Green-painted green body and doors.   10 15 20 25

(B) Light green-painted green body, green-painted gray doors, metallic red overstamped "Seasons Greetings 1973" in gold. C. Lang Collection.   60 80 100 125

(C) Same as (B), but dark green-painted green body.   60 80 100 125

(D) Green-painted white body, green-painted gray doors.   10 15 20 25

(E) Same as (D), but green-painted white doors.   10 15 20 25

(F) Same as (A), but green-painted gray doors, Type IX body, Type II frame. C. Rohlfing Collection.   10 15 20 25

9743 SPRITE: Type IX body, Symington-Wayne trucks, Type II frame, dark green lettering. This car and the next two entries listed were part of an uncatalogued 1463 Coca-Cola switcher set in 1974. C. Lang comment.

(A) Light green-painted light green body, green-painted green door.   7 9 12 15

(B) Medium green-painted dark green body, doors same as (A).

| | 7 | 9 | 12 | 15 |

(C) Light green-painted white body, green-painted white doors.

| | 7 | 9 | 12 | 15 |

(D) Same as (C), but green-painted green doors. 7 9 12 15

(E) Medium green-painted white body, green-painted white doors, KMT overstamping "75th Anniversary". 7 9 12 15

(F) Medium green-painted medium green body, medium green-painted dark green doors. 7 9 12 15

9744 TAB: Type IX body, white lettering, Symington-Wayne trucks, Type II frame.

(A) Medium magenta-painted light red body, magenta-painted red doors.

| | 7 | 9 | 11 | 15 |

(B) Dark magenta-painted dark red body, magenta-painted red doors.

| | 7 | 9 | 11 | 15 |

(C) Medium magenta-painted white body, magenta-painted white doors.

| | 7 | 9 | 11 | 15 |

(D) Light magenta-painted white body, magenta-painted red doors.

| | 7 | 9 | 11 | 15 |

(E) Same as (D), but pink body painted light magenta, doors.

| | 7 | 9 | 11 | 15 |

(F) Dark magenta-painted white body, magenta-painted white doors, KMT overstamping "75th Anniversary". 7 9 11 15

9745 FANTA: Type IX body, black lettering, Symington-Wayne trucks, Type II frame.

(A) Light orange-painted orange body, orange-painted orange doors.

| | 7 | 9 | 11 | 15 |

(B) Flat medium orange-painted orange body, same doors as (A).

| | 7 | 9 | 11 | 15 |

(C) Shiny medium orange-painted orange body, same doors as (A).

| | 7 | 9 | 11 | 15 |

(D) Same body as (C), orange-painted white doors. 7 9 11 15

(E) Dark orange-painted orange body, same doors as (A). 7 9 11 15

(F) Light orange-painted white body, same doors as (A). 7 9 11 15

(G) Medium orange-painted white body, orange-painted white doors.

| | 7 | 9 | 11 | 15 |

(H) Medium orange-painted orange body, same doors as (A), KMT overstamping "75th Anniversary". 7 9 11 15

9746: Not used

9747 CHESSIE SYSTEM: 1975-76, double-door automobile car, blue-painted blue doors; yellow lettering, Symington-Wayne trucks, Type II frame:

(A) Flat blue-painted blue body. 5 7 10 14

(B) Slightly darker, shiny blue-painted blue body. 5 7 10 14

9748 CP RAIL: 1975-76, Type IX body, white lettering, Symington-Wayne trucks, Type II frame, medium blue-painted medium blue doors: (A) through (G), medium blue-painted white doors: (H) through (N).

A-G: Medium blue-painted medium blue doors.

(A) Dark blue-painted dark blue body.	6	8	10	12
(B) Medium blue-painted dark blue body.	6	8	10	12
(C) Medium light blue-painted dark blue body.	6	8	10	12
(D) Medium light blue-painted medium blue body.	6	8	10	12
(E) Dark light blue-painted medium blue body.	6	8	10	12
(F) Medium dark blue-painted medium blue body.	6	8	10	12
(G) Medium blue-painted medium blue body.	6	8	10	12

H-N: Medium blue-painted white doors

(H) Flat medium dark blue-painted medium blue body.	6	8	10	12
(I) Medium dark blue-painted medium blue body.	6	8	10	12
(J) Medium light blue-painted medium blue body.	6	8	10	12
(K) Medium light blue-painted white body.	6	8	10	12
(L) Medium dark blue-painted white body.	6	8	10	12
(M) Lightest blue-painted white body.	6	8	10	12
(N) Royal sides but lighter royal top on royal body.	6	8	10	12

9739   9739

9740   9742

9743   9744

9745   9747

(O) Royal-painted royal body, royal-painted royal doors. **6 8 10 12**

(P) Royal-painted medium blue body, royal-painted white doors. **6 8 10 12**

(Q) Royal-painted sides and medium blue top on medium blue body, light blue painted white doors. **6 8 10 12**

(R) Purple-painted medium blue body, purple-painted white doors. **6 8 10 12**

(S) Royal-painted light blue body, royal-painted royal doors. **6 8 10 12**

9749 PENN CENTRAL: 1975-76, Type IX body, white and red lettering, Symington-Wayne trucks, Type II frame

(A) Green-painted green body, green-painted gray doors. **6 8 10 12**

(B) Same as (A), but green-painted jade doors. **6 8 10 12**

(C) Same as (A), but green-painted lime green doors. **6 8 10 12**

(D) Slightly darker green-painted green body, green-painted gray doors. **6 8 10 12**

(E) Lightest green-painted white body, green-painted white doors. **6 8 10 12**

(F) Same as (A), but green-painted green doors. **6 8 10 12**

9750 DT&I: 1975-76, Type IX body, yellow lettering, Symington-Wayne trucks, Type II frame, glossy green body except (E).

(A) Medium green-painted dark green body, medium green-painted dark green doors. **5 6 8 10**

(B) Same as (A), but medium green-painted clear doors. **5 6 8 10**

(C) Medium green-painted light green body, medium green-painted dark green doors. **5 6 8 10**

(D) Medium green-painted white body, medium green-painted dark green doors. **5 6 8 10**

(E) Flat green-painted light green body, flat green-painted light green doors. **5 6 8 10**

(F) Light green-painted white body, medium green-painted dark green doors. **5 6 8 10**

(G) Same as (A), but large yellow square "RIDIN' THE RAILS" logo with picture of Johnny Cash to left of doors. The authenticity of this car has been questioned. F. Cordone Collection. **NRS**

9751 FRISCO: 1975-76, Type IX body, white lettering, Symington-Wayne trucks, Type II frame, red-painted red doors.

(A) Flat red-painted red body. **6 8 10 12**

(B) Shiny red-painted red body. **6 8 10 12**

9752 LOUISVILLE & NASHVILLE: 1975-76, Type IX body, yellow lettering, Symington-Wayne trucks, Type II frame.

(A) Light blue-painted royal blue body, medium blue-painted royal blue doors. **6 8 10 12**

(B) Medium blue-painted navy blue body, same doors as (A). **6 8 10 12**

(C) Light blue-painted royal blue body, medium blue-painted white doors. **6 8 10 12**

(D) Medium blue-painted navy blue body, same doors as (C). **6 8 10 12**

9753 MAINE CENTRAL: 1975-76, Type IX body, green lettering, Symington-Wayne trucks, Type II frame.

(A) Medium yellow-painted yellow body, dark yellow-painted yellow doors. **6 8 10 12**

(B) Light yellow-painted yellow body, light yellow-painted white doors. **6 8 10 12**

(C) Medium yellow-painted yellow body, same doors as (B). **6 8 10 12**

(D) Darker yellow-painted yellow body, medium yellow-painted white doors. **6 8 10 12**

(E) Light yellow-painted white body, same doors as (D). **6 8 10 12**

(F) With NETCA (New England Division, Train Collectors Association) imprint. **— — 20 25**

9754 NEW YORK CENTRAL: 1976-77, "Pacemaker FREIGHT SERVICE", Type IX body, white lettering, Symington-Wayne trucks, Type II frame, red-painted red doors. Essentially similar to postwar 6464-125. C. Lang comment.

(A) Light flat red-painted red body.	8	10	12	15
(B) Medium red-painted red body.	8	10	12	15
(C) Dark red-painted red body.	8	10	12	15
(D) With METCA (Metropolitan Division, Train Collectors Association) imprint.	—	—	20	25
(E) Same as (B), but Type III frame. LaVoie Collection.	8	10	12	15
(F) Same as (C), but Type III frame. C. Rohlfing Collection.	8	10	12	15

9755 UNION PACIFIC: 1975-76, Type IX body, white lettering, Symington-Wayne trucks, Type II frame.

(A) Tuscan-painted brown body, tuscan-painted brown doors.	6	8	12	15
(B) Tuscan-painted white body, tuscan-painted white doors.	6	8	12	15
(C) Tuscan-painted brown body, tuscan-painted white doors.	6	8	12	15

9757 CENTRAL OF GEORGIA: Type IX body, red lettering, Symington-Wayne trucks, Type II frame, tuscan car with large silver oval on side. Uncatalogued; came as part of dealers' year-end special package. See introduction for details.

(A) Tuscan-painted brown body, silver-painted gray doors, lightly speckled oval.	10	15	20	25
(B) Same as (A), but medium speckled oval.	10	15	20	25
(C) Same as (A), but shiny silver oval.	10	15	20	25
(D) Same as (A), but silver-painted clear doors, shiny silver oval.	10	15	20	25

(E) Same as (A), but silver-painted yellow doors, shiny silver oval.	10	15	20	25
(F) Tuscan-painted clear body, silver-painted yellow doors, shiny silver oval.	10	15	20	25

See also Factory Errors and Prototypes.

9758 ALASKA: 1976-77, Type IX body, lettering usually yellow, Symington-Wayne trucks, Type II frame, blue car with yellow stripe.

(A) Blue-painted dark blue body, blue-painted white doors.	10	12	15	20
(B) Same as (A), but blue-painted blue doors.	12	10	15	20
(C) Blue-painted medium blue body, blue-painted white doors.	10	12	15	20
(D) Blue-painted white body, blue-painted white doors.	10	12	15	20
(E) Same as (D), but white lettering, yellow stripe above lettering and logo. R. M. Caplan Collection.	—	—	325	350
(F) Blue-painted blue body, blue-painted blue doors, white lettering.	—	—	—	325

See also Factory Errors and Prototypes.

9759 PAUL REVERE: Type IX body, white sides, red-painted white plastic roof and ends, blue or dark blue-painted white plastic door, blue lettering, Symington-Wayne trucks, Type II frame. This and the next two entries were part of the Liberty Special uncatalogued set made in 1975-76. C. Rohlfing and C. Lang comments.

	10	12	15	20

9760 LIBERTY BELL: White Type IX body, dark blue-painted white roof and ends, red-painted red plastic door; blue lettering, Symington-Wayne trucks, Type II frame. C. Rohlfing comment.

	10	12	15	20

9761 GEORGE WASHINGTON: White Type IX body, red-painted white roof and ends, dark blue-painted white plastic door; blue lettering, Symington-Wayne trucks, Type II frame. C. Rohlfing comment.

	10	12	15	20

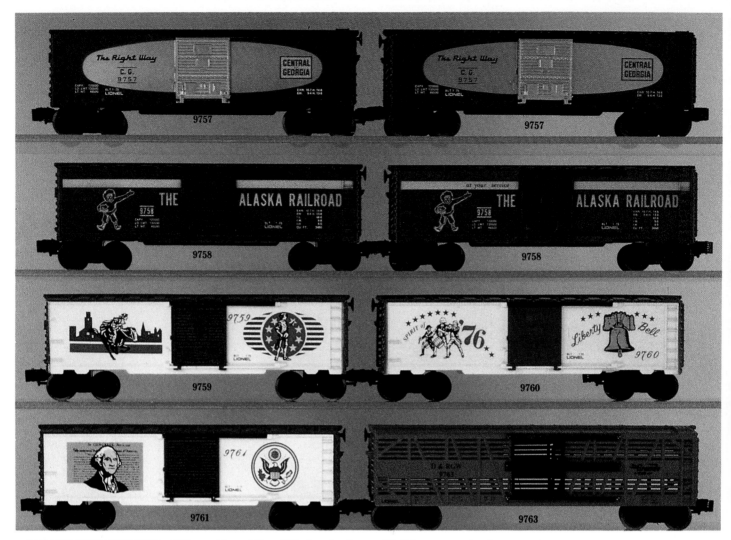

9757   9757

9758   9758

9759   9760

9761   9763

9762 WELCOME TOY FAIR: 1975, uncatalogued, Type IX body, red and silver painted white plastic body, red-painted red plastic door; metallic silver lettering, "9762" does not appear on car.   —   **75   100   125**

9763 RIO GRANDE: Stock car, orange-painted orange plastic body, black painted black plastic door; black lettering, Symington-Wayne trucks, Type I frame, metal door guides.
(A) Bright orange paint.   **6   8   10   12**
(B) Dull orange paint.   **6   8   10   12**

9764 GRAND TRUNK WESTERN: Double-door boxcar, blue-painted blue plastic body, blue-painted dark blue door; white lettering, Symington-Wayne trucks, Type II or III frame, all rivet detail missing.   **6   8   10   14**

9765: Not used

9766: Not used

9767 RAILBOX: Type IX body, yellow-painted yellow plastic body, black painted black plastic door; black lettering, Symington-Wayne trucks.
(A) Light yellow paint, Type III frame.   **6   8   10   12**
(B) Medium yellow paint, Type II frame.   **6   8   10   12**
(C) Dark yellow paint, Type II frame.   **6   8   10   12**

9768 BOSTON AND MAINE: 1976-77, Type IX body, black and white lettering, Symington-Wayne trucks, black-painted black doors.
(A) Glossy blue-painted gray body, Type II frame.   **6   8   10   12**
(B) Flat blue-painted gray body, Type III frame.   **6   8   10   12**
(C) Same as (B), but Type III frame, LaVoie Collection. **6   8   10   12**

9769 B.&L.E.: 1976-77, Type IX body, black and white lettering, Symington-Wayne trucks.
(A) Flat orange-painted orange body, orange-painted white doors, Type II frame.   **6   8   10   12**
(B) Shiny orange-painted orange body, orange-painted orange doors, Type III frame.   **6   8   10   12**

(C) Shiny orange-painted orange body, orange-painted white doors, Type III frame.   **6   8   10   12**
(D) Same as (C), but Type II frame.   **6   8   10   12**

9770 NORTHERN PACIFIC: 1976-77, Type IX body, orange-painted orange doors; white and black lettering, Symington-Wayne trucks.
(A) Glossy orange-painted orange body, Type II frame. **6   8   10   12**
(B) Flat orange-painted orange body, Type III frame. **6   8   10   12**
(C) Flat orange-painted opaque-white body, Type III frame.
                             6   8   10   12

9771 NORFOLK AND WESTERN: 1976-77, Type IX body, white lettering, Symington-Wayne trucks. This car was included as part of 1762 Wabash Cannonball steam engine freight set in 1977 as well as a separate sale item. C. Lang comment.
(A) Dark blue-painted blue body, dark blue-painted blue doors, Type III frame.   **4   6   8   10**
(B) Same as (A), but dark blue-painted gray body.   **4   6   8   10**
(C) Same as (A), but dark blue-painted white doors, Type II frame.
                             4   6   8   10
(D) Same as (A), but stamped "TCA Museum & National Headquarters" in silver at lower right of doors.   —   —   **20   25**

9772 GREAT NORTHERN: Type IX body, green and orange-painted green body, green and orange-painted green door; yellow and black lettering, Symington-Wayne trucks, Type III frame; part of 1665 Empire State Express set.   **20   25   30   35**

See also Factory Errors and Prototypes.

9773 NYC: Double-door stock car, black-painted black doors, black lettering, Symington-Wayne trucks, Type I frame; part of 1665 Empire State Express set. C. Lang comment.
(A) Light yellow-painted yellow body.   **12   15   20   25**
(B) Dark yellow-painted yellow body.   **12   15   20   25**

9764

9767

9768

9769

9770

9771

9772

9773

9774 THE SOUTHERN BELLE: 1975, uncatalogued, Type IX body, orange sides and silver roof and ends painted on orange body, green-painted white doors; green and black lettering, Symington-Wayne trucks, Type II frame, 1975 TCA National Convention car.   —   —   **25**   **30**

9775 MINNEAPOLIS & ST. LOUIS: Type IX body, uncatalogued, red-painted red doors; white lettering, Type II frame, Standard 0 trucks; from Service Station set.

(A) Light red-painted red body.   **12**   **15**   **20**   **25**
(B) Dark red-painted red body.   **12**   **15**   **20**   **25**

9776 SOUTHERN PACIFIC: Uncatalogued, Type IX body, black-painted body, black-painted black doors; white and gold lettering, Standard 0 trucks, Type II frame, from Northern Pacific Service Station set of 1976. C. Lang comment.

(A) Black-painted black body.   **15**   **20**   **25**   **30**
(B) Black-painted opaque-white body.   **NRS**

See also Factory Errors and Prototypes.

9777 VIRGINIAN: 1976-77, Type IX body, yellow lettering, Symington-Wayne trucks.

(A) Blue-painted light blue body, dark blue-painted dark blue doors, Type II frame.   **8**   **10**   **12**   **15**
(B) Blue-painted light blue body, light blue-painted light blue doors, Type III frame.   **8**   **10**   **12**   **15**
(C) Blue-painted medium blue body, light blue-painted light blue doors, Type III frame.   **8**   **10**   **12**   **15**
(D) Blue-painted light blue body, blue-painted white doors, Type II frame.   **8**   **10**   **12**   **15**

9778 SEASONS GREETINGS 1975: Uncatalogued, Type IX body, blue-painted blue body, silver-painted gray doors; silver lettering, Symington-Wayne trucks, Type II frame.   —   **100**   **150**   **180**

9779 TCA 9700-1976: Uncatalogued, Type IX body, red roof and ends, white sides painted on white body, blue-painted blue doors; Symington-

Wayne trucks, Type II frame, flying eagle electrocal to left of door, 1976 TCA National Convention car. **Note:** "Philadelphia" misspelled on all cars in production run as "PHILADEPHIA." C. Lang comment.
    —   **20**   **30**   **40**

9780 JOHNNY CASH: Uncatalogued, Type IX body, black roof, silver sides painted on gray body, black-painted black doors; black lettering, Symington-Wayne trucks, Type III frame.   —   **25**   **30**   **40**

9781 DELAWARE & HUDSON: 1977-78, Type IX body, yellow-painted yellow door, Symington-Wayne trucks, Type III frame.

(A) Light yellow-painted yellow body, blue lettering.   **6**   **8**   **10**   **12**
(B) Medium yellow-painted yellow body, dark blue lettering.
    6   **8**   **10**   **12**

9782 THE ROCK: 1977-78, Type IX body, white and black lettering, Symington-Wayne trucks, Type III frame.

(A) Blue-painted gray body, blue-painted gray doors.   **6**   **8**   **10**   **12**
(B) Blue-painted light blue body, blue-painted blue doors.
    6   **8**   **10**   **12**

9783 BALTIMORE & OHIO: 1977-78, Type IX body, blue sides and ends, silver roof painted on blue body, blue-painted blue doors; white and blue lettering, Symington-Wayne trucks, Type III frame, "Time Saver Service". Essentially similar to postwar 6464-400. C. Lang comment.
    6   **8**   **10**   **12**

9784 ATSF: 1977-78, Type IX body, red-painted red body and red doors; white lettering, flat black-painted roof and ends, Symington-Wayne trucks, Type III frame.   **8**   **10**   **12**   **15**

See also Factory Errors and Prototypes.

9785 CONRAIL: 1977-79, Type IX body, white lettering, Symington-Wayne trucks, Type III frame.

(A) Medium blue-painted blue body and doors.   **6**   **8**   **10**   **12**
(B) Same as (A), but overprinted "TCA MUSEUM EXPRESS", only 108 examples made. Pinta and Rohlfing observations.   **NRS**

9774	9775					

(C) Light blue-painted blue body and doors. This was not a normal paint variation, but an attempt by Fundimensions to correct the car's color. The sample paint chip sent by Conrail to Fundimensions was too dark to match the Conrail prototypes. This variety is much more scarce than the medium blue version. R. LaVoie comment, R. Vagner Collection.

           — — 30 35

9786 CHICAGO AND NORTHWESTERN: 1977-79, Type IX body, tuscan-painted tuscan doors; white lettering, Symington-Wayne trucks, Type III frame.

(A) Tuscan-painted gray body.   **4 6 8 10**

(B) Tuscan-painted tuscan body, stamped "TCA MUSEUM EXPRESS"; only 144 examples made. C. Rohlfing comment.   **NRS**

9787 CENTRAL OF NEW JERSEY: 1977-79, Type IX body, Brunswick green-painted green body and doors; metallic gold lettering, Symington-Wayne trucks, Type III frame.   **6 8 10 12**

9788 LEHIGH VALLEY: 1977-79, Type IX body, cream-painted cream body and doors; black lettering, Symington-Wayne trucks, Type III frame.

(A) Decal on door.   **6 8 10 12**

(B) No decal on door.   **6 8 10 12**

9789 PICKENS: Type IX body, blue-painted blue body and doors; white lettering, circular red, white and blue arrow logo, Symington-Wayne trucks, Type III frame, from Rocky Mountain Special set of 1977.

          10 15 25 30

9801-9809: STANDARD "0" SERIES

9801 BALTIMORE & OHIO: 1975, boxcar, gray mold, silver body.

(A) Light blue stripe.   **10 15 20 25**

(B) Dark blue stripe.   **10 15 20 25**

See also Factory Errors and Prototypes.

9802 MILLER HIGH LIFE: 1975, reefer, white mold, red lettering and logo.   **10 12 15 20**

See also Factory Errors and Prototypes.

9803 JOHNSON'S WAX: 1975, boxcar, red mold, black and white lettering.

(A) Painted red, white and dark blue. **10 12 15 20**

(B) Painted red, white, light blue.   **10 12 15 20**

9805 GRAND TRUNK: 1975, reefer, gray mold, silver paint; black lettering.   **15 20 25 30**

9806 ROCK ISLAND: 1975, boxcar, red mold, tuscan paint; white lettering.   **20 25 30 40**

9807 STROH'S BEER: 1975-76, reefer, red mold, red paint; gold and white lettering.   **40 50 60 70**

9808 UNION PACIFIC: 1975-76, boxcar.

(A) White mold painted dark yellow, yellow door mold painted light yellow.

         40 50 65 75

(B) Light yellow mold painted dark yellow, yellow door mold painted light yellow.   **40 50 65 75**

9809 CLARK: 1975-76, reefer, red mold, blue lettering.

(A) Medium red paint.   **10 12 15 20**

(B) Dark red paint.   **10 12 15 20**

9811 PACIFIC FRUIT EXPRESS: 1980, yellow-painted yellow plastic body, tuscan-painted tuscan plastic roof, yellow-painted yellow plastic doors; gold diamond FARR Series 2 logo, red, white and blue UP shield, blue SP logo, part of Famous American Railroad Series 2; available as separate sale only.   **— — 20 25**

9812 ARM & HAMMER: 1980, billboard reefer, yellow sides, red roof and ends, Symington-Wayne trucks, yellow and red electrocal.

         — — 10 12

9813 RUFFLES: 1980, billboard reefer, dark blue roof and ends, Symington-Wayne Trucks, red and blue electrocal.

(A) White sides   **— — 10 12**

(B) Light blue sides. Samson and Rogers Collections. **— — 10 12**

9814 PERRIER: 1980, water billboard reefer, dark Brunswick green sides,

9782

9783

9784

9784

9785

9785

9786

9787

light yellow ends and roof, Symington-Wayne trucks. "PERRIER" electrocal to right of door, mountain spring electrocal to left of door shows a Perrier bottle bubbling from beneath the earth. — — 20 25

See also Factory Errors and Prototypes.

9815 NEW YORK CENTRAL: Scheduled for 1985, Standard 0 refrigerator car, orange body, maroon roof, black catwalk; blue NYRB lettering, "Early Bird" logo, Standard 0 trucks. Price is estimated at introduction; actual retail may be higher. — — — 25

9816 BRACHS: 1980, billboard reefer, white sides, brown roof and ends, disc-operating couplers. — — 9 12

9817 BAZOOKA: 1980, billboard reefer, white sides, red and blue Bazooka electrocal, Symington-Wayne trucks.
(A) Red roof and ends. — — 10 12
(B) Orange roof and ends. C. Rohlfing Collection. — — 12 15

9818 WESTERN MARYLAND: 1980, reefer, orange-red sides, Standard 0 sprung die-cast trucks; part of 1070 Royal Limited set.
(A) Black roof, ends and lettering. — — 20 25
(B) Brown roof, ends and lettering. Griggs Collection. **NRS**

9819 WESTERN FRUIT EXPRESS: 1981, reefer, yellow sides and ends, Great Northern goat logo, FARR Series 3 logo, disc-operating couplers, part of Famous American Railroad Series 3, available as separate sale only.
— — 12 15

9825 SCHAEFER: 1976-77, reefer, white body, red lettering and roof, Standard 0 Series. 15 20 25 30

9826 P&LE: 1976-77, reefer, white lettering, Standard 0 Series.
(A) Flat green, first run, 500 manufactured. 40 50 60 70
(B) Shiny green. 15 20 30 40

9827 CUTTY SARK: 1984-85, favorite spirits reefer, yellow sides and doors, black roof and ends; black lettering, black and white sailing ship electrocal, Symington-Wayne trucks. — — — 15

9828 J&B: 1984-85, favorite spirits reefer, dark gold sides and doors, white roof and ends; red and black lettering, red, black and white herald electrocal, Symington-Wayne trucks. — — — 15

9829 DEWARS WHITE LABEL: 1984-85, favorite spirits reefer, white sides and doors, red roof and ends; dark red and black lettering, green and gold bagpiper electrocal, Symington-Wayne trucks. — — — 15

9830 JOHNNIE WALKER RED: 1984-85, favorite spirits reefer, 1984-85: yellow-gold sides and doors, tuscan roof and ends, dark red lettering, deep red rectangular logo with gold lettering, red, white and gold Johnnie Walker electrocal, Symington-Wayne trucks. — — — 15

9831 PEPSI COLA: 1982, reefer, white sides, light blue ends and roof; red, white and blue Pepsi electrocal, Symington-Wayne trucks.
— — 10 14

9832 CHEERIOS: 1982, reefer, yellow body; black lettering, black Cheerios electrocal, Symington-Wayne trucks. — — 10 14

9833 VLASIC: 1982, reefer, white sides, yellow roof and ends; black lettering, Symington-Wayne trucks. — — 10 14

9834 SOUTHERN COMFORT: 1983, Favorite Spirits reefer, white body, gold roof and ends; black lettering, black oval Southern mansion electrocal, Symington-Wayne trucks. C. Lang and C. Rohlfing comments.
— — — 15

9835 JIM BEAM: 1983, Favorite Spirits reefer, white sides, red roof and ends; white and black lettering, red, white and black logo to right of door, Symington-Wayne trucks. C. Lang and C. Rohlfing comments.
— — — 15

9836 OLD GRANDDAD: 1983, Favorite Spirits reefer: orange body, gold roof and ends, black-edged gold and brown lettering, orange, white and black electrocal to right of door, Symington-Wayne trucks. C. Lang and C. Rohlfing comments. — — — 15

9837 WILD TURKEY: 1983, Favorite Spirits reefer, light yellow body,

9813

9814

9818

9833

9834

9835

9836

9837

9854

9875

dark brown roof and ends; red, dark brown and white lettering, dark brown lettering and turkey electrocal to right of door, Symington-Wayne trucks. C. Rohlfing comment. — — — 15

9840 FLEISCHMANN'S GIN: Announced for 1985, favorite spirits reefer, light tan sides, brown roof and ends; dark blue and brown lettering, blue and gold eagle electrocal, Symington-Wayne trucks. — — — 16

9841 CALVERT GIN: Announced for 1985, favorite Spirits reefer, dark blue body, silver roof and ends; silver lettering, red and silver herald electrocal, Symington-Wayne trucks. — — — 16

9842 SEAGRAM'S GIN: Announced for 1985, favorite Spirits reefer, cream sides, black roof and ends; dark blue, red and gold lettering, blue and cream shield electrocal, Symington-Wayne trucks. — — — 16

9843 TANQUERAY GIN: Announced for 1985, favorite Spirits reefer, white sides, black roof and ends; dark red and black lettering, dark red and black circular electrocal, Symington-Wayne trucks. — — — 16

9849 LIONEL: 1983, bright orange refrigerator car with orange doors and blue roof; very large circular old-fashioned "LIONEL" logo in red, white and blue to the right of the door. Lionel "lion" electrocal to the left of the door. The number to the immediate right of the lion is portrayed as 5718 in the 1983 Collector Center brochure, but 9849 is the number of the production models. This car and others in this series may have been prompted by the unauthorized repainting and sale of Lionel rolling stock in

similar fashion by a small New England firm. Symington-Wayne trucks. R. LaVoie and C. Lang comments. — — 35 45

9800 SERIES REEFER BODY TYPES
By Donald J. Mitarotonda
Type I

Two metal door guides.
Two metal bars running underneath frame, secured in center by one Phillips-head screw.
Trucks secured to metal.
Doors, underneath the ladders on each side of the body, are wider than the ladders.
Roof has three ice hatches, third ice hatch in one corner.

Type II

Same as Type I, but doors underneath the ladders are the same width as the ladders, roof has two ice hatches in opposing corners.

Type III

Two plastic door guides.
No metal bars underneath frame.
Trucks secured to the frame with a plastic pin.
Doors underneath the ladders are the same width as the ladders.
Roof has two ice hatches in opposing corners.

9850 BUDWEISER: 1973-76
(A) Type I body, light red roof, white body and door, red and black lettering.

7	9	11	14

(B) Same as (A), but with medium red roof.

7	9	11	14

(C) Same as (A), but Type I body with dark red roof.

7	9	11	14

(D) Same as (A), but large period after "BEER CAR" at lower right.

9	11	15	20

(E) Same as (A), but Type II body.

7	9	11	14

9851 SCHLITZ: 1973-76
(A) Type I body, shiny brown roof, white body and door, brown lettering.

6	8	10	12

(B) Same as (A), but with Type II body with dull brown roof.

6	8	10	12

9852 MILLER: 1973-76
(A) Type I body, shiny brown roof, white body and door, black lettering.

4	5	6	8

(B) Same as (A), but with Type II body with dull brown roof.

4	5	6	8

(C) Same as (B), but Type III body. Confirmation requested. **NRS**

9853 CRACKER JACK
(A) Type I body, brown roof, light caramel body, dark caramel door; red and black lettering, with border around Cracker Jack.

15	20	25	35

(B) Same as (A), but with medium caramel body and door.

15	20	25	35

(C) Same as (B), but with no border. Reportedly, fewer than 50 made.

80	100	125	150

(D) Type I body, brown roof, white body and door, red and black lettering, with border, rare. **NRS**

(E) Same as (D), but circled "R" registration mark and without border.

5	7	10	14

(F) Same as (E), but red roof and ends.

5	7	10	14

(G) Same as (E), but no registration mark.

5	7	10	14

(H) Same as (E), but Type II body. Confirmation requested. **NRS**

9854 BABY RUTH: 1973-76
(A) Type I body, red roof, white body and door, red and blue lettering.

6	8	10	12

(B) Same as (A), but with no "R" registration mark.

8	10	12	14

(C) Same as (B), but with Type II body.

6	8	10	12

(D) Same as (A), but Type II body. C. Rohlfing Collection.

6	8	10	12

(E) Same as (A), but darker red roof and lettering.

6	8	10	12

9855 SWIFT: 1974-76
(A) Type I body, black roof, silver body and door, black lettering, "BLT 1-73".

6	8	10	12

(B) Same as (A), but with "BLT 1-7".

15	20	30	40

(C) Same as (A), but Type II body.

6	8	10	12

(D) Same as (A), but Type III body. Confirmation requested. **NRS**

9856 OLD MILWAUKEE: 1974-76
(A) Type II body, gold roof, red body and door; white and black lettering.

8	10	12	15

(B) Same as (A), but Type III body. Confirmation requested. **NRS**

9858 BUTTERFINGER: 1973-76
(A) Type I body, flat blue roof, orange body and door; white and black lettering.

6	8	10	12

(B) Same as (A), but with blue gloss roof.

6	8	10	12

(C) Same as (B), but Type II body.

6	8	10	12

(D) Same as (B), but Type III body. Confirmation requested. **NRS**

9859 PABST: 1974-75

(A) Type I body, medium blue roof, white body and door; blue and red lettering.   6   8   10   12

(B) Same as (A), but with Type II body.   6   8   10   12

(C) Same as (A), but gloss blue roof. Roof could be switched from 9858, so existence of this version from factory is questionable. Confirmation requested.   **NRS**

9860 GOLD MEDAL: 1973-76

(A) Type I body, bright orange roof, white body and door, black lettering. This is reportedly the version found in separate sale boxes.
    6   8   10   12

(B) Same as (A), but dull dark orange. This version was probably produced for the 1974 Grand National set. It may also have been sold separately; reader comments requested.   6   8   10   12

(C) Same as (A), but Type II body.   6   8   10   12

(D) Same as (A), but Type III body. Confirmation requested.   **NRS**

9861 TROPICANA: 1975-77

(A) Type II body, flat green roof, white body and door; green and orange lettering. Only available in set 1560 North American set. C. Lang comment.   12   15   25   30

(B) Same as (A), but with Type III body, shiny green roof, opaque-white body and door.   6   8   10   12

(C) Type III body, translucent white body and roof; green and orange lettering.   6   8   10   12

9862 HAMMS: White roof, blue body and door; red and white lettering.

(A) Type II body.   10   12   15   20

(B) Type III body. Confirmation requested.   **NRS**

9863 RAILWAY EXPRESS AGENCY:

(A) Type II body, green roof, green body and door, gold lettering, no electrocals (rubber-stamped).   15   20   25   30

(B) Same as (A), but with electrocals.   10   15   20   25

(C) Same as (B), light green roof, with electrocals (gray mold).   10   15   20   25

(D) Same as (C), but with Type III body and green roof.   10   15   20   25

9864 TCA: 1974 Convention Car, 9800-series reefer construction, Type II body with metal door guides and channel, Symington-Wayne trucks. White body with medium royal blue roof, ends and doors, black, red and blue Seattle World's Fair Space Needle Tower logo at left of door; "1954-1974" in red and TCA logo in black above large blue "20" at right of door.
    —   —   30   35

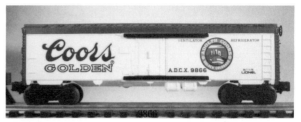

9866 COORS:

(A) Type III body, brown roof, white body and doors; black and dark yellow lettering, no "R" registration mark.   10   12   15   20

(B) Same as (A), but has low "R" registration mark.   12   15   20   25

(C) Same as (A), but with high "R" registration mark.   10   12   15   20

(D) Same as (B), low "R" registration mark touching the "S" in "COORS" logo. Hard to find.   30   40   50   60

9867 HERSHEY'S: Type III body, silver roof, chocolate brown body and door, silver lettering.   10   12   15   20

9868 TTOS: 1980, national convention car, 9800-style reefer, yellow body, dark blue roof and ends. Further details requested. C. Rohlfing comment.
    NRS

9869 SANTA FE: Type III body, brown roof, white body, brown door, black lettering, Standard 0 trucks. Part of 1672 Northern Pacific Service Station Special set in 1976. C. Lang comment.   15   20   30   35

9870 OLD DUTCH CLEANSER: Type III body, red roof, yellow body, red door; white and black lettering, red, black, yellow and white Old Dutch cleaning lady electrocal.   6   8   10   12

9871 CARLING BLACK LABEL: Type III body, black roof, dark red body and door; white, gold and black lettering and electrocal.

           6   8   10   12

9872 PACIFIC FRUIT EXPRESS: 1978-79:
(A) Type III body, silver roof, orange body and door, black and white lettering.   **6   8   10   12**
(B) Same as (A), but overstamped "MIDWEST DIV. TCA 1979"; only 300 examples made. C. Rohlfing comment.   **NRS**

9873 RALSTON PURINA: 1978-79, Type III reefer, blue plastic ends and roof painted blue, white plastic sides painted white; elaborate Ralston-Purina electrocal in red, white and blue on car side states "Car used 1945-64", Symington-Wayne trucks.   **6   8   10   12**

9874 LITE: 1978-79, (Miller Lite), Type III reefer, blue plastic roof painted blue, white plastic sides painted white, white doors painted gold; gold and blue electrocal, dark blue "LITE", Symington-Wayne trucks.

           6   8   10   12

9875 A&P: 1979, Type III reefer, brown-painted roof, mustard-painted sides; red and black A&P electrocal, Symington-Wayne trucks.

           6   8   10   12

9876 CENTRAL VERMONT: 1978, Type III reefer, black plastic roof painted black, gray sides painted silver; green lettering, silver door, Standard 0 trucks, part of 1867 Milwaukee Special freight set. C. Lang comment.   **—   —   20   25**

9877 GERBER: 1979, Type III reefer, dark blue-painted roof and ends, medium blue-painted sides; famous baby shown on black and white electrocal, white lettering. C. Rohlfing comment. **6   8   10   12**

9878 GOOD AND PLENTY: 1979, Type III reefer, magenta-painted roof, white painted sides, Good and Plenty box electrocal. **6   8   10   12**

9879 KRAFT PHILADELPHIA CREAM CHEESE: Originally shown in 1979 advance catalogue with gray sides, dark blue roof and ends; blue and white Kraft Philadelphia Cream Cheese electrocal. After the prototype, now in the Fundimensions archives, was made up, the Kraft Company withdrew

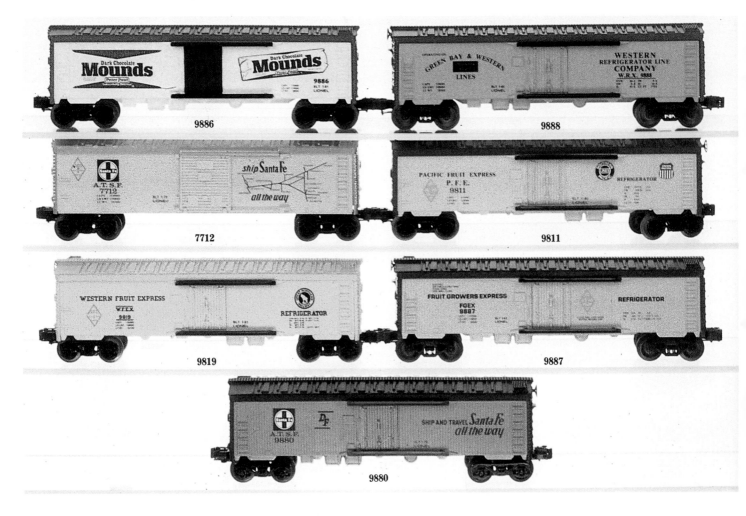

9886   9888

7712   9811

9819   9887

9880

its permission to use the name and logo, and the number was reassigned to the next entry. **Not Manufactured**

9879 HILLS BROS: 1979, Type III reefer, yellow-painted roof and ends, red-painted sides, coffee can electrocal.   6   8   10   12

9880 SANTA FE: 1979, Type III reefer, tuscan-painted roof and ends, orange-painted sides; black cross logo and "SHIP AND TRAVEL SANTA FE ALL THE WAY", gold diamond-shaped FARR 1 logo, from Famous American Railroad series 1.   20   25   30   35

9881 RATH PACKING: 1979, billboard reefer, yellow sides, tuscan roof and ends, black; yellow and white Rath electrocal, Standard 0 trucks; available only as part of 1970 Southern Pacific Limited set.
   —   —   25   35

9882 NYRB: 1979, (New York Central reefer), Type III reefer, tuscan painted roof and ends, orange-painted sides; Early Bird Service electrocal, black lettering, Standard 0 trucks; from Quaker City Limited set.
   —   20   25   30

9883 NABISCO: 1979, Type III reefer, blue-painted roof, gray-painted sides; Oreo cookie package electrocal.   10   12   15   20

9884 FRITOS: 1982, Type III reefer, yellow-orange sides, red roof and ends, dark red doors; Fritos logo electrocal, Symington-Wayne trucks. C. Rohlfing comment.   —   8   10   12

9885 LIPTON 100 TEA BAGS: 1981, Type III reefer, deep red and yellow sides, dark brown roof and ends, Symington-Wayne trucks. C. Rohlfing comment.   —   8   10   12

9886 MOUNDS: 1981, Type III reefer, white sides, red roof and ends, brown-maroon doors, Mounds package electrocal. C. Rohlfing comment.
   —   8   10   12

9887 FRUIT GROWERS EXPRESS: 1983, Type III reefer, yellow sides, dark green roof and ends, St!.dard 0 trucks, FARR 4 gold diam-nd logo, FARR Series 4, car sold separately. Caponi comment.   —   —   20   25

9888 GREEN BAY & WESTERN: 1983, Type III reefer, gray sides, dark red roof and ends; black lettering, Standard 0 trucks, only sold as part of 1361 Gold Coast Limited set. Catalogue showed car with white sides. Caponi comment.   —   —   30   40

More information needed on the numbers of the following cars:
SEASON'S GREETINGS: 1975, 9700-style boxcar, silver-gray body, black roof and ends, red and black 75th Anniversary circle electrocal to right of door. C. Lang comment.   **NRS**

SEARS: 1985, short 027 boxcar, white body, green and black "SEARS/ NEW CENTURY" to right of door and black "CENTENNIAL/ CELEBRATION/1886-1986" to left of door, black lower stripe, Symington-Wayne trucks. Part of Sears set, catalogue number 95339C, identical to Chessie System set 1402, except that this car replaces short stock car.   **NRS**

5717   5719

Chapter V
CABOOSES

It is ironic that Fundimensions is producing the best cabooses ever seen in tinplate just as these cars are being phased out on real railroads across the nation. The caboose is a car steeped in nostalgia. Who of us hasn't seen a picture of a train crew enjoying breakfast cooked over a coal stove in one of these waycars? For most of us, a freight train without a caboose is unthinkable. However, the caboose complicates switching assignments, and its need has been considerably lessened by detachable signal devices for the last car on the train and the commodious, air-conditioned cabs of the modern diesel locomotives. Real railroaders do not feel quite as romantically attached to the caboose; veterans of the rails would be quick to tell you that these cars were not all cozy little houses on rails. Unless the caboose was quite modern, it was drafty in winter despite the heat of the coal stove and, in summer, somewhere west of the Eternal Inferno. Thus, cabooses are becoming highly specialized or nonexistent in today's railroading.

This is not to deny that real railroading lacks the color and romance we ascribe to it — far from it. As an example of the unexpected influence of railroading in our lives, consider the streetcars of Brooklyn in the 1890s. The motormen who ran these cars had no idea of the potential power of electric traction since they had learned their trade with horse-drawn cars. As a result, they were extremely reckless drivers who endangered pedestrians every day.

The local baseball team's players had to cross the streetcar tracks to get to their ball field, and several team members had close shaves with these trolleys. As a result, their team eventually became known as the Brooklyn Dodgers! The name remains today, long after the cars have gone. (This and other transportation stories of interest can be found in George Gipe's **The Last Time When:** (New York: World Almanac Publications, 1981.))

Tinplate railroading, however, demands cabooses for its trains, romantic or not, and Fundimensions has responded with a fine variety of these cars. Some are modeled after their prewar predecessors, like the N5C porthole caboose, while others, such as the magnificent extended vision cabooses, are unique to Fundimensions.

THE SOUTHERN PACIFIC SQUARE-CUPOLA CABOOSES

The square-cupola Southern Pacific caboose has been produced from the first year of 1970; this is fitting, since this caboose was the mainstay of postwar production. The Fundimensions version of the SP caboose has a new plastic undercarriage which snaps onto the cab.

Most of the SP cabooses have been used for inexpensive sets and have been unlighted, but a few of these, such as the 9166 Rio Grande and the 9178 Illinois Central Gulf, are lighted and have translucent white plastic window inserts. These "deluxe" SP cabooses are mostly to be found in early collector sets from the mid-1970s. Some, like the 9172 Penn Central and the 9173 Jersey Central, were offered for separate sale. Recent production of these cabooses in traditional sets has featured "glow-in-the-dark" window inserts.

The most desirable of the SP cabooses are the ones from the sets, but no SP caboose produced by Fundimensions can be considered truly rare. Some of the earliest unlighted SP cabooses marketed for Canadian production are in fact very difficult to find, but collectors have not shown too much interest in them — yet.

THE N5C PORTHOLE CABOOSES

The N5C Porthole caboose has been one of the mainstays of Fundimensions production, along with the bay window caboose. In real life, this caboose type was used only by the Pennsylvania Railroad, but that hasn't stopped Fundimensions from issuing this caboose in dozens of railroad names and colors. Since all these cabooses are lighted and the design is very attractive, it's no wonder that they are so plentiful. Production of the N5C has languished in recent years in favor of the bay window cabooses and the new extended vision cabooses, but in 1985 a new Pennsylvania porthole caboose was issued with the set of cars intended for the new 6-8-6 steam turbine locomotive. This particular example is unique to the N5C line because it uses 027 die-cast passenger trucks instead of the usual Symington-Wayne plastic trucks. (Of course, the caboose would look better with Standard "O" trucks, but these trucks cannot be adapted for a light roller pickup.)

The first of the N5C cabooses was the 9160 Illinois Central of 1970. Early production used AAR trucks with old postwar wheel sets, but these quickly changed to Symington-Wayne trucks and fast-angle wheels. Canadian National, Pennsylvania and Santa Fe models were quick to follow, and in subsequent years these cabooses were produced in a considerable variety of road names. Special issues accompanied the Bicentennial, 75th Anniversary and Disney sets, while others were made to match the available diesel locomotives in the Fundimensions line.

In all, about 25 of these cabooses have been produced in one guise or another. Their availability is highly variable today. Even some of the regular issues have become hard to find, and the cabooses from the sets only turn up occasionally. The most difficult to find seems to be the red 9165 Canadian Pacific, which was only found in a Service Station set. Many others, such as the 9161 CP Rail, are quite common. These little high-quality cabooses are bright additions to the beginning collector's rolling stock. In recent years, they have fallen under the shadow of the bay window and extended vision cabooses, so they are usually available at good prices.

THE BAY WINDOW CABOOSES

Lionel's postwar model of the Bay Window caboose was issued in only two regular production varieties, but when Fundimensions revived this handsome car, the firm produced a considerable number and variety of them. The first Fundimensions bay window caboose came as part of the Empire State Express set of 1976 in green New York Central markings. The original intent of Fundimensions was to limit this caboose to special sets, but the demand for the caboose became so acute that it soon entered regular cataloguing and production.

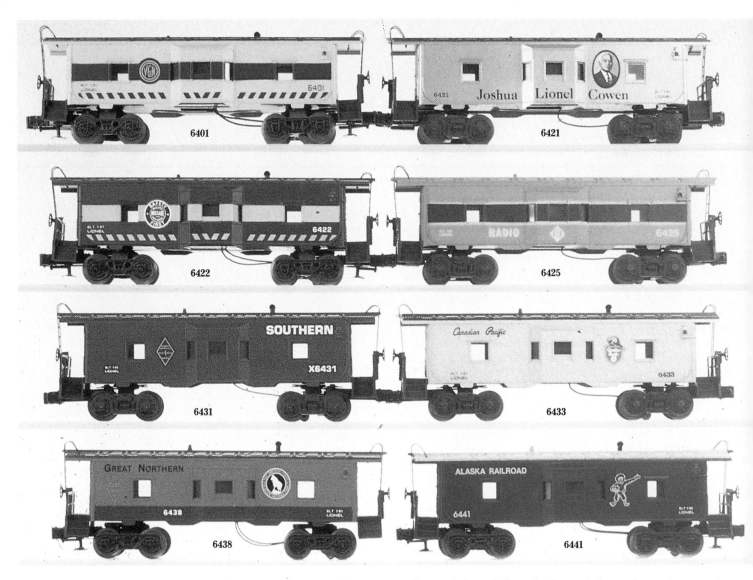

6401　6421

6422　6425

6431　6433

6438　6441

Two examples of the bay window cabooses illustrate collector insistence upon matching locomotives and cabooses, no matter what the practice on the prototype railroad. In 1976, Fundimensions issued the Northern Pacific Service Station Special set with a black and gold Northern Pacific GP-9 locomotive and a green, silver and yellow Northern Pacific Bay Window caboose, true to the prototype. Collectors didn't like the fact that the caboose wasn't a color match for the locomotive, so the company issued a black and gold Northern Pacific bay window caboose which did match the GP-9. Where the New York Central caboose had Symington-Wayne plastic trucks with long coupler extensions, both Northern Pacific cabooses had die-cast 027 passenger trucks. Since then, the bay window cabooses have come with both types of trucks.

Two years later, in 1978, history repeated itself. Fundimensions produced a magnificent Santa Fe SD-18 six-wheeled locomotive in blue and yellow freight colors. The bay window caboose meant to accompany this locomotive was made in red and black colors, just as the real railroad issued them. Once more, collectors howled that the caboose didn't match the engines, so Fundimensions ceased making the 9274 red and black model in favor of a 9317 Santa Fe Bay Window caboose in blue and yellow colors. This means, of course, that the red and black caboose has become a real collector's item; reportedly, fewer than 3,000 were made.

It wasn't long before the bay window caboose became the dominant caboose of the Fundimensions lineup. Beginning in the late 1970s and through the current years, several new issues have turned up in every catalogue and other new ones have been used in limited edition sets. About 35 of these cabooses have been produced since their introduction in 1976 — an average of almost four new ones per year!

The reasons for the popularity of the bay window caboose are not hard to understand. The construction of this caboose is excellent. It retains the stamped metal frame of the postwar cabooses, and its metal ladder trim adds an authentic touch. The lighting system is a little curious, but it is effective. Clear plastic rods reach from the light bulb to the little red marker lights on the rear of the caboose, providing a fiber-optic pathway for the illumination. The windows in the central bay are shaded by black paper so that the clear plastic windows on the caboose sides receive most of the light. The light bulb on this caboose and many other pieces of Fundimensions rolling stock and locomotives is a 12-volt plug-in clear lamp used in quite a few automotive applications. (Lamps designed for Chrysler Corporation side marker, instrument panel and turn signal lights are exact duplicates of the Fundimensions light bulbs.) All versions of these cabooses have two operating couplers, whether the trucks are plastic or die-cast.

Many of the bay window cabooses are common enough for

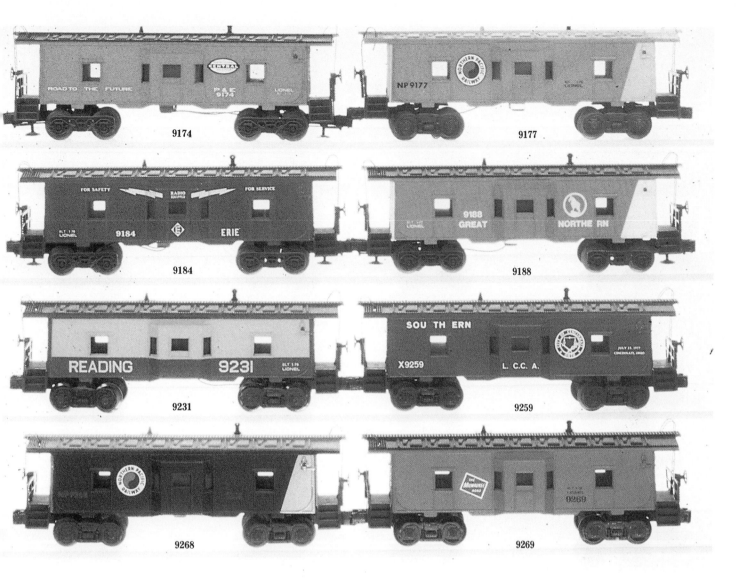

9174

9177

9184

9188

9231

9259

9268

9269

the beginning collector to acquire a fair-sized collection. On the other hand, several of the bay window cabooses offered only in sets are very hard to acquire. The toughest ones to get are probably the 9174 New York Central P&E from the Empire State Express set, the X9259 Southern issued for the 1977 LCCA Convention, the 9274 Santa Fe in red and black and the 9316 Southern Pacific in silver and black.

THE FUNDIMENSIONS EXTENDED VISION CABOOSES

In 1982, Fundimensions issued a fine collector train set in Norfolk and Western markings known as the Continental Limited. The handsome maroon SD-24 six-wheeled locomotive had an electronic horn, and the rolling stock was all of very high quality. However, the real surprise was reserved for the caboose, which was unlike anything ever seen in tinplate. The Extended Vision caboose is a large, scale-length square-cupola caboose which on the real railroad illustrates the state of the art in caboose construction. Many collectors regard this caboose as the finest tinplate caboose ever produced. The extended vision cabooses produced to date have all been limited edition items.

The Fundimensions extended vision caboose has a stamped metal frame with a black plastic battery box and brake cylinder piece attaching to the frame by means of a black plastic channel. All of these cabooses are equipped with 027 passenger-style die-cast trucks with two operating couplers. The sides, ends and roof are molded in one piece with a large

hole in the roof. A separately molded cupola piece is snapped onto the roof atop this hole; it is secured by projections in the body shell on the sides. Sometimes this separate cupola piece can lead to problems. On the 6905 Nickel Plate Road caboose, the lettering "Nickel Plate High Speed Service" goes across the top of the sides in such a way that one of the words is on the cupola. If the cupola is snapped onto the body in reverse, the sides will read "Nickel Speed High Speed Service" and "Nickel Plate High Plate Service". This is not a factory error — just an incorrectly installed cupola.

The sides of the extended vision cabooses are absolutely smooth except for molded grab-rails near the platform, two large square windows per side and molded signal lamps at both ends. Inside the car, four clear plastic rods lead to the signal lamps for brighter illumination, and all the windows on the sides and on the cupola are lighted as well. Plastic snap-in end railing pieces and a tall plastic chimney complete the decor of the caboose — or do they? Some of these cabooses have been produced with slots cut into the ends of the roofs so that metal trim ladders can be attached as they are on the bay window cabooses. However, the extended vision cabooses have no roof catwalks! The 6900 Norfolk and Western and the 6901 Ontario Northland cabooses do not have these ladders, but the 6903 Santa Fe does. In some cases the caboose is pictured in the catalogues without the ladders, but the production pieces have them. In other cases the reverse is true. These now-you-see-

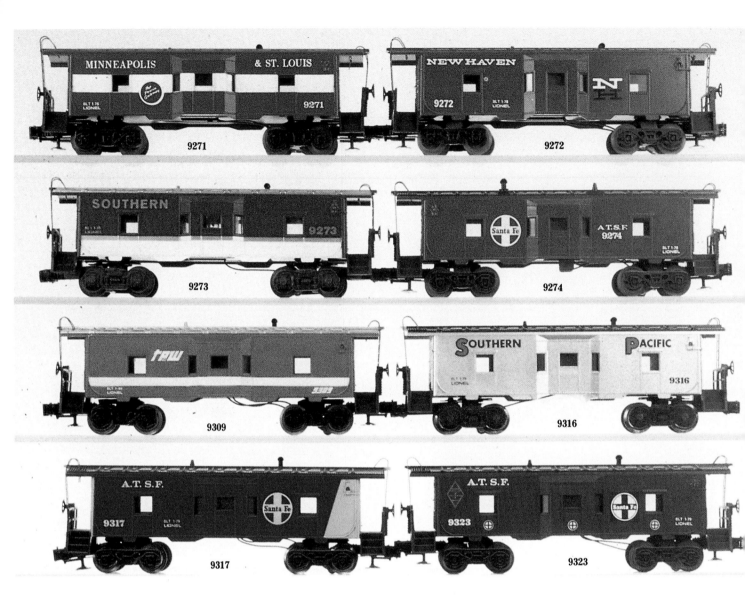

9271   9272

9273   9274

9309   9316

9317   9323

them, now-you-don't ladders could make for some interesting variations. (We would like to hear from our readers about whether their samples have the ladders or not. It is quite possible that some pieces were made both ways!)

Because of their handsome scale appearance and high demand, most of the extended vision cabooses command substantial price premiums. The one exception seems to be the 6901 Ontario Northland caboose, which has not been in much demand. The 6910 New York Central Pacemaker Extended Vision caboose might become the most scarce of these cabooses because of extreme demand from scale Hudson, New York Central F-3 and New York Central GP-9 owners. The 6903 Santa Fe is also appreciating very rapidly.

These cabooses are also magnificent matches for the new SD-40 scale diesels. Besides the Norfolk and Western, Ontario Northland, Nickel Plate, Santa Fe and New York Central examples, extended vision cabooses in Union Pacific and Erie-Lackawanna colors have been made, and a Burlington Northern one is scheduled for 1985 production.

SOME OTHER FUNDIMENSIONS CABOOSES

Besides those mentioned above, there are three other styles of Fundimensions cabooses, two of them particular to Fundimensions alone. Several work cabooses have been issued

for the Fundimensions traditional series ever since the first years of the company, beginning with the 9021 Santa Fe in 1970. This little caboose featured a "convertible" cab which could be taken off so that the car could be used as a simple flatcar. This example was followed by a similar D.T.&I. model in 1971 and a Soo Line work caboose in 1975. Other work cabooses have been made for the Trains and Trucking and Working on the Railroad sets of 1977 and 1978, but by and large these cabooses have been supplanted by the newer center-cab maintenance caboose. One example, the 6916 New York Central, is planned for 1985 production as part of a steam switcher work train; this piece will have some of the deluxe trim items lacking on previous production. None of these cabooses attracts much attention, except for a few early varieties of the 9021 Santa Fe.

The four-wheeled bobber caboose was first made for the Kickapoo Valley and Northern set of 1972. It is an all plastic car completely new with Fundimensions production. Although it looks small and it has been used only on lower-priced sets, it is surprisingly faithful to its prototype, some of which can be seen on the Strasburg Railroad in Strasburg, Pennsylvania. Along with the 9090 Mini-Max boxcar, it is the only four-wheeled car in the Fundimensions repertoire. This caboose has been made in Chessie, Santa Fe, Rock Island and Reading colors over the years; the Reading in green was even

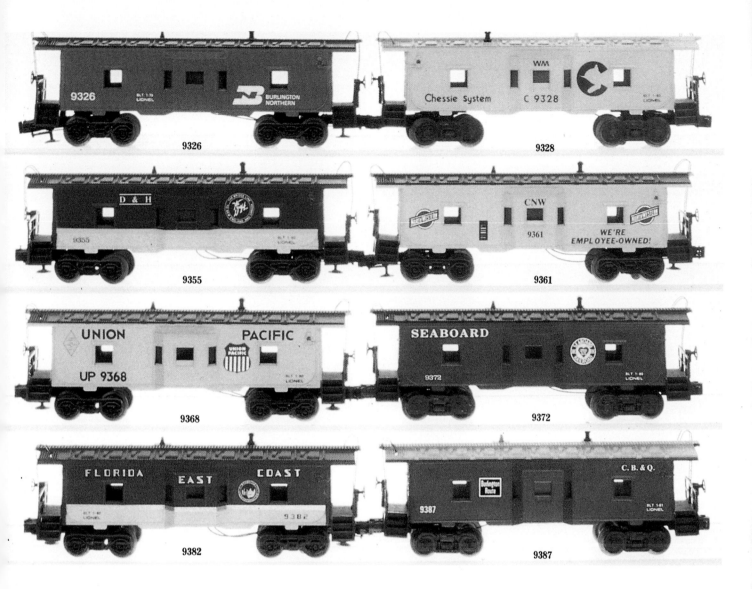

9326   9328

9355   9361

9368   9372

9382   9387

available for separate sale. A version with extra trim pieces is scheduled for production as part of a Santa Fe dockside switcher set in 1985. These whimsical, rather cute cabooses are good additions to a collection, although as part of the lower-priced lines they do not attract much collector attention.

Finally, in 1981, a new type of caboose emerged with the production of the Reading Yard King set. This was the Maintenance caboose, sometimes called the Transfer caboose. Essentially, this caboose consists of a flatcar with pipe-style railings on both sides leading to a small square cab mounted at the center of the flatcar. Another version of the Reading caboose was produced for separate sale, with the green and yellow colors reversed from the one included with the Yard King set. Several other cabooses of this design have emerged in recent years, among them Chicago and Northwestern, Burlington Northern and Erie-Lackawanna examples. Despite the fact that this caboose design is of relatively recent vintage, it has an old-time look about it which looks very good with a string of wood-sided reefers in a train. The separate-sale Reading and the Burlington Northern are the easiest ones to acquire, but the collector can expect several more examples of this caboose in the Traditional series in years to come.

With its cabooses, Fundimensions has achieved a nice balance of the old-fashioned railroad and the contemporary scene. The new designs are very praiseworthy, especially the

extended vision models, and the older designs have been carried into graphics and railroad lines far beyond anything produced in the postwar years. As with many other Fundimensions lines, the variety is welcome.

CABOOSES

SP Caboose Types

To the best of our knowledge, Fundimensions did not reuse Lionel molds I through IV and began its production with a new model (Type V).

Type V

1. Two rivets on side bottom corners.
2. No window frames on front and back cupola windows.
3. Plain plastic handrail stanchions on cupola roof.
4. Slightly larger door knobs.
5. Plainer plastic handrail stanchions by front and rear doors.
6. Steps not built into car mold.
7. Horizontal window bars.
8. Missing short vertical row of rivets on body under cupola between cupola windows, no rivets on ledge over side windows.

Type VI

1. Two rivets on side bottom corners.
2. No window frames on front and back cupola windows.
3. Plain plastic handrail stanchions on cupola.
4. Slightly larger door knobs.

5. Plainer handrail stanchions by front and rear doors.
6. Steps not built into car mold.
7. Horizontal window bars.
8. Missing short vertical row of rivets on body under cupola.
9. Wood-grained catwalk and hatches.

Type VII

1. Two and a half rivets on side bottom corners.
2. No window frames on front and back cupola windows.
3. Plain plastic handrail stanchions on cupola.
4. Small door knobs.
5. Plainer handrail stanchions by front and rear doors.
6. Steps not built into car mold.
7. Horizontal window bars.
8. Missing short vertical row of rivets on body under cupola.
9. No wood-grained catwalk.

S P End Types

Type I: Smooth walkway surface.

Type II: Rough walkway surface.

N5C Caboose Types

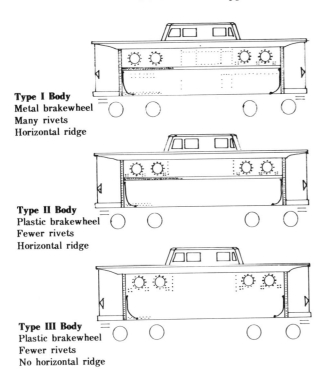

Type I Body
Metal brakewheel
Many rivets
Horizontal ridge

Type II Body
Plastic brakewheel
Fewer rivets
Horizontal ridge

Type III Body
Plastic brakewheel
Fewer rivets
No horizontal ridge

	Gd	VG	Exc	Mt

1776 N&W: 1976, N5C Type II, white sides, red roof, gold lettering; from N&W Spirit of '76 set.

	Gd	VG	Exc	Mt
(A) Flat red roof.	9	12	15	20
(B) Shiny, darker red roof.	9	12	15	20

6401 VIRGINIAN: Bay window, yellow sides with broad blue stripe through center, including bay; yellow and blue safety striping along lower side, "VGN" logo with yellow letters inside circular blue field surrounded by yellow and blue rings; blue, heat-stamped, sans-serif lettering "BLT 1-81/LIONEL" in two lines at one end and "6401" at other end, Symington-Wayne trucks with disc couplers. Brewer Collection. Catalogued on page 22 of the small 1981 catalogue. Matches 8950 Virginian Fairbanks-Morse. Also a good match for 8659 Virginian rectifier electric and Virginian SD-18 pair, 8071-72. — — 15 20

6420 READING: 1981-82, work caboose, dark yellow shanty on flatcar with dark green base; available only as part of Reading Yard King freight set 1154. — — 10 15

6421 COWEN: 1982, bay window, gold and dark tuscan with picture of Cowen; lettered "JOSHUA LIONEL COWEN" and "BLT 1-81 LIONEL", 027-style die-cast passenger trucks; issued as a limited edition in the "Spring Collector Series". — — 25 30

6422 DULUTH MISSABE: 1981-82, bay window, tuscan body; yellow stripes, black lettering, Symington-Wayne trucks, illuminated. — — 15 20

6425 ERIE-LACKAWANNA: 1983-84, bay window caboose, gray body; maroon striping edged with yellow stripes, yellow lettering, yellow ends, Symington-Wayne trucks. Matches 8369 GP-20 and 8759 GP-9 diesels. C. Lang and R. LaVoie Collections. — — 15 20

6426 READING: 1982, maintenance caboose, yellow flatcar, green cab, yellow diamond; reverse color scheme from Yard King set caboose, Symington-Wayne trucks. — — 7 10

6428 CHICAGO & NORTHWESTERN: 1984, maintenance/transfer caboose (both terms are used for this caboose), dark green wood-scribed flatcar body, dark green plastic pipe-style handrails, yellow center cab, white flatcar lettering, black cab lettering. Part of 1314 Northern Freight Flyer set. C. Lang comment. — — — 12

6431 SOUTHERN: 1983, Bay Window, red sides, silver roof, FARR logo on sides, 027-style die-cast passenger trucks, illuminated, (shown in catalogue with green sides), gold diamond-shaped FARR logo, part of FARR 4 series and available only as a separate sale item. Caponi comment. — — 25 30

6432 UNION PACIFIC: 1981, S.P. Type, part of Number 1151 U.P. Thunder Freight. Description needed. — — 5 6

6433 CANADIAN PACIFIC: 1981, Bay Window, gray with maroon roof and lettering, 027-style die-cast passenger trucks, illuminated, part of Number 1158 Maple Leaf Limited set. — — 30 40

6435: Unlettered 1983, maintenance caboose, olive drab with two railings on one side of shanty and dual gun on other, Symington-Wayne trucks, one fixed coupler; part of set 1355 Commando Assault train, came without lettering on car, decals furnished with set. — — — 10

6438 GREAT NORTHERN: 1981, bay window, dark orange and dark green body and ends, dark green roof; dark green stripe along bottom, black lettering, diamond-shaped FARR 3 logo in gold, yellow, black and white mountain goat logo, illuminated, die-cast 027-style passenger trucks, only sold separately. C. Rohlfing comment. — — 20 25

6439 READING: 1984-85, bay window caboose, green roof, yellow and green body; yellow lettering, lighted, Symington-Wayne trucks. — — — 20

6441 ALASKA: 1982, bay window, dark blue painted blue body and roof, yellow lettering and logo, Symington-Wayne trucks, lighted. C. Lang and C. Rohlfing comments. — — 15 20

6449 WENDY'S: 1981-82, N5C, white body, red lettering, yellow roof; part of Favorite Food Series, sold separately only. — — 20 25

6482 NIBCO: 1982, SP type, part of special promotional set 1264; see entry 8182 in Chapter I for background. Unlighted but with "glow-in-the-dark" windows. Red unpainted plastic body, black plastic railings; silver and black "NIBCO EXPRESS" script logo between third and fourth side windows, Symington-Wayne trucks. Very hard to find. Raber Collection. **NRS**

6483 NEW JERSEY CENTRAL: 1982, SP-type caboose, made for LCCA convention. Unpainted red Type VII plastic body, Type II ends, white lettering, "BLT. 9-82", one operating and one dummy coupler attached by metal rivets, Symington-Wayne trucks. Reportedly only 503 examples made. C. Lang comments, C. Darasko and C. Rohlfing Collections. Hard to find. **NRS**

6485 CHESSIE SYSTEM: 1984-85, SP-type caboose, yellow plastic body with black trim, blue lettering and logo, one operating coupler, Symington-Wayne trucks; part of set 1402. — — — 10

6491 ERIE-LACKAWANNA: Scheduled for 1985, maintenance/transfer caboose, black flatcar body and handrail piping, dark red cab, black roof and stack, white lettering and logo, Symington-Wayne trucks. — — — 12

6506 L.A.S.E.R.: 1981-82, Security Car with gun, black base, chrome-

6901   6903

6905   6904

finished cab, blue cab lettering; part of 1150 L.A.S.E.R. Train set.

| | | 15 | 20 |

6900 N&W: 1982, extended vision caboose, dark red body, black roof; white lettering, no ladders to roof on ends, die-cast 027-style passenger trucks; part of 1260 Continental Limited set, shown as "7301" in 1982 catalogue illustration.

| | | 35 | 45 |

6901 ONTARIO NORTHLAND: 1982, extended vision caboose, yellow and dark blue body, turquoise cupola roof; die-cast 027-style passenger trucks dark blue "triple lightning" logo on sides. Separate sale item from 1982 Fall Collector Center.

| | | 25 | 30 |

6903 SANTA FE: 1983, extended vision, blue and yellow body, yellow main roof, blue cupola sides and roof, yellow lettering, ladders at ends, black smokestack, 027-style die-cast passenger trucks, illuminated. Separate sale item from 1983 Collector Preview brochure. C. Rohlfing and R. LaVoie Collections.

| | | 35 | 40 |

6904 UNION PACIFIC: 1983, extended vision, yellow body, gray and red lettering, red line along roof edge, silver main and cupola roofs, black smokestack, 027-style die-cast passenger trucks; part of 1361 Gold Coast Limited set and only available as part of the set.

| | | 45 | 55 |

6905 NICKEL PLATE ROAD: 1983-84, extended vision caboose, dark red body, white lettering on body side, gray stripe with black "NICKEL PLATE HIGH SPEED SERVICE" lettering, "NICKEL PLATE ROAD" in old fashioned white serif letters, below cupola, number in white below lettering. Some cars came with cupolas installed incorrectly; these are not factory errors in the usual sense, since reversing the cupola produces the correct lettering. 027-style die-cast passenger trucks. Designed to match 8215 Nickel Plate Road 2-8-4 Berkshire locomotive. Separate sale item from 1983 Fall Collector Center. LaVoie comment.

| | | 40 | 45 |

See also Factory Errors and Prototypes.

6906 ERIE-LACKAWANNA: 1984-85, extended vision caboose, gray, maroon and yellow paint scheme, 027 die-cast passenger trucks; part of Erie-Lackawanna Limited set.

| | | | 45 |

6908 PENNSYLVANIA: 1984-85, N5C porthole caboose, deep maroon body, black main roof, yellow-painted cupola and cupola roof, white lettering, white and black PRR Keystone, diamond-shaped FARR 5 logo, lighted, 027-style die-cast passenger trucks (the only N5C to be thus equipped to date).

| | | | 35 |

6910 NEW YORK CENTRAL: 1984-85, extended vision caboose, red upper sides and ends, gray lower sides ("Pacemaker" paint scheme), black roof; "NYC/6910" in black on the gray area and New York Central oval in white on the red area, ladders to roof, 027-style die-cast passenger trucks. Separate sale item from 1984 Spring Collector Center. This caboose is in great demand because it matches the 8406 Hudson steam engine and the 8477 New York Central GP-9 — not to mention numerous other New York Central locomotives produced in the past. R. LaVoie comment and Collection.

| | | 55 | 60 |

6912 REDWOOD VALLEY EXPRESS: 1983-84, SP-type caboose, tuscan body, yellow lettering and logo, unlighted, one operating coupler, archbar trucks, part of Redwood Valley Express set 1403.

| | | | 10 |

6913 BURLINGTON NORTHERN: Announced for 1985, extended vision caboose, Cascade green body, yellow ends, gray roof; white BN logo and lettering, 027-style die-cast passenger trucks; from Burlington Northern Limited collector set of 1985.

| | | | 45 |

6916 NEW YORK CENTRAL: Announced for 1985, work caboose, black flatcar base, gray cab and tool bin; black NYC oval logo, white lettering, Symington-Wayne trucks, one operating coupler; from Yard Chief switch engine set.

| | | | 12 |

7508 LIONEL: 1975-76, N5C Type II, silver sides, 75th ANNIVERSARY SPECIAL, "BLT 1-75", lights, enclosed windows; broad red stripe runs halfway across body, circular 75th Anniversary logo, Symington-Wayne trucks.

| 7 | 11 | 15 | 20 |

7600

7600 FRISCO: 1975-76, N5C Type II, red, white and blue sides, lights, enclosed windows, Spirit of '76 Series.

(A) Flat red roof.	6	8	20	25
(B) Shiny red roof.	6	8	20	25
(C) Stamped "MIDWEST DIVISION, TCA". H. Azzinaro Collection.	—	—	—	50

9021 SANTA FE: 1970-74, work caboose, black frame with yellow lettering, caboose converts into "wood" deck flatcar.

(A) Medium red cab, light red toolbox, "9201" on frame, AAR trucks, plastic wheels, one manumatic coupler, one fixed coupler. (Note: A "manumatic" coupler operates, but it does not have the thumb tack pressed into the armature shaft so that a remote track will pull it down. Obviously, any manumatic coupler can be quickly made into a remote control uncoupler.)   3   5   7   10

(B) Same as (A), but light red cab, two manumatic couplers.   3   5   7   10

(C) Dark shiny cab and toolbox, Symington-Wayne trucks, one operating coupler, one fixed coupler, "9021" not on frame.   3   5   7   10

(D) Same as (A), but orange cab. Came in early sets; somewhat difficult to find.   12   15   20   25

9025 DETROIT, TOLEDO & IRONTON: 1971-74, work caboose, black frame with white lettering, orange cab with black lettering, dark orange toolbox, metal wheels, magnetic coupler in front, fixed rear coupler.   4   6   8   10

9027 SOO: 1975, work caboose, black frame with white lettering, red cab with white lettering, dark red toolbox, plastic wheels, one manumatic coupler in front, caboose converts into flatcar with stakes.
     4   6   8   10

9057 CP RAIL: 1978-79, SP Type VII, yellow unpainted plastic body, black-painted trim on sides, black lettering, Type II ends, Symington-Wayne trucks, one manumatic coupler, one dummy; stack, from Great Plains Express set, no lights.   5   7   9   11

9058 LIONEL LINES: 1978-79, SP Type VII, orange unpainted plastic; black lettering, Type II ends, Symington-Wayne trucks, plastic wheels, manumatic couplers, unlighted.   3   5   6   8

9060 NICKEL PLATE: 1970-71, SP Type VI or VII, maroon or brown body, white lettering, MPC logo, Type I ends, tuscan or black frame.

(A) Type VI, maroon body.	3	5	6	8
(B) Type VII, maroon body.	3	5	6	8
(C) Type VII, brown body.	3	5	6	8

9061 ATSF: 1970-71, 78, SP Type V or VII, red body, yellow lettering.

(A) SP Type V, MPC logo, AAR trucks, Type I end.   3   5   6   8

(B) SP Type VII, Symington-Wayne trucks, one manumatic coupler, Type II ends, metal wheels.   3   5   6   8

(C) Same as (B), but with Type I ends.   3   5   6   8

9062 PC: 1970-71, SP Type V or VII, green body; white lettering, Type I ends.

(A) SP Type V, MPC logo, AAR trucks.	2	3	5	9
(B) SP Type VII, MPC logo.	2	3	5	9
(C) SP Type VII, no MPC logo.	2	3	5	9

9063 GRAND TRUNK: 1970, SP Type V or VI, light orange or maroon body, white lettering, AAR trucks, MPC logo, Type I ends.

(A) SP Type V, orange body.	10	15	20	25
(B) SP Type V, dark orange body.	8	10	15	20
(C) SP Type VI, maroon body, Canadian release. Somewhat hard to find.	15	20	25	30

9064 C&O: 1971, Type VI or VII, yellow body, red stripe, blue lettering, Type I ends, MPC logo.

(A) SP Type VI, light yellow body, light red stripe, light blue lettering.
     3   5   7   10

(B) SP Type VI, medium light yellow, red stripe, blue lettering.
     3   5   7   10

(C) SP Type VI, medium yellow, red stripe, blue lettering.
     3   5   7   10

(D) SP Type VII, medium light yellow, red stripe, blue lettering.
     3   5   7   10

9065 CANADIAN NATIONAL: 1971-72, SP Type VI, maroon with white lettering, Type I ends, MPC logo, Canadian release. Somewhat hard to find.   10   15   20   25

9066 SOUTHERN: SP Type VI, white lettering, Symington-Wayne trucks, Type III SP body, Type I end, no MPC logo.

(A) Red body.	5	6	8	10
(B) Very dark red body (almost maroon). C. Rohlfing Collection.				NRS

9067 KICKAPOO VALLEY & NORTHERN: 1972, bobber, black frame, four wheels, gold lettering. Came only in the Kickapoo Valley and Northern set of 1972.

(A) Red body.	3	5	7	10
(B) Yellow body.	3	5	7	10
(C) Green body.	3	5	7	10

9068 READING: 1973-75, bobber, green body, yellow lettering, black frame. Came as separate sale item in Type II box.   3   5   6   8

9069 JERSEY CENTRAL: 1973-74, SP Type VII, brown body, white lettering, Type I ends.   3   5   6   8

9070 ROCK ISLAND: 1973-74, SP Type VII, gray with black and gray lettering, Type I ends.   6   8   10   12

9071 AT&SF: 1974-75, bobber, red body, white lettering, black frame, uncatalogued, Sears Set 79C9715C (Sears catalogue number).
     5   6   8   10

9073 COKE: 1973, SP Type VII, red body, white lettering, Type I ends, no MPC logo. Came as part of Coca-Cola switcher set.

(A) Light red body.	3	5	8	10
(B) Medium red body.	3	5	8	10
(C) Dark flat red body.	3	5	8	10

9075 ROCK ISLAND: SP Type VII, red body, white lettering, Type 1 ends, no MPC logo.   5   6   8   10

9076 WE THE PEOPLE: SP Type VII, white and red sides, blue roof, white and blue lettering, American flag, Type I ends, no MPC logo. Came as part of Liberty Special set.   4   7   9   11

9077 RIO GRANDE: 1977-79, 1981, SP Type VII, orange body, black lettering, Type II ends, no MPC logo.   3   4   6   8

9078 ROCK ISLAND: 1977, 1979, bobber, red body, white lettering, black frame.   3   5   6   8

9079 ATSF: 1979, details needed.   NRS

9080 WABASH: 1977, SP Type VII, red body, black roof, white lettering, Type II ends, no MPC logo. Part of Wabash Cannonball steam engine set.
     5   7   10   11

9085 ATSF: 1980-81, work caboose, plastic trucks and wheels, one operating coupler, one fixed coupler.   3   4   5   6

9160 IC: 1971, N5C Type II except for (B).

(A) Darker flat orange sides and roof, black lettering, white "ic", Symington-Wayne trucks, one operating coupler.   10   15   20   25

(B) Flat light orange sides and roof, black lettering, white "ic", AAR trucks, pre-1970 wheels, operating couplers, Type I body. Earliest production; hard to find.   15   20   25   30

(C) Darker flat orange sides and roof, black lettering, white "ic", black circle.   10   15   17   20

(D) Darker flat orange sides and roof, yellow "ic".   10   15   20   25

(E) Orange and white sides, white roof, black lettering, white "ic", white areas added by Glen Uhl, an Ohio Lionel dealer.   NRS

(F) Flat light orange roof, orange sides, black lettering, white "ic", Symington-Wayne trucks, one disc coupler, one fixed coupler.
     10   15   17   20

9160 IC: 1975, ITT Cable Hydrospace; ITT sticker obscures all but IC

9057

9058

9060

9061

9062

9063

9064

9065

9066

9069

9070

9073

131

emblem on side, one coupler. Type N5C II body, see 8030(C) in Chapter I, valued with set.

9161 CANADIAN NATIONAL: 1971, N5C Type II, orange body, white lettering, black roof, lights, "BLT 1-72", Symington-Wayne trucks. Can have one or two operating couplers. Many examples have heavy blurred lettering, especially built date and MPC logo. Slight price premium (about $3.00) for crisp, clear lettering.   **5   7   9   12**

9162 PENNSYLVANIA: 1972-76, N5C Type II, tuscan, white lettering, Symington-Wayne trucks; includes green or red marker lights, illuminated.- Somewhat difficult to find.   **10   12   15   20**

9163 ATSF: 1973-76, N5C Type II, red painted gray body with white lettering, lights, blue Santa Fe herald, Symington-Wayne trucks. Part of 1388 Golden State Arrow set of 1973; available as a separate sale item thereafter. C. Lang comment.   **6   8   10   12**

9165 CANADIAN PACIFIC: 1973, N5C Type II, red with white lettering, lights; came in C.P. Service Station Special. Difficult to find.
15   20   25   30

9166 RIO GRANDE: 1974, SP Type VII, yellow body, silver roof and stripes, black lettering, no MPC logo, lights, stack, enclosed windows, Type I ends.

(A) Light yellow sides.   **6   8   12   15**
(B) Medium yellow sides.   **6   8   12   15**

9167 CHESSIE: 1974-76, N5C Type II, light yellow sides, silver roof, orange stripe, blue lettering. Part of Grand National set of 1974; available as a separate sale item thereafter.   **4   6   8   12**

9168 UNION PACIFIC: 1975-76, N5C Type II, yellow sides, red or green lettering, black roof, lights, enclosed windows.

(A) Red lettering.   **6   8   10   12**
(B) Green heat-stamped lettering; scarce.   **—   —   —   335**

9169 MILWAUKEE ROAD: 1975, SP Type VII, brown sides, black roof, red lettering, lights, enclosed windows, Type I ends. Part of Milwaukee Service Station Set of 1975, but unlike previous year's 9166 Rio Grande, never offered for separate sale.   **10   12   15   20**

9170 N&W: 1976, listed under 1776.

9171 MISSOURI PACIFIC: 1975-77, SP Type, red sides and roof, white lettering, lights, stack, enclosed windows, Type I ends.

(A) SP Type VI.   **6   8   10   12**
(B) SP Type VII.   **6   8   10   12**

9172 PC: 1975-77, SP Type VII, black sides and roof, white lettering, lights, stack, enclosed windows, Type I ends.   **8   10   12   15**

9173 JERSEY CENTRAL: 1975-77, SP Type VI or VII, red sides and roof, white lettering, lights, stack, enclosed windows, Type I ends.

(A) SP Type VI.   **6   8   10   12**
(B) SP Type VII.   **6   8   10   12**

9174 P&E: 1976, (New York Central), bay window, green sides, black roof; white lettering, Symington-Wayne trucks; from Empire State Express set of 1976. Difficult to find.   **20   30   40   50**

9175

9175 VIRGINIAN: 1975-77, N5C Type II, dark blue sides, yellow roof; yellow lettering, lights, Symington-Wayne trucks, enclosed windows.

8	10	12	15

9176 BANGOR & AROOSTOOK: 1976, N5C Type II, red, white and blue with red roof, lights, enclosed windows, 1976 Bicentennial Issue; came with 8665 engine in one long box. Seldom sold separately from engine.

12	15	20	25

9177 NORTHERN PACIFIC: 1976, bay window, silver roof, green and dark or medium yellow sides; black lettering, red and white NP logo, 027-style die-cast passenger trucks, from Northern Pacific Service Station Special set. This was the first bay window caboose to use die-cast trucks. C. Lang comment.

(A) Dark yellow sides.	9	15	20	25
(B) Medium yellow sides.	9	15	20	25

9178 ILLINOIS CENTRAL GULF: SP Type VII, light or dark orange, silver roof, black lettering, white "IC", Type II ends, part of 1976 Illinois Central Gulf freight set and never offered for separate sale.

(A) Light orange.	10	12	15	20
(B) Dark orange.	10	12	15	20

9179 CHESSIE: 1979, bobber, yellow body, blue lettering, black frame, four plastic wheels.

3	5	6	8

9180 ROCK: 1977-78, N5C blue, black and white sides, white roof, lights, enclosed windows, Symington-Wayne trucks.

(A) Type II body.	6	8	10	12
(B) Type III body. C. Rohlfing Collection.	6	8	10	12

9181 BOSTON & MAINE: 1977, N5C, blue, black and white body, lights, enclosed windows, Symington-Wayne trucks.

(A) Type II body.	6	8	10	12

(B) Type III body. C. Rohlfing Collection.	6	8	10	12

9182 NORFOLK & WESTERN: 1977-80, N5C, black body, white lettering, lights, enclosed windows, Symington-Wayne trucks.

(A) Type II body.	6	8	10	12
(B) Type III body. C. Rohlfing Collection.	6	8	10	12

9183 MICKEY MOUSE: 1977-78, N5C, white sides, red/orange roof, Type III body, Mickey and lettering decal in yellow, black, red and blue; Symington-Wayne trucks, one operating coupler.

12	15	20	25

9184 ERIE: 1977-78, bay window, red and white lettering, Symington-Wayne trucks, two operating couplers.

10	12	15	20

9185 GT: 1977, N5C, gray plastic painted blue, orange ends, white lettering, red marker lights, Symington-Wayne trucks, one tab coupler, lights.

(A) Type II body.	6	8	10	12
(B) Type III body. C. Rohlfing Collection.	6	8	10	12

9186 CONRAIL: 1977-78, N5C, gray plastic painted blue, black roof; white lettering, red marker lights, Symington-Wayne trucks, one tab coupler, lights.

(A) Type II body.	6	8	10	12
(B) Type III body. C. Rohlfing Collection.	6	8	10	12

9187 GULF MOBILE & OHIO: 1977-78, SP Type, gray plastic painted red, black roof, white lettering, Type VII SP body, Type II ends, lights, metal wheels, Symington-Wayne trucks, one tab operating coupler. From Heartland Express set; not offered for separate sale. C. Rohlfing Collection.

10	12	15	20

9188 GREAT NORTHERN: 1977, bay window, blue and white sides, black roof; white lettering, two operating couplers, lights; from Rocky Mountain Special set.

13	15	25	35

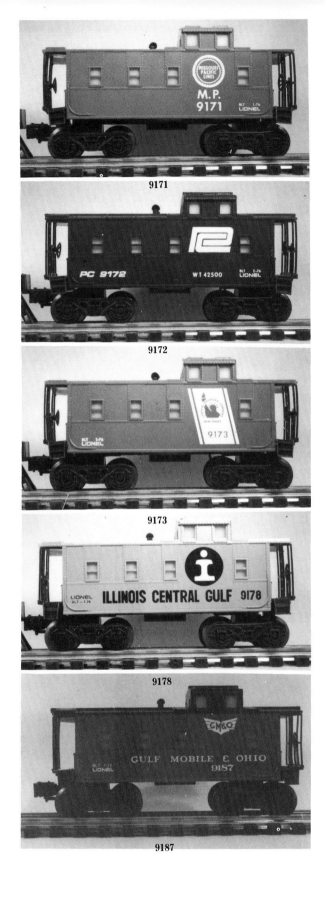

9075

9076

9077

9080

9166

9169

9171

9172

9173

9178

9187

9231 READING: 1979, bay window, green and yellow sides, yellow lettering, green roof, Symington-Wayne trucks; part of Quaker City Limited set. **15   20   25   30**

9239 LIONEL LINES: 1983, N5C, bright orange sides, dark blue roof; red, white and blue "LIONEL" circular logo centered on car side, "LIONEL LINES" in blue modern sans-serif letters, over and underscored by two blue stripes which run the length of the car, black railings, platforms and steps, number at lower right in blue, lighted, Symington-Wayne trucks; matches 8380 engine. R. LaVoie comment.   —   —   **30   35**

9259X SOUTHERN: 1977, bay window, LCCA Convention car, red body, 4,500 made.
(A) White lettering. Kruelle Collection.   —   —   **35   40**
(B) Gold lettering. C. Lang Collection.   —   —   **35   40**

9268 NORTHERN PACIFIC: 1976, bay window, black and gold sides; yellow hash marks, red lettering, gold ends and roofs, die-cast 027-style passenger trucks. Made in response to collector complaints that the 9177 Northern Pacific bay window caboose did not match the locomotive in that year's Service Station Special set. See 9274 entry for a similar situation.   —   **20   25   30**

9269 MILWAUKEE ROAD: 1978, bay window, dull orange and black, red logo, die-cast 027-style passenger trucks. Part of Milwaukee Special freight set of 1978.   —   **20   25   30**

9270 NORTHERN PACIFIC: Type III N5C orange-painted gray body, white letters. C. Rohlfing Collection.   **6   8   10   12**

9271 MINNEAPOLIS & ST. LOUIS: 1978-79, bay window, red sides with large white stripe, blue roof, white lettering, lights, two operating couplers, 027-style die-cast passenger trucks. Part of 1868 Minneapolis & St. Louis Service Station set.   **12   15   20   25**

9272 NEW HAVEN: 1978-80, bay window, dark red body, white and black lettering, lights, two operating couplers, Symington-Wayne trucks.
    8   10   12   15

9273 SOUTHERN: 1978, bay window, green and white body, gold stripes
    10   15   20   25

9274 SANTA FE: 1979, bay window, black roof, red sides, white letters, two operating couplers, Symington-Wayne trucks. Reportedly, only 3,000 made because collectors complained that it did not match the Santa Fe SD-18 diesels made the previous year. Fundimensions stopped making this caboose in favor of the blue and yellow 9317 in response.
    20   30   40   50

9276 TEXAS & PACIFIC: 1980, SP Type, dark blue with white lettering; catalogued as part of freight set but not made.   **Not Manufactured**

9287 SOUTHERN: 1978, Type III N5C body, gray plastic painted red, red roof, white lettering, red markers, Symington-Wayne trucks, one tab coupler, lights. C. Rohlfing comment.   **6   8   10   12**

9288 LEHIGH VALLEY: 1978, 1980, Type III N5C body, gray plastic painted red, yellow roof; yellow lettering, red markers, Symington-Wayne trucks, one tab coupler, lights. C. Rohlfing comment.   **6   8   10   12**

9289 CHICAGO & NORTH WESTERN: 1978, 1980, Type III N5C gray plastic body painted yellow, Brunswick green roof; black lettering, red marker lights, Symington-Wayne trucks, one tab coupler, lights. C. Rohlfing comment.
(A) As described above.   **6   8   10   12**
(B) Same as (A), except two disc couplers. Dunn Collection.
    6   8   10   12
(C) Same as (B), but overstamped "TCA MUSEUM EXPRESS, MARCH 8, 1980". Only 144 examples made. C. Rohlfing comment.   **NRS**

9309 TOLEDO, PEORIA & WESTERN: 1980-81, bay window, orange body with silver roof and white lettering, Symington-Wayne trucks, from 1072 Cross Country Express set. Shown in red in catalogue, but not made for production that way, although we have reports of a red example which may be a prototype. C. Lang, C. Rohlfing and I. D. Smith comments.
(A) Orange body, silver roof and white lettering. G. Kline Collection.
    —   —   **15   20**
(B) Same as (A), but red body. Possible prototype. Reader comments requested. W. Eddins Collection.   **NRS**

9316 SOUTHERN PACIFIC: 1979, bay window, silver with black roof, illuminated, 027-style die-cast passenger trucks, from 1970 Southern Pacific Limited set.   —   —   **35   40**

9317 ATSF: 1979, bay window, blue and yellow body, yellow ends; yellow lettering, Symington-Wayne trucks, lights; matches ATSF SD-18 engine. See entry 9274 for story behind this caboose.   **9   12   15   20**

9323 ATSF: 1979, bay window, tuscan body; white lettering, black and white Santa Fe cross logo, gold diamond-shaped FARR 1 logo, Symington-Wayne trucks, lights, from FARR Series I; available as separate sale only.
    20   25   30   35

9326 BURLINGTON NORTHERN: 1979-80, bay window, green-painted body; white lettering, Symington-Wayne trucks, lights.   —   **9   12   18**

9328 WM CHESSIE SYSTEM: 1980, bay window, yellow with silver roof; blue lettering and logo, 027-style die-cast passenger trucks; from 1070 Royal Limited set.   —   —   **25   30**

9341 ATLANTIC COAST LINE: 1979-82, SP Type, red with white lettering, glow-in-the-dark windows, Symington-Wayne trucks, from Number 1960 Midnight Flyer set.   —   —   **6   8**

9346 WABASH: 1979, SP Type, dark red sides, white lettering, black roof; from 1991 Wabash Deluxe Express. Young Collection.
    —   —   **6   8**

9355 DELAWARE & HUDSON: 1980, 1982, bay window, dark blue and gray body, yellow stripe, Symington-Wayne trucks, illuminated; matches 8050 - 8051 D H U36C diesels.
(A) 1980, as described above.   —   —   **20   25**
(B) 1982, same as (A), but TTOS decal added. C. Rohlfing comment.   **NRS**

9357 SMOKEY MOUNTAIN LINE: 1979, bobber, red unpainted plastic body; white lettering, one-piece plastic cab and roof, one-piece black unpainted plastic frame, two black unpainted plastic end railing units, plastic wheels on metal axles, fixed plastic coupler fastened to frame by metal screw (for a total of three metal parts), body and frame highly detailed, frame underside lettered "LIONEL MPC 9067-10"; came with 1965 Smokey Mountain Line set.
(A) As described above. G. Halverson and G. Salamone Collections.
    2   4   5   6
(B) Unpainted green plastic body, black heat-stamped lettering "SML", logo between windows.   **2   4   5   6**

9361 CHICAGO & NORTHWESTERN: 1980, bay window, yellow sides, Brunswick green roof, illuminated, Symington-Wayne trucks. Previous to the production of this caboose, several Midwestern train shops repainted other bay window cabooses into this color scheme. C. Rohlfing and R. LaVoie comments.   —   —   **15   20**

9368 UNION PACIFIC: 1980, bay window, yellow with red roof and lettering, Symington-Wayne trucks; red, white and blue UP shield logo, diamond-shaped FARR 2 logo, Famous American Railroad series number two, only sold separately.   —   —   **15   17**

9372 SEABOARD: 1980, bay window, dark red body, black roof, white lettering, red, white and black circular Seaboard logo, die-cast 027-style passenger trucks, from 1071 Mid Atlantic Limited set.
    —   —   **22   25**

9380 NEW YORK, NEW HAVEN & HARTFORD: 1980, SP-Type, silver-painted body, black roof and cupola, unlighted; black New Haven script lettering, Symington-Wayne trucks, two operating couplers; came with 1050 New Englander set. Zylstra Collection.   —   —   **10   12**

9381 CHESSIE: 1980, SP-Type, yellow sides and end, silver roof, blue lettering; from 1052 Chesapeake Flyer set.   —   —   **8   10**

9382 FLORIDA EAST COAST: 1980, bay window, red and yellow with white stripe, illuminated, Symington-Wayne trucks; matches 8064 and 8065 GP-9 diesels.   —   —   **15   20**

9387 BURLINGTON: 1981, bay window, red sides, white lettering, illuminated, 027-style die-cast passenger trucks; from 1160 Great Lakes Limited set.   —   —   **25   35**

We need a number for the following entry:
ATSF: Scheduled for 1985, bobber caboose, blue body, silver frame, end rails and stack, dummy couplers. From 1985 Midland Freight set.   **NRS**

9068

9071

9078

9179

9021

9025

9027

Chapter VI

ACCESSORIES

By Roland E. LaVoie and Glenn Halverson

In 1958, amid the placid years of Eisenhower, the "Silent Generation" and the rude awakening posed by "Sputnik", author and social critic Vance Packard published a book called **The Waste Makers**, which climbed rapidly to the top of the best-seller lists. In this book, Packard castigated the hitherto sacred cow of business by detailing the operational concept of planned obsolescence. He accused businessmen of forcing American consumers to buy manufactured goods by making them stylistically unacceptable or, worse, by designing them to wear out just as they were paid for. Given the stylistic excesses of the American automobiles of the period and the notorious tendency of the good old washing machine to self-destruct, Packard made a good case for his thesis.

For one company, the Lionel Corporation, that thesis did not hold true. Even when the business climate for toy trains took a sharp downturn, the legacy of Joshua Lionel Cowen was too strong for the company to ignore until the end of the decade, when Cowen sold his shares and finally retired. Nowhere was the commitment to quality better demonstrated than with Lionel's operating accessories, those little animated joys which seemed destined to last forever. One of the main reasons for this durability was the dependence of these accessories upon solenoid relays and rugged vibrator motors for their operation. Take an old Lionel accessory out of its box after it has been unearthed from a 30-year stay in a dusty attic, and likely as not, the mechanism will operate perfectly. It's not unusual to see even prewar accessories in active use on layouts, day after day.

Building something to last is commendable indeed, but Lionel's commitment to durability in its accessories posed a very unusual marketing problem for the fledgling Fundimensions firm in 1970. The firm found itself in competition with its own past! How could Fundimensions expect people to buy its accessories when so many of the old ones were still out there working perfectly?

The obvious answer to that question was to build new kinds of accessories. Even here, the engineering excellence of the old Lionel Corporation seemed to haunt Fundimensions at every turn. For every reissue of the old accessories which was improved, such as the 2494 Rotating Beacon, which worked much better than its 394 and 494 predecessors, other reissues emphasized the inexperience of the firm at making these toys. You will read articles about the 2125 Whistle Shack and the 2156 Station Platform in this chapter which detail the more painfully obvious engineering goof-ups.

Thus, it took quite a while for Fundimensions to find its own niche for its accessory line, and even longer to get out of the shadow of its illustrious past. Many of the earliest accessories were direct copies of the older line with subtle differences. These were produced in very limited quantities and are well worth seeking today; they include the three accessories mentioned above, the 2199 Microwave Relay Tower and a few others. In fact, Fundimensions had a copious supply of leftover production which it re-packaged into its own boxes! Thus, it is quite possible to find a 2154 blinking crossing signal which is absolutely identical to the postwar version but is packed in a

Type I Fundimensions box. Only when these supplies were exhausted, around the beginning of 1972, did Fundimensions market its own lines — and even then these were no different from their predecessors except cosmetically. How many collectors know that the postwar 252 crossing gate and its Fundimensions 2152 successor can only be told apart by the gate prop at the end of the gate? It is metal in postwar production and black plastic in Fundimensions production. The bases of the 2152 gates even carry 252 Lionel Corporation markings!

The first stirrings of Fundimensions' individuality came in 1973, when the firm began the sales of scale 0 Gauge building kits. This is quite understandable, given the long background of model building possessed by the Craft Master and Model Products Corporation people now running Lionel. These attractive kits have been a staple of the Fundimensions line ever since that year. However, it was not until 1976 that Fundimensions introduced accessories which could truly be called its own — and it did so with a vengeance! One accessory, partly derivative from older forms, was the 2127 diesel horn shed, which worked from a 9-volt battery through a speaker hidden in a shack shaped like the one used for the 2126 whistling freight shed, also introduced (or re-introduced, if you prefer) that year. The others were original in every way. One was an ingenious 2175 Sandy Andy ore tower kit which used a system of weights to dump coal into a little ore car which traveled down a rack and dumped its contents into a waiting coal car. It was a devil to keep in adjustment, but it was amusing when it worked. Another was a coaling station kit which dumped coal into a car underneath the building.

The most spectacular of the accessories, however, was a fully operating 2317 automatic drawbridge. This terrific accessory used the same operating principles as the fabled 313 bascule bridge of the early postwar years, but it added the dimension of an over-and-under layout. If a train on the upper track approached an open drawbridge, it would stop until the bridge was lowered, a bell ringing all the while. If the train were on the lower level and encountered a closed drawbridge, it would stop until the bridge was raised. The accessory could be wired for continuous operation using insulated tracks or contactors. Though difficult to hook up, this was a fine accessory which brought great action to a layout and looked handsome.

But the lure of nostalgia proved too strong for Fundimensions to resist. In 1980, the fine 454 sawmill was revived by the firm, using the number 2301. This was the first revival of the truly magnificent and complex accessories from the glory days of the Lionel Corporation, and it sold very well. Also revived in that year was a manual version of the old 282 gantry crane, and operators realized that a remote control version could not be far behind. The meticulously detailed 0 Gauge switches were once again made in 1980, and in the next year the popular oil derrick made its appearance.

The year 1982 was accessory heaven as a steady parade of resurrections began apace. In that year, the colorful animated newsstand and the imposing icing station appeared. A nice revival of the old 256 freight station appeared as the 2129 in

1983, as well as the American Flyer oil drum loader, the 2316 remote control gantry crane, the 2315 overhead coaling station and the 2318 operating control tower. Most of these accessories were delayed in production, but that only whetted the collector and operator appetite for more. In 1984, more did indeed follow. The good die-cast bumpers reappeared in two colors, the dwarf signal made an appearance and the old 356 operating freight station and 445 operating control towers came out as the 2323 and 2324, respectively. No new accessories of this type were announced for 1985, perhaps to give Fundimensions time to produce those already announced and to catch its collective breath after the production delays the firm experienced in 1983 and 1984.

Perhaps it is easy to chastise Fundimensions for relying on the old tried and true Lionel accessories so much, but when the company has had a good thing going for it, one cannot blame anybody for sticking to a successful formula. With few exceptions, the operating accessories have been very brisk sellers. In addition, there have been some technical innovations worthy of praise. In the new operating gantry crane and overhead coal loader, the rugged but ponderous and noisy Lionel AC electric motors have been replaced by quiet, efficient AC/DC can motors which work more smoothly, never need lubrication (though the gears do) and use fewer volts than their predecessors. This means that more accessories can be activated on less power, not to mention the maintenance-free features. The good old solenoids and vibrator motors produced by Fundimensions work just as well as their elder Lionel cousins.

Will there be further revivals of older Lionel operating accessories? If you need convincing that this will indeed be so, just look through the Lionel catalogues of the middle to late 1950s. There you may view the big water tower, the culvert loader and unloader, the overhead gantry signal, the barrel and coal ramps, the helicopter launching station and many, many other candidates for revival. Will there be entirely new accessories added to the Fundimensions line? The answer to this is less certain, but eventually the supply of subjects for revival will run low. Then, perhaps Fundimensions will make accessories found in the old Lionel archives but never produced. Possibly, we could see some accessories with a modern twist, such as a dockside container ship unloading gantry (which would really be a spectacular accessory!).

Yet, the tradition lives on. Only in 1985 did one accessory finally disappear from the catalogue after a continuous 50-year run in one form or another. This was the Operating Gateman, a little fellow who rushed out of his shack as the train went by, swinging his lantern mightily. From 1935 to 1984, this accessory was produced in 45, 045, 45N, 145 and 2145 configurations. It was truly the toy train equivalent of the Ford Model "T"! Don't sell the little gateman short, either...he may just be taking a well-deserved vacation in Hawaii before he returns once more to uphold one of the great truths about Lionel Toy Trains: "Not just a toy...A tradition!"

Gd VG Exc Mt

ACCESSORIES

2110 GRADUATED TRESTLE SET: 1971-83, twenty-two pieces graduated from 3/16 to 4-3/4 high.   5   7   10   12

2111 ELEVATED TRESTLE SET: 1971-83, ten 4-3/4 inch piers.
(A) Gray plastic.   5   7   10   12
(B) Brown plastic.   5   7   10   12

2113 TUNNEL PORTALS: 1984-85, gray plastic stonework, "LIONEL" and circular "L" logo molded into portal.   —   —   5   6

2115 DWARF SIGNAL: 1984-85, gray body, black twin-light lens hood; uses pin-type bulbs; Type III box.   —   —   11   13

2117 BLOCK TARGET SIGNAL: 1985, black base, white pole, black two-light lens hood.   —   —   —   18

2122 EXTENSION BRIDGE: 1977-83, two gray plastic piers, plastic bridge, requires assembly; 24" long by 5" wide, piers 7" high, overall height with piers is 11-3/4".
(A) Brown sides and top.   —   10   12   20
(B) Brown sides and maroon top, Piker Collection.   —   10   12   20

OOPS! BACK TO THE DRAWING BOARD, BOYS! (OR, THE STRANGE SAGA OF THE 2125 FUNDIMENSIONS WHISTLE SHACK)

With the assistance of Glenn Halverson

During its first two years of existence, Fundimensions was noted for the rather offbeat accessories it produced. From the first, the company realized that action accessories had to be provided for its trains to sell well and build a new toy train market. Sometimes Fundimensions was successful in making a postwar accessory work better; this was certainly the case with the Fundimensions 2494 Rotating Beacon. Other times, the adaptation didn't quite work out as Fundimensions had planned it. There was always the unforeseen and the unexpected.

One accessory became an engineering error on the part of Fundimensions, the 2125 Whistle Shack. It was quite understandable that Fundimensions wanted to add a steam whistle to its accessory lineup; after all, what young railroader didn't thrill to the sound of the melodious whistle? So, late in 1970, the Fundimensions engineering people secured some of the old postwar 125 Whistle Shacks and prowled around the leftover parts inventory to see what the firm had inherited from the old Lionel Corporation. Sure enough, a good number of the excellent 125 Whistle Shack motors and whistle casings were available.

Therefore, Fundimensions decided to market a whistle shack for 1971, calling it the 2125 Whistle Shack. This accessory is portrayed in the catalogue in its late postwar colors — a red roof, white house and light gray base. However, the Fundimensions whistle shack emerged in a very strange amalgamation of colors. The house and the roof bear 145 part numbers, showing clearly their derivation from the popular 145 Operating Gateman. But the colors do not fall into any inherited pattern; nor do they look like the whistle shack shown in the 1971 catalogue.

The base of the Fundimensions 2125 is not light gray; it is dark brown. The identifying logo on the bottom of the base has been changed to read "2125 WHISTLE STATION / LIONEL MPC / MT. CLEMENS, MICH. / MADE IN U.S. OF AMERICA". The 2125 has the good postwar motor, impeller and casing assembly; the whistle casing is black plastic and is attached to the structure by two Phillips-head screws.

The house is white unpainted plastic. The door, toolshed roof and window inserts are red, but a rather strange translucent red plastic instead of the solid red color on postwar models. It is the same translucent red color found on the Fundimensions distribution of the 6560 Crane Car in the same year. Instead of a red roof, the roof of the 2125 is a medium pea green. None of the colors used match with each other very well. Aside from the old 125 with a green base the 2125 is the only whistle shack which was produced with four different

2122

2125

2127

2133

2140

2145

2152

2154

2162

2163

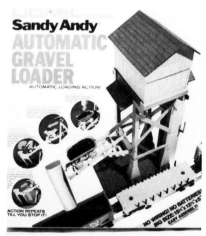

2175

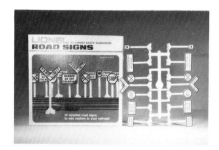

2180

colors. The accessory came in a square Type I Fundimensions box.

The real surprise is the "improvement" Fundimensions decided to incorporate into this whistle shack. Someone came up with (you'll hopefully excuse the pun) the bright idea to illuminate the shack. To accomplish this, Fundimensions used a little light clip similar to the ones used in the N5C Porthole Cabooses. This clip was attached to the oval slot atop the station and incorporated a 12-volt automotive plug-in bulb. Two black wires led from this clip to the wire terminals used for making the electrical connections to the transformer.

So far, so good. However, the engineers had forgotten that three connections were needed for constant illumination, not two. The failure of the engineers to realize this fact meant that the light would go on only when the whistle button was pressed to operate the station! That would, of course, really call attention to where the whistle sound was coming from, but that was not quite the intent of the engineers!

The 2125 Whistle Shack was quickly withdrawn from service after only one year of production. Not until 1976 did Fundimensions market another whistle shack, the 2126. This time, the base and roof were brown with a cream house, green door, green windows and brown toolshed roof. The motor was an entirely new diode-operated design; it wasn't quite as strong as the postwar motor, but it worked reliably. It was soon joined by a 2127 Diesel Horn Shed which operated from a 9-volt battery. Oh, yes — the 2126 omitted the illumination feature! Ironically, a small promotional accessory catalogue in 1975 showed a complex layout loaded with accessories. Guess which whistle shack is visible on the layout? Right — the 2125!

Fundimensions may have "goofed" in the production of the 2125 Whistle Shack, but in the process it created an interesting little curio of an accessory which is very scarce but has not received much attention. Since the 2125 was catalogued for just a year, not very many of them could have been made — remember that the toy train market was quite small in 1971. This little accessory might show great appreciation value once collectors realize just how scarce it is. An educated guess would be that fewer than 1,000 of these whistle shacks were produced, since there could not have been very many of the postwar motors left over. Significantly, 1971 was also the year when Fundimensions used spare parts to make the 6560 Crane Car and the 2156 Station Platform with its prewar light bulbs. Whatever the quantity, the 2125 Whistle Shack seldom shows up at toy train shows. For the Fundimensions collector, the 2125 is a highly interesting little "sleeper".

2125 WHISTLING FREIGHT STATION: 1971, white shed body, translucent red door, window inserts and toolshed lid, dark brown base embossed "2125", postwar-type motor. Type I box; mint condition requires presence of box. Roof and base are Fundimensions products; shed parts and motor are postwar carry-overs. Has 12-volt automotive-type light connected to clips; light only works when whistle is blown! Very hard to find.
(A) Green roof. G. Halverson and R. LaVoie Collections.
                    20   25   35   40
(B) Tuscan roof. C. Rohlfing Collection.
                    20   25   35   40

2126 WHISTLING FREIGHT SHED: 1976-83, brown plastic base, off-white yellow shed, green door and windows, opaque window in non-opening door, green toolshed lid, brown plastic roof, whistle. Found with two types of doors: one type has two large windows; the other has twelve smaller windows.
(A) Brown plastic roof.   10   12   15   20
(B) Same as (A), but green plastic roof; possibly leftover roof from 2125 production. J. Cusumano Collection.   10   12   15   20

2127 DIESEL HORN SHED: 1976-83, height 4-7/8", base 6" x 6", battery-operated by nine-volt transistor battery not included. Diesel horn remote controlled, light tan plastic base, red building, white toolshed lid, white door, frosted window, gray roof. Same door variation as 2126 above.
                      10   12   15   20

2128 AUTOMATIC SWITCHMAN: 1983, animated blue switchman waves flag as train approaches. Green metal painted base with green cardboard bottom. Appears to be a reissue of 1047 from 1959-61. Reader comments requested on differences, if any.   —   —   25   30

2129 FREIGHT STATION: 1983, maroon platform, tan building with brown windows and door, green roof, black picket fence with billboards reading "Cheerios", "Wheaties", and "Gold Seal". Also several wall posters, illuminated by one interior bulb. The catalogue shows the station with white walls. 15" long, 5" wide and 5-1/2" high. This is a reissue of 256 from 1950-53. Reader comments appreciated on the differences between 2129 and 256.   —   —   16   20

2133 FREIGHT STATION: 1972-83, maroon plastic base, white plastic sides; box at one time made by Stone Container Corporation, Detroit, Michigan, white corrugated box with colored picture of station on lid. Reissue of 133 from 1957-66. Earliest versions use metal clip-on bayonet base light socket, rather than the postwar version, in which the light socket is riveted to the bracket. Later Fundimensions stations have plastic clip-on socket using a 12-volt automotive-type bulb. T. Rollo comment.
(A) Early; medium green roof, green door and window inserts, brown chimney, maroon base. G. Halverson Collection. 10   12   18   25
(B) Later; pea green chimney, windows, doors and roof, maroon base. G. Halverson and T. Rollo Collections. 10   12   18   25
(C) Latest; darker Penn Central green roof, door and window inserts, dark brown base. G. Halverson Collection. 10   12   18   25

2140 AUTOMATIC BANJO SIGNAL: 1970-83, as train approaches, red light turns on, "stop" arm swings, die-cast construction; 7-1/2" high.
(A) "LIONEL CORPORATION" stamped on underside of base; postwar carry-over. Came in Type I Fundimensions box. G. Halverson Collection.
                     8   10   15   25
(B) MPC logo on base, Type II Fundimensions box. G. Halverson Collection.   8   10   15   20

2145 AUTOMATIC GATEMAN: 1970-84: 1985 marks the 50th anniversary of the most famous and long-lived of all Lionel accessories. This little shed was first offered in 1935 as the 45 for Standard Gauge and the 045 for 0 Gauge (differing only in the type of special insulated track or contactor included with the accessory). In 1946 its number changed to 45N, and in 1950 it was substantially revised and changed to the 145. Its spectacular market success reflects its great play value. The gateman, who is really a watchman, rushes from his lighted shed as the train approaches. He warns pedestrians and vehicles with his swinging lantern and returns to the shed after the train passes. The accessory came with a pressure contactor and a lockon. Refer to Prewar and Postwar Guides for further history of this accessory.
(A) 1970, green metal base, white shed with brown door and window, frosted plastic window inserts, maroon roof and toolshed lid. Mint value must have the Fundimensions Type I box; this accessory was actually a postwar 145 piece in the new Fundimensions packaging. G. Halverson Collection. 10   15   20   30
(B) 1971-84, same as (A), but brown roof and toolshed lid, Type II box. G. Halverson Collection. 10   12   15   20

2151 SEMAPHORE: 1978-83, brown plastic base, white pole, white and black-striped semaphore arm, red and green jewel lights; raises as train approaches.   8   10   15   20

2152 AUTOMATIC CROSSING GATE: 1977-83, black plastic base, white plastic gate with gray weights, on bottom "#252 Crossing Gate", with pressure contactor. The Fundimensions version can be distinguished from its postwar 252 counterpart by the presence of a black plastic gate rest at the end of the gate arm rather than the metal one used in the postwar version. Many postwar examples were repacked into Fundimensions Type I boxes. Some examples were sold in Type III rolling stock boxes with black print; "6-2152/AUTOMATIC CROSSING GATE" on the ends. R. LaVoie comment, G. Halverson Collection.   7   10   15   20

2181

2199

2214

2310

2312

2313

2314

2317

2494

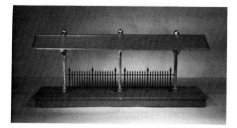

2256

2256

2280
2290

2154 AUTOMATIC HIGHWAY FLASHER: 1970-83, red light blinks alternately as train passes; 8-3/4" high with special track clip, the 154C contactor. This device clamps over the track and has two thin metal plates which are insulated from the rail. The device is wired so that the train wheels run across the metal flanges, completing the circuit to each of the two bulbs in turn. Thus the left light goes on and off as the wheels pass over the left plate, and the right light goes on and off with the right plate, giving the flashing appearance of the accessory. This clever contactor first appeared in 1940 with the first versions of the 154. Fundimensions production has been observed in several colors. Reader comments are needed with the specific examples.

(A) White plastic crossbuck with raised black lettering, gray unpainted post with chrome finial cap. This is a postwar 154 packaged in a Type I Fundimensions box. G. Halverson Collection.
    8 10 15 20

(B) Black crossbuck with raised white lettering, black finial cap, MPC logo stamped on underside of base. G. Halverson Collection.
    8 10 15 20

2156 STATION PLATFORM: 1971, rerun of 156 with changes; pea green plastic base, medium red roof, lighted with two large prewar round or acorn light bulbs, underside of base reads, "CAT. NO. 2156 STATION PLATFORM", and "LIONEL MT. CLEMENS MICH. MADE IN USA". Mint value must have original light bulbs and Type I box. Grossano, Halverson and Rollo Collections.
    — 25 35 50

See article on page 147 about 2156 Station Platform by Thomas S. Rollo.

2162 AUTOMATIC CROSSING GATE AND SIGNAL: 1970-83, black plastic base, black crossbuck with white lettering and simulated bell at top, white gate, red bulbs with pins, pressure contactor, lockon.

(A) Red-painted diagonal stripes, metal support rod on gate, Type I box, postwar markings on base. Postwar carry-over in Fundimensions box. G. Halverson Collection.
    10 12 15 20

(B) Same as (A), but black-painted diagonal stripes, black plastic support rod on gate, Type II box, postwar markings on base blanked out. G. Halverson Collection.
    10 12 15 20

2163 AUTO BLOCK TARGET SIGNAL: 1970-78, green light switches to red as train approaches; 7-1/2" high, contactor, L-19R red bulb, L-19G green bulb, both with pins.

(A) Light tan base, Type I or Type II box.   **8 10 15 20**
(B) Medium tan base, Type II box. R. LaVoie Collection. **8 10 15 20**
(C) Dark tan base, brass-colored wire thumbscrews instead of nickel. Box type not known. G. Halverson Collection.   **NRS**

2170 STREET LAMPS: 1970-83, three per package. Earliest versions carry postwar stamping on underside of base but are packaged in Type I shrink wrap. Later versions have Lionel MPC markings.

(A) Dark green pole, dark green pole top, cream globe, pin-type bulbs; same bulb was used for postwar 76 lamp post. G. Halverson and T. Rollo Collections.   **7 10 15 20**

(B) Light green pole, mismatched dark green pole top, white globe, small foreign-made midget bulb with screw base (note that a "midget lamp" is any lamp 1/4" or less in diameter). Cole comment, G. Halverson Collection.   **10 15 20 25**

(C) Light green pole and pole top, white globe, midget screw-base bulb, Type II shrink-wrap packaging. G. Halverson Collection. **7 10 12 15**

2171 GOOSE NECK LAMPS: 1980-83, two lamps, reissue of 1961-63.
    8 10 12 15

2175 SANDY ANDY: 1976-79, mechanically-operated gravel loader, light brown structure, dark brown roof and base, gray plastic girders, light brown ore car. Top of silo is loaded with coal. Car is attached to string with weight. When lever holding weight is released, weight brings car to top of incline, where it pushes against lever which uncovers hole releasing coal into car. When weight of coal overcomes brass weight on line attached to car, car travels down girders and is tripped into chute which unloads coal into waiting car. Cycle then begins again. Difficult to adjust properly, but action is delightful when accessory works properly. Plastic kit. R. LaVoie comment.   **10 15 20 30**

2180 ROAD SIGN SET: 1977-83, plastic signs, attached as shown.
    — — 2 3

2181 TELEPHONE POLES: 1977-83, ten poles, each 7" high.
    — — 2 4

2195 FLOODLIGHT TOWER: 1970-72, eight lights, unpainted gray tower, light bracket and reflectors, tan base, "LIONEL" on two tabs near top of tower, transitional hybrid; unpainted gray plastic tower structure with unpainted gray "LIONEL" signs (postwar version has red-painted "LIONEL"), postwar microwave relay top on tower, postwar markings on base, Type I box. Very hard to find. B. Thomas and G. Halverson Collections.   **— — 40 50**

2199 MICROWAVE TOWER: 1972-75, black plastic base, gray plastic tower, black plastic top with three operating blinking light tips, postwar markings on base, Type II box. The gray color of the tower structure is significantly darker than that of the postwar version, and the "LIONEL" plates on the side of the tower are not painted red. R. LaVoie Collection.
    10 15 25 30

2214 GIRDER BRIDGE: 1970-83, metal base, black or brown-painted or brown-anodized, gray plastic side embossed "LIONEL", comes knocked down or assembled. If knocked down plastic sides must be screwed on with eight Phillips-head screws; 10" long, 4-1/2" wide.

(A) As described above, Type I or Type II box. C. Rohlfing Collection.
    — 3 5 8

(B) Earliest version, Type I box, knocked down assembly, gray plastic sides, method of attaching base differs from later versions — fits in slots molded into girder sides and has no screws for assembly, snap-together. Blackened metal base. G. Halverson Collection.   **— 8 12 15**

2256 STATION PLATFORM: 1973-81, green plastic base, metal posts, black plastic center fence, red unpainted plastic roof, not lighted.

(A) As described above.   **3 5 6 10**
(B) TCA special issue: Penn Central green base, lighter red roof than regular issue, overprint heat-stamped in white; "21 TCA National Convention, Orlando, Florida, June 19-26, 1975". G. Halverson Collection.
    — 15 20 30

2260 BUMPER: 1970-73, same mold used as for postwar 26 and 260 die-cast bumpers, but black plastic body, four screws at corners, translucent red cap, takes 14-volt bayonet base bulb. Came in Type I box or Type II shrink-wrap packaging. Somewhat hard to find.

(A) Bottom fiber plate marked "NO. 260/THE LIONEL CORPORATION" in white, hex nut holds plate to chassis. This is identical to late postwar Hagerstown production except for the translucent lens cap. G. Halverson Collection.   **NRS**

(B) Same as (A), but later production, no lettering on bottom fiber plate. R. LaVoie Collection.   **NRS**

2280 BUMPERS:
(A) 1973-75, three to a package, early version with open area, Type I box.
    — 1 3 5
(B) 1974-80, 1983, later version with closed area. **— — 3 5**

2282 BUMPER: 1983, black die-cast body which attaches to the track with screws; black plastic shock absorber, red illuminated jewel atop body. Reissue of 260 bumper from the 1950s with a color change. Illustrated in the 1983 Fall Collector's Brochure. Type V box. LaVoie comment. Price per pair.   **— — 15 20**

2283 BUMPER: 1984-85, tuscan-painted die-cast body identical in construction to 2282 above. Made in Hong Kong and sold as part of Traditional Series in pairs in Type III boxes. Price per pair.   **— — 10 12**

2290 LIGHTED BUMPERS: 1974-83, similar in construction to 2280, but with copper contact and small screw-base red bulbs. Type III box. Price per pair.   **3 4 6 8**

2292 STATION PLATFORM: 1985, dark red base, black plastic roof supports, black fencing, dark green roof, chromed acorn nut roof fasteners; unlighted.   **— — — 6**

2300 OIL DRUM LOADER: 1983, reissue of 779 American Flyer accessory from 1955-56. Reader comments and differences between 779 and 2300 appreciated. Listed here as well as in our American Flyer book because it appeared in a Fundimensions catalogue and will be found with Lionel trains.
    — — 65 75

2301 OPERATING SAWMILL: 1981-83, maroon plastic base, white mill building, red door, gray shed, red lettering on window facing track, white crane; simulates the transformation of logs into dressed lumber, vibrator mechanism moves lumber; length 10-1/2", width 6", height 6". Reissue of 464 from 1956-60.   **— — 55 65**

2302 U.P. GANTRY CRANE: 1981-82, maroon crane housing and boom, black platform spans track and runs on its own wheels, manually-operated, reproduction of 282 from 1954 but without motor and remote control.

           —   —   10   15

2303 SANTA FE: 1980-81, manual operating gantry crane, dark blue plastic cab, yellow boom and lettering, gray superstructure. Came as kit in 1072 Cross Country Express set.   —   —   20   25

2305 OIL DERRICK: 1981-83, walking beam rocks up and down, bubbling pipe simulates oil flow, hand-operated winch; ladder, barrels, red-painted sheet metal base; reissue of 455 from 1950-54.   —   —   60   70

2306 OPERATING ICE STATION: 1982-83, with reefer, reissue of 352 from 1955-57.   —   —   85   100

2307 BILLBOARD LIGHT: 1983-84, black die-cast post, hooded black light casting; attaches to base of billboard and blinks by thermostatic control.

           —   —   10   12

2308 ANIMATED NEWSSTAND: 1982-83, reissue of 128 from 1957-60.

           —   —   70   80

2309 MECHANICAL CROSSING GATE: 1982-83, operated by weight of train.   —   —   2   4

2310 MECHANICAL CROSSING GATE AND SIGNAL: 1973-75, activated by weight of train; black and white plastic, requires assembly.

           —   2   3   5

2311 MECHANICAL SEMAPHORE: 1982-83, operated by weight of train.   —   —   2   4

2312 MECHANICAL SEMAPHORE: 1973-75, activated by weight of train, flag raises and green signal illuminates as train approaches, flag lowers and red signal illuminates after train passes contact track .

           —   3   5   6

2313 OPERATING FLOODLIGHT TOWER: 1975-83, black plastic base, red plastic tower, black plastic top, eight miniature lights, two binding posts on bottom.   7   10   15   20

2314 OPERATING SEARCHLIGHT TOWER: 1975-83.
(A) Gray plastic tower and dark gray base, two searchlights; rare. G. Halverson Collection.   NRS
(B) Black plastic tower and base, red tower top, two searchlights. Somewhat hard to find. G. Halverson Collection.   15   20   25   30
(C) Same as 2314(A) but red tower, black base, red tower top. W. Eddins Collection.   7   10   15   20

2315 COALING STATION: 1984-85, reissue of 497 from 1953-58. Originally scheduled for number 2324, but that number was used later for the revival of the postwar 445 operating switch tower. Dark red metal structure, gray support base, black pillars, gray coal tray, gray roof. (Postwar version had maroon coal tray and green roof, and color of paint was lighter red.) This version uses the new Fundimensions can motor instead of the postwar motor, so it runs more quietly at lower voltage.   —   —   70   80

2316 NORFOLK & WESTERN: 1983-84, remote control gantry crane, essentially similar to the postwar 282R, but with several important construction changes. Dark maroon cab, gold lettering and cab base, maroon boom, gray superstructure. Does not have electromagnet found on the 282R. The single motor and gearing of the 282R has been replaced by two Fundimensions can motors mounted under the superstructure, one for each operation of the crane (swiveling of body and hook operation). Compared to the 282R, this crane is not as strong a lifting device, but it operates much more quietly than the 282R on much lower voltage. R. LaVoie Collection.   —   —   75   85

2317 DRAWBRIDGE: 1975-81, brown plastic piers, gray span, five pressure binding posts visible on right side of illustration, olive green tender house with terra cotta roof, brown door and steps, with one full length of 0-27 track and two half sections.   —   15   25   30

2318 CONTROL TOWER: 1983-84, red roof, yellow building, black superstructure, gray base (postwar 192 predecessor had orange and green colors). Two men move in circles around the building interior; powered by vibrator motor. Caution: many examples of both the postwar accessory and this version have damaged roofs caused by heat from the light bulb. The socket cannot be bent down, since the men pass under it. To prevent roof damage, replace the 14-volt light bulb supplied with the accessory with an 18-volt bayonet bulb. Fasten aluminum foil, shiny side out, to the underside of the

roof just above the light bulb. R. LaVoie comment and Collection.

           —   —   50   55

2319 WATCHTOWER: 1975-80, lighted non-operating version of postwar 445 switch tower. White body, maroon base and staircase, Penn Central green roof, red chimney, green door and window inserts.

           —   10   15   20

2320 FLAG POLE KIT: 1983, reissue of 89 from 1956-58. Reader comments on the similarities and differences between 89 and 2320 would be appreciated.   —   —   3   5

2323 OPERATING FREIGHT STATION: 1984-85, essentially similar to postwar 356. Dark red base, black baggage cart pathway, light tan housing, dark green roof, two green luggage carts (shown this way in catalogue, but production may differ), stick-on billboards, black fence with poster ads. Baggage carts move around station in alternation.   —   —   —   50

2324 OPERATING SWITCH TOWER: 1984-85, essentially similar to postwar 445. Dark red base, steps and upper doorway, tan building with dark brown door and window inserts, brown balcony, dark green roof with red chimney. One man runs into station house; other man comes down stairs; illuminated.   —   —   —   45

2494 ROTARY BEACON: 1972-74, red sheet metal tower with revolving beacon powered by vibrator motor, beacon projects red and green illumination, over 11-1/2" high, red stamped metal base 5" x 5"; black ladder, black-lettered aluminized foil nameplate on base, two clips on underside of base for wires. Construction of light hood differs from postwar 494; black plastic light hood rotates on circular metal collar which is frequently missing from used examples. Box at one time made by Stone Container Corporation; some have glue-on paper overlay with black and white picture of accessory, while other boxes lack this picture. This is one of the scarcest of all the Fundimensions accessories. Cole, Halverson and LaVoie comments; Halverson, Kruelle and LaVoie Collections.

          15   20   30   40

2709 RICO STATION: 1981-83, large plastic kit; 22" long by 9" wide, different versions were reportedly made. The 2797 from 1976 was made in different colors. Reader comments about specific colors appreciated.

          10   15   20   25

2710 BILLBOARDS: 1970-84, five plastic frames in box with strip of five billboards. Cardstock billboards have lavender bordering instead of dark green used on postwar examples; green frames have "STANDARD" in oval on ribbed bottom. Inside of frames stamped "2710 BILL BOARD MT. CLEMENS, MICH./MADE IN U.S.A." and Lionel logo.
(A) 1970-72, light green frames, MPC logo on inside of frame, Type I box. One sample observed had one dark green postwar and four Fundimensions frames. R. LaVoie and G. Halverson Collections.   3   4   5   6
(B) 1973-84, slightly darker green frames, Type II or Type III box, Lionel logo on inside of frame.   1   2   3   4

FUNDIMENSIONS BILLBOARD LISTINGS
 The following is our first listing of billboards produced by Fundimensions. Unless otherwise stated, dates reflect catalogue period for a particular billboard. We welcome additions to this list, especially since we suspect that there are many more uncatalogued billboards in existence. In addition, descriptions of the color and lettering schemes are needed with some of the billboards. The examples listed are from the collections of I. D. Smith, G. Halverson and R. LaVoie.
1. "BUY U. S. SAVINGS BONDS", 1970-71 stack of $50 bonds wrapped in red, white and blue flag wrapper on white background.
2. "EDUCATION IS FOR THE BIRDS (The Birds Who Want To Get Ahead)", 1970-71, uncatalogued; blue and red lettering on plain white background.
3. "GET A DODGE.", 1970-71, uncatalogued; cartoon figure of mule in brown tones, blue lettering on white background.
4. SHERATON HOTELS, 1970-71, blue and red rectangles; white lettering and white Sheraton logo.
5. BETTY CROCKER, 1970, blue script lettering on white background.
6. CHEERIOS, 1970, blue General Mills "G" and red lettering on white background.
7. LIONEL MPC, 1970-71, red "LIONEL" in modern typeface; red and blue lettering; red and blue MPC logo on white background.
8. AUTOLITE, 1970-71, uncatalogued; description needed.

2285

2787

2788

2791

2792

2793

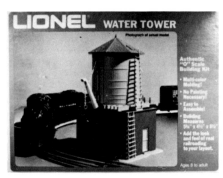

2789

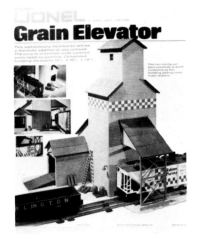

2796

2905

2927

9. PLAY-DOH, 1970-71, uncatalogued; description needed.

10. FOAM VILLAGE FOR LIONEL BY MYCO, 1971, uncatalogued; conveyor belt carries housing structures out of factory.

11. LIONEL, 1972-84, picture of Santa Fe F-3 locomotive in red, silver, black and yellow; "LIONEL" in modern red typeface.

12. FAMOUS PARKER GAMES, 1971-76, dark orange background, black lettering and black Parker Brothers "swirl" logo.

13. CRAFT MASTER, 1971-84, blue square at left with black and white Craft Master logo and white lettering, light brown portrait of mountain range at right.

14. MPC MODEL KITS, 1971-84, dark blue and white MPC logo, red lettering, cars, rocket and train on yellow and white background.

15. KENNER TOYS, 1972-76, yellow and red cartoon bird at right, white lettering on blue background.

16. SCHLITZ BEER, 1977-84, beer can and white lettering on red background.

17. BABY RUTH, 1977-84, picture of candy bar wrapper, red lettering on white background.

18. NIBCO WASHERLESS FAUCETS, 1982, uncatalogued; black Nibco logo, red lettering and picture of faucet on white background.

19. RIDE THE NIBCO EXPRESS, 1982, uncatalogued; black and white lettering and script on dark red background.

2714 TUNNEL: 1975-77, 15-1/2" x 13-1/2" x 10", two-piece construction.
2 3 5 7

2717 SHORT EXTENSION BRIDGE: 1977-83, 10" x 6-1/2" x 4-1/2"; plastic kit.
— 2 3 5

2718 BARREL PLATFORM: 1977-83, plastic kit includes figure, barrels, tools, lamp, ladder and building, 4" x 4" x 3-1/2".
— 1 2 4

2719 SIGNAL TOWER: 1977-83, described as "Watchman Shanty" in catalogue; 7" high, 4 x 4-1/2", plastic kit.
— 1 2 4

2720 LUMBER SHED: 1977-83, plastic kit includes workman, shed, table, lumber, tools, ladder; 4" high, 6" long, 3-1/2" wide .
— 1 2 4

2721 LOG LOADING MILL: 1979, red plastic kit, manual operation, pressing a lever causes plastic log to be released and roll down ramp; part of inexpensive "Workin' On The Railroad" sets.
NRS

2722 BARREL LOADER: 1979, green plastic kit, manual operation, workman pushes barrel down a chute; part of inexpensive "Workin' On The Railroad" sets.
NRS

2723 BARREL LOADER: 1984, brown plastic kit, manual operation, workman pushes barrel down chute; part of set 1403.
NRS

2729 WATER TOWER BUILDING KIT: 1985, orange-brown pump house with gray door and window insert, light tan base, gray ladder, green tower support frame, light tan tank, gray spout, green tank roof. Pictured in the 1985 Traditional Catalogue, but cancelled from dealer order sheets in September 1985.
Not Manufactured

2784 FREIGHT PLATFORM: 1981-83, snap together realistic 0 scale plastic kit with opening door.
2 3 6 9

2785 ENGINE HOUSE: 1974-77, plastic kit. Very similar kits have been produced in the past few years by Pola and others. This kit is very hard to find.
— 20 30 40

2786 FREIGHT PLATFORM: 1974-77, freight shed with platform, plastic kit.
— 3 4 7

2787 FREIGHT STATION: 1974-77, 1983, highly detailed 0 scale plastic kit.
3 5 7 10

2788 COALING STATION: 1975-77, plastic kit, coal may be mechanically dumped.
8 10 15 20

2789 WATER TOWER: 1975-80, water tower on brick structure, plastic kit.
— 3 7 10

2790 BUILDING KIT ASSORTMENT: 1983, details needed.
NRS

2791 CROSS COUNTRY SET: 1970-71, Type I box, five telephone poles, twelve railroad signs, watchman's shanty with crossing gate; 17-1/4" black trestle bridge; contents wrapped in brown paper inside box. Hard to find in unused condition. G. Halverson Collection.
— 15 20 25

2792 LAYOUT STARTER PAK: 1980-83, snap-together extension bridge kit, barrel platform kit, lumber shed kit, 10 telephone poles, 14 road signs, five billboards and a Track Layout Book.
— — 15 20

2792 WHISTLE STOP SET: 1970-71, details of contents needed.
— 10 15 20

2793 ALAMO JUNCTION SET: 1970-71, details of contents needed.
— 10 15 20

2796 GRAIN ELEVATOR: 1977, 16" high, 16" long, 13" wide, plastic kit.
— 15 20 25

2797 RICO STATION: 1976, large plastic kit 22" x 9" x 9" high, modeled after Rico, Colorado, station. See also 2709.
— 20 25 30

2900 LOCKON: 1970-85.
.20 .50 1 1.25

2901 TRACK CLIPS: 1970-85, 12-pack.
— 1 2 5

2905 LOCKON & WIRE: 1972-85, blister pack.
— .70 .85 1.50

2909 SMOKE FLUID: 1977-85, for locomotives made after 1970.
— 1 1.50 3

2927 MAINTENANCE KIT: 1977-85, consists of lubricant, oiler, track cleaning fluid, track cleaner, rubber eraser, all mounted on a piece of cardboard and shrink-wrapped.
(A) Type I packaging (same scheme as Type I box), oil, lubricant, eraser-type track cleaner and liquid track cleaner; materials are leftover postwar production with Hillside, N.J. factory address. G. Halverson Collection.
— — 7 10
(B) Type II or III packaging, Fundimensions-produced materials.
1 2 3 5

2951 TRACK LAYOUT BOOK: 1976-80, 83, several editions have been issued; see paper listings.
— .50 .75 2

2952 TRACK ACCESSORY MANUAL: See paper listings.
— — .75 1

2953 TRAIN & ACCESSORY MANUAL: 1977-85, several editions have been issued; see paper listings.
— — 1.25 2

2960 LIONEL 75TH ANNIVERSARY BOOK: 1975, see paper listings for description.
— 6 8 10

2980 MAGNETIC CONVERSION COUPLER: 1979 and probably other years as well, kit for replacing other types of couplers with magnetic operating couplers. Consists of plate assembly and coupler. I. D. Smith comment.
— — 1 2

8190 DIESEL HORN: 1981, electronic package that can be adapted to engines or rolling stock, operated by whistle button on older transformer. Type V box includes circuit board, speaker, two double-sided adhesive pads and instructions. Roller pickup assembly must be purchased separately if it is needed; unit can be installed with existing roller pickups. Price for unused unit only.
— — — 25

8251-50 HORN/WHISTLE CONTROLLER: 1972-74, rectangular push-button box for early Fundimensions horns and whistles. Easily burned out if contacts stick in closed position, as they often did. Came in black or red case with matching push button. R. LaVoie comment, G. Halverson Collection.
— — 2 3

9195 ROLLING STOCK ASSORTMENT: 1979. Lionel offered a 12-car assortment of its inexpensive cars for mass market sales (contrasted with collector market sales). Lionel provided two each from the following categories: short boxcar, short hopper, long gondola, short tank, work caboose and flatcar with fences. Each car has Bettendorf plastic trucks with one operating disc coupler and one fixed coupler. However, the specific road names and colors included probably changed during the production period to fit Fundimensions' convenience. We would appreciate reader listings of the contents of their assortments. Some cars needed assembly by purchaser. Bohn comment.

TRANSFORMERS

4045 SAFETY TRANSFORMER: 1970-71, black case, variable AC output, lever controls speed, automatic circuit breaker, two binding posts with one serving as forward and reverse button, 45-watt output. G. Halverson Collection.
1 2 3 4

4050 SAFETY TRANSFORMER: 1972-79, same as 4045, but red case.
1 2 3 4

4060 POWER MASTER: 1980-83, black case, fixed AC and variable DC output, direction reverse switch, automatic circuit breaker.
6 9 12 30

4090 POWER MASTER: 1978-81, 1983, AC output, right lever controls speed, left lever controls direction; fixed voltage taps, automatic circuit breaker.

10	15	20	55

4150 TRAIN MASTER TRANSFORMER — 3 6 12

4250 TRAIN MASTER TRANSFORMER — 3 6 12

4651 TRAIN MASTER: 1978-79, lever controls speed, two posts with button on one post for forward and reverse, automatic circuit breaker.

—	—	2	3

5900 AC/DC CONVERTER: 1979-81, 1983. — — 4 6

027 TRACK

5012 CURVED TRACK: 1980, 1983, four on card. — — 2.20 3.50

5013 CURVED TRACK .10 .30 .50 .55

5014 HALF-CURVED TRACK: 1980-83. .20 .40 .50 .75

5017 STRAIGHT TRACK: 1980-83, four on card. — — 3.50 3.50

5018 STRAIGHT TRACK .20 .40 .50 .75

5019 HALF-STRAIGHT TRACK .20 .40 .50 .75

5020 90 DEGREE CROSSOVER 1.50 3 3.50 4.75

5023 45 DEGREE CROSSOVER 1.50 3 4 6.50

5025 MANUMATIC UNCOUPLER: 1971-75, small Type I box with three black plastic uncoupling devices which clamp to track. Pushing a button raises two extensions between the rails; these are supposed to catch the coupler discs and pull them down. As a rule, these uncouplers do not work very well. Packed three to a box; instructions printed on the box. G. Halverson and R. LaVoie Collections. — — 1 2

5030 TRACK EXPANDER SET: 1972 Catalogue refers to this as "Switch Layout Expander Set". Type I box. Contains pair of manual switches, two sections of curved 027 track and six sections of straight 027 track. Made for distribution in Canada by Parker Brothers. See next entry for American production. G. Halverson Collection. — — — 25

5030 LAYOUT BUILDER SET: 1978-80, 83, pair of manual switches, two curved, six straight track. 10 14 17 25

5033 CURVED TRACK: Bulk packed, but sold individually.

.10	.20	.30	.75

5038 STRAIGHT TRACK: Bulk packed, but sold individually.

.10	.20	.30	.75

5041 0-27 INSULATOR PINS: 12 per pack. — — .50 1

5042 0-27 STEEL PINS: 12 per pack. — — .40 .75

5113 0-27 WIDE RADIUS TRACK: 16 sections make a 54 inch diameter circle per piece. — — 1.10 1.50

5149 REMOTE UNCOUPLING TRACK — 2.50 3.50 7.25

0-27 SWITCHES

5021 MANUAL SWITCH, LEFT 4 7 8 13

5022 MANUAL SWITCH, RIGHT 4 7 8 13

5027 PAIR MANUAL SWITCHES 8 13 15 26

5090 THREE PAIR MANUAL SWITCHES: 1983 — — 60 80

5121 REMOTE SWITCH, LEFT 7 11 14 20

5122 REMOTE SWITCH, RIGHT 7 11 14 20

5125 PAIR REMOTE SWITCHES 14 20 28 40

5823 45-DEGREE CROSSOVER: Type I or Type II shrink-wrap packaging, comes in light brown or dark brown base. G. Halverson Collection. — — 4 6

0 GAUGE TRACK, SWITCHES AND UNCOUPLERS

550S STRAIGHT TRACK: 1970, 10" long. .25 .30 .75 1.25

550C CURVED TRACK: 1970, 10-7/8" long. .25 .30 .75 1.25

UCS REMOTE CONTROL TRACK: 1970, accessory rails, two-button controller, magnet. 2 3 5 8

5132 REMOTE SWITCH, RIGHT: With controller. 15 20 33 40

5133 REMOTE SWITCH, LEFT: With controller. 15 20 33 40

5193 THREE PAIR REMOTE SWITCHES: 1983 — — 90 110

5500 STRAIGHT TRACK: 1971, 10" long. — .30 .75 1.25

5501 CURVED TRACK: 1971, 10-7/8" long. — .30 .75 1.25

5502 REMOTE CONTROL TRACK: 1971, 10" long. 2 3 5 8

5510 CURVED TRACK — .30 .75 1.25

5520 90 DEGREE CROSSOVER: 1971 2 3 5 7

5530 REMOTE UNCOUPLING SECTION: With controller.

6	9	11	13

5540 90 DEGREE CROSSOVER 3 5 7 8

5543 INSULATOR PINS: 1970, 12 per pack. .25 .50 .75 1

5545 45 DEGREE CROSSOVER: 1982. — — — 13

5551 STEEL PINS: 1970, 12 per pack. .25 .50 .75 1

5572 WIDE RADIUS CURVED TRACK: 16 pieces make a circle with a 72" diameter. Price per piece. .50 .75 1.25 2.50

TRUTRACK SYSTEM ITEMS, 1973-74

In 1973 and 1974, Fundimensions attempted a major innovation in its operating system with the introduction of "Trutrack". Trutrack featured a realistic T-shaped rail made from aluminum, wood-grained plastic ties at relatively close intervals, wide-radius curves and a thin, less conspicuous center rail. The track used a snap-lock assembly with rail joiners. The system featured separate pieces of rubberized ballasted roadbed which snapped onto each track or switch piece. The 1973 catalogue listed remote and manual switches, switch roadbed and lockons as well as the straight and curved track sections and their roadbed pieces. Unfortunately, aluminum track is not compatible with magnetraction. Although some sources have stated that Fundimensions had problems with the switches, which were supposed to have been made in Italy, we suspect that the incompatibility with magnetraction is the reason why the track was dropped from production after only small amounts were produced, since magnetraction was more important to Lionel's operating system than an improved track appearance. We have only confirmed the existence of straight track, straight roadbed and curved roadbed. G. Halverson comment.

5600 CURVED TRACK: 1973, not confirmed as produced.

5601 CARD OF FOUR CURVED TRACK: 1973, not confirmed as produced.

5600 CURVED TRACK: 1973, not confirmed as produced.

5601 CARD OF FOUR CURVED TRACK: 1973, not confirmed as produced.

5602 CARD OF FOUR ROADBED BALLAST FOR CURVED TRACK: 1973-74, actually came fastened together with rubber band inside packaging. G. Halverson Collection. — — 4 8

5605 STRAIGHT TRACK: 1973. G. Halverson Collection.

—	—	1	2

5606 CARD OF FOUR STRAIGHT TRACK: 1973, actually came fastened with rubber band inside packaging. G. Halverson Collection.

—	—	4	8

5607 CARD OF FOUR ROADBED BALLAST FOR STRAIGHT TRACK: 1973, actually came fastened together with rubber band inside packaging, Type II packaging. G. Halverson Collection. — — 4 8

5620 LEFT MANUAL SWITCH: 1973, not confirmed as produced.

5625 LEFT REMOTE SWITCH: 1973, not confirmed as produced.

5630 RIGHT MANUAL SWITCH: 1973, not confirmed as produced.

5635 RIGHT REMOTE SWITCH: 1973, not confirmed as produced.

5640 CARD OF TWO LEFT SWITCH ROADBED PIECES: 1973, not confirmed as produced.

5650 CARD OF TWO RIGHT SWITCH ROADBED PIECES: 1973, not confirmed as produced.

PERIPHERAL ITEMS

JC-1 LIONEL JOHNNY CASH RECORD ALBUM: 33-1/3 speed.

—	2	3	6

7-1100 HAPPY HUFF'N PUFF: 1975, train set, Fundimensions preschool toy push train similar to those made by Fisher-Price and Playskool, whimsical old-fashioned four-wheel steamer and two gondolas embossed with two large squares on their sides. Train is made of plastic simulated to look like wood. Wheels fastened with metal axles. Locomotive has smile-mouth and eye decorations. Came with a circle of two-rail plastic track and a story booklet showing "how Happy Huff'n Puff got his name". Bohn and LaVoie comments. — **4   7   9**

7-1200 GRAVEL GUS: 1975, a three-piece road construction set consisting of a grader with a large squared head seated on the chassis (presumably Gus) and two side dump cars. The grader has four large wheels and swivels in the center with a removable pusher blade. The two cars each have one axle with two large wheels, with the first car resting on the grader and the second car resting on the rear of the first car. The set is made from plastic simulated to resemble wood. It came with a full-color story booklet. Weisblum comment. **NRS**

7-1300 GRAVEL GUS JUNIOR: 1975, appears to be identical to 7-1200 Gravel Gus, except has only one side dump car. Bohn comment. **NRS**

7-1400 HAPPY HUFF'N PUFF JUNIOR: 1975, essentially similar to 7-1100 Happy Huff'n Puff, except does not include circle of track, locomotive has much thicker smokestack and gondolas are not embossed with large squares. These four pre-school toys were apparently offered only in 1975 through large toy outlets. Their success would have been an asset to Fundimensions, but they were launched into the teeth of a highly competitive pre-school market long dominated by giants such as Fisher-Price and Playskool. Bohn and LaVoie comments. **NRS**

2390 LIONEL MIRROR: 1981, old-fashioned mirror with dark walnut wood frame, gold, red and black decoration showing 1920-era boy with train set. — — **35   40**

NO NUMBER LIONEL CLOCK: 1976-77, made by American Sign and Advertising Services, Inc., 7430 Industrial Road, Industrial Park, Lawrence, Kentucky, 41042; white dial with black hand, red second hand, red field on bottom with white "LIONEL", available to Service Stations for $20.00 to $25.00. — — **25   30**

NO NUMBER LIONEL PENNANT: Plastic, white background, black trim on edge, black "LIONEL", left arrow red, right side arrow blue, "A LIFETIME INVESTMENT IN HAPPINESS" in black; 45" wide, 29-1/2" high. — — **2   4**

NO NUMBER BLACK CAVE VINYL PLAYMAT: 1982, from 1254 Black Cave Flyer set; 30" x 40"; from set 1355. — — — **10**

NO NUMBER COMMANDO ASSAULT TRAIN PLAYMAT: 1983, 30" x 40"; from set 1355. — — — **10**

NO NUMBER ROCKY MOUNTAIN FREIGHT PLAYMAT: 1983, 36" x 54", from set 1352. — — — **3**

NO NUMBER STATION PLATFORM: 1983, 23" x 3-1/2" x 5" similar to 2256 Station Platform, details requested; part of set 1351.
— — — **10**

NO NUMBER CANNONBALL FREIGHT VINYL PLAYMAT: 1982, 36" x 54"; two-piece mat, from set 1155. — — — **5**

NO NUMBER L.A.S.E.R. VINYL PLAYMAT: 1982, 36" x 54"; mat from set 1150. — — — **5**

A CREATION FROM A TINPLATE CHINESE MENU: THE FUNDIMENSIONS 2156 STATION PLATFORM

By Thomas S. Rollo

(Editor's Note: Tom Rollo is a Milwaukee collector of long experience. His interest in prototype traction is shown by his writing for the official magazine of the Minneapolis Transportation Museum, the **Minnegazette**. He is working on articles for our next edition of Lionel Postwar; these will include pieces on the Madison passenger cars, the 6454 boxcars, the Lionel Corporation's boxes and a light bulb study. He is also planning a comprehensive study of Lionel's freight and passenger stations. To round out his wide-ranging interests, Mr. Rollo also collects antique telephones.)

The earliest Fundimensions accessories were indeed a mixed lot. The company sought to make the most efficient use of the resources on hand. Sometimes this meant using leftover postwar stock by reissuing it in Fundimensions boxes.

Sometimes, Fundimensions combined leftover parts and assemblies in some unexpected ways. The 2156 Station Platform offers an interesting study in the use of resources by Fundimensions. This station was one of only a handful of accessories produced by MPC during the first two years of production. Yet, for such a simple accessory, the thought and research that went into the station is truly remarkable.

The photograph accompanying this article shows three generations of station platforms with roofs removed to reveal some important construction details. The station at the top of the photo is the original 156 Station Platform which was produced from 1939 to 1942 and again from 1945 to 1949. In the middle is the 157 Station Platform which was catalogued from 1952 to 1955 and from 1958 to 1959. At the bottom of the picture is the MPC-Fundimensions version of this station with lighting, the 2156, which was produced only in 1970 and 1971. A careful examination of these stations reveals that the Fundimensions station is a crossbreed between the two earlier stations.

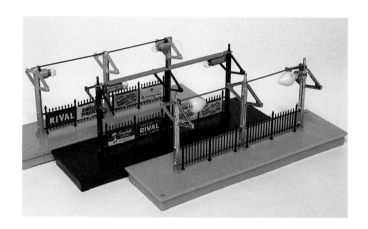

The "grandfather" version, the 156, has a base and roof made of compression-molded thermoset material marketed under the trade name of Bakelite. This station has a base painted Lionel's traditional green and a vermilion-painted roof. The roof supports are die-cast, with integral screw-base lamp sockets on each end support. To create the series electrical circuit for illumination, there is a metal rod passing the length of the platform between the two outermost roof supports. This rod bridges the two lamp base contacts together. With the end supports themselves, this arrangement creates the series circuit. The bulbs used were 6 to 8 volt number 50 miniature screw-base lamps. Lionel's catalogue number for these bulbs was 156-13.

The revival of the station platform in 1952 created an entirely new product. Unpainted injection-molded thermoplastic replaced the thermoset material. The roof supports were still die-cast, but new tool work for them was designed which omitted the lamp sockets and added the words "LIONEL LINES" vertically above the part number. These supports were now chemically blackened. The lamp sockets were relocated and changed to bayonet-based pieces which were part of a stamped metal clip which fit over the tips of the roof supports. The bulbs were changed to 6 to 8 volt number 51 bayonet bulbs; Lionel catalogued these as Q-90. Electrically, the new platform functioned the same as its 156 predecessor, even though the only pieces which were not changed cosmetically were the picket fence sections.

In 1970, after an absence of eleven years, the station platform returned as Fundimensions' 2156. One would expect that Fundimensions would use leftover postwar parts and molds to produce this station, but that is only partially true — and that is where the real interest lies in this piece. To be sure, the base and roof were injection-molded, using the tooling from the 157 of the 1950s. As would be expected, the engraving on the underside of the base was changed extensively to replace Lionel Corporation markings with MPC data and to mask out the G.E. (General Electric) letters in the lamp replacement information.

The roof supports of the 2156 are the surprise. They appear to be either entirely new tool work or old prewar tool work which has been extensively remodeled! Whatever these supports are, they certainly had their inspiration in the 156 station produced 21 years earlier. The roof is bright red and the base green; the color shades are quite close to those of the old 156 rather than the more recent 157.

The most amazing part of the 2156 station is the set of light bulbs issued with the piece. They are incredibly old! One station examined had original bulbs labeled "G.E. 18V". These are the round bulbs intended for use in the bracket lights on either side of the doors of the 115 Station, the prewar 116 Double Station, the 128 Station and Terrace, the 129 Terrace and the 155 Standard Gauge Freight Shed! This bulb bore the Lionel number 40-3. The bulb showing the operating voltage only instead of the manufacturer's lamp number dates the bulb as having been made prior to 1952, eighteen years before the production of the 2156!

Another 2156 had a pair of bulbs labeled "G.E. 14V". These bulbs are just as old as the others; they were intended for use in the number 58 Lamp Post, which took this acorn-shaped bulb. Lionel's number for these bulbs was 39-3. Had both of these bulbs been produced after 1952, when the light bulb codes were changed, they would have been numbered 1442W for the 18-volt and 1441W for the 14-volt. Apparently, someone at Fundimensions forgot that the circuitry for the 2156 was wired in series rather than in parallel. Series wiring meant that twice the voltage of the lamps was needed to light them. In other words, the proper operating voltage for the twin 14 volt lamps was 28 volts and the voltage for the two 18-volt lamps had to be a staggering 36 volts! An old T, K, V or Z transformer cranked up all the way could produce only 25 volts!

Why was the 2156 Station Platform produced in this way?

The answer probably lies in two areas: Fundimensions' desire to use all the parts on hand to minimize its costs and their practice of subcontracting. It seems reasonable to assume that Fundimensions inherited a great quantity of the old white-enameled bulbs when it took over the assets of the Lionel Corporation in 1970. In addition, the stamped metal cross rod of the 157 was probably subcontracted; therefore, the tooling for it was not available.

After the station was eliminated from the catalogue in 1972, Fundimensions reissued the station in 1973, deleting the lighting and changing the number to 2256. Curiously, the old die-cast roof supports in bright metal are still there, although the metal electrical cross rod has been omitted and the lamp sockets have been reduced to hollow untapped cylinders. This non-lighted version lasted through 1981. After an absence of a year, the station reappeared in 1983 as part of the Baltimore and Ohio "General" passenger train set. It had a brown base and a gray roof, but was still unlighted. This time, the roof supports were made in black unpainted plastic. Although it continued in the Baltimore and Ohio set through 1984, this station was not offered for separate sale. Finally, in 1985, Fundimensions resurrected the station platform once more, assigning it the number 2292. Like its predecessors, this station has a red roof and a green base, but both shades are much darker than the 2256. This parallels the development of the 157, when Lionel issued its later production with a dark red base instead of a maroon one and a deep green roof instead of a medium green one. Like the station accompanying the B&O set, the 2292 has unpainted black plastic roof support posts and is unlighted. Its price is considerably lower than its predecessors, no doubt because of the elimination of the die-cast roof supports. Judging from the way Fundimensions keeps resurrecting this little station platform, it also appears to have at least nine lives!

The 2156 Station Platform and its successors are eloquent testimony for the thought and research which went into Fundimensions' early product line. By merging the specifications for two different products, the firm achieved the most attractive colors, efficient production using injection molding and effective use of a leftover inventory of light bulbs, even if the voltage mistake is taken into account. Clearly, the early team of Fundimensions executives exhausted every effort to succeed when every decision was a risk.

Chapter VII
GONDOLAS

On real railroads, no piece of rolling stock takes as much steady abuse as the gondola car. Big loads of scrap steel, 55-gallon drums, machine parts, crushed automobiles and other assorted refuse of our highly industrialized society are routinely dropped with a bang into these decidedly non-glamorous cars with nary a thought for the car's appearance or shape. One never sees gondolas in new condition, it would seem. Instead, they are observed in varying stages of abuse and decay; some have rusted sides, some are dented beyond belief, but somehow all of them keep rolling on the rails and doing their jobs.

In a way, the Lionel gondolas were subjected to their own kind of abuse in the postwar period. Innumerable New York Central gondolas were made in black, red, green and blue versions, and because these cars were meant to be loaded and played with, they probably took more abuse at the hands of young railroaders than any other cars. Look through a tinplate junkpile at a train show, and chances are that most of the junk cars are gondolas. Not only that, but the cars were cheapened as the years went by. The postwar gondolas began with impressive metal frames and trucks and finished with absolutely bare undersides and cheap non-operating trucks and couplers.

In recent years Fundimensions may have reversed that trend by bringing some style to the lowly gondola car. Several of the most recent gondola issues have been equipped with the magnificent Standard "0" trucks; some have even been offered as separate-sale limited production items, such as the 6208 B&O meant to complete the Royal Limited set. New colors and rail markings have brightened the car considerably, and even the less expensive short gondolas have been at least made in brighter colors than their postwar predecessors.

Basically there have been three types of gondola bodies used by Fundimensions, one of a completely new design. The first one is the reissue of the short 6142 type of the postwar years. Typical of these direct reissues is the 9032 Southern Pacific gondola of 1975. Like all the new Fundimensions versions of the gondola, this car has molded brakewheels on each side rather than the older practice of separately installed metal ones or no brakewheels at all.

The second gondola is also a short car, but it is a version which is new with Fundimensions. This car is illustrated by the 9033 Penn Central of 1977. If you look closely, you can distinguish this car from the earlier carry-over model by the thick rim on the long sides of the car and the smaller molded brakewheel on the car sides. Like the other short gondola, this car has been used in inexpensive sets.

The third type of gondola is by far the most numerous and the most varied in type; it is the long 6462-type gondola. This car shows several construction variations from its later postwar predecessors. The Fundimensions car has molded brakewheels, where the older car either had metal ones or none at all. In the later postwar cars the bottom was absolutely smooth and devoid of all ornamentation. Fundimensions added girder and rivet work to the bottom of its 6462-type gondolas, and they look much better as a result.

If you look closely at the bottom of the Fundimensions gondolas, you will see a circle with the numbers "6462-2" and either "1" or "2" under the part number. This marking was present on the postwar cars as well. The presence of "1" and "2" numbering does not mean that a separate mold was used. It refers to the side of the mold from which the car emerged after the plastic injection process. The mold for the 6462-type cars was made in such a way that two cars were made at a time. The "1" and "2" numbers merely tell you which mold side your particular car came from.

The first of the early long gondolas was the 9140 Burlington model of 1970. This car was made in at least three shades of green, none being particularly more scarce than another. However, there is one version of the 9141 Burlington Northern from 1971 which is genuinely rare. Most of the 9141 production was green, but a few were made in tuscan. This car is highly prized. So is the 9143 Canadian National gondola made for Canadian sets distributed by Parker Brothers in 1971. This car is also very hard to find. Two Santa Fe gondolas of similar design can cause confusion as well. One of them, the 9284, was available in 1977 and 1978 in some sets; this car had a red and yellow body in a "half-and-half" paint configuration. In 1980 a black and yellow Santa Fe gondola of the same design was made for the Cross Country Express set. The black and yellow one is harder to find, although neither is really scarce. To add to the confusion, Republic Steel models have been made in different numbers in yellow, blue and green cars, all with the same Republic Steel logos and markings. All these are fairly common, though the yellow 9055 model is less frequently seen.

Since the Quaker City Limited collector set of 1978, most of the collector sets have included a gondola in colorful markings with Standard "0" trucks. Many of these gondolas, and some more common ones, have included round canisters like those of the postwar era. These canisters can be found in varying shades of orange, white, silver-gray and red. A few cars have the square radioactive waste canisters without the lighting apparatus.

There have been other gondolas in the Fundimensions lineup from time to time, some of them quite remarkable. Scale Standard "0" gondolas were produced for the Standard "0" Series beginning in 1973. These cars were scale-length with the sprung trucks typical of the series, and they also included a highly realistic coal load. They came in Wabash, Southern Pacific, Grand Trunk and New York Central markings. In the case of the Wabash, two examples of the car have been reported in gray rather than in black. Needless to say, these are probably factory prototypes and are extremely rare. Another Standard "0" gondola, again in New York Central markings, is scheduled for production in 1985.

Some gondolas were made to operate, using as models two highly successful operating cars from the postwar era. The 9307 Erie animated gondola is a direct reissue of the 3444 model of the postwar era. In this amusing and colorful car, the pull of a lever sets off a vibrator motor which turns a length of 35 mm film around two spools. Attached to the film by little metal clips are figures of a policeman and a hobo. The film and

6201

6205

6206

6208

9131

9136

9141

9142

spools are cleverly concealed by a load of crates, making it appear that the policeman is chasing the hobo around and around the crates. A less expensive version of this car came in Union Pacific markings. This car used a rubber band drive rather than a vibrator motor, and it would only work when the car was in motion. The other operating gondola, the 9290 Union Pacific model issued in 1983 as part of the Gold Coast Limited collector set, is a revival of the popular operating barrel car. A vibrator motor sends six wooden barrels up a chute built into the car; at the top of the chute, a workman kicks them off the car into a bin (or onto the postwar barrel ramp, which has not been reissued). This car was made in black and yellow Union Pacific markings. A tuscan Conrail barrel car was scheduled for 1984 production, but it was delayed until September, 1985. The Union Pacific car even has the old postwar bar-end metal trucks because this is the only truck which can be equipped with the sliding shoe contacts needed for the car's operation. Unfortunately, it is quite scarce. The handsome Conrail barrel car should make this type of car more available to operators and collectors.

The Fundimensions production of the gondola has added some much-needed color and attractiveness to this usually humdrum piece of rolling stock. The special collector series cars and some of the scarce variations in the earlier production are well worth a search by the Fundimensions collector.

	Gd	VG	Exc	Mt

6200 F.E.C.: 1981, orange body, yellow numbers and letters, three silver-finished plastic canisters; part of 1154 Reading Yard King set.

— — 8 10

6201 UNION PACIFIC: 1983, yellow body, tan crates, red lettering, animated car with rubber band belt drive from axle; railroad cop chases hobo around crates only when car is moving. See 9307 for vibrator motor version. — — 13 15

6202 WESTERN MARYLAND: 1982, black with white lettering, black plastic coal load, Standard 0 trucks; part of 1260 Continental Limited set. To date, this is the only gondola outside of the large Standard 0 series which is equipped with a coal load. C. Lang comment. — — 20 25

6205 CANADIAN PACIFIC: 1983, tuscan with white lettering, CP electrocal, Standard 0 trucks, two gray canisters; available as separate sale item. — — 15 20

6206 CHICAGO & ILLINOIS MIDLAND: 1983, red with white lettering, two gray atomic energy type canisters without lights and lettering, Symington-Wayne trucks; part of 1354 Northern Freight Flyer set.

— — 8 10

6207 SOUTHERN: 1983, black with white lettering, two red canisters, Symington-Wayne trucks; part of 1353 Southern Streak set.

— — 6 8

6208 B&O: 1983, dark blue body, yellow "B&O" and "6208" at left of car, yellow Chessie cat at center, and yellow "Chessie System" at right; reporting marks along lower girders, Standard 0 trucks, two gray canisters; designed to be added to the 1980 Royal Limited set, Type V box. LaVoie Collection. — — 15 20

6209 NEW YORK CENTRAL: 1985, Standard 0 gondola, black body, white lettering, Standard 0 trucks, simulated coal load. — — — 25

6210 ERIE-LACKAWANNA: 1984-85, black body, white lettering and Erie logo, Standard 0 trucks, two gray unlettered atomic energy containers; from Erie-Lackawanna Limited set. — — — 25

6211 CHESAPEAKE & OHIO: 1984-85, unpainted black body, yellow lettering and logo, two yellow canisters, Symington-Wayne trucks; from set 1402. — — — 10

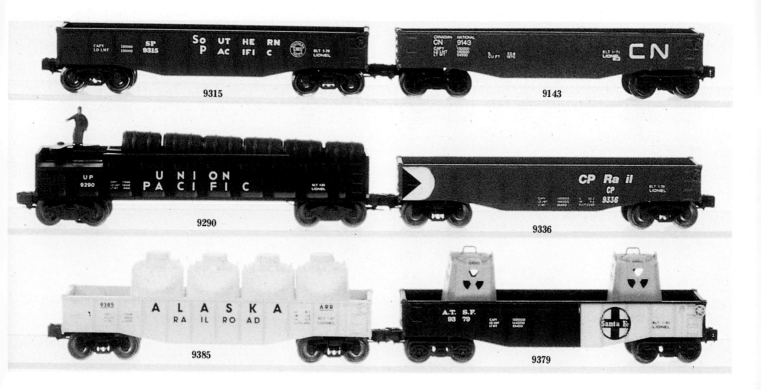

9315   9143

9290   9336

9385   9379

6214 LIONEL LINES: 1983-84, orange body and interior, last four outer panels on right painted dark blue, "LIONEL/LINES" in dark blue across orange panels; red, white and blue "L" circular herald on blue area; car number under and overscored, Symington-Wayne trucks.

—   —   25   30

6258 ATSF: Announced for 1985, short gondola, blue body, yellow lettering and logo, Symington-Wayne trucks, dummy couplers; part of Midland Freight set. —   —   —   6

6260 NEW YORK CENTRAL: Announced for 1985, gray body, black lettering and oval NYC logo, two black canisters, Symington-Wayne trucks; part of Yard Chief switcher set. —   —   —   9

9017 WABASH: 1978, 1980-81, red with white lettering, Symington-Wayne trucks, three canisters. —   —   4   5

9030 KICKAPOO VALLEY AND NORTHERN: 1972, black base.
(A) Green top.   2   3   5   7
(B) Red top.   1   2   3   4
(C) Yellow top.   2   3   4   6

9031

9031 NICKEL PLATE: 1974, 1979, 1983, brown body, white lettering, Symington-Wayne trucks; fixed couplers 1974, 1979, operating couplers 1983. We do not know if the 1983 version has small or large brakewheel. The 1983 version came as part of 1253 Heavy Iron set.
(A) Large brake wheel.   2   3   5   7
(B) Small brake wheel.   2   3   5   7

9032

9032 SOUTHERN PACIFIC: 1975, 1978, red body, white lettering, Symington-Wayne trucks, fixed couplers.
(A) Light red body, small brakewheel.   1   2   3   4
(B) Dark red body, small brakewheel.   1   2   3   4
(C) Medium red body, large brakewheel.   1   2   3   4

9033

9033 PENN CENTRAL: 1977, 1979, 1981, 1982, light green body, white lettering, Symington-Wayne trucks, fixed couplers, small brakewheel.

1   2   3   4

9055 REPUBLIC STEEL: 1977-81, yellow body, dark blue lettering, one fixed coupler, one manumatic coupler, Symington-Wayne trucks, three silver canisters, plastic wheels.   4   6   8   10

9131 RIO GRANDE: 1974, orange body, black lettering, Symington-Wayne trucks, one disc coupler, one fixed coupler, no MPC logo.
(A) Light orange body.   1   2   3   4
(B) Medium orange body.   1   2   3   4
(C) Darker orange body.   1   2   3   4

9136 REPUBLIC STEEL: 1972-79, blue body, white lettering, Symington-Wayne trucks, one manumatic coupler, one fixed coupler, plastic wheels, MPC logo.
(A) Lighter blue.   1   2   3   4
(B) Medium blue.   1   2   3   4
(C) Darker blue.   1   2   3   4
(D) Darker blue, MPC logo dropped, post-1972 production. C. Rohlfing comment.   1   2   3   4

9140 BURLINGTON: 1970-71, 1980-81, green body, white lettering, one manumatic coupler, one fixed coupler, plastic wheels.
(A) 1970, light green body, AAR trucks, flat surface brakewheel, MPC logo.   1   2   3   4
(B) 1971, medium light green body, Symington-Wayne trucks, raised brakewheel, no MPC logo.   1   2   3   4
(C) 1971, medium dark green body, Symington-Wayne trucks, no MPC logo.   1   2   3   4

(D) 1971, dark green body, Symington-Wayne trucks, no MPC logo.

                                             1   2   4   5

See also Factory Errors and Prototypes.

9140

9141 BURLINGTON NORTHERN: 1971, green body, white lettering, Symington-Wayne trucks (except C), one manumatic coupler, one fixed coupler, metal wheels, MPC logo, flat surface brakewheel.
(A) Light green body.   **1   2   3   4**
(B) Medium green body.   **1   2   3   4**
(C) Dark green body, AAR trucks. C. Rohlfing comment.
                                         3   4   5   6
(D) Tuscan body, Canadian production only; very hard to find. When sold separately, came in Parker Brothers Type I box with small cellophane window and black Parker Brothers logo. G. Halverson Collection.
                                  —   —   95 115

See also Factory Errors and Prototypes.

9142 REPUBLIC STEEL: 1971, green body, white lettering, Symington-Wayne trucks, one manumatic coupler, one fixed coupler, plastic wheels, MPC logo.
(A) Dark green body.   **1   2   3   4**
(B) Medium green body, recessed whirley brakewheel. Rohlfing Collection.   **1   2   3   4**
(C) Medium green body, flat brakewheel, stamped "LCCA". Rohlfing Collection.   **NRS**

See also Factory Errors and Prototypes.

9143 CANADIAN NATIONAL: 1973, maroon body, white lettering, Symington-Wayne trucks, one manumatic coupler, one fixed coupler, metal wheels, MPC logo; sold primarily in Canada; somewhat hard to find.
                              10 15 20 25

9144

9144 RIO GRANDE: 1974, black body, yellow lettering, Symington-Wayne trucks, two disc couplers, metal wheels, no MPC logo.
                                 1   2   4   5

See also Factory Errors and Prototypes.

9225 CONRAIL: 1984-85, operating barrel car, tuscan body, black chute, white lettering and Conrail "wheel" logo, blue man with flesh-colored hands and face, six varnished barrels, postwar bar-end metal trucks, includes black dump tray. At press time, this car had not yet been distributed; the latest information is that it will in fact be made, despite persistent stories to the contrary. Estimated price at introduction.
                               —   —   —   40

9283

9283 UNION PACIFIC: 1977, yellow body, red lettering, Symington-Wayne trucks, metal wheels, no MPC logo; part of 1760 Heartland Express set. C. Lang comment.   **2   5   8 10**

9284

9284 SANTA FE: 1977-78, red and yellow body, yellow and red lettering, Symington-Wayne trucks, metal wheels, no MPC logo; part of 1762 Wabash Cannonball set. C. Lang comment.   **6   8 10 12**

9290 UNION PACIFIC: 1983, operating barrel car, man "unloads" barrel, vibrator mechanism, six varnished wooden barrels, plastic unloading bin, black body, yellow lettering. Postwar bar-end metal trucks used because Standard 0 trucks were not adaptable to sliding shoe mechanism. Reissue of 3562-type car from 1954-58 although with new road name. Only available as part of 1361 Gold Coast Limited set. C. Lang comment.
                                 —   —   —   60

9307 ERIE: 1979-80, red with white lettering and Erie logo, 027-style die-cast passenger trucks, gray crate load with black lettering, animated car with vibrator motor; railroad cop chases hobo around crates when lever is pulled.
(A) Partially painted hobo.   **—   — 33 40**
(B) Completely painted hobo. Mellan Collection. Other observations show differences in the cop and hobo figures, such as elaborate hand-painting on either or both figures which may be factory production. Further reader comments are invited.   **NRS**

See also Factory Errors and Prototypes.

9315 SOUTHERN PACIFIC: 1979, brown plastic body painted brown, white lettering, "BLT 1-79", Southern Pacific decal with white letters on black background, built-in small brakewheel, part of Southern Pacific Special set, Standard 0 trucks.   **12 15 20 25**

9336 CP RAIL: 1979, red plastic car, 9-9/16" long, white lettering, brakewheels embossed in car ends, black and white logo appears at end opposite brakewheel, Standard 0 trucks; came in Type IV box, 6462 mold designation on underside; from 1971 Quaker City Limited set. Miller observation.   **— 12 15 20**

9340 ILLINOIS CENTRAL GULF: 1979-81.
(A) Orange body with black lettering, yellow canisters, plastic wheels, Symington-Wayne trucks.   **—   —   3   5**
(B) Red body with white lettering, no canisters, Symington-Wayne trucks; part of 1159 Midnight Flyer set made for Toys 'R Us. G. Kline Collection.
                                  NRS

9370 SEABOARD: 1980, tuscan with yellow lettering, three silver-finished plastic canisters, Standard 0 trucks; from 1071 Mid-Atlantic Limited set.
                                  — 12 15 20

9379 ATSF: 1980, black and yellow, two gray plastic canisters, Symington-Wayne trucks; came with 1072 Cross Country Express.
                                — 10 12 15

9385 ALASKA: 1981, yellow with black lettering, four white canisters, Standard 0 trucks; part of 1160 Great Lakes Limited set.
                                — 12 15 20

9820 WABASH: 1973-74, simulated coal load, Standard 0 series with Standard 0 trucks.
(A) Black body, white lettering.   **20 25 30 35**
(B) Brown body, coal load, not produced with trucks or truck mounting holes. Produced by Lionel on special order for 0 Scale modelers to mount own trucks; originally sold by dealer Andrew Kriswalus. C. Lang Collection.   **NRS**
(C) Same as (B), but black body and coal load. C. Lang Collection.   **NRS**

See also Factory Errors and Prototypes.

9821

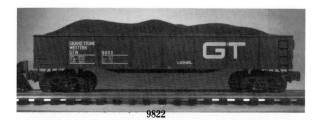

9822

9824

9821 SOUTHERN PACIFIC: 1973-74, brown or black body, white lettering, simulated coal load, Standard 0 series with Standard 0 trucks.

(A) Brown body.	**20**	**25**	**30**	**35**
(B) Black body; hard to find.	—	—	**175**	**200**

See also Factory Errors and Prototypes.

9822 GRAND TRUNK: 1974, blue body, white lettering, simulated coal load, Standard 0 series with Standard 0 trucks. **20 25 30 35**

9824 NEW YORK CENTRAL: 1975, black body, white lettering, simulated coal load, Standard 0 series with Standard 0 trucks. **20 25 30 35**

Chapter VIII
TANK AND VAT CARS

9050
9051
6301
6302
6304
6305
6306
6315-1972

As of a few years ago, Fundimensions has revived all the major tank car styles used in the postwar years. The last such style to be revived was the 6465-type two-dome tank car which emerged in Shell markings in 1983. It is not too surprising that Fundimensions has paid a great deal of attention to tank cars, even though in the real railroad world these cars are far more common in refinery areas than they are in other parts of the country. After all, one of the largest sales markets for toy trains is on the East Coast, where tankers are rather common.

What is surprising is that Fundimensions has not produced its own original versions of tank cars. On the real railroads, tank cars exist in astonishing variety, and many scale model firms have issued much more modern tank car varieties than has Fundimensions. Perhaps it is a simple matter of projected sales versus tooling costs. Now that the firm is producing scale-length locomotives such as the SD-40 and scale cabooses like the extended vision model, perhaps we will see more scale

cars in tinplate in the future. It's a promising direction for Fundimensions to take; new types of rolling stock tend to revitalize a toy train maker's line.

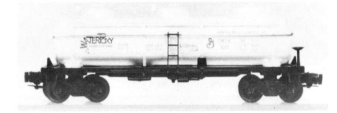

9250 Waterpoxy Tank Car with bar-end trucks. This is believed to be the first piece of rolling stock produced by Fundimensions and sold to the general public. Note that the brakewheel is on a raised stalk, like postwar tank cars. The later version has a brakewheel placed flat on the frame. R. LaVoie Collection, G. Stern photograph.

154

6357   9250

9150   9158

9278   9313

9321   9324

The Fundimensions tank cars begin in early 1970 with the interesting 9250 GMCX "Waterpoxy" tank car with three domes. The construction differences between the Fundimensions cars and those made in the postwar era are more or less minor. The postwar cars had their brakewheels on a raised shaft; most of these are mounted directly on the frame without the shaft in Fundimensions production. The 9250 tank car had several interesting varieties, and one of them may have been the first freight car actually made by Fundimensions. The earliest version of the 9250 came with leftover bar-end metal postwar trucks; it was made in Hillside, not Mount Clemens. (Other collectors dispute this theory, citing the fact that the 9250 was not catalogued until 1971. We invite your opinion.) Soon, the car came with regular-issue Symington-Wayne trucks. The latest production of the 9250 featured lettering and coloring which was much brighter than its predecessors; in addition, where these had come in a large Type I box, this last version was shoehorned into a small Type I box.

The three-dome tank car has had many successors since the 9250. It has come in Sunoco, DuPont, Bakelite, Gulf, Magnolia and many other real railroad and corporate names. Strangely, there are not too many variations of these cars, and none of the three-dome tank cars is especially rare. The hardest ones to acquire are the ones in limited sets, such as the 9138 black Sunoco and the 9313 Gulf.

In the same beginning year of 1970, Fundimensions also revived the excellent postwar 6315-type single-dome platform tank car. This first appeared as a white-bodied car with black and orange Gulf lettering which is a little more difficult to find than most other tank cars. Typically, the orange and black lettering is not too sharp; it is often fuzzy and blurred. Fundimensions soon corrected its early logo problems, however, and most of the single-dome tank cars have good, clear logos.

There are two different tank ends found on the single-dome tank cars. The first type was used up to the 9153 Chevron tank car in 1974; this tank car end had "Lionel" lettering just above the wire railing, as did all the postwar single-dome tank cars. The second type omits this lettering; and the Chevron car is the only one which has both types of ends.

There is another curious tank car body available; it is found inside a boxcar! This car-within-a-car was issued for the Lionel Collectors' Club of America as the 97330 Airco. Many collectors have taken the tank out of the boxcar body and added a frame, railings and a platform to create a 97330 Airco tank car to match the boxcar. This curious arrangement has not been duplicated since.

Another unusual situation occurred with two nearly identical yellow Shell single-dome tank cars. Fundimensions issued the

97330 Airco Tank and Boxcar with broken truck.

9151 Shell tank car in 1972 with a yellow body, red lettering and yellow ends. Apparently, somebody thought the car looked a little too plain, because in the next production year the car's number was changed to 9152, the lettering became a little more bold and the ends were made black instead of yellow. As a result, the all-yellow 9151 is a great deal more difficult to find than many collectors believe.

Some innovative decorating schemes have made their debuts with the single-dome tank car. In 1975 Fundimensions surprised collectors with its Borden tank car which featured a shiny, simulated chrome-plated body. Black lettering and black ends gave it an extremely formal look which was popular with many collectors. This example was soon followed by others in Gulf, Sunoco, Texaco and Mobilgas markings. In 1978 Fundimensions hit a jackpot with an unusual and fanciful car which won a great following for its bright decoration. This was the 9278 Lifesavers tank car; the body of the car was covered by an incredibly bright pressure-sensitive decal to make the car look like a large roll of multicolored Lifesavers candy rolling down the tracks. This car sold so well that Fundimensions next issued a single-dome tank car which looked like a Tootsie Roll candy package.

Another candy tanker was scheduled for production but was deleted before the advance catalogue came out in early 1979. This was the Pep-O-Mint tank car, which would have been similar to the Life Savers tank car except for stripes in pink, black and white. Although the car was never produced, the decals were in fact printed, and some have gotten into circulation. The collector should know that any such car is a product of decal application outside of the factory rather than actual production. It is not clear why the car was withdrawn, especially in view of the huge success of the Lifesavers car. Perhaps the candy company withdrew its permission to use its trademark very late in the production cycle. That did, in fact, happen with the 9879 Kraft Philadelphia Cream Cheese refrigerator car, for which a few prototypes exist in the Mount Clemens archives. The 9879 number was hurriedly reassigned to the Hills Brothers car.

A small, all-plastic single-dome tank car similar to postwar models has also been made for inexpensive sets by Fundimensions. This car has been made in Mobilgas (two colors), Firestone, Alaska and Sunoco markings on a plastic frame rather than the postwar metal frame. The 9050 yellow Sunoco is a little harder to find than all the others, probably because it was the first and an exact remake of the postwar 6015 yellow

car. These small tank cars do not attract too much collector attention (except for the Alaska tank car) and are usually easy to find at inexpensive prices.

The two-dome tank car modeled upon the omnipresent postwar 6465 Sunoco tank car has been a recent addition to the Fundimensions line in Shell and Gulf markings. It illustrates a curious phenomenon reported by many dealers in its Shell configuration — yellow cars and locomotives do not, as a rule, sell very well. Nobody seems to know why this is so, unless it is because the public does not perceive yellow as a prototypical color and therefore judges the rolling stock as unrealistic.

The Fundimensions vat car is a curious but attractive creation. A metal frame is the foundation for a low-slung open framework car with a roof supported by girder work on the sides and ends. Within this open framework are four round vats anchored to the car base. The roof has simulated hatches atop each of the vats. The first Fundimensions vat car to emerge was the Heinz pickle car in 1974. Like its postwar predecessor, this car has several variations, including unmarked vats as an interesting factory error. This car was followed by a Libby pineapple vat car in 1975 and a Mogen-David wine car in 1977.

Only two other vat cars have been produced since the first three, but these two may indicate a new direction for the vat cars. In 1983 an extremely handsome Budweiser beer vat car was produced in red, white and silver markings. It was such a good seller that it was followed by a blue and white Miller Lite beer vat car. These two cars may mean that Fundimensions plans on marketing its future vat cars in beer markings; this strategy would create an interesting series of cars for collectors.

Although very few of the Fundimensions tank cars are true rarities, they are certainly colorful, and a good collection can be built by the beginning collector at relatively modest prices. The tank cars from the collector sets, such as the 9277 Cities Service, the 9331 Union 76 and the 6305 British Columbia, show excellent potential for appreciation in value because of their limited production.

TANK AND VAT CARS

Fundimensions adopted the 6315 chemical tank car (the platform, single tank car) as its preferred style. It modified the 6315 tank by replacing the brakewheel on a standing post with a low brakewheel on the frame. Fundimensions created two types of platform, single-dome cars.

Type 1: Lettering on the ends above the railing.
Type 2: No lettering on the car ends.
9153 Chevron comes with both Type 1 and 2 ends. Starting with 9154 Borden, circa 1975, only Type 2 ends are found.

	Gd	VG	Exc	Mt
303 STAUFFER CHEMICAL: 1985, single-dome, special production for Lionel Operating Train Society. Unpainted dark gray tank with wide painted black band at center; design similar to original postwar 6315 Gulf model. Black dome top, orange Stauffer Chemicals logo, black "Stauffer Chemical Co." script, "SCHX 303/CAPY." on tank ends, black-painted metal railings instead of usual chrome, Symington-Wayne trucks, Type III box. T. Herner Collection.	—	—	30	35
6300 CORN PRODUCTS: 1981, yellow body, three-dome, black lettering, Symington-Wayne trucks; from 1154 Reading Yard King set.	—	—	14	16
6301 GULF: 1981-82, single-dome, white with orange "Gulf", Symington-Wayne trucks.	—	—	10	12
6302 QUAKER STATE: 1981-82, dark green body; white lettering, black frame, Symington-Wayne trucks, three-dome. C. Rohlfing comment.	—	—	15	18

6304 GREAT NORTHERN: 1981, dark green tank, black platform, single-dome, white lettering, black and white Great Northern logo, gold FARR Series 3 logo, Standard 0 trucks, from Famous American Railroads Series 3, only available as separate sale. C. Rohlfing comment. — — **15 18**

6305 BRITISH COLUMBIA: 1981, light green tank, black platform, single-dome; white lettering, Standard 0 trucks; from 1158 Maple Leaf Limited set. — — **30 35**

6306 SOUTHERN: 1983, single-dome: silver tank, black lettering, gold FARR 4 series emblem, Standard 0 trucks; separate sale item.

— — **20 25**

6307 PENNSYLVANIA: 1984-85, single-dome, deep maroon tank, black frame, black ladders, catwalk and dome top; white lettering, gold FARR 5 logo, Standard 0 trucks. — — **25**

6308 ALASKA: 1982, short single-dome, dark blue tank, black frame; yellow lettering and eskimo logo, one operating and one fixed coupler, Symington-Wayne trucks. — — **10 12**

6310 SHELL: 1983, 6465-style two-dome, yellow tank body; red lettering and logo, black stamped-steel frame, Symington-Wayne trucks; separate sale item. Caponi comment. — — **8 10**

6312 CHESAPEAKE & OHIO: 1984-85, 6465-style two-dome, black tank body; yellow lettering, stamped metal frame, Symington-Wayne trucks; part of set 1402. — — — **10**

6313 LIONEL LINES: 1983-84, single-dome, bright orange tank body, blue tank ends; red, white and blue circular Lionel logo at left and "LIONEL/LINES" in dark blue at right, Symington-Wayne trucks. Limited production. — — **30 35**

6315 TCA PITTSBURGH: 1972, single-dome, made for TCA annual convention at Pittsburgh. Orange tank body, black dome; black "7-11" lettering, postwar bar-end metal trucks. — — **65 75**

6317 GULF: 1984-85, 6465-style two-dome, white tank body; orange lettering, orange and white Gulf logo, stamped metal frame, Symington-Wayne trucks. — — — **10**

6357 FRISCO: 1983, single-dome, black tank; white lettering, yellow tank cover, Standard 0 trucks. Only available as part of 1361 Gold Coast Limited set. — — **30 40**

9036 MOBILGAS: 1978-80, single-dome, small frame, 7-7/16 inches long, white plastic tank painted white with red lettering, black ends, one brakewheel; Symington-Wayne trucks, one disc coupler with tab, one fixed coupler, metal wheels.
(A) As described above. **1 2 3 5**
(B) Same as (A), but LCCA meet car overstamp, 1978-79. C. Rohlfing comment. **NRS**

9039 MOBILGAS: 1978, 1980, red single-dome plastic tank painted red, black ends; white lettering, black frame, one brakewheel, Symington-Wayne trucks, metal wheels, one disc coupler with tab, one fixed coupler.
1 2 3 5

9050 SUNOCO: 1970-71.
(A) Yellow-orange body, blue lettering, AAR trucks, one operating coupler, one fixed coupler, MPC logo, medium orange-yellow background in Sunoco logo. **4 5 7 9**
(B) Medium yellow body, blue lettering, Symington-Wayne trucks, one operating coupler, one fixed coupler, MPC logo, medium orange-yellow background in Sunoco logo. **4 5 7 9**
(C) Same as (B), but dark yellow body. **4 5 7 9**
(D) Same as (B), but light yellow body, light orange-yellow background in Sunoco logo. **4 5 7 9**
(E) Same as (B), but with green lettering. **NRS**

9051 FIRESTONE: 1974-75, short car, Symington-Wayne trucks, one operating coupler, one fixed coupler, no MPC logo.
(A) Unpainted shiny white body, light blue lettering.
3 4 5 7
(B) Painted flat white body, blue lettering. **3 4 6 8**

9106 MILLER BEER: 1984-85 vat car, dark blue body and roof; white lettering, metal chassis, four white vats with red, gold and blue Miller logo, Symington-Wayne trucks. — — — **12**

9128 HEINZ: 1974-76, red roof, gray sides, red lettering on frame, Symington-Wayne trucks.

(A) Medium yellow vats, green lettering.	6	8	10	12
(B) Light yellow vats, green lettering.	6	8	10	12

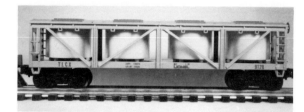

(C) Medium yellow vats, no lettering.	15	20	25	35
(D) Light yellow vats, light turquoise lettering.	12	15	20	25
(E) Medium yellow vats, turquoise lettering.	12	15	20	25

9132 LIBBY'S CRUSHED PINEAPPLE: 1975-77, green roof, gray sides, yellow vats; red and brown lettering on vats, green lettering on frame, Symington-Wayne trucks. **6 8 10 12**

9138 SUNOCO: 1978, three-dome, black tank body; white lettering, Sunoco decal, "BLT 1-78", black plastic frame, black brakewheel, Standard 0 trucks, disc couplers with tabs; part of 1868 Minneapolis and St. Louis Service Station set. **15 20 25 30**

9146 MOGEN DAVID: 1977-79, silver roof, blue sides, tan vats; blue vat lettering, white frame lettering, Symington-Wayne trucks.
6 8 10 12

9147 TEXACO: 1977, single-dome, chrome and black body; red and black lettering, Symington-Wayne trucks, two operating couplers, no MPC logo. **8 10 12 15**

9148 DUPONT: 1977-79, 1981, three-dome, cream, yellow and green body; green lettering, red logo, Symington-Wayne trucks, no MPC logo, operating couplers. **6 8 10 12**

9150 GULF: 1971, single-dome, white body; black and orange lettering and logo, Symington-Wayne trucks, operating couplers, MPC logo. Typically, many examples of this car have fuzzy, ill-defined markings. Slight premium for well-marked example.
(A) Black and orange lettering. **10 15 20 25**
(B) Black and dark orange lettering. P. Piker Collection.
10 15 20 25

9151 SHELL: 1972, single-dome, yellow body, yellow ends, yellow tank top; red lettering, Symington-Wayne trucks, operating couplers, MPC logo. This car most likely came only in sets. **8 10 12 15**

9277   9331

9334   9344

9353   9354

9367   9369

9373   9386

9152 SHELL: 1973-74, single-dome, yellow body, black ends, black tank top; red lettering (bolder and darker than on 9151), Symington-Wayne trucks, operating couplers, no MPC logo. This car came in sets and was offered for separate sale. Early production had postwar-style tank ends with "L" in a circle, as on the postwar 6315. Later production did not have this circle. G. Halverson comment. Same comment applies to next entry.

(A) Light yellow body.	6	7	9	12
(B) Medium yellow body.	6	7	9	12

9153 CHEVRON: 1974-76, single-dome, silver and blue body; blue lettering, Symington-Wayne trucks, operating couplers, no MPC logo.

(A) Light blue and red decals.	6	8	10	12
(B) Dark blue and orange decals.	6	8	10	12

9154 BORDEN: 1975-76, single-dome, chrome and black body, black lettering, Symington-Wayne trucks, operating couplers, no MPC logo. This was the first Fundimensions tank car to feature a chromed finish.

                                6   8   10   12

9155 MONSANTO: 1975, LCCA Convention car, white single-dome tank body; black lettering, red "M" logo on left of tank, Symington-Wayne trucks. C. Rohlfing comment.   —   —   50   60

9156 MOBILGAS: 1976-77, single-dome, chromed tank body; red and blue lettering and logo, Symington-Wayne trucks, operating couplers.

                                8   10   12   15

9159 SUNOCO: single-dome, chrome and blue body; blue lettering, Symington-Wayne trucks, operating couplers, no MPC logo; available only in sets.   20   25   30   35

9189 GULF: single-dome, chrome and black body; blue lettering, Symington-Wayne trucks, operating coupler, no MPC logo; available only in sets.   15   20   25   30

9193 BUDWEISER: 1983, silver roof, red sides, red and white vats, red vat lettering, Symington-Wayne trucks; separate sale item that has sold well. C. Rohlfing and Caponi comment.   —   10   12   15

9250 WATERPOXY: 1971, three-dome, white body, blue and green lettering, MPC logo. One sample observed came in Type I box dated July 1971. T. Rollo comment.

(A) Postwar bar-end metal trucks, two old-type raised brakewheel stands. This was the first freight car made by Fundimensions; it was manufactured at the old Lionel Hillside, New Jersey plant before the firm moved to Mount Clemens, Michigan. (See Introduction.) R. LaVoie comment.

7	10	15	20

(B) Symington-Wayne trucks, two operating couplers, one plastic brakewheel.

6	8	10	12

(C) Same as (B), but white-painted translucent tank and ends, much brighter green and blue lettering than (A) or (B), Symington-Wayne trucks, came in smaller Type I box with black "9250/G.M.C.X./TANK CAR" stamped in black on ends. Probably very late production. R. LaVoie collection.

8	10	12	15

9277 CITIES SERVICE: 1977, single-dome, green body and dome, metal ladder and platform around dome, black plastic frame, one brakewheel, handrails run nearly completely around tank, Standard 0 trucks. Part of Milwaukee Special set of 1977.

10	15	20	25

9278 LIFESAVERS: 1978-79, platform, single-dome; extraordinarily bright pressure sensitive decal showing five flavors, tank and dome car chrome-plated, metal walk and ladders, metal handrails run nearly completely around car, one brakewheel, Symington-Wayne trucks.

10	12	15	20

9279 MAGNOLIA: 1978-79, three-dome, white plastic body painted white, black ends, black lower third of tank, shiny metal handrails, black metal ladders, black plastic frame, Symington-Wayne trucks.

6	8	10	12

9313 GULF: 1979, three-dome, black plastic painted shiny black; white lettering, orange and black Gulf logo, shiny metal handrail, black metal ladders, one brakewheel, Standard 0 trucks; part of Southern Pacific Limited set.

—	20	25	30

9321 A.T.S.F.: 1979, single-dome, silver-painted body, metal walkway, black metal ladders, dull metal handrail almost all the way around, black plastic frame, Symington-Wayne trucks, black and white Santa Fe decal, FARR Series 1 logo.

10	12	15	20

9324 TOOTSIE ROLL: 1979, 1981-82, single-dome, white ends, brown center tank section; white lettering, Symington-Wayne trucks.

6	8	10	15

9327 BAKELITE: 1980, three-dome, white upper body, red lower tank body; red lettering, red and white UNION CARBIDE logo, Symington-Wayne trucks.

—	—	12	14

9331 UNION 76: 1979, single-dome, dark blue tank body; orange lettering and UNION 76 logo, Standard 0 trucks; from 1071 Quaker City Limited set. C. Rohlfing comment.

—	15	20	25

9334 HUMBLE: 1979, single-dome, silver-painted tank; red and blue lettering, Symington-Wayne trucks.

6	8	10	12

9344 CITGO: 1980, white, three-dome, blue lettering, red and blue CITGO logo, Standard 0 trucks; from 1070 The Royal Limited.

—	15	20	25

9347 NIAGARA FALLS: 1979, TTOS National Convention car, powder blue tank, black lettering.

—	—	40	50

9353 CRYSTAL: 1980, red, three-dome, white lettering, Symington-Wayne trucks.

—	—	11	13

9354 PENNZOIL: 1981, chrome-finished, single-dome, Symington-Wayne trucks; yellow and black logo.

—	10	12	15

9356 LIFE SAVERS STIK-O-PEP: 1980, single-dome tank car; planned for 1980 release and shown in the Toy Fair catalogue of that year, this car was pulled from production at the last minute for unknown reasons; our guess is withdrawal of corporate permission or the demand of a royalty. The pressure-sensitive decals for the car had been contracted and already made; presumably, all such decals would have been stored or destroyed after production was canceled. However, one surviving set of decals has been found and applied to a chrome-plated tank car after the original decorations had been removed, leaving just the chromed tank body. It is not known how many of these decals have survived, but any 9356 tank car in existence was definitely produced outside the factory. F. Fisher Collection. Reader comments invited.   **Not Manufactured**

9367 UNION PACIFIC: 1980, single-dome, silver-painted tank body; black lettering, gold FARR Series 2 logo; available only as separate sale. C. Rohlfing comment.

(A) Red, white and blue Union Pacific shield decal.

—	—	12	15

(B) Same as (A), but Union Pacific shield is smaller and darker colored and is an electrocal rather than a decal. This was probably a running change implemented because the decals had a tendency to peel. L. Lefebvre Collection.

—	—	15	20

9369 SINCLAIR: 1980, single-dome, medium green tank; white lettering and logo, Standard 0 trucks; from 1071 Mid Atlantic set.

—	—	20	25

9373 GETTY: 1980-81, white single-dome, orange logo, Symington-Wayne trucks; from 1072 Cross Country Express set.

—	—	12	15

9386 PURE OIL: 1981, single-dome, cream tank body; dark blue lettering and logo, Standard 0 trucks; from 1160 Great Lakes Limited set. C. Rohlfing comment.

—	—	20	25

Chapter IX
FLATCARS

In the postwar years, the Lionel Corporation made the flatcar its most versatile freight carrier. The long plastic flatcar was used to haul just about every load under the sun, from transformers to Christmas trees. If the load could not be put onto the flatcar directly, Lionel saw to it that the car was adapted to the purpose. For example, Lionel would fit a flatcar with bulkheads and put a liquified gas container between them.

Fundimensions has not come close to making the flatcar the all-around performer of the postwar years, but the company has made excellent use of the flatcar in many areas. Essentially, there have been three types of flatcars used by Fundimensions in its production.

One of the first cars to emerge was a new design for a short flatcar, typified by the 9020 Union Pacific. This car has a wood-scribed top and bottom, and as issued in sets the car came with little plastic stakes which fit into small holes around the perimeter of the car. These stakes are seldom found with the cars when they show up on dealers' tables at train shows. This little flatcar was issued in Santa Fe, Chesapeake & Ohio, MKT and Republic Steel markings as well as Union Pacific logos. The scarcest of them is a tuscan 9020 with AAR trucks, probably from the earliest stages of production. The car was also equipped with bulkheads and logs; since it was a car which was usually in inexpensive sets, it usually had one operating and one dummy coupler.

A second type of flatcar is the re-release of the Lionel 1877-type "General" flatcar. This is another short flatcar which was originally issued with plug-in fences and horses as part of the rolling stock meant to accompany the "General" locomotive of 1977. Since then, it has been used as a base for many different flatcars in inexpensive sets. None to date have been issued with the metal truss rods which were used on some of the postwar versions of the car.

The third type of flatcar has been the full 11-inch flatcar which was so common in postwar production. Fundimensions has revived both of the basic molds for this car. The 6424-11 mold has been used most often for the TOFC flatcars with trailers, while the 6511-2 mold has shown up as the base for the Fundimensions searchlight cars and the derrick cars. This flatcar, in Chesapeake and Ohio markings, was the one used for the revival of the excellent Harnischfeger crane-carrying car in 1976; it was joined almost immediately by a Penn Central car carrying a big steam shovel. Both of these came in large boxes as kits to be assembled by the purchaser, just as the postwar versions did. A 9121 Louisville and Nashville car came with both a bulldozer and a scraper; this car was included in some deluxe sets beginning in 1974 and was available separately for several years. The dozer and scraper kits themselves, if in intact condition, are worth more than the car!

The most frequent use of the long flatcar in the Fundimensions era has been with the TOFC flatcars with trailers. ("TOFC" is the railroad abbreviation for "Trailer On Flat Car.") Since its first years, the company has issued approximately fifteen of these cars, and they are in keeping with MPC's desire to use its graphic capabilities well. These flatcars would look better with a single longer trailer instead of two short trailers, but Fundimensions is merely repeating postwar practice by using the two small vans. The real TOFC cars can be used both ways.

The first of the TOFC cars was the 9120 Northern Pacific in 1970, one of the first cars issued by the new company. This car was green with white lettering, and it had two white vans with corrugated sides and no markings. The trailers were constructed a little differently from their postwar predecessors. The postwar trailers had a separate metal tongue riveted to the underside of the trailer which held the plastic prop wheels. This metal piece was riveted to the trailer. Fundimensions cast the trailer body in one plastic piece, including the tongue support. The flatcar has plug-in side slip barriers, just as did the postwar original, and the trailers are all single-axled and double-wheeled.

One of the scarcer TOFC flatcars was issued in early 1972. It was another Northern Pacific TOFC car with the same color scheme as the 9120, but with the number 9122 and a 1972 built date. This car came in a Type II box, where its predecessor had a Type I box. The plastic cover for the trailer axles on the 9120 was black; on the 9122, the axle was green. Very early in the production run, the colors of the 9122 were changed to a tuscan flatcar and gray trailers. As a result, the green 9122 is one of the scarcer TOFC cars.

By 1976 Fundimensions had made the decision to expand its line of TOFC cars to add a modern look to its rolling stock. To dress up the car, the firm made the trailers smooth-sided instead of corrugated; this allowed the use of bright modern railroad logos on the trailers. The first of these cars was the Cascade green 9133 Burlington Northern; it was quickly followed by cars in CP Rail, IC Gulf, Great Northern, Southern Pacific, Chicago and Northwestern and Union Pacific markings, among several others. The latest of these cars is an Express Mail TOFC flatcar scheduled for 1985 production.

One of the more interesting TOFC flatcars is the one made in 1976 for the Lionel Collectors' Club of America convention in Atlanta, Georgia. This trailer car is not on a regular flatcar but on a newer tri-level automobile car without the second and third racks. The trailers themselves are not Lionel and are much larger than the style Lionel uses. Fundimensions apparently sent the whole shipment to the LCCA with only one side of the flatcars stamped. The club offered to have members' cars restamped on demand, but on the whole the version with one side stamped is still more common.

A few other flatcar types have made random appearances at times. One was the Fundimensions revival of the Radioactive Waste car in two versions, one as part of a limited edition set and one for separate sale. On this flatcar, two rails are laid for the length of the car, and two lighted canisters are clipped onto the rails. As the car rides along, the canisters blink red warning lights — scarcely a romantic addition to a layout, but a definite curiosity! The big four-truck die-cast transformer car has also been revived for separate sale as part of the Mid-Atlantic Limited set of 1980. The set car was painted brown and had the old postwar bar-end metal trucks. A second four-truck flatcar was offered for separate sale in that year; it was gray-painted and had the die-cast 027 passenger trucks. It carried two maroon bridge girders instead of a transformer. Finally, one of the nicest flatcars ever made for tinplate was produced as part of the Standard "0" Series in 1976. This was the 9823 Santa Fe flatcar, which was scale-length and came with a plastic crate load. Another version of this scale flatcar, this time in New York Central markings, is scheduled for production in 1985.

Fundimensions' use of the flatcar has been clearly different from the use made of the car in the postwar years. The flatcar has been used more to give a modern look to Fundimensions' freight line than to serve as a "do-it-all" platform. Although very few of these cars are scarce, they can form an important part of the collector's freight consist, especially the rather nice TOFC cars.

	Gd	VG	Exc	Mt

6500: See entry 9233, this chapter.

6504 L.A.S.E.R.: 1981-82, helicopter on black flatcar, similar to Lionel 3419; from 1150 L.A.S.E.R. set. — — 12 15

6505 L.A.S.E.R.: 1981-82, satellite tracking car, similar to Lionel 3540; black car, light blue housing, from 1150 L.A.S.E.R. set. — — 12 15

6506 L.A.S.E.R.: 1981-82, security car, see Chapter VI, Cabooses. — — 12 15

6507 L.A.S.E.R.: 1981-82, A.L.C.M. cruise missile on black flatcar; from 1150 L.A.S.E.R. set. C. Rohlfing comment. — — 12 15

6509 LIONEL: 1981, depressed-center die-cast flatcar with four trucks, gray-painted die-cast body, two maroon bridge girders with white "LIONEL" attached to car by rubber bands, four sets die-cast 027-style passenger trucks, bottom of base reads "MACHINERY CAR/PART NO./6418-4/LIONEL/MT. CLEMENS, MICH./48045". This was the car sold as a separate sale item; it was one of the first cars to be packaged in a Type IV collector box. C. Lang comment, W. Barnes Collection. — — 35 40

6521 NEW YORK CENTRAL: 1985, Standard 0 flatcar, tuscan body, scribed floor, white lettering and logo, Standard 0 trucks, 24 tall plastic stakes supplied with car to fit into holes around car perimeter, no load included. — — — 25

6531 EXPRESS MAIL: Scheduled for 1985, TOFC flatcar, blue 6424-11 flatcar body, white lettering, two blue vans with orange roofs, white lettering and orange and white Express Mail logo, Symington-Wayne trucks. — — — 15

6561: 1983, unlettered, olive drab flatcar with cruise missile, fixed couplers; from 1355 Commando Assault Train, decals furnished with set. Caponi comment. — — — 10

6562: 1983, unlettered, olive drab flatcar with crates and barrels, fixed couplers; from 1355 Commando Assault Train, decals furnished with set. Caponi comment. — — — 10

6564: 1983, unlettered, olive drab flatcar with two tanks, fixed couplers; from 1355 Commando Assault Train, decals furnished with set. Caponi comment. — — — 10

6573 REDWOOD VALLEY EXPRESS: 1984-85, flatcar with log dump bin, 1877-style tuscan flatcar body with yellow lettering, gray bolsters and log bin, three brown-stained logs, arch bar trucks; part of set 1403. — — — 10

6575 REDWOOD VALLEY EXPRESS: 1984-85, flatcar, 1877-style flatcar body with yellow lettering, yellow fence-style stakes around car perimeter, crate loads, arch bar trucks; part of set 1403. — — — 10

6670 DERRICK: See Operating Cars Chapter.

9014 TRAILER TRAIN: 1978, yellow body, black lettering and stakes, plastic trucks and wheels, manumatic couplers; from 1864 Santa Fe Double Diesel set. — 3 4 6

9019 FLATCAR: 1978, a base that came with either a superstructure for a box or crane car, work caboose, or log loader; as part of 1862 Logging Empire or 1860 Timberline set. — — 1 2

9020

9020 UNION PACIFIC: 1970-77, plastic wheels, one manumatic coupler, one fixed coupler.

(A) Medium yellow body, black lettering.	2	3	4	5
(B) Light yellow body, light blue lettering.	2	3	4	5
(C) Dark yellow body, dark blue lettering.	2	3	4	5
(D) Medium yellow body, blue lettering.	2	3	4	5
(E) Medium light yellow body, blue lettering.	2	3	4	5
(F) Medium yellow body, blue lettering, wood-grained floor.	2	3	4	5
(G) Medium light yellow body, blue lettering, wood-grained floor.	2	3	4	5

(H) 1970, early production, unpainted tuscan plastic, heat-stamped, yellow-lettered, "CAPY 100000 LD LMT 121800 LT WT 47200 UP 9020 UNION PACIFIC BLT 1-70", wood-grained floor, 16 stakes, AAR trucks, one fixed, one disc-operating coupler. Came as part of early set with 8041 New York Central 2-4-2 steam locomotive with red stripe but no whistle or smoke; 9141 green BN long gondola with white lettering, three red canisters and AAR trucks; 9010 GN hopper car and 9062 PC caboose. C. Anderson and Wolf Collections. — — 12 15

(I) Same as (H), but dark red body, no wood graining on floor. C. Rohlfing Collection. — — 12 15

9022

9022 A.T.&S.F.: 1971, 1975, 1978, yellow lettering, metal wheels, one operating coupler, one fixed coupler, eight plastic stakes, bulkheads, four unstained dowel-cut logs; part of 1586 Chesapeake Flyer freight set. C. Lang comment.

(A) Red body, wood-grained floor.	3	4	5	7
(B) Red body, plain floor.	3	4	5	7
(C) Black body.	3	4	5	8

9023

9023 MKT: 1973-74, 1978, black body, white lettering, metal wheels, one operating coupler, one fixed coupler, eight plastic stakes, bulkheads, four unstained dowel-cut logs; part of 1386 Rock Island Express freight set. C. Lang comment. 1 2 3 4

9024 CHESAPEAKE & OHIO: 1974, yellow body, blue lettering, plastic wheels, fixed couplers. 1 2 3 4

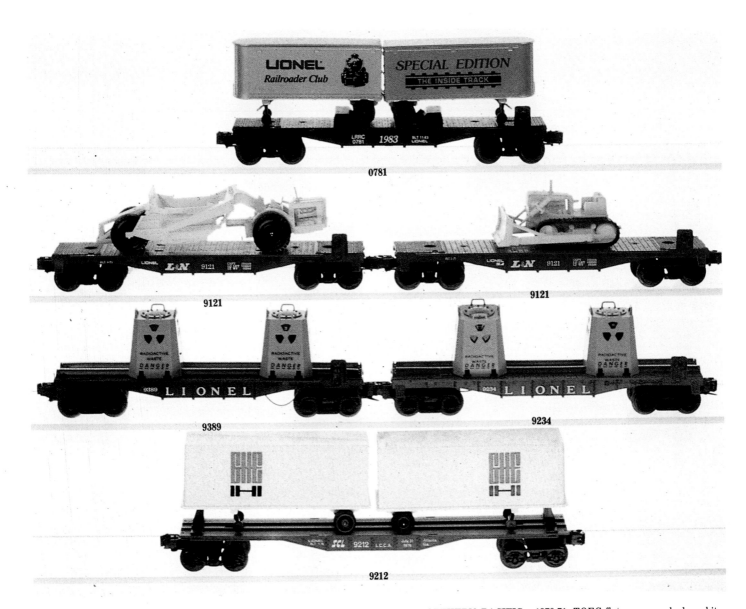

0781

9121   9121

9389   9234

9212

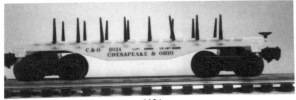

9024

9025 DTI: 1978, probably yellow body, black lettering and stakes; reportedly came with 1964 Santa Fe Double Diesel as an optional insert, verification requested.   **NRS**

9026 REPUBLIC STEEL: 1975-77, 1980, blue body, white lettering, plastic wheels, one manumatic coupler, one fixed coupler, wood-grained floor.

                                            1   2   3   4

9120

9120 NORTHERN PACIFIC: 1970-71, TOFC flatcar, green body, white lettering, white vans with corrugated sides and no lettering, two operating couplers, wheel stops.

(A) AAR trucks, MPC builder's plates, no side slip bars. Some examples have vans with postwar body shells and Fundimensions roofs. G. Halverson comment.   **6   8   10   12**

(B) Same as (A), but later production; Symington-Wayne trucks, no MPC builder's plates, with side slip bars.   **6   8   10   12**

9121 L&N: 1971, 1974, 1976, 1978-79, some versions with yellow dozer and scraper kit, Symington-Wayne trucks, mold 6424-11, die three.

(A) 1971, brown body, white lettering as follows, "BLT 1-71/LIONEL/[MPC logo]/L & N/CAPY 100000/LD LMT 103800/LT WT 65200". Came in Type I box with yellow dozer and scraper kits, AAR trucks; also offered in early sets. R. Loveless Collection.   **8   10   12   15**

(B) Same as (A), but maroon flatcar body. This version somewhat hard to find. G. Halverson Collection.   **15   20   25   30**

(C) Same as (A), but without "BLT 1-71" and MPC logo under "LIONEL". R. Loveless Collection.   **6   8   10   12**

(D) 1974-76, 1978-79, brown body, white lettering, came in special Type II box when offered for separate sale, included both kits. Also part of Grand National set in 1974 and 1560 North American set in 1975. Kaiser Collection.   **6   8   10   12**

See also Factory Errors and Prototypes.

9122 NORTHERN PACIFIC: 1972-75, flatcar, Symington-Wayne trucks, 6424-11 body mold.

(A) Green body, white lettering and white unlettered vans with corrugated

9233

6509

9282

9333

9383

9352

9122

sides, black axle covers, Symington-Wayne trucks, identical to 9120 except for number and "2-72" built date, came in early Type II box. R. LaVoie Collection. 10 12 15 20

(B) Tuscan flatcar body with white lettering, unlettered gray vans with corrugated sides and green axle covers. 6 8 10 12

(C) Same as (B), but vans are postwar leftover pieces. G. Halverson Collection. 6 8 10 12

(D) Tuscan flatcar body, yellow grader kit (no dozer kit); part of 1560 North American set. J. Breslin Collection. 6 8 10 12

9124 PENN CENTRAL: Green unpainted plastic body, lettered "PC PENN CENTRAL BLT 1-73 CAPY 14000 LD LMT 136700 LT WT 63300", comes with three logs, two black plastic ribs, mold number "6424-11" on

underside, arch bar trucks, one operating coupler with plastic semi-disc for manual operation (known as manumatic coupler), one fixed coupler.

(A) As described above. Cunningham and Ristau Collections.

  — 5 6 8

(B) Same as (A), but dozer kit instead of logs, "Capy 140,000, "LD. LMT. 156,700", Symington-Wayne trucks; came as part of 1866 Great Plains Express set. C. Rohlfing Collection. 5 6 8 10

9133 BURLINGTON NORTHERN: 1976, 1980, green body, white lettering and logo, mold 6424-11, die 3, Symington-Wayne trucks.

(A) No load. 4 5 6 8

(B) 1980, two matching Burlington Northern vans with smooth sides and white BN logo. 6 8 10 12

9133

9149

9149 CP RAIL: Red body, white lettering, silver, white, and black vans with white letters, Symington-Wayne trucks.   **5   7   10   12**

9157

9157 C&O: 1976-78, 1981, blue body, yellow lettering, P&H yellow crane kit, Symington-Wayne trucks.

(A) Gray rubber treads on crane cab.   **8   10   12   15**
(B) Black rubber treads on crane cab.   **8   10   12   15**

9158

9158 PENN CENTRAL: 1976-77; 1980, green body, white lettering, steam shovel kit, Symington-Wayne trucks.

(A) Gray rubber treads on steam shovel cab.   **8   10   12   15**
(B) Black rubber treads on steam shovel cab.   **8   10   12   15**

9212 LCCA: 1976, Atlanta, flatcar with vans, originally stamped only on one side, LCCA offered to restamp them for members and many were restamped, 3500 made.

(A) One side stamped.   **—   —   25   30**
(B) Two sides stamped.   **—   —   30   35**

9222 L&N: 1983, TOFC flatcar: two "L&N" gray vans with black lettering.

(A) Tuscan flatcar with white lettering. C. Lang Collection.   **—   —   12   14**

(B) Maroon flatcar with pale yellow lettering. C. Lang Collection.   **—   —   12   14**

9226 DELAWARE & HUDSON: 1984, TOFC flatcar, bright blue flatcar body with yellow lettering and logo, gray vans with black lettering and yellow D&H logo, Symington-Wayne trucks.   **—   —   —   14**

9232 ALLIS CHALMERS: 1980, gray atomic reactor load, orange base, blue lettering; rerun of 6519 from 1958-61; part of 1072 Cross Country Express set. C. Lang comment.   **—   —   20   25**

9233 TRANSFORMER: 1980, tuscan-painted depressed-center die-cast flatcar with red transformer with white insulators, lettered "LIONEL TRANSFORMER CAR", four trucks with 16 wheels; part of 1071 Mid Atlantic Limited set. Originally scheduled for number 6500, but 9233 was the actual production number.   **—   —   35   40**

9234 RADIOACTIVE WASTE: 1980, red flatcar with white-lettered "LIONEL", two rails run car length, two removable energy containers with flashing red lights; part of 1070 Royal Limited set. C. Lang comment.   **—   —   30   35**

9282 GREAT NORTHERN: 1978, 1981-82, TOFC flatcar, mold 6424-11, die three, orange body, green lettering, black plastic brakewheel easily broken, green vans with elaborate GN orange and green decal, trailer undersides marked "LIONEL" with "MPC 1000" without letters "MPC", van with hole for tractor and tractor lift.   **5   7   9   13**

9285 IC GULF: black body, mold 6424-11, die 3, white lettering, silver vans with black lettering, IC orange and black "pig on wheels" logo on van sides, Symington-Wayne trucks; came as part of 1785 Rocky Mountain Special set and never offered for separate sale. C. Lang comment, R. LaVoie Collection.   **12   15   20   25**

9306 ATSF: 1980, brown base and fence, two horses; part of 1053 The James Gang Set.   **—   —   9   13**

See also Factory Errors and Prototypes.

NOTE: 9325 is used on several different cars.

9325 NW: 1980-81, part of uncatalogued 1157 Wabash Cannonball set and 9196 Rolling Stock Assortment. Black plastic body, 8-1/2" long, with heat-stamped white letters on side; "BLT 1-79 N&W 9325 NORFOLK AND WESTERN LIONEL". Simulated wood grain floor, partial floor cut-out about 9/16" in diameter, plastic brakewheel, two-rung tan plastic fencing around floor perimeter, with three plastic pieces offset to clear brakewheel on end, Symington-Wayne trucks, plastic wheels, one operating and one dummy coupler. Bottom stamped "9325-T-5A LIONEL MT. CLEMENS MICH. 48045". Came in box with ends marked "LIONEL 027 GAUGE FLAT CAR WITH FENCES 6-9325". B. Smith and Runft Collections.   **—   3   4   5**

9325 NW: 1978-79, flatcar with cab and boom, red plastic flatcar with yellow plastic cab and boom, "NW" in white. Unassembled; purchaser snaps car together. Symington-Wayne trucks, two dummy couplers. Car came in box numbered 9364, but number on car is 9325. This number also used on companion dump car. Catalogued with "dump car and crane car assortment".   **—   3   4   5**

9325 DUMP CAR: 1978-79, came with "dump car and crane car assortment"; details needed.   **NRS**

9333 SOUTHERN PACIFIC TOFC: 1980, flatcar, tuscan body, Symington-Wayne trucks, white lettering, one brakewheel, two white vans with black wheels and black "SOUTHERN PACIFIC" lettering on sides with red-outlined large "S" and "P". D. Griggs Collection.   **—   —   10   14**

9352 CHICAGO & NORTHWESTERN: 1980, Brunswick green flatcar with two yellow Chicago & Northwestern vans, lettered "FALCON SERVICE" with bird logo. C. Rohlfing comment.   **—   8   10   14**

9379 LIONEL: Catalogued in 1980 as part of Texas and Pacific diesel set, but never made, flatcar with derrick.   **Not Manufactured**

9383 UNION PACIFIC: 1980, TOFC flatcar, dark gray flatcar with white lettering, light yellow vans with red lettering and stripe and red, white and blue UP shield logo, gold diamond-shaped FARR 2 logo. This was the extra freight car marketed separately to accompany the Union Pacific Famous American Railroads set. C. Rohlfing and C. Lang comments, R. LaVoie Collection.   **—   —   20   25**

9389 RADIOACTIVE WASTE: 1981, maroon body flatcar, white "LIONEL" lettering and number, two rails run car length, two removable gray energy containers with flashing red lights, 027-style die-cast passenger trucks. Separate sale item in Type III box identical to 9234 set car except for number and flatcar color. R. LaVoie comment.   **—   —   20   25**

9553 WESTERN & ATLANTIC: 1978-79, brown base and fence, gold lettering, six horses, arch bar trucks, operating couplers, metal wheels, available separately; matches General locomotive and coaches.

(A) As described above.   **—   —   15   20**
(B) Same as (A), except yellow fencing; hard to find. G. Halverson Collection.   **—   —   35   45**

9823 A.T.&S.F.: 1976, Standard O flatcar, tuscan body, white lettering, Standard O trucks; two sets of tan plastic crates, 24 pointed black stakes supplied with car fit into holes around car perimeter.   **20   25   30   35**

Chapter X

PASSENGER CARS

One of the real pleasures of tinplate railroading has always been to start up a train layout, turn off all the lights and watch the lighted layout by "night". If the layout was a well-equipped one, street and signal lights would shine, searchlights would beam onto the platform, and the locomotive would come flying around a curve, its headlight reflecting off the tracks. If the operator looked at the train coming at him at eye level, he could watch the locomotive speed past him, followed by a long string of lighted passenger cars, possibly with little human silhouettes in the windows.

Obviously, tinplate doth not live by freight cars alone. That is why Fundimensions tried to respond as quickly as possible to repeated requests for a new passenger car series. In 1973 Fundimensions began the production of its 9500 Series passenger cars with the Milwaukee Special set. In this set, an 8304 4-4-2 locomotive in Milwaukee Road markings pulled three dull orange Milwaukee passenger cars with maroon lettering and roofs. These cars were excellent models of the heavyweight cars used during the 1920s on almost every American railroad. They were lighted and highly detailed, with little vents in the clerestories, detailed closed vestibules and translucent window inserts. The only sore points about the cars were the their length (it didn't quite match the length of the classic Irvington cars) and their couplers. These were non-operating and mounted directly onto the car bodies; if the track was not level or had rough spots, the cars could easily uncouple accidentally. Some operators went so far as to put twist-ties around the coupler knuckles to keep them together!

The Milwaukee Special was followed during the next two years by a Broadway Limited set with Pennsylvania cars in tuscan and black with gold lettering and a Capitol Limited with Baltimore and Ohio cars in blue and gray with gold lettering. (Unfortunately the color of the B&O cars did not match the 8363 B&O F-3 diesels.) The three set cars soon had several stablemates. In 1975 separate sale Pullman cars were produced to match all three sets. In the next year full baggage cars came out, and the end of 1976 saw many observation cars made into the Campaign Special series with Presidential posters, bunting and an American flag decorating the cars in all three series. One Milwaukee car, the 9511 Minneapolis, was offered as part of a coupon deal. In all, there were ten Milwaukee cars, nine Pennsylvania cars and eight Baltimore and Ohio cars when production was complete.

As problems arose with these cars, attempts were made to solve them. It was found that the lights in the cars shone through the car roofs. At first, Fundimensions tried silver paint on the tops of the light bulbs in the cars, but that cut down the illumination too much. Eventually, cardboard inserts were placed into the roofs, and that solved the problem handily. Getting at the light bulbs to change them was a horrendous problem never fully solved. The roof and translucent window pieces were made of one casting which snapped into the car bodies. At first, there were tabs on the car bottoms, but these actually had to be cut off to remove the roof! Later, the tabs were eliminated in favor of projections in the translucent window inserts which snapped into the window frames. Even

with this arrangement, getting the roofs off these cars has always been a job to tax the most patient of people.

In 1977 the cars were issued in a different railroad scheme, this time with operating couplers. A baggage car, a combine, two Pullman coaches and an observation car were made in green and gold Southern markings to match the 8702 Southern 4-6-4 Hudson. These made up the Southern Crescent set (though the items were always sold separately, not as a complete set). Coincidentally, these cars also matched the Southern F-3 diesel pair produced in 1975. The next year, the cars were produced in the Blue Comet set with a significant improvement — the die-cast six-wheel passenger trucks. Several changes were made to the casting of the car underside to accommodate these trucks, and unfortunately earlier cars cannot be retrofitted with them. The same five-car scheme was used for the Chessie Steam Special set in 1980 and the Chicago and Alton set of 1981. Over the years, several of these cars were also made as TCA special cars in dark Brunswick green. Another similar set in yellow was made for the Toy Train Operating Society.

In 1976 Fundimensions reissued the short 027 streamlined passenger cars of the postwar period as the Lake Shore Limited set. These cars were pulled by an Alco in Amtrak markings with four matching cars. Later on, three more cars were added as separate sale items to expand the set. They had the same plastic wooden beam-style trucks as the earlier 9500 cars (odd, since these were archaic trucks for cars of a modern design) and were illuminated. These cars were produced in coach, Vista Dome and observation configurations. They have also been used for the TCA Bicentennial set and the Quicksilver Express set of 1982.

In 1978 Fundimensions revived the "General" style baggage and coach cars to accompany their reissue of the "General" engine the year before. This old-time car has also been used in Rock Island and Peoria three-car sets, Baltimore and Ohio cars and in one unlighted version as part of the James Gang set. These cars were faithful reproductions of the postwar issues.

Nice as these cars were, they were not the passenger cars everyone was waiting for. Those emerged in 1979 with the reissue of the big extruded aluminum cars from the fabled Congressional Limited in beautiful Pennsylvania markings. Instead of the flat finish of the postwar issues, the Fundimensions cars had a polished aluminum finish which looked great behind the Pennsylvania F-3 twin-motored diesels also produced in that year. A baggage car, two passenger coaches, a Vista Dome car and an observation car formed the original set, but later Fundimensions added a diner car, a combine and an extra passenger car to the set. These cars were an outstanding success for Fundimensions, and it was inevitable that more would follow.

That is exactly what happened in 1980. A startling Burlington Zephyr set was produced with chrome-plated twin F-3 diesels and the same five basic cars with authentic Zephyr-style lettering. As with the Pennsylvania cars, the extra cars were soon produced. Perhaps the most breathtaking set of all came the next year, when Fundimensions issued the J

9570

9571

9573

9572

9574

class Norfolk and Western steam engine and six stunning aluminum Powhatan Arrow passenger cars painted deep maroon with black roofs and gold lettering and striping. Many collectors believe this set to be the most beautiful passenger set ever produced in tinplate; unfortunately, the quality was reflected in the stiff price exacted for the cars, especially the diner, which was produced later in extremely limited quantities.

The follow-up to the Powhatan Arrow set was impressive, too. In 1982 Fundimensions produced the long-awaited Southern Pacific Daylight set. This set was originally pulled by an F-3 pair of diesels, but in 1983 the J class die was used to produce a terrific model of the GS-4 Daylight steam engine. The passenger cars were done in bright red, orange and black colors made famous by the elite West Coast train of the 1940s. As before, separate sale cars came out later. Unfortunately, S.P. fans noted deviations in the color schemes from the original. Like the Norfolk and Western set, the Daylight set has attracted a big following because of its beautiful color scheme.

By this time, Fundimensions was really "on a roll", producing set after beautiful set of these passenger cars in colors and styles no postwar aluminum set could hope to match. In 1983, however, Fundimensions changed the style of the cars. All of the previous aluminum cars had been made with stylish fluted sides and roofs, just as their postwar predecessors were. With the New York Central cars of 1983, Fundimensions eliminated the scribed sides and roofs and produced the cars with smooth sides and roofs. To be sure, the cars were still very attractive, but collectors soon voiced complaints about them. For one thing, the smooth-sided cars would fingerprint very easily, and the fingerprints were difficult to remove. Worse than that, the paint on the cars would chip all too easily, leaving unsightly aluminum marks through the paint. This was, of course, one way Fundimensions could keep the cost of these very expensive cars down, but for many collectors the New York Central set represented a distinct decline in quality. As before, the cars were accompanied by New York Central F-3 diesels, and separate sale cars have been added to the set.

The 1984 set, in Union Pacific Overland Limited colors, sparked vehement complaints. Two distinctly different shades of yellow were used for the locomotives, and more often than not they did not match. Collectors would thus have to hunt through many boxes to find locomotive units with the colors matching properly. Worse, the plastic doors used on the passenger cars did not match the color of the paint used on the cars, and there were even two shades of yellow paint. The observation cars did not match the rest of the set. In addition, collectors complained that the red striping on the cars was very poorly applied, giving the smooth-sided cars a rather cheap look. Fundimensions was in fact having production problems at the time, and it is unfortunate that such a fine set fell victim to the difficulties the factory was experiencing. These sets have sold very poorly as a result.

For 1985 Fundimensions has planned a smooth-sided set in brown and orange Illinois Central "City of New Orleans" colors. Reports are that the initial sets have solved the quality control problems, but the question remains whether Fundimensions has repeated its set formula too many times with this production. This would be the sixth set issued as aluminum passenger cars pulled by F-3 premium diesels. The tremendous expense of these sets raises the question of how extensive the resources of Fundimensions collectors really are. Regardless of the problems, one must admit that these aluminum cars have formed the consist of some truly magnificent sets which illustrate the apex of tinplate achievement.

Overall, Fundimensions has met the challenge of producing passenger cars extremely well. The beginning collector can secure quite a few passenger cars (aside from the aluminum ones) without severe damage to the wallet. The earliest Pennsylvania, Milwaukee and Baltimore and Ohio cars are readily available, except for the full baggage cars, which are very scarce items. The Amtrak 027 cars are not very difficult to find, either. With the right locomotive, the beginner can make up a very nice passenger train. For example, a Pennsylvania S-2 steam turbine, an old postwar 675 or 2025 K-4 steam locomotive or the 8551 Pennsylvania EP-5 Electric all look great pulling a string of the Pennsylvania cars — and so does the 8753 GG-1 Electric. The 8558 Milwaukee EP-5 looks fine at the head of the Milwaukee cars, and the Baltimore and Ohio F-3 diesels are a great match for the Baltimore and Ohio cars, color disparity notwithstanding. The Chessie Steam Special cars are fairly easy to get; they can be pulled by an 8603 Chesapeake and Ohio Hudson or a Chessie U36B, U36C or GP-20. They even have the extremely nice six-wheel die-cast passenger trucks. It is possible to get a decent passenger set on a modest budget, comparatively speaking, unless you must have the aluminum cars. With such sets, you too can return to an apparently much more innocent day than ours, when miniature passenger trains ran without a care or a schedule on a tinplate layout. The power to enthrall is still there!

	Gd	VG	Exc	Mt

577 NORFOLK & WESTERN: See 9562.

578 NORFOLK & WESTERN: See 9563.

579 NORFOLK & WESTERN: See 9564.

580 NORFOLK & WESTERN: See 9565.

581 NORFOLK & WESTERN: See 9566.

0511 TCA ST. LOUIS: 1981, convention baggage car, 9500-series type heavyweight car, Brunswick green body with black roof, "THE GATEWAY TO THE WEST/ST. LOUIS" in rubber-stamped gold lettering, gold stripes above and below windows run the length of the car, "0511" on box only, "1981" at both ends of car, white TCA logo, six-wheel die-cast passenger trucks. J. Bratspis Collection.   —   —   —   60

1973

1973 TCA BICENTENNIAL SPECIAL: 1973, 1974, 1975, red, white and blue; set of three cars. Price for set.   —   —   125   150

1973 only.   —   —   40   50

1974 TCA BICENTENNIAL SPECIAL: Matches 1973.   —   —   40   50

1975 TCA BICENTENNIAL SPECIAL: Matches 1973.   —   —   40   50

6403 AMTRAK: 1976-77, Vista Dome, aluminum with red and blue window stripes. This car and 6404, 6405 and 6406 were part of the 1663 Lake Shore Limited set. C. Lang comment.   10   12   15   20

6404 AMTRAK: Matches 6403, Pullman.   10   12   15   20

6405 AMTRAK: Matches 6403, Pullman.   10   12   15   20

6403

6406 AMTRAK: Matches 6403, observation.   10   13   15   20

6410 AMTRAK: Matches 6403, Pullman. This and the 6411 and 6412 cars were offered as separate sale items to expand the Lake Shore Limited set. C. Lang comment.   8   10   12   16

6411 AMTRAK: Matches 6403, Pullman.   8   10   12   16

6412 AMTRAK: Matches 6403, Vista Dome.   8   10   12   16

7200 QUICKSILVER: 1982-83, Pullman, blue and silver, lighted; part of 1253 Quicksilver Express.   —   —   20   25

7201 QUICKSILVER: 1982-83, Vista Dome, matches 7200.   —   —   20   25

7202 QUICKSILVER: 1982-83, observation, matches 7200.   —   —   20   25

7203 NORFOLK AND WESTERN: 1983, dining car, matches 9562, 9563, etc.   —   —   200   225

7204 SOUTHERN PACIFIC: 1983, dining car, matches 9594. See 9594 for background.   —   —   175   200

7205 TCA DENVER: 1982, Convention combine car, matches 0511; "7205" on box only, gold-lettered "THE ROCKY MOUNTAIN ROUTE/UNITED STATES MAIL/RAILWAY POST OFFICE/DENVER". J. Bratspis Collection.   —   —   —   60

7206 TCA LOUISVILLE: 1983, Convention Pullman car, matches 0511; "7206" on box only, gold-lettered "GREAT LAKES LIMITED/LOUISVILLE".   —   —   —   60

7207 NEW YORK CENTRAL: 1983, extruded aluminum dining car, "TWENTIETH CENTURY LIMITED"; matches 9594 and other New York Central passenger cars.   —   —   100   125

7208 PENNSYLVANIA: 1983, dining car, "JOHN HANCOCK"; matches Pennsylvania "Congressional Limited" passenger cars 9569 to 9575.   —   —   100   125

7210 UNION PACIFIC: 1984, smooth-sided dining car, see 9546 for description.   —   —   —   65

7211 SOUTHERN PACIFIC: 1983, Vista Dome car, "Daylight"; matches Southern Pacific Daylight passenger cars 9590 through 9593.   —   —   175   200

7212 TCA PITTSBURGH: 1984, convention car, matches 0511. F. Stem and J. Bratspis Collections.   —   —   —   60

7215 BALTIMORE AND OHIO: 1983, blue sides, gray roof, white window striping and lettering, General-style coach; part of 1351 Baltimore & Ohio set with 7216 and 7217.   —   —   15   20

7216 BALTIMORE AND OHIO: 1983, matches 7215. C. Rohlfing comment.   —   —   15   20

See also Factory Errors and Prototypes.

7217 BALTIMORE AND OHIO: 1983, baggage, large eagle electrocal on side; matches 7215 and 7216.   —   —   15   20

7220 ILLINOIS CENTRAL: Announced for 1985, "City Of New Orleans" baggage car, smooth-sided medium brown body (although pictured in dark brown in catalogue, production pieces will be lighter in shade); orange and gold striping, gold "ILLINOIS CENTRAL", brown "RAILWAY EXPRESS AGENCY" and "BAGGAGE" lettering, smooth black roof, unlighted (the other cars in the set are illuminated), black ends, brown doors, die-cast 0 gauge four-wheel passenger trucks with operating couplers.   —   —   —   70

7221 ILLINOIS CENTRAL: Announced for 1985, "Lake Ponchartrain" combine; matches 7220, lighted, silhouettes in windows.   —   —   —   70

7222 ILLINOIS CENTRAL: Announced for 1985, "King Coal" passenger coach; matches 7221.   —   —   —   70

7223 ILLINOIS CENTRAL: Announced for 1985, "Banana Road" passenger coach; matches 7221.   —   —   —   70

7224 ILLINOIS CENTRAL: Announced for 1985, "General Beauregard" dining car; matches 7221.   —   —   —   70

7225 ILLINOIS CENTRAL: Announced for 1985, "Memphis" observation car, red rear lights, lighted rear "City of New Orleans" drumhead; otherwise matches 7221.   —   —   —   70

8868 AMTRAK: See Diesels Chapter.

8869 AMTRAK: See Diesels Chapter.

8870 AMTRAK: See Diesels Chapter.

8871 AMTRAK: See Diesels Chapter.

9500 MILWAUKEE ROAD: 1973, Pullman, "CITY OF MILWAUKEE", flat orange, flat maroon roof, lights, roof fastened with tabs through floor.   10   15   25   30

9501 MILWAUKEE ROAD: Pullman, "CITY OF ABERDEEN".
(A) Flat orange, flat maroon paint.   10   15   22   25
(B) Shiny orange and shiny maroon paint.   10   15   25   30

9502

9502 MILWAUKEE ROAD: Observation, "PRESIDENT WASHINGTON"; matches 9500.   12   18   25   30

9503 MILWAUKEE ROAD: Pullman, "CITY OF CHICAGO"; matches 9500.   12   15   20   25

9504 MILWAUKEE ROAD: 1974, Pullman, "CITY OF TACOMA", flat orange, flat maroon roof, lights.
(A) Roof fastened with tabs through floor.   12   15   20   25
(B) Roof fastened through windows.   12   15   20   25

9505 MILWAUKEE ROAD: 1974, Pullman "CITY OF SEATTLE", flat orange, flat maroon roof, lights.
(A) Tabs through floor hold roof.   12   15   20   25
(B) Tabs through windows.   12   15   20   25

9506 MILWAUKEE ROAD: 1974, baggage combine, "U.S. MAIL", flat orange sides, flat maroon roof.   12   15   20   25

9507

9507 PENNSYLVANIA: 1974, Pullman, "CITY OF MANHATTAN", tuscan with black roof, gold lettering, lighted; one center rail pickup roller, ground pickup contacts on other truck, fully detailed undercarriage.   15   20   25   30

9508 PENNSYLVANIA: Pullman, "CITY OF PHILADELPHIA"; matches 9507.   15   20   25   30

9509 PENNSYLVANIA: Observation, "PRESIDENT ADAMS"; matches 9507.   15   20   25   30

9510 PENNSYLVANIA: 1974, baggage-mail-coach combine; matches 9507, lights, "UNITED STATES MAIL RAILWAY POST OFFICE" in gold heat-stamped letters.   10   15   20   25

9511 MILWAUKEE ROAD: 1973, Pullman, "CITY OF MINNEAPOLIS", special coupon car, lights.   15   25   30   35

9512 SUMMERDALE JUNCTION: 1974, special for TTOS, yellow with maroon roof, lights.   —   —   35   40

9513 PENNSYLVANIA: 1975, Pullman, "PENN SQUARE", lights; matches 9507.   10   15   20   25

9512

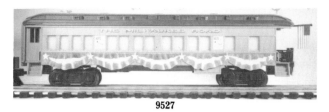

9527

9514 PENNSYLVANIA: 1975, Pullman, "TIMES SQUARE", lights; matches 9507.

| | 10 | 15 | 20 | 25 |

9515 PENNSYLVANIA: 1975, Pullman, "WASHINGTON CIRCLE"; matches 9507, lights.

| | 10 | 15 | 20 | 25 |

9516 BALTIMORE & OHIO: 1976, Pullman, "MOUNTAIN TOP", matches 9517.

| | 10 | 15 | 22 | 30 |

9517

9517 BALTIMORE & OHIO: 1975, coach, "CAPITAL CITY", blue, gray windows, yellow stripes, gray roof, lights.

| | 20 | 25 | 30 | 40 |

9518 BALTIMORE & OHIO: 1975, observation, "NATIONAL VIEW"; lights, matches 9517.

| | 20 | 25 | 30 | 40 |

9519 BALTIMORE & OHIO: 1975, baggage combine, "UNITED STATES MAIL", lights, matches 9517.

| | 15 | 20 | 25 | 30 |

9520

9520 TOY TRAIN OPERATING SOCIETY: 1975, special for National Convention; matches 9512.

(A) No decal.

| | — | — | 35 | 45 |

(B) With Phoenix decal for convention attendees.

| | — | — | 45 | 55 |

9521 PENNSYLVANIA: 1975, double-door baggage, tuscan with black roof, lights.

| | 40 | 50 | 65 | 75 |

9522 MILWAUKEE ROAD: 1975, double-door baggage, flat orange, flat maroon roof, lights.

| | 40 | 50 | 65 | 75 |

9523 BALTIMORE & OHIO: 1975, double-door baggage, "AMERICAN RAILWAY EXPRESS", lights; matches 9517.

| | 20 | 25 | 35 | 40 |

9524 BALTIMORE & OHIO: 1976, Pullman, "MARGARET CORBIN", lights; matches 9517.

| | 10 | 15 | 20 | 25 |

9525 BALTIMORE & OHIO: 1976, Pullman, "EMERALD BROOK"; matches 9517.

| | 10 | 15 | 20 | 25 |

9526

9526 TOY TRAIN OPERATING SOCIETY: 1976, special for National Convention; matches 9512.

(A) No Utah decal.

| | — | — | 35 | 45 |

(B) With Utah decal for convention attendees.

| | — | — | 45 | 55 |

9527 MILWAUKEE: 1976, "ROOSEVELT", campaign observation, red, white and blue bunting on car sides, small flag on rear platform.

| | 10 | 12 | 15 | 20 |

9528 PENNSYLVANIA: 1976, "TRUMAN", campaign observation, lights; matches 9507.

| | 10 | 12 | 15 | 20 |

9529 BALTIMORE & OHIO: 1976, "EISENHOWER", campaign observation; matches 9517.

| | 10 | 12 | 15 | 20 |

9530 SOUTHERN: 1978, baggage, "JOEL CHANDLER HARRIS", dark green body and roof; light apple green window stripe, gold edge striping and gold lettering, four-wheel wood-beam plastic trucks with operating truck-mounted couplers. (Previous cars in the 9500 heavyweight series had non-operating body-mounted couplers.)

| | 15 | 20 | 25 | 30 |

9531 SOUTHERN: 1978, combination, "ANDREW PICKENS"; matches 9530.

| | 15 | 20 | 25 | 30 |

9532 SOUTHERN: 1978, Pullman, "P. G. T. BEAUREGARD"; matches 9530.

| | 15 | 20 | 25 | 30 |

9533 SOUTHERN: 1978, Pullman, "STONEWALL JACKSON"; matches 9530.

| | 15 | 20 | 25 | 30 |

9534 SOUTHERN: 1978, observation, "ROBERT E. LEE"; matches 9530.

| | 15 | 20 | 25 | 30 |

9535 TOY TRAIN OPERATING SOCIETY: 1977, special for National Convention; matches 9512.

(A) No Ohio decal.

| | — | — | 35 | 45 |

(B) With Ohio decal for convention attendees.

| | — | — | 45 | 55 |

BLUE COMET SERIES

9536 THE BLUE COMET: 1978, baggage, "BARNARD", blue unpainted plastic sides, dark blue roof; cream stripe through windows, gold lettering, gold stripes above and below windows, illuminated, die-cast six-wheel trucks, full detailed undercarriage, two disc couplers, glazed windows.

| | 10 | 15 | 20 | 25 |

9537 THE BLUE COMET: 1978, combination, "HALLEY"; matches 9536.

| | 10 | 15 | 20 | 25 |

9538 THE BLUE COMET: 1978, Pullman, "FAYE"; matches 9536.

| | 15 | 20 | 25 | 30 |

9539 THE BLUE COMET: 1978, Pullman, "WESTPHAL"; matches 9536.

| | 15 | 20 | 25 | 30 |

9540 THE BLUE COMET: 1978, observation, "TEMPEL", matches 9536.

| | 10 | 15 | 20 | 25 |

9541 SANTA FE: 1980, 1982, baggage, "RAILWAY EXPRESS AGENCY", light tan body, cherry red roof, black lettering and Santa Fe cross logo, unlighted, arch bar trucks, plastic wheels; part of 1053 The James Gang set.

| | — | — | 15 | 20 |

9544 TCA CHICAGO: 1980, convention Pullman car; matches 0511, "9544" on box only, gold-lettered "LAND OF LINCOLN/CHICAGO".

| | — | — | — | 60 |

9545 UNION PACIFIC: 1984, smooth-sided baggage car, yellow body; red striping and lettering, gray roof and ends, unlighted. (The rest of the cars in the set are illuminated). Part of the "Overland Limited" passenger set.

| | — | — | 60 | 65 |

9546 UNION PACIFIC: 1984, combine, illuminated, silhouettes in windows; otherwise matches 9545.

| | — | — | 60 | 65 |

9547 UNION PACIFIC: 1984, observation car, red taillights on rear, illuminated "Overland Limited" drumhead; otherwise matches 9546. There have been vehement complaints from collectors that the yellow color on this car is much darker than the other cars in the set, and the doors do not match the body color. Numerous examples observed validate these complaints.

| | — | — | 60 | 65 |

9548 UNION PACIFIC: 1984, "Placid Bay" passenger coach; matches 9546.

| | — | — | 60 | 65 |

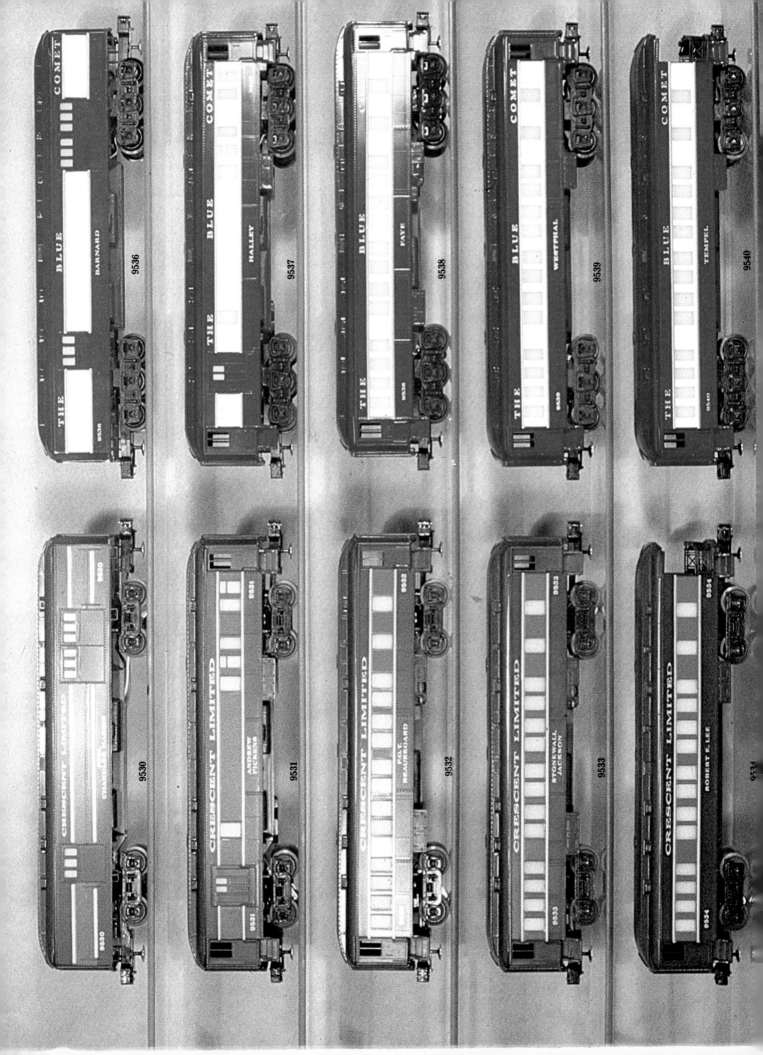

9549 UNION PACIFIC: 1984, "Ocean Sunset" passenger coach, matches 9546. — — 60 65

9551 WESTERN & ATLANTIC: 1977-79, 1860-type baggage car for General set, yellow body, tuscan platforms and roof; tuscan lettering, black stacks and ventilators, arch bar trucks. — 15 20 25

9552 WESTERN & ATLANTIC: 1860-type coach for General set; matches 9551. — 15 20 25

THE ALTON LIMITED: Includes locomotive and tender.

9554 ALTON LIMITED: 1981, baggage, "ARMSTRONG", 9500 series heavyweight-style, dark maroon body, silver roof; dark red window striping, gold lettering, die-cast six-wheel passenger trucks. — — 25 30

9555 ALTON LIMITED: 1981, combine, "MISSOURI"; matches 9554. — — 25 30

9556 ALTON LIMITED: 1981, coach, "WILSON"; matches 9554. — — 25 30

9557 ALTON LIMITED: 1981, coach "WEBSTER GROVES"; matches 9554. — — 25 30

9558 ALTON LIMITED: 1981, observation, "CHICAGO"; matches 9554. — — 25 30

9559 ROCK ISLAND & PEORIA: 1981 combo, 1860s General-style car, light tan body, maroon roof and platforms, maroon lettering, black stacks and ventilators, illuminated, arch bar trucks; matches 9560 and 9561 and goes with 8004 locomotive; all only available as separate sale. — — 20 25

9560 ROCK ISLAND & PEORIA: 1981, coach; matches 9559. — — 20 25

9561 ROCK ISLAND & PEORIA: 1981, coach; matches 9559. — — 20 25

THE POWHATAN ARROW: Includes locomotive and tender. **NRS**

(9562) NORFOLK AND WESTERN: 1981, baggage, "577" and in script "The Powhatan Arrow", first painted extruded aluminum passenger car made by Lionel, with black roof, maroon sides, gold striping and lettering; catalogue number is stamped on the boxes, not the cars. — — 65 75

(9563) NORFOLK AND WESTERN: 1981, combine, "578"; matches 9562. — — 65 75

(9564) NORFOLK AND WESTERN: 1981, coach, "579"; matches 9562. — — 65 75

(9565) NORFOLK AND WESTERN: 1981, coach, "580"; matches 9562. — — 65 75

(9566) NORFOLK AND WESTERN: 1981, observation, "581"; matches 9562. — — 65 75

(9567) NORFOLK AND WESTERN: 1981, Vista Dome, matches 9562. — — 85 100

9569 PENNSYLVANIA: 1981, combination, "PAUL REVERE"; matches 9571. — — 65 75

9570 PENNSYLVANIA: 1979, "RAILWAY EXPRESS AGENCY", small door baggage, mirror polished aluminum, plastic ends, same trucks as original Lionel baggage cars but with fast angle wheels. — 50 60 75

9571 PENNSYLVANIA: 1979, "WILLIAM PENN", Pullman, mirror polished aluminum, iridescent maroon stripes; spring loaded lamp receptacle, rerun of 1950s 2543, but 2543 had flat finished aluminum, brown flatter stripes, 252 crossing gate light unit with sliding shoe or rivet end contact. — 50 60 75

9572 PENNSYLVANIA: 1979, "MOLLY PITCHER", Pullman; matches 9571. — 50 60 75

9573 PENNSYLVANIA: 1979, "BETSY ROSS", Vista Dome; matches 9571. — 50 60 75

9574 PENNSYLVANIA: 1979, "ALEXANDER HAMILTON", observation, matches 9571, "Lionel Limited" on back door inside of protective gate. — 50 60 75

9575 PENNSYLVANIA: 1979, Pullman, "THOMAS A. EDISON", aluminum passenger car; matches 9571. — — 100 125

TEXAS ZEPHYR: Includes 8054, 8055 and 8062 engines and 9588 Vista Dome. **NRS**

9576 BURLINGTON: 1980, extruded aluminum baggage, "SILVER POUCH", four-wheel 0 Gauge die-cast passenger trucks, 16" long, for 0 Gauge track; only available for separate sale. — — 55 60

9577 BURLINGTON: 1980, coach, "SILVER HALTER"; matches 9576. — — 55 60

9578 BURLINGTON: 1980, coach, "SILVER GLADIOLA"; matches 9576. — — 55 60

9579 BURLINGTON: 1980, Vista Dome, "SILVER KETTLE"; matches 9576. — — 55 60

9580 BURLINGTON: 1980, observation, "SILVER VERANDA"; matches 9576. — — 55 60

CHESSIE STEAM SPECIAL: Includes 8003 Loco and Tender. **NRS**

9581 CHESSIE: 1980, baggage, yellow sides, gray roof, blue ends and lettering, vermilion stripe on sides. — — 25 30

9582 CHESSIE: 1980, combine; matches 9581. — — 25 30

9583 CHESSIE: 1980, coach; matches 9581. — — 25 30

9584 CHESSIE: 1980, coach; matches 9581. — — 25 30

9585 CHESSIE: 1980, observation; matches 9581. — — 25 30

9588 BURLINGTON: 1980, Vista Dome, "SILVER DOME"; matches 9576. — — 65 75

SOUTHERN PACIFIC DAYLIGHT

9589 SOUTHERN PACIFIC: 1982, extruded aluminum baggage with distinctive red, orange, white and black "daylight" colors; part of Spring Collector Series; includes four matching cars and a matching pair of F-3 diesels (8260 and 8262), all sold separately. Part of Spring Collector Series for 1982 with four matching cars and a matching pair of F-3 diesels (8260 and 8262). In the 1983 Collector Series Catalogue the set was offered again. Then in the 1983 Fall Collector Series, the 7211 Vista Dome was added. Also in 1983 a 7204 Dining Car and an 8261 Diesel B unit were offered. The three later cars were apparently intentionally made in quantities lower than market demand, causing a dramatic short term price appreciation. It will be most interesting to see if the price differentials hold. — — 65 75

9590 SOUTHERN PACIFIC: 1982-83, Combo; matches 9589. — 50 65 75

9591 SOUTHERN PACIFIC: 1982-83, Pullman; matches 9589. — 50 65 75

9592 SOUTHERN PACIFIC: 1982-83, Pullman; matches 9589. — 50 65 75

9593 SOUTHERN PACIFIC: 1982-83, observation; matches 9589. — 50 65 75

9594 NEW YORK CENTRAL: 1983, double-door, extruded aluminum baggage, painted gray with white lettering and black roof, gray ends; sold as a separate item, with matching diesels 8370, 8371, 8372 and matching cars 9595, 9596, 9597, 9598 and 7207; four-wheel 0 Gauge die-cast passenger trucks, operating couplers. We have had reports that the smooth-sided cars in this and subsequent series have paint which can chip easily if mishandled. In addition, the dark gray color of the paint on these cars shows fingerprints easily, and these prints, once present, are hard to remove. — — 65 75

9595 NEW YORK CENTRAL: 1983, extruded aluminum combine, illuminated; matches 9594. — — 65 75

9596 NEW YORK CENTRAL: 1983, extruded aluminum coach, "WAYNE COUNTY" Pullman, illuminated; matches 9594. — — 65 75

9596 NEW YORK CENTRAL: 1983, extruded aluminum coach, illuminated, "HUDSON RIVER" Pullman; matches 9594. — — 65 75

9598 NEW YORK CENTRAL: 1983, extruded aluminum, observation, "MANHATTAN ISLAND", illuminated; matches 9594. — — 65 75

Chapter XI

OPERATING CARS

Many of the operating cars produced by Fundimensions have been mentioned in the various introductions to other chapters in this book because they are best categorized within a larger area of production. Examples of these are the operating boxcars, gondolas and hopper cars. However, some of the operating cars in the Fundimensions line do not fit too readily into those categories. These are the log and coal dump cars, the crane cars, the searchlight cars and the derrick cars.

The Fundimensions log dump car is modeled after the late Lionel Corporation examples. It is an all plastic car with an open flatcar body and a central log cradle attached to a spring-loaded plunger. When the magnet in an operating track pulls down the plunger, the cradle tilts and dumps three wooden dowels serving as logs. The mechanism works well, but the logs sometimes flip off the cradle on sharp curves during operation.

Over the years, Fundimensions has produced its log cars in four railroad markings. The first one catalogued was a tuscan Louisville and Nashville car in 1970, but that car was never produced. The first of the log cars was a green 9300 Penn Central, which ran from 1970 through 1974 and again in 1977. In 1974 the car was changed to yellow Union Pacific markings as the 9303 — or 9305. The car was designated as a 9305 if the customer purchased it with a remote track included, though the number was always 9303 on the car. This car ran from 1974 through 1978 and again in 1980. The car changed to a red Santa Fe model in 1979 through 1983, and for 1984 a Northern Pacific model in dark green was made. A Pennsylvania log dump car in tuscan is scheduled for production in 1985.

The Fundimensions coal dump car is essentially a modified log dump car with a tilting coal bin attached to the cradle. It is a bit ungainly and does not interest collectors very much. In operation, some people had complaints about the coal supplied with the car; it was made of PVC plastic pellets which would pick up static electricity and stick to everything on the layout, including the operator when he/she tried to put the coal back in the car.

The first of the Fundimensions coal dump cars came out in 1974 with a dark blue color scheme and yellow Chesapeake and Ohio lettering. As with the log car, the number of the car was different in 1974 if the buyer purchased a package with a remote track. The car carried the number 9304 without the track; the package with the track was designated 9306, but 9304 was the car's marking. This car ran from 1974 through 1978, after which it was replaced by a yellow Union Pacific model running from 1979 through 1982. In 1983 a coal dump car was included as part of the Northern Freight Flyer; this car had a black flatcar body with a gray bin and white Chicago and Northwestern lettering and was not offered for separate sale. The separate sale car for 1983 and 1984 was a tuscan Pennsylvania car with gold lettering and a red Keystone. A New York Central coal dump car is portrayed in the 1985 catalogues for separate sale.

The Fundimensions searchlight car is modeled after the 6822 "Night Crew" postwar searchlight car, except that the rubber man of the postwar model is missing from the Fundimensions car. It uses a 6511-2 flatcar base and the same parts and assembly methods as its postwar predecessor. The first Fundimensions searchlight car was a car of long duration, the tuscan 9302 Louisville and Nashville car with a gray superstructure and black light hood. This car ran from 1973 through 1978, a long run of six years. The earliest models had an MPC logo on the car side; they are less common than the car without the logo. There is another scarce version of the car with white lettering instead of yellow.

In 1979 the 9302 was replaced by an attractive 9312 Conrail car with a blue flatcar base. The car was pictured with an orange superstructure in the 1979 advance catalogue, but the pictures in all the regular catalogues showed the superstructure as gray. As it turns out, the car was made both ways. Some collectors believe that the example with the orange superstructure is scarcer than the gray example, but this is not so. Apparently, there are significant regional differences which account for the scarcity of one example or another of this car. In the Philadelphia area, for example, nobody had any trouble locating Conrail searchlight cars with orange superstructures; in fact, the gray examples were a little harder to find. In other areas, the reverse is true. We believe that the car was made in about equal quantities of orange and gray superstructures. However, reader comments are still invited about this car. The Conrail searchlight car was produced through 1983.

After producing only two versions of the car over its first thirteen years, Fundimensions decided to diversify its production a bit. In 1983 a Chicago and Northwestern searchlight car with a black base and a gray superstructure was made for the Northern Freight Flyer set but was not available for separate sale. The 1984 and 1985 catalogues show two new searchlight cars; one is an attractive Reading model in green and yellow colors, and the other is a U.S. Marines model in olive-drab camouflage painting. In addition to these cars, the 1985 catalogue shows a New York Central model which is scheduled for production as part of a work train set with a steam switcher engine.

In addition to the controversial and confusing 6560 Crane car revival of 1971 described elsewhere, Fundimensions has made seven different crane cars. However, the first of them did not emerge until 1979, when two of them were produced, both with Standard "O" trucks. The first one was a Reading crane in green and yellow included with the Quaker City Limited set; the other was designated (apparently at the last minute) as the sixth car of the Famous American Railroads Set One. It carries the diamond-shaped F.A.R.R. logo (not many collectors seem to be aware of this) and was a separate sale item. This was the attractive blue and yellow 9348 Santa Fe Crane car.

The next crane cars had a significant innovation — the six-wheel die-cast passenger trucks which had been introduced on the Blue Comet passenger cars in 1978. The 9329 Chessie Crane came in the usual bright yellow and blue Chessie "cat" paint scheme and was part of the Royal Limited collector set of 1980. From this point on, all of the crane cars were made for special collector sets. The next one came in the maroon and gray colors of the Canadian Pacific as part of the Maple Leaf

Limited set of 1981. A 6510 Union Pacific crane was made in 1983 for the Gold Coast Limited set and a pretty Erie-Lackawanna model came out in 1984 for the Erie-Lackawanna Limited set. For 1985 a New York Central crane in black with white lettering has been planned for the New York Central steam switcher set; unlike the others, this crane will have plastic trucks.

The Fundimensions derrick car is a sort of baby crane car without the cab and is modeled after a postwar Lionel car. This car has a 6511-2 flatcar as its base, and the derrick assembly is riveted to the car. The derrick is collapsible and snaps into position when raised; it operates with a hand crank and swivels.

In 1980 a version just like the postwar derrick in Lionel markings with a red flatcar was scheduled for a Texas and Pacific set headed by an Alco diesel, but that set was never made. Instead the Lionel car came out the next year as part of the Reading Yard King set. The next derricks both came out in 1983. One was a Chicago and Northwestern derrick which was part of the Northern Freight Flyer set; the other was a yellow 9235 Union Pacific derrick which was available for separate sale in that year and in 1984. The most recent derrick car is a black Illinois Central car, which had been planned for 1985 production, but was canceled just prior to press time.

Obviously, the most desirable of these operating cars are the crane cars, which can sometimes be found for separate sale because the set they came in has been split up by dealers. The separate-sale Santa Fe crane is a nice car which is still readily available. Aside from the extremely scarce 6560 revival of 1971, it is a little too soon to tell which of these crane cars will be the scarcest, but preliminary indications show that the Canadian Pacific is a big favorite, thanks to its color scheme. However, the other crane cars are bright and colorful, too. The derrick cars are very good for the beginning collector; they make good operating cars and they are very reasonably priced, even the ones in the sets. The searchlight cars make an interesting group when they are all together; the Louisville and Nashville car is very common, while the Reading car shows signs of being in some demand by collectors. The log and coal dump cars do not as a rule interest collectors too much, but there is a Chesapeake and Ohio blue coal dump car without lettering, a little-known factory error which is probably very scarce.

Like all the other operating cars produced by Fundimensions, these cars add action and animation to an operating layout. As with other freight cars in the Fundimensions lineup, the variety of these cars adds to the attractiveness of a collection of them.

	Gd	VG	Exc	Mt

6109: See Hoppers Chapter.

6201: See Gondolas Chapter.

6251 NEW YORK CENTRAL: Announced for 1985, coal dump car, black body, grating pieces added to car ends (earlier varieties did not have these pieces), black bin, white lettering, Symington-Wayne trucks. Comes with simulated coal and dumping bin. — — — 15

6670: See 9378 entry in this chapter.

7900: See Boxcars Chapter.

7901: See Boxcars Chapter.

8868 AMTRAK: See Diesels Chapter.

8869 AMTRAK: See Diesels Chapter.

8870 AMTRAK: See Diesels Chapter.

8871 AMTRAK: See Diesels Chapter.

9217: See Boxcars Chapter.

9218, 9219, 9221: See Boxcars Chapter.

9238 NORTHERN PACIFIC: 1983-84, log dump car, dark green body and log cradle, white lettering, five stained wooden logs, Symington-Wayne trucks. — — — 14

See Factory Errors and Prototypes.

9241 PENNSYLVANIA: 1983-84, log dump car, tuscan body, grating pieces added to ends of car, gold lettering, Symington-Wayne trucks. Comes with three stained large logs and dumping bin. — — 12 15

9300

9300 PENN CENTRAL: 1970-73, log dump mechanism, green body, white lettering, MPC logo, Symington-Wayne trucks, two disc couplers.

(A) With helium tank. 6 8 10 12

(B) With log. 5 7 9 10

9300

9301: See Boxcars, Chapter V.

9303

9303 UNION PACIFIC: 1974, 1979, log dump, yellow body, red lettering, Symington-Wayne trucks, one disc coupler, one fixed coupler.

4 6 8 10

9304

9304 CHESAPEAKE & OHIO: 1974, coal dump, dark blue body and coal bin, yellow lettering, Symington-Wayne trucks, one disc coupler, one fixed coupler.

(A) White "coal" from raw plastic pellets. 4 5 8 10

(B) Black "coal". 4 5 8 10

See also Factory Errors and Prototypes.

9305 UNION PACIFIC: 1974, 1979 log dump car. This number was used to refer to the package which included a remote control track, although the car number remained 9303. Add $4.00 to values of 9303 for presence of track in original package. **NRS**

9306 C&O: 1974-76, coal dump car. This number was used to refer to the package which included a remote control track, although the number on the car remained 9304. Add $4.00 to values of 9304 for presence of track in original package.

9307: See Gondolas Chapter.

9308: See Boxcars Chapter.

9310 A.T.S.F.: 1978-79, 1981-82, log dump, red body, yellow lettering, "BLT 1-78", Symington-Wayne trucks, one operating coupler, one fixed coupler, operating disc on underside; when plunger is pulled down load dumps three dowels about six inches long, 5/8 inch diameter.

5 7 9 13

9310

9311 UP: 1978-82, yellow coal dump with black coal, Symington-Wayne trucks, one operating coupler, one fixed coupler; when operating disc pulled down load dumps.   **5   7   9 13**

9311

9398 PENNSYLVANIA: 1983, coal dump, tuscan frame and bin, gold lettering, red and gold rubber-stamped Keystone, mechanism activated by special track, Symington-Wayne trucks, one operating and one dummy coupler, with dumping bin and simulated coal; separate sale item.   **—   — 12 15**

9399 CHICAGO & NORTHWESTERN: 1983-84: coal dump, black frame, gray bin, plunger mechanism activated by special track, Symington-Wayne trucks, one operating and one dummy coupler; sold as part of 1354 Northern Freight Flyer set.   **— — — 14**

CRANES, DERRICKS AND SEARCHLIGHT CARS

6325 NEW YORK CENTRAL: Announced for 1985, crane car, black base, cab and boom; white lettering and white New York Central oval logo, Symington-Wayne trucks. Part of Yard Chief switcher set.   **— — — 18**

6508 CANADIAN PACIFIC: 1981, crane car, maroon base and boom with white letters, gray cab with maroon lettering, die-cast six-wheel passenger trucks; part of 1158 Maple Leaf Limited set.   **— — 35 40**

6510 UNION PACIFIC: 1982, crane car, yellow cab with silver roof, gray plastic base, red "UNION PACIFIC" lettering, tall stack, notched boom at high end, die-cast six-wheel passenger trucks. From Gold Coast Limited set. Weisblum Collection.   **— — 45 50**

6522 CHICAGO & NORTHWESTERN: 1984-85, searchlight car, black body, gray superstructure, white lettering, Symington-Wayne trucks; sold as part of Number 1354 Northern Freight Flyer set.   **— — — 15**

6524 ERIE-LACKAWANNA: 1984-85, crane car, yellow base with maroon logo and lettering, maroon cab with white lettering, gray cab roof and boom, die-cast six-wheel passenger trucks; from Erie-Lackawanna Limited set.   **— — — 40**

6526 U.S. MARINES: 1984-85, searchlight car, camouflage-painted olive and yellow flatcar, superstructure and searchlight hood, Symington-Wayne trucks. Matches 5726 U.S. Marines bunk car in paint scheme as well as 8485 U.S. Marines diesel switcher. Came with sheet of decals to be applied to car by purchaser.   **— — — 14**

LOWERING THE BOOM ON THE CRANE CAR,
OR,
WILL THE REAL 6560 PLEASE STAND UP?

With the assistance of Glenn Halverson

The 6560 Crane car was one of the staples of the old Lionel Corporation for many years. In fact, production of the 6560 and its predecessors, the 2460 and the 6460, goes all the way back to the late 1940s. In any form, it was a brisk seller because of its excellent play value. Like any Lionel crane, the cab could swivel, the hook could be lowered and raised and the boom could be adjusted.

No wonder, then, that even in its declining years the Lionel Corporation would want to continue production of this popular car. It is the production of the 6560 in the last years of the Lionel Corporation which has raised problems for postwar and Fundimensions collectors alike. In 1966 the Lionel Corporation auctioned off a great deal of its plant at Hillside, New Jersey so the company could consolidate its production of all its toys, including the trains, in Hagerstown, Maryland. The tooling returned to Hillside in 1969, the last year the Lionel Corporation made trains. When Fundimensions took over the train manufacturing rights in 1970, quite an inventory of miscellaneous parts came as part of the deal. Obviously, since the parts were already available, selling trains made from them would convey considerable advantage to the young firm.

And so, in 1971, Fundimensions advertised the 6560 Crane car in its consumer catalogue. For quite some time, many collectors wondered whether Fundimensions had actually marketed the crane. The right answer is that Fundimensions did not actually make the crane car; rather, the firm assembled it from existing parts and distributed it in its own boxes. This practice was quite common in 1970 and 1971, since original postwar accessories can often be found in Fundimensions boxes in brand-new condition.

The real problem comes about when the Fundimensions box is not present with the crane. How can the collector tell the Fundimensions crane from those made in Hillside and Hagerstown? The answers to this question have been a long time in coming, and further confirmation is needed, but at last a true picture is beginning to emerge. It is important to get a clear picture, too, because the Fundimensions 6560 is scarcer than either the common Hillside production or the somewhat hard to find Hagerstown production from 1968 and 1969.

Regular Hillside production of the 6560 Crane car, even the later ones with AAR plastic trucks instead of the older bar-end metal trucks, is relatively easy to distinguish from the other varieties. The cab is a solid, bright red plastic with white lettering. The base and boom are black plastic. The wheels near the top of the boom which hold the wire assembly are fastened to a plate which in turn is fastened to the boom by a round-headed, slotted black screw. The U-shaped bracket which holds the boom to the cab is blackened, and so are the rivets used to fasten the boom at this point. On the later Hillside 6560 Cranes, both cab wheels are solid instead of slotted; that is the way they appear on the other two cranes as well. The crane came in a regular Lionel orange, blue and white box.

The Hagerstown production of the 6560 was quite another matter. Since Lionel had auctioned off its injection molding machines, the firm subcontracted the manufacture of the plastic pieces to Richmond Plastics of Richmond, Virginia. There are some significant differences in the plastic pieces because of this. Some of the car bases made in Hagerstown are black, and a few came through blank with no lettering. However, most of the 6560 bases were a very dark blue; this is best observed from the underside of the car. The boom plastic color always matched the color of the base. The cab color is strikingly different from the previous production. A few were an orange-red, but most were a translucent light red color. The plastic is very different in character from the Hillside cranes. In the Hagerstown cranes, the red plastic has an almost "see-through" quality, as if one could shine a light through it. The Hillside cranes show more gloss and more solid red in the color of the cabs. This translucent red cab is a critical factor in identifying these cranes.

6560   **6560**

9332   **9329**

6508   **6510**

The wire assembly near the top of the boom is fastened with a chromed rivet instead of a black screw, and the U-shaped bracket at the bottom of the boom is bronzed instead of black. The Hagerstown cranes can come with AAR operating or dummy trucks; most have two operating trucks. The box is orange and white; the end panels are marked "THE LIONEL TOY CORPORATION / HAGERSTOWN, MARYLAND" and "No. 6560-25 / OPERATING / CRANE CAR". The box part number is 12-247; unlike most of the Hagerstown boxes, the car description is printed in orange rather than rubber-stamped in black. To add to the possible confusion, only the number 6560 is found on the crane, though the number on the box has a 25 suffix. A few years earlier, Lionel actually had produced a 6560-25 crane with the full number on the car base!

Now comes the real problem — distinguishing the Fundimensions 6560 from the Hagerstown 6560 in the absence of the Fundimensions box. The Fundimensions crane also has a dark blue base and boom, AAR trucks with older Lionel wheels, solid cab wheels and a translucent red cab! Can these two cranes be distinguished from one another?

The answer seems to be a qualified yes. Certain subtle differences do show up when the Hagerstown and Fundimensions cranes are placed side by side. The Fundimensions cab has the same washed-out, translucent color as the Hagerstown crane, but the color of the red plastic is clearly darker. The same color and texture appear on the door and window pieces used in the 2125 Whistle Shack, also made only in 1971. We suspect that the red roof of the 2156 station has the same color, but this needs confirmation. Like the Hagerstown crane, the Fundimensions crane has its wire assembly fastened to the boom by a rivet, but the Fundimensions rivet is blackened, unplated or bronzed instead of chromed. The U-shaped bracket at the bottom of the Fundimensions boom is also blackened, but bronzed brackets may also exist. Therefore, in the absence of the Fundimensions box, the best way to tell the Fundimensions 6560 from the Hagerstown 6560 is through the darker red translucent color of the cab and the blackened or bronzed rivet at the wire assembly.

The blue-based Hagerstown 6560 Crane is hard to find; it was offered as part of a set with a 2029 locomotive made in Japan for Lionel, and it was also offered for separate sale. The Fundimensions crane was assembled as a separate sale item only and is extremely difficult to find. This is one of the rare occasions when the original box will bring a substantial premium because of its use to positively identify the piece. Both of these cranes are very desirable pieces, but the Fundimensions 6560 is a real prize for anyone's collection. Since the Fundimensions cranes were only distributed for one year, chances are that only a small quantity of them were made at all. Incredibly, Fundimensions did not issue another crane car until 1979, when the Quaker City Limited set included a crane in Reading green and yellow colors.

The Fundimensions 6560 Crane car remains one of the great undiscovered secrets of the first years of the company. Slowly but inevitably, collectors are beginning to be aware of the scarcity of this piece. It is also a historically significant piece because it shows how Fundimensions maximized the use of its resources at a critical time for the company. It is a prime candidate for real appreciation in value over the next few years, along with some of the early accessories and small steam engines.

We do not think that we have all the pieces of the Fundimensions 6560 puzzle assembled yet. Therefore, we would like to hear from owners of both Hagerstown and Fundimensions cranes, especially those in their original boxes for positive identification. The key variables are the cab color, the base and boom color, the wire assembly rivet and the boom base bracket. Perhaps with a few more responses, we will be able to find information which will help collectors tell the Hagerstown and Fundimensions cranes apart, once and for all.

6560 BUCYRUS ERIE: 1971, crane car, very dark blue base and boom (best seen from underside), translucent red plastic cab (darker than Hagerstown postwar examples), solid operating wheels, white lettering on base sides, blackened, unplated or bronzed rivet holds wire assembly at top of boom, blackened or bronzed U-shaped rivet holds boom crank at base of boom, open AAR trucks, postwar wheels which turn on axles, two operating couplers.

(A) Came in Fundimensions Type I box with red lettering on box end label and picture of car. Mint value must include this box.   P. Catalano, C. Rohlfing and R. LaVoie comments, G. Halverson Collection.

60	75	100	125

(B) Canadian distribution; came in Type I box with smaller cellophane window and Parker Brothers black printed logo. One example observed in Montreal. We would like to know if there are any differences between this version and the one assembled for American production. G. Halverson comment.   **NRS**

6574 REDWOOD VALLEY EXPRESS: 1984, short crane car, 1877-style yellow flatcar base with dark brown lettering, tuscan plastic cab with yellow logo, gray boom, arch bar trucks; part of 1403 Redwood Valley Express set.

—	—	—	12

6576 ATSF: Announced for 1985, short crane car, dark blue scribed 1877-style flatcar body, dark blue cab, gray boom, gray log cradle and cab attachment piece, yellow lettering and Santa Fe cross logo, Symington-Wayne trucks, dummy couplers. From Midland Freight set.

—	—	—	12

6670: See entry 9378.

9235 UNION PACIFIC: 1983, yellow base with black derrick, Symington-Wayne trucks; separate sale item.

—	—	10	12

9236 CHICAGO & NORTHWESTERN: 1983, black base with yellow derrick, Symington-Wayne trucks; sold as part of 1354 Northern Freight Flyer set.

—	—	13	16

9245 ILLINOIS CENTRAL: Announced for 1985, derrick car, black 6511-2 flatcar base with white lettering and logo, bright orange swiveling boom riveted to flatcar, Symington-Wayne trucks. Canceled from dealer order sheets in September, 1985.

9247 NEW YORK CENTRAL: Announced for 1985, searchlight car, black 6511-2 flatcar body, white lettering, gray superstructure, black lens hood, Symington-Wayne trucks; part of Yard Chief switcher set.

—	—	—	15

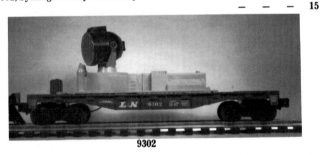

9302

9302 LOUISVILLE & NASHVILLE: 1973-74, searchlight, brown body, mold 6511-2, Symington-Wayne trucks with disc couplers, gray superstructure with mold 6812-5. Yellow lettering on flatcar base. Superstructure embossed "TRACK MAINTENANCE" and has two shovels, wire, control

panel and oxygen tanks molded in as part of mold 6812-5. The searchlight is not a part of the superstructure as such, but it is fastened to the superstructure by a circular metal fastener and is not intended to be removed. Griggs Collection.

(A) MPC logo.	8	10	12	15
(B) No MPC logo.	6	8	10	12
(C) All white lettering.	—	—	50	65

9312

9312 CONRAIL: 1979-82, searchlight, blue body, white lettering, mold "No. 6511-2", gray or orange plastic superstructure, mold "No. 3520-12", with box embossed "Track Maintenance" and tools, wire, control panel, oxygen tanks and searchlight unit.

(A) Unpainted gray superstructure, plastic rivet holding trucks. Nordby observation.

—	10	12	15

(B) Orange assembly, metal rivet holding trucks. Rohlfing and Nordby observations. This version was shown only in the 1979 advance catalogue. Apparently, both versions were produced in about the same numbers, but there were distinct regional differences in distribution which led collectors to believe that the orange superstructure version was scarce. It carries only a small premium over the gray superstructure version. R. LaVoie and Bryan Smith observations.

—	12	15	20

9329 CHESSIE SYSTEM: 1980, crane car, blue base, yellow cab with silver roof, die-cast six-wheel passenger trucks; came with 1070 The Royal Limited.

—	—	35	40

9332 READING: 1979, crane car, green base, yellow cab, green roof, yellow boom, yellow and green lettering and logo, Standard 0 trucks; from Quaker City Limited set.

—	—	25	35

9345 READING: 1984-85, searchlight car, dark green 6511-2 flatcar body with yellow lettering, cream superstructure with black and white Reading diamond-shaped pressure-sensitive decal on both sides, black searchlight hood, Symington-Wayne trucks.

—	—	—	14

9348 SANTA FE: 1979, crane car, blue base with yellow lettering, blue cab with yellow lettering and Santa Fe cross logo, gold diamond-shaped FARR 1 logo on cab, yellow boom, Standard 0 trucks, came in special Type III box. This crane was issued as the extra car for the first Famous American Railroads set of 1979. R. LaVoie Collection..

—	—	30	35

9378 LIONEL: 1981, red flat with yellow derrick, pictured as 6670 in catalogue, but produced as 9378. Symington-Wayne trucks; from 1154 Reading Yard King set. R. DuBeau and W. Barnes comments.

—	—	15	20

Chapter XII
AUTOMOBILE CARRIERS

1973 TCA: 1973, convention automobile carrier, black body, Symington-Wayne trucks. TCA logo in gold on one letter board, "NATIONAL CONVENTION/DEARBORN, MICH./1973" in gold on second letter board, same side, all lettering deep heat-stamped; came in 9123 Lionel Type II automobile carrier box, but 9123 does not appear on car side; gold "TRAILER TRAIN" reporting marks on flatcar side. C. Lang Collection.

$$- \quad - \quad - \quad 45$$

9123 CHESAPEAKE & OHIO: 1974, two or three-tier body, either one or two boards lettered, Symington-Wayne trucks, operating couplers.
(A) Three-tier black body, yellow lettering, upper board on each side lettered "C&O". Johnson Collection.   10   12   15   20
(B) Three-tier blue body, yellow lettering, one board lettered.

4   6   8   10

(C) Two-tier black plastic body, yellow lettering, "C&O FOR PROGRESS" on boards, "TRAILER TRAIN RTTX 9123" and "BLT 1-73" on frame, Symington-Wayne trucks, metal wheels, disc-operating couplers, not catalogued, came in factory sealed 1386 Rock island Express set in lieu of the 9125 blue N&W two-tier automobile carrier shown on the box and in the 1973-74 catalogues. Johnson Collection.   **NRS**

See also Factory Errors and Prototypes.

9125 NORFOLK & WESTERN: 1974, two-tier blue or black body, white lettering, single-board lettered, Symington-Wayne trucks, operating couplers; sold only in sets.
(A) Blue body, lettered with road name, number and built date, "TRAILER TRAIN".   8   11   15   25
(B) Black body. Wilson Collection.   8   15   20   40

9126 CHESAPEAKE & OHIO: 1973-74, three-tier body, either one or two boards lettered, Symington-Wayne trucks, operating couplers. Came in 1388 Golden State Arrow and 1460 Grand National sets; Grand National set also had 9123 C&O blue three-tiered car instead of 9126. C. Lang comment.

(A) Yellow body, blue lettering, one board lettered.   6   8   10   12
(B) Light yellow body, light blue lettering, one board lettered.

3   6   9   12

(C) Light yellow-painted yellow plastic body, bright royal blue lettering. The painted body is unusual for this car. Reader comments requested. G. Halverson Collection.   **NRS**

See also Factory Errors and Prototypes.

9129 NORFOLK & WESTERN: 1975, brown body, white lettering, single board stamped, Symington-Wayne trucks, two operating couplers.

4   6   8   10

9139 PENN CENTRAL: 1977, green body, white lettering, single board stamped, Symington-Wayne trucks, two operating couplers; part of Illinois Central Gulf freight set. C. Lang comment.   6   8   10   12

9145 ILLINOIS CENTRAL GULF: 1977, orange body, black lettering, single board stamped, Symington-Wayne trucks, two operating couplers.

4   6   8   10

9216 GREAT NORTHERN: 1978, blue plastic, white lettering, from Milwaukee Special set, black car stops on each level, Standard 0 trucks. To date, this is the only Fundimensions automobile carrier issued with die-cast trucks.   10   12   15   20

9281 A.T.S.F.: 1978-79, two-level carrier in red plastic, white lettering, white and red Santa Fe electrocal on upper boards on both sides, lower boards blank, "BLT 1-78", black vehicle stops on ends, Symington-Wayne trucks.   4   6   8   10

9351 PENNSYLVANIA: 1980, three-tier tuscan body, gold lettering with old-style red and gold keystone insignia on upper board, blank lower board.

6   8   10   12

Chapter XIII

FACTORY ERRORS AND PROTOTYPES

Gd VG Exc Mt

6464-1971 TCA SPECIAL: Disneyland, same as regular issue, but Mickey Mouse logo shows half-smile rather than full smile on each side. R. M. Caplan Collection. — — — **250**

6464-1 WESTERN PACIFIC: Probably late 1969 or early 1970, boxcar, orange-painted orange body and door, white lettering, Type VII body with 9200 end plates, metal door guides, postwar bar-end metal trucks. Prototype for reissue of 6464-type boxcars by Fundimensions, but this version never produced; believed to be one of a kind. R. M. Caplan Collection. — — — **1500**

6905 NICKEL PLATE ROAD: Extended vision caboose, gray stripe and script lettering completely missing from one side. Other types of factory errors may also exist; reader comments invited. **NRS**

7216 BALTIMORE AND OHIO: 1983, General-style passenger coach, no white striping along windows. R. LaVoie observation. **NRS**

8030 ILLINOIS CENTRAL: GP-9, Type II railings, lettering and numbering missing from one side. G. Halverson Collection. **NRS**

8050 DELAWARE & HUDSON: U-36C, "Delaware & Hudson" and "8050" missing from one side. G. Halverson Collection. **NRS**

8104 UNION PACIFIC: 1981, 4-4-0, General-type locomotive, green cab, pilot, lamp, wheel spokes and bell, black stack, chrome-finished boiler, "3" appears on side of headlamp and under cab window, green plastic "General"-style tender with one arch bar truck on front of tender and one Symington-Wayne truck on rear and simulated wood pile. This locomotive was sold by J.C. Penney as an uncatalogued special called "The Golden Arrow"; locomotive with wooden base and plastic cover. Moyer Collection. — — **195 225**

8252 DELAWARE & HUDSON: Alco powered A Unit. Factory prototype as shown in 1972 catalogue with lighter blue, almost powder blue paint, number-boards read "8022", D&H decal on side but road name and number not printed out. Road name and number shown in 1972 catalogue are printer overlay. Front coupler, side ladder steps do not line up with door, believed to be one of a kind. P. Catalano Collection. — — — **550**

8253 DELAWARE & HUDSON: Dummy Alco, light blue, almost powder blue, yellow sticky strip along bottom, ladders do not line up with door. With D&H decal but without number or name on side. 1972 catalogue shows prototype with name and number but these are printer overlay. P. Catalano Collection. — — — **550**

8359 B&O: GM 50th Anniversary GP-7.
(A) Without "B&O" and "GM 50" but with nose decal. **NRS**
(B) No nose decal or numbers on sides, but "B&O" present. G. Halverson Collection. **NRS**

8460 MKT: NW-2 Switcher, deeper red than usual production, lettering missing from one side. G. Halverson Collection. **NRS**

8556 CHESSIE SYSTEM: NW-2 Switcher, Chessie System lettering and logo missing from both sides. G. Halverson Collection. **NRS**

8763 NORFORLK AND WESTERN: GP-9, black-painted plastic body with white lettering, red overspray inside cab, painted over 8666 Northern Pacific cab, frame riveted instead of spot-welded. Prototype displayed at 1978 Toy Fair. G. Halverson Collection. **NRS**

8900 ATSF: 4-6-4, boiler front in silver has feed water heater; no evidence of removal or alteration. G. Parsons Collection. — — — **320**

9010 GREAT NORTHERN: 1971, short hopper, lettering missing from one side. G. Halverson Collection. **NRS**

9111 NORFOLK & WESTERN: 1972, quad hopper, Tuscan body, white decal lettering, prototype, rare. C. Lang comment. **NRS**

9121 L&N: 1975, flatcar with dozer and scraper, brown flatcar body, white lettering on one side only. J. Breslin Collection. **NRS**

9123 C&O: 1973-76, automobile carrier.
(A) Three-tier black body, C&O markings on both upper and lower boards on each side. This is a legitimate factory error. Any attempt to fake this piece by combining tiers from two different cars can be detected easily by the absence of the "TRAILER TRAIN" lettering on the lower board. G. Halverson comment. **15 20 25 30**
(B) Three-tier blue body, yellow lettering, two boards lettered. G. Halverson Collection. **12 15 20 45**
(C) Three-tier yellow body, blue lettering, "BLT 1-73", only upper board lettered; only ten in existence. Fuhrmann Collection. — — **400** —
(D) Two-tier blue plastic body, no road name, white lettering, "BLT 1-73" and "9123"; only six made. Fuhrmann Collection. — — **600** —

9126 CHESAPEAKE & OHIO: 1973-74, automobile carrier car, light yellow body, two boards lettered. — **15 20 45**

9134 VIRGINIAN: 1976-77, covered hopper, silver roof cover instead of blue. This is a legitimate factory error, not a switched cover, because the silver cover is painted over the normal blue unpainted cover. When the hatches are lifted, the blue shows through, and there are silver paint specks on the inside of the car, which is unpainted gray. Most likely, this car was run through the paint spray booth with the cover installed. R. LaVoie comment, G. Halverson and C. Lang Collections. — — — **100**

9140 BURLINGTON: 1971, long gondola, flush-molded brakewheel, lettering on one side only. G. Halverson Collection. **NRS**

9141 BURLINGTON NORTHERN: 1973, long gondola, flush molded brakewheel, lettering on one side only. G. Halverson Collection. **NRS**

9142 REPUBLIC STEEL: 1973, long gondola, lettering on one side only. G. Halverson Collection. **NRS**

9144 RIO GRANDE: Long gondola, recessed brakewheel molding, lettering on one side only. G. Halverson Collection. **NRS**

MX 9145 AUTOLITE: 1972 apparent prototype of 9042 Autolite short 027 boxcar. The lettering on the left side of the car is hand-lettered with a brush and a Rapidograph type pen. There are guide lines visible for the lettering. The words "AUTOLITE/SPARK PLUGS" are somewhat larger than those on the production 9042. The car does not have MPC or 9040 Series embossed on the end plates. The body is embossed "Part No. 100 4-3" on the inside. The technical data on the right is simulated by rough "chicken scratch" writing. There is no "LIONEL" or "BLT. 1-71". The "MX" lettering may indicate "MOTORCRAFT EXPERIMENTAL". Symington-Wayne trucks, one operating and one dummy coupler. R. DuBeau Collection. **NRS**

9200 ILLINOIS CENTRAL: Boxcar, Unpainted orange Type VI body, IC close, open AAR trucks, metal door guides; preproduction sample. G. Halverson Collection. **NRS**

9202 SANTA FE: Boxcar, orange-painted orange body, black-painted black door, black lettering; prototype, one of 69. — — **800 900**

9207 SOO: Type VII body, Type I frame.
(A) White-painted sides and black-painted roof on white plastic body with red-painted red door, black lettering, metal door guides, Symington-Wayne trucks; preproduction sample, one of twenty-four. — — — **225**
(B) Same as (A), but all white-painted car. — — — **225**

9238 NORTHERN PACIFIC: 1984-85, log dump car, same as catalogued issue, but mirror imaged lettering on both sides of car; electrocal was applied in reverse. G. Wilson Collection. — — — **75**

9304 C&O: 1973-76, coal dump car, no lettering on either side. **NRS**

9306 ATSF: Flatcar with two horses; from 1053 James Gang set, one arch bar and one AAR truck. R. Grandison Collection. **NRS**

9307 ERIE: 1979-80, animated gondola.
(A) Lettering and numbering completely absent from one side of car; probable factory error. Moss Collection. **NRS**

(B) Unpainted turquoise gondola body, unpainted tan crate load, no lettering or numbering; possible prototype. A. Otten Collection. **NRS**

9308 AQUARIUM CAR: 1981-83, unpainted and unlettered clear plastic. A. Otten collection. **NRS**

9602 ATSF: 1977, all markings to right of door on both sides are missing.

— — — 350

9700 SOUTHERN: Boxcar, tuscan-painted tuscan Type IX body, tuscan-painted tuscan doors, Symington-Wayne trucks, Type II box. Possible pre-production sample for 9711 Southern boxcar, which was produced in this color. Two examples examined and known to exist. J. LaVoie Collection.

NRS

9701 BALTIMORE & OHIO: Double-door boxcar.
(A) Black-painted sides, silver roof painted on blue plastic, yellow-painted yellow doors, yellow lettering, Type II frame; 12 made. — — 400 —
(B) Black sides and silver roof painted on gray plastic body, light blue-painted light blue doors, light blue lettering, Type II frame, preproduction sample. **NRS**
(C) Deep blue-painted deep blue plastic body, black-painted black doors, yellow lettering, printed on only one side, Type II frame. R. M. Caplan Collection. — — — 1000
(D) Unpainted blue plastic body, yellow lettering, one side blank. R. M. Caplan collection. — — — 1000

9703 CP RAIL: Boxcar, dark green-painted light green body, dark green-painted light green doors, Type II frame; one of five preproduction samples, one side blank. — — — 600

9705 DENVER & RIO GRANDE: Boxcar.
(A) Silver-painted gray Type IX plastic body, red-painted red doors, Type I frame, red lettering, 16 made. Red doors installed outside factory. R. Vagner comment. Preproduction sample. — — 400 —
(B) Same as (A), but Type II frame. Red doors installed outside factory. R. Vagner comment. Preproduction sample. — — 400 —
(C) Silver-painted Type IX gray plastic body, orange lettering, Type II frame; ten made. — — 500 —

9706 C&O: Boxcar, black-painted gray plastic, black-painted door, Type II frame; four preproduction samples known. — — 700 —

9708-9709 U.S. MAIL/BAR: Same color scheme on both sides, but one side is lettered for 9708 U. S. Mail car and one side for 9709 BAR State of Maine car. R. M. Caplan collection. — — — 1500

9709 BAR STATE OF MAINE:
(A) Same as (D) in listings, but no printing on the white areas of either side. — — — 125
(B) Blue and light red-painted gray body, blue and red-painted gray doors, white and black-painted lettering, number stamped on angle.

30 45 60 70

9757 CENTRAL OF GEORGIA: Tuscan-painted brown body, silver-painted gray doors, number misprinted. **NRS**

9758 ALASKA:
(A) Blue-painted white body, blue-painted white doors, white lettering, without "at your service". — 150 225 325
(B) Blue-painted dark blue body and doors, yellow lettering, without "at your service." R. Vagner Collection. — — 325 350

9772 GREAT NORTHERN:
(A) Missing number and "GN" on one side. We wish to learn how many of this variety are in collector hands. Reader comments are invited. **NRS**
(B) Same as (A), but completely missing GN logo on right. Black lettering and underscoring on left side is present, but has shifted downward so that the underscoring is through the yellow line. Breslin Collection. We wish to learn how many of this variety are in collector hands. Reader comments are invited. **NRS**

9776 SOUTHERN PACIFIC: Black-painted body and black doors, white and gold lettering, double-stamped lettering and emblems.

— — 35 50

9784 ATSF: 1977-78, dark maroon-painted body, flat black roof and ends, white lettering "washed out" with tinge of pinkish-maroon. Meisel comment, R. Vagner Collection. — — — 600

9801 BALTIMORE AND OHIO:
(A) Dark blue lower stripe, B&O decal is misplaced on one side only. Klaassen Collection. **NRS**
(B) No lettering in upper left corner of one side. D. Newman Collection. **NRS**

9802 MILLER HIGH LIFE: Standard 0 reefer, gray plastic body, red doors and lettering, "BLT 1-73", red plastic snap-on walkway, die-cast sprung trucks, disc-operating couplers, the "2" in 9802 is slightly higher than "980", probable prototypes, five known to exist. Fuhrmann Collection. — — 700 —

9814 PERRIER: 1980 billboard reefer, perrier bottle missing from mountain spring electrocal. McCabe Collection. We do not know how rare this variety is. Reader comments requested. **NRS**

9820 WABASH: Gray body, black lettering, simulated coal load, Standard 0 series with Standard 0 trucks, die-cast sprung trucks, disc couplers; only two in existence. Barbret Collection. — — 800 —

9821 SOUTHERN PACIFIC: 1973-74, Standard 0 gondola, black body, white lettering, "Blt 1-73", Southern Pacific decal, no brakewheel but hole for brakewheel, only three known. Fuhrmann Collection.

— — 800 —

Chapter XIV

SETS

FUNDIMENSIONS SETS - U.S. MARKET

By Donna Price and Glenn Halverson
With the assistance of Brenda Patterson,
Dan Johns and Chris Rohlfing

Lionel has produced a remarkable number of sets since 1970. Some of these sets were illustrated and described in either Lionel's consumer catalogues or the collector center brochures. These we refer to as Lionel Catalogue Sets and are listed below by year.

Lionel's catalogue record is moderately accurate. However, since each year's catalogue was prepared considerably before the sets actual production, some production changes were made that are not reflected in the catalogue. This report is based on the catalogue record and when deviations are known, we have reported the actual set components. If you note differences in your set(s) from those listed in this chapter, we would appreciate your describing the differences to us.

This chapter includes all known sets: catalogued and uncatalogued. The sets for Canadian distribution are listed separately later in the chapter. We have arranged Lionel catalogue sets for each year by set number and have dropped the prefix "6" which was used from 1971 on by Fundimensions. For each year we also have a listing of "Other Sets". Other sets are sets Fundimensions made for major toy retailing outlets such as Sears, Lionel Leisure (Kiddie City stores), J.C. Penney, True Value Hardware Stores and others. Each set has a set number, the name (if any) and the retail outlet for which the set was produced. If no retail outlet is named, the set was available through regular Lionel distributors. Although our listing is extensive, it is not complete and we look forward to reader reports on sets not listed here.

Editors Note: Donna Price, a staff editor, and Brenda Patterson, a word processor, prepared the listing of catalogued sets. Glenn Halverson, a tele-communications major at Michigan State University and a resident of Clifton Park, New York has been one of the major researchers for this book. He is responsible for substantial changes in the text, especially in the accessories and steam engines chapters. During his research for this segment, he contacted Fundimensions, where he was ably assisted by Dan Johns, the Director of Customer Relations for the firm. Mr. Johns has been most helpful in this and other areas. Chris Rohlfing has provided superb editorial assistance to a number of our publications. He carefully reviewed his collection for this chapter.

1970
LIONEL CATALOGUE SETS

1081 WABASH CANNONBALL: 8040 locomotive and tender, 9140 or 9141, 9021, 9060, 4045, eight 5013s, two 5018s, new mechanical automatic uncoupler, 2CTC, wires, owner's maintenance and instruction manual.

1082 YARD BOSS: 8010 diesel, 9140 or 9141, 9010, 9021, 4045, eight 5013s, two 5018s, new automatic uncoupler, 2CTC, wires, owner's maintenance and instruction manual.

1083 PACEMAKER: 8041 locomotive and tender, 9010, 9140 or 9141, 9020, 9062, 5020, twelve 5013s, four 5018s, 4045, train crew - three figure set, 2911, mechanical automatic uncoupler, 2CTC, wires, owner's maintenance and instruction manual.

1084 GRAND TRUNK & WESTERN: 8042 locomotive and tender, 9010, 9040, 9020, 9063, 5149, eight 5013s, three 5018s, 4045, train crew - three figure set, 2911, 2CTC, wires, owner's maintenance and instruction manual. (9050 Sunoco tank car is pictured but not included in set description.)

1085 SANTA FE EXPRESS DIESEL FREIGHT: 8020 twin-diesel, 9050, 9120, 9041, 9010, 9140 or 9141, 9061, 5149, 5020, twelve 5013s, seven 5018s, 4045, train crew - three figure set, 2CTC, wires, owner's instruction and maintenance manual.

1086 THE MOUNTAINEER: 8062 locomotive and tender, 9300, 9120, 9130 (catalogue states C&O but picture shows B&O), 9202, Great Northern steel caboose, 5149, eight 5013s, seven 5018s, 4090, train crew - three figure set, 2911, 2CTC, wires, owner's maintenance and instruction manual. Catalogued but not manufactured.

1087 MIDNIGHT EXPRESS: 8030 diesel, 8031 dummy, 9300, Penn Central communications satellite car, 9120, 9130, 9203, 9160, ten 5013s, eleven 5018s, 5022L, 5022R, 5149, 4090, train crew - three figure set, 2CTC, wires, owner's maintenance and instruction manual. Catalogued but not manufactured.

OTHER 1970 SETS

1091 Sears Special: 8043 locomotive, 8040T, 9140, 9011, 9060.

49N9707 Sears: 8040 locomotive and slope-back tender, gondola, boxcar, 9300, bobber caboose, 25-watt transformer, eight 5013s, two 5018s.

49N97092 Sears: 8041 locomotive and tender, gondola, NYC bobber caboose, eight 5013s, 25-watt transformer.

79N97081C Sears: 8042 locomotive and tender, gondola, 9010, flatcar, 9063, eight 5013s, four 5018s, three figures, 2909, 4045.

79N97082C Sears: 8040 locomotive and tender, 9140, 9010, 9060, two 5018s, eight 5013s, manual, 4045.

1971
LIONEL CATALOGUE SETS

1081 WABASH CANNONBALL: 8040 or 8043 locomotive and tender, 9142, 9020, 9060, eight 5013s, two 5018s, mechanical uncoupler, 25-watt Trainmaster transformer, 2900, wires, instructions.

1085 SANTA FE TWIN DIESEL: 8020 twin-diesel, 9040, 9141, 9050, 9012, 9120, 9061, 4050, push-button electric uncoupling track, twelve 5013s, seven 5018s, 5020, two figures, 2900, wires, instructions, foam model buildings.

1182 THE YARDMASTER: 8111 diesel, 9090, 9142, 9300, 9021, eight 5013s, four 5018s, mechanical uncoupler, 25-watt Trainmaster transformer, 2900, wires, instructions.

1183 THE SILVER STAR: 8141 locomotive and tender, 9010, 9020, 9142, 9062, twelve 5013s, four 5018s, 5020, 4050, two figures, mechanical uncoupler, 2900, wires, instructions.

1184 THE ALLEGHENY: 8142 locomotive and tender, 9022, 9040, 9012, 9141, 9064, eight 5013s, five 5018s, push-button electric uncoupling track, 4050, two figures, 2900, wires, instructions, foam model buildings.

1186 CROSS COUNTRY EXPRESS: 8030 diesel, 9135, 9200, 9250, 9121, 9300, 9160, ten 5013s, eleven 5018s, 5149, 5121, 5122, 4090, mechanical uncoupler, two figures, 2900, wires, instructions.

OTHER 1971 SETS

1190 Sears Special #1: 8140 locomotive, 8040T, i9140, 9020, 9060.

1195 J.C. Penney Special: 8022 diesel, 9140, 9011, 9021.

79C95204C Sears: 8020 diesel, boxcar, gondola, 9012, 9050, 9012, 9061, (catalogue shows two hoppers), five 5018s, twelve 5013s, push-button remote track, 5020, two figures, three canisters, 50-watt transformer.

79C97101C Sears: 8040 or 8043 locomotive and tender, 9141, 9020, 9060, two 5018s, eight 5013s, 25-watt transformer.

79C97105C Sears: 2-4-2 locomotive and tender, 9141, 9142, hopper, 9063, (catalogue shows two gondolas), four 5018s, eight 5013s, uncoupling unit, two figures, two canisters, 50-watt transformer.

The following train set is from the Sears catalogue pages that list the three preceding sets. Although the page heading is "Lionel", it is not known if this set was made by Fundimensions.

79C95265C SPEEDRAIL: Modernistic metal and plastic engine, streamlined boxcar, flatcar and gondola, 18" x 44" elevated figure-eight layout, see-through tunnel, 39-piece trestle set, 16-watt power pack.

1972
LIONEL CATALOGUE SETS

1081 WABASH CANNONBALL: 8040 locomotive and tender, 9136, 9020, 9060, eight 5013s, two 5018s, mechanical uncoupler, 25-watt Trainmaster transformer.

1182 YARDMASTER: 8111 diesel, 9300, 9136, 9013, 9025 or 9061, eight 5013s, four 5018s, mechanical uncoupler, 25-watt Trainmaster transformer. Distributed in Canada as T-1272.

1183 SILVER STAR: 8203 locomotive and tender, 9136, 9013, 9020, 9062, twelve 5013s, four 5018s, 5020, mechanical uncoupler, 4150. Distributed in Canada as T-1273.

1186 CROSS COUNTRY EXPRESS: 8030 diesel, 9111, 9151, 9121, 9700, 9701, 9160, ten 5013s, eleven 5018s, 5149, remote switches, figures, 4090.

1280 KICKAPOO VALLEY & NORTHERN: 8200 locomotive, operating dump car, 9020, 9067, eight 5013s, two 5018s, 25-watt Trainmaster transformer. Distributed in Canada as T-1280.

1284 ALLEGHENY: 8204 locomotive and tender, 9042, 9141, 9012, 9022, stakes and load, 9064, eight 5013s, five 5018s, 5149, figures, whistle controller, 4150.

1285 SANTA FE TWIN DIESEL: 8020 diesel, 8021 dummy, 9700, 9140 or 9141, 9300, 9012, 9122, 9061, twelve 5013s, seven 5018s, 5149, 5020, figures, 4150.

1287 PIONEER DOCKSIDE SWITCHER: 8209 locomotive and tender, 9013, 9136, 9060, nine 5018s, eight 5013s, manual switch, 4150.

OTHER 1972 SETS

1290: 8140 locomotive, 8040T, 9136, 9020, 9060.

79C95204C Sears: 8020 diesel, boxcar, gondola, 9012, 9050, 9012, 9061, (catalogue shows two hoppers), five 5018s, twelve 5013s, push-button remote track, 5020, two figures, three canisters, 50-watt transformer.

79C97101C Sears: 8040 or 8043 locomotive and tender, 9141, 9020, 9060, two 5018s, eight 5013s, 25-watt transformer.

79C97105C Sears: 2-4-2 locomotive and tender, 9141, 9142, hopper, 9063, (catalogue shows two gondolas), four 5018s, eight 5013s, uncoupling unit, two figures, two canisters, 50-watt transformer.

The following train set is from the Sears catalogue pages that list the three preceding sets. Although the page heading is "Lionel", it is not known if this set was made by Fundimensions.

79C95265C SPEEDRAIL: Modernistic metal and plastic engine, streamlined boxcar, flatcar and gondola, 18" x 44" elevated figure-eight layout, see-through tunnel, 39-piece trestle set, 16-watt power pack.

Sears 79N9552C: 8141 locomotive and tender, 9012, 9020, 9140, 9062, 5020, four 5018s, twelve 5013s, canisters, 5025, 4150.

Sears 79N9553C: 8020 diesel, 9300, 9040, 9140 or 9141, 9011, 9141, 9061, 5020, eight 5018s, twelve 5013s, canisters, 5025, 4150.

Sears 79N97101C: 8042 locomotive, slope-back tender, 9136, 9011, 9060, two 5018s, eight 5013s, 25-watt transformer.

1973
LIONEL CATALOGUE SETS

1380 U.S. STEEL INDUSTRIAL SWITCHER: 8350 diesel, 9031, 9024, 9068, eight 5013s, DC power pack.

1381 CANNONBALL: 8300 or 8502 locomotive and tender, 9031, 9024, 9061, eight 5013s, two 5018s, 25-watt transformer.

1382 YARDMASTER: 8111 diesel, 9136, 9013, 9300, 9025, eight 5013s, four 5018s, 25-watt transformer.

1383 SANTA FE FREIGHT: 8020 diesel, 9300, 9136, 9013, 9021, eight 5013s, six 5018s, 25-watt transformer.

1384 SOUTHERN EXPRESS: 8140 locomotive and tender, 9013, 9140, 9020, 9066, twelve 5013s, four 5018s, 5020, 4150.

1385 BLUE STREAK FREIGHT: 8303 locomotive and tender, 9013, 9136, 9043, 9140, 9020, 9066, eight 5013s, six 5018s, 4150.

1386 ROCK ISLAND EXPRESS: 8304 locomotive and tender, 9125, 9131, 9023, 9015, 9070, eight 5013s, six 5018s, 4150.

1387 MILWAUKEE SPECIAL: 8305 locomotive and tender, 9500, 9501, 9503, eight 5013s, six 5018s, 4150.

1388 GOLDEN STATE ARROW: 8352 diesel, 9135, 9126, 9707, 9152, 9708, 9163, 4150, ten 5013s, eleven 5018s, 5149.

OTHER 1973 SETS

1390 Sears Seven-Unit: 8310 locomtive, 8310T, 9013, 9020, 9136, 9040, 9060.

1392 Sears Eight-Unit: 8308 locomotive, 8308T (1130T-type), 9124, 9136, 9013, 9020, 9043, 9069.

1395 J.C. Penney: 8311 locomotive, 8311T (1130T-type), 9140, 9013, 9024, 9043, 9050, 9066.

49C95225 Sears: Heritage trestle train set, pictured on Lionel 027 page but not made by Fundimensions.

79C95223C Sears: 8351 diesel, 9043, hopper, 9136, 9020, ATSF caboose, eight 5013s, two 5018s, 25-watt transformer.

79C95224C Sears: 8303 locomotive and tender, flatcar with stakes, 9043, 9136, hopper, flatcar, 9069, ten 5013s, twelve 5018s, two manual switches, 4150.

1974
LIONEL CATALOGUE SETS

1380 U.S. INDUSTRIAL SWITCHER: 8350 diesel, 9024, 9031, 9068, eight 5013s, DC power pack.

1381 CANNONBALL: 8300 locomotive and tender, 9031, 9024, 9163, eight 5013s, two 5018s, transformer.

1382 YARDMASTER: 8111 diesel, 9136, 9120, 9013, 9025, eight 5013s, four 5018s, transformer.

1383 SANTA FE FREIGHT: 8351 diesel, 9013, 9020 or 9300, 9136, 9021, eight 5013s, six 5018s, transformer. Reader reports requested.

1384 SOUTHERN EXPRESS: 8302 locomotive and tender, 9013, 9136, 9020, 9066, transformer, twelve 5013s, four 5018s, 5020.

1385 BLUE STREAK FREIGHT: 8303 locomotive and tender, 9140, 9020, 9136, 9043, 9013, 9069, transformer, eight 5013s, six 5018s.

1386 ROCK ISLAND EXPRESS: 8304 locomotive and tender, 9015, 9131, 9023, 9125, 9070, transformer, eight 5013s, six 5018s.

1388 GOLDEN STATE ARROW: 8352 diesel, 9135, 9707, 9126, 9301, 9152, 9163, transformer, 5149, ten 5013s, eleven 5018s.

1460 GRAND NATIONAL: 8470 diesel, 9860, 9303, 9121, 9114, 9126 or 9123, 9740, 9167, two remote-controlled switches, 5149, 5020, transformer, twenty-three 5018s, eighteen 5013s.

1487 BROADWAY LIMITED: 8304 locomotive and tender, 9507, 9508, 9509, eight 5013s, six 5018s, transformer.

1489 SANTA FE DOUBLE DIESEL: 8020 diesel, 8021 dummy, 9013, 9140, 9042, 9036, 9024, 9061, eight 5013s, six 5018s, transformer.

OTHER 1974 SETS

1492 Sears Seven-Unit: 8310 locomotive, 8308T (1130T-type, 9124, 9136, 9013, 9043, 9069.

1493 Sears: Same as 1492, but with Mailer.

1499 J.C. Penney Great Express: 8311 locomotive, 8311T (1130T-type), 9136, 9013, 9020, 9066.

79N95223C Sears: 8351 diesel, 9020, 9013, 9043, 9142, 9061, eight 5013s, two 5018s, uncoupler, 7-1/2-watt transformer.

79N96178C Sears: 8502 locomotive and tender, gondola with canisters, 9071, eight 5013s.

79N96185C Sears: 8310 locomotive and tender, flatcar with logs, 9136, 9013, 9043, 9069, eight 5013s, eight 5018s, manual switch, bumper, uncoupler, 25-watt transformer.

1975
LIONEL CATALOGUE SETS

1380 U.S. STEEL INDUSTRIAL SWITCHER: 8350 diesel, 9031, 9024, 9067, eight 5013s, DC power pack.

1381 CANNONBALL: 8502 locomotive and tender, 9024, 9031, 9061, eight 5013s, two 5018s, transformer.

1384 SOUTHERN EXPRESS: 8302 locomotive and tender, 9136, 9013, 9020, 9066, twelve 5013s, four 5018s, 5020, transformer.

1388 GOLDEN STATE ARROW: 8352 diesel, 9135, 9707, 9126, 9301, 9152, 9163, transformer, 5149, ten 5013s, eleven 5018s.

1461 BLACK DIAMOND: 8203 locomotive and tender, 9136, 9020, 9043, 9140, 9013, 9052, eight 5013s, six 5018s, transformer.

1487 BROADWAY LIMITED: 8304 locomotive and tender, 9507, 9508, 9509, eight 5013s, six 5018s, transformer.

1489 SANTA FE DOUBLE DIESEL: 8020 diesel, 8021 dummy, 9020, 9013, 9140, 9136, 9042, 9061, eight 5013s, six 5018s, transformer.

1560 NORTH AMERICAN EXPRESS: 8564 diesel, 9121, 9861, 9303, 9129, 9260, 9755, 9168, two remote control switches, twenty-three 5018s, eighteen 5013s, 5020, 5149.

1581 THUNDERBALL FREIGHT: 8500 locomotive and tender, 9011, 9020, 9032, 9052, eight 5013s, two 5018s, transformer.

1582 YARD CHIEF: 8569 diesel, 9140, 9044, 9011, 9026, 9027, eight 5013s, two 5018s, transformer.

1584 N&W SPIRIT OF AMERICA: 1776 diesel, 9135, 9153, 9707, 9129, 9301, 9176, 5149, ten 5013s, eleven 5018s, transformer.

1585 75TH ANNIVERSARY SPECIAL: 7500 U36B diesel, 7507, 7502, 7501, 7504, 7503, 7505, 7506, 7508.

1586 CHESAPEAKE FLYER: 8304 locomotive and tender, 9131, 9125, 9016, 9022, 9064, eight 5013s, four 5018s, two canisters, transformer.

1587 CAPITAL LIMITED: 8304 locomotive and tender, 9517, 9518, 9519, eight 5013s, four 5018s, transformer.

OTHER 1975 SETS

1594 Sears: 8563 diesel. Details needed.

1976
LIONEL CATALOGUE SETS

1384 SOUTHERN EXPRESS: 8302 locomotive and tender, 9136, 9013, 9020, 9066, 5020, transformer, eight 5013s, four 5018s.

1489 SANTA FE DOUBLE DIESEL: 8020 diesel, 8021 dummy, 9013, 9136, 9042, 9140, 9020, 9061, eight 5013s, six 5018s, transformer.

1581 THUNDERBALL FREIGHT: 8500 locomotive and tender, 9011, 9020, 9032, 9172, eight 5013s, two 5018s, transformer.

1582 YARD CHIEF: 8569 diesel, 9026, 9044, 9140, 9011, 9027, girders, eight 5013s, two 5018s, transformer.

1585 LIONEL ANNIVERSARY SPECIAL: 7500 diesel, 7507, 7504, 7503, 7506, 7505, 7501, 7502, 7508.

1586 CHESAPEAKE FLYER: 8304 locomotive and tender, 9016, 9125, 9131, 9022, 9064, eight 5013s, four 5018s, two canisters, transformer.

1660 YARD BOSS: 8670 diesel, 9032, 9026, 9179, DC power pack, eight 5013s.

1661 ROCK ISLAND LINE: 8601 locomotive and tender, 9033, 9020, 9078, die-cut freight station, bridge and tunnel, eight 5013s, two 5018s, transformer.

1662 THE BLACK RIVER FREIGHT: 8602 locomotive, 9021, 9016, 9140, 9026, 9077, two canisters, twenty-two telephone poles and road signs, die-cut freight station, bridge and tunnel, trestle set, eight 5013s, four 5018s, transformer.

1663 AMTRAK LAKE SHORE LIMITED: 8664 diesel, 6403, 6404, 6405, 6406, eight 5013s, four 5018s, transformer.

1664 ILLINOIS CENTRAL FREIGHT: 8669 diesel, 9767, 9139, 9606, 9852, 9121, 9178, 5021, 2280, 2317, 5149, twelve 5013s, nine 5018s, two 5019s, six trestles, transformer.

1665 NYC EMPIRE STATE EXPRESS: 8600 locomotive and tender, 9772, 9773, 9266, 9159, 9174, eight 5013s, ten 5018s, transformer.

OTHER 1976 SETS

1594 Sears: 8563 diesel. Details needed.

1693 Toys-R-Us Rock Island Special: 8601 locomotive, 8601T, 9047, 9020, 9078.

1694 Toys-R-Us Black River Special: 8602 locomotive, 8602T (1130T-type), 9026, 9048, 9140, 9077.

1696 Sears: 8604 locomotive, 1130T, 9020, 9044, 9140, 9011, 9069.

1698 True-Value: 8601 locomotive and tender, 9020, 9046, 9078.

1977
LIONEL CATALOGUE SETS

1585 LIONEL ANNIVERSARY SPECIAL: 7500 U36B diesel, 7507, 7502, 7501, 7504, 7503, 7505, 7506, 7508. Nine-unit train commemorating Lionel's 75th anniversary.

1586 THE CHESAPEAKE FLYER: 8304 locomotive and tender, 9016, 9125, 9022, 9131, 9064, eight 5013s, four 5018s, two canisters, transformer.

1661 ROCK ISLAND LINE: 8601 locomotive and tender, 9033, 9020, 9078, three canisters, six wood railroad ties, die-cut freight station, bridge and tunnel, eight 5013s, two 5018s, transformer.

1662 THE BLACK RIVER FREIGHT: 8602 locomotive and tender, 9140, 9016, 9026, 9077, two canisters, twenty-two telephone poles and road signs, die-cut freight station, bridge and tunnel, trestle set, eight 5013s, four 5018s, transformer.

1663 AMTRAK LAKE SHORE LIMITED: 8664 diesel, 6403, 6404, 6405, 6406, eight 5013s, four 5018s, transformer.

1664 ILLINOIS CENTRAL FREIGHT: 8669 diesel, 9767, 9139, 9606, 9852, 9121, 9178, 5021, 2280, 2317, 5149, twelve 5013s, nine 5018s, two 5019s, six trestles, transformer.

1760 STEEL HAULERS: 8769 diesel, 9016, 9020, 9033, 9071, Peterbilt tractor with die-cast chassis, trailer, operating crane kit, pull cart, eight 5013s, two 5018s, DC power pack, die-cut factories and shed. Plastic loads include pipes, I-beams, engine blocks, culverts, posts, train wheels, crates with loads, warehouse skids.

1761 CARGO KING: 8770 diesel, 9026, 9032, 9016, (9021, 9025 or 9027), Mack and Peterbilt tractors, two trailers, two operating crane kits, pull cart, eight 5013s, four 5018s, die-cut buildings, transformer. Plastic loads include cement blocks, barrels, wood stacks, I-beams, culverts, pipes, crates, warehouse skids, posts.

1762 THE WABASH CANNONBALL: 8703 locomotive and tender, 9851, 9079, 9284, 9771, 9080, canisters, 2110, twelve 5013s, fourteen 5018s, transformer.

1764 THE HEARTLAND EXPRESS: 8772 diesel, 7808, 9302, 9116, 9283, 9187, 5027, ten 5013s, seven 5018s, transformer.

1765 ROCKY MOUNTAIN SPECIAL: 8771 diesel, 9789, 9610, 9286, 9189, 9285, 9188, 5125, two 2290s, three-piece trestle, 5149, nine 5013s, twenty-three 5018s, transformer.

OTHER 1977 SETS

1790 Lionel Leisure Steel Hauler: 8769 diesel, 9033, 9034, 9020, 9071.

1791 Toys-R-Us Steel Hauler: 8769 diesel, 9033, 9049, 9020, 9071.

1792 True-Value: Same as 1698, except 9053 True-Value boxcar replaces 9046 True-Value boxcar.

1793 Toys-R-Us Black River Freight: 8602 locomotive, 8602T (1130T-type), 9026, 9052, 9140, 9077.

1796 J.C. Penney: 8770, 9026, 9032, 9054, 9025, 4651.

1978
LIONEL CATALOGUE SETS

1662 BLACK RIVER FREIGHT: 8602 locomotive and tender, 9140, 9016, 9026, 9077, 2180, 2181, die-cut girder bridge, tunnel and freight station, eight 5013s, four 5018s, twelve-tier graduated trestle set, 2905, transformer.

1760 TRAINS N' TRUCKIN' STEEL HAULER: 9769 diesel, 9020, 9011, 9033, 9071, Peterbilt tractor, truck with stakebed trailer, operating 10" crane kit, eight 5013s, two 5018s, DC power pack, two die-cut buildings. Plastic loads include I-beams, train wheels, crates, warehouse skids, barrels.

1761 TRAINS N' TRUCKIN' CARGO KING: 8770 diesel, 9032, 9026, 9016, 9027, 2905, eight 5013s, six 5018s, transformer. Mack truck with stake bed trailer, Peterbilt truck with a flatbed trailer, two 10" tall operating cranes, three die-cut buildings, cargo and accessories. Plastic cargo includes I-beams, train wheels, crates, warehouse skids, barrels.

1860 WORKIN' ON THE RAILROAD TIMBERLINE: 8501 locomotive, slope-back tender, operating log dumper car, operating crane car, 9021, plastic operating log loading mill, four figures, throttle, eight 5013s, two 5018s, transformer.

1862 WORKIN' ON THE RAILROAD LOGGING EMPIRE: 8501 locomotive, slope-back tender, operating dumper car with logs, operating crane car, 9019, 9043, flatcar with fences, 9025, 2721, 2722, four plastic workman, throttle, twelve 5013s, six 5018s, 5020, transformer.

1864 SANTA FE DOUBLE DIESEL: 8861 diesel, 8862 dummy, 9035, 9018, 9033, 9014, 9058, eight 5013s, six 5018s, manual uncoupler, 2905, 2717, transformer.

1865 CHESAPEAKE FLYER: 8800 locomotive, 8800T, 9036, 9017, 9035, 9018, 9058, 2717, 2180, eight 5013s, six 5018s, 2905, manual uncoupler, 2909, transformer.

1866 GREAT PLAINS EXPRESS: 8854 diesel, 9729, 9036, 9121, 9011, 9140, 9057, 2717, ten 5013s, seven 5018s, 5027, transformer.

1867 MILWAUKEE LIMITED: 8855 diesel, 9277, 9276, 9216, 9411, 9876, 9269.

OTHER 1978 SETS

1860 Timberline: 8803 locomotive, 8803T-5, 9019-5, 9019-14, 9019-25, 9019-35, 9019-45, 9019-26, 9019-27, 9019-250, 3207-45, 9019-30, 8803-T10.

1862 Logging Empire: Same as 1860, but with additional track and building.

1892 J.C. Penney Logging Empire: Same as 1862.

1893 Toys-R-Us Logging Empire: Same as 1862, but with special decal sheet.

79N98765C: 8601 locomotive, ATSF slope-back tender, log dump car, crane car, boxcar, caboose, plastic log loader building, barrel loader building, four plastic figures, four plastic logs, twelve 5013s, six 5018s, 5020.

1979
LIONEL CATALOGUE SETS

1864 SANTA FE DOUBLE DIESEL: 8861 diesel, 8862 dummy, 9035, 9018, 9033, 9014, 9058, 2717, eight 5013s, six 5018s, transformer, 2905.

1865 CHESAPEAKE FLYER: 8800 locomotive and tender, 9036, 9017, 9035, 9018, 9058, 2717, 2180, eight 5013s, six 5018s, 2905, transformer.

1866 GREAT PLAINS EXPRESS: 8854 diesel, 9417, 9036, 9121, 9011, 9140, 9057, 2717, ten 5013s, seven 5018s, 5027, transformer.

1960 MIDNIGHT FLYER: 8902 locomotive, 8902T, 9339, 9340, 9341, eight 5013s, two 5018s, DC power pack, 2905.

1962 WABASH CANNONBALL: 8904 locomotive and tender, 9016, 9035, 9036, 9080, eight 5013s, four 5018s, AC transformer, 2905.

1963 BLACK RIVER FREIGHT: 8903 locomotive and tender, 9136, 9016, 9026, 9077, 2717, eight 5013s, six 5018s, DC power pack, 2181, 2180, manumatic uncoupler, 2905.

1964 RADIO CONTROL EXPRESS: 8901 locomotive and tender, boxcar, gondola, operating dump car, work caboose, log loading mill, barrel loader, ten 5113s, 5027. Shown in the Toy Fair catalogue but never manufactured.

1965 SMOKEY MOUNTAIN LINE: 8905 locomotive, operating dump car, gondola, bobber caboose, 2180, eight 5013s, two 5018s, DC power pack.

1970 THE SOUTHERN PACIFIC LIMITED: 8960 diesel, 8961, 9313, 9881, 9732, 9315, 9320, 9316.

1971 QUAKER CITY LIMITED: 8962 diesel, 9882, 9332, 9331, 9338, 9336, 9734, 9231.

OTHER 1979 SETS

1960 Midnight Flyer: 8902 locomotive, 8902T, 9339, 9340, 9341.

1962 Wabash Cannonball: 8904 locomotive, 8904T (1130T-type), 9036, 9035, 9016, 9346.

1963 Rio Grande: 8903.

1990 Mystery Glow Midnight Flyer: Same as 1960, but with glow decals, road signs and barrel loader.

1991 Wabash Deluxe Express: 8904 locomotive, 8906T (1130T-type), 9325, 9035, 9346, barrel loader, short bridge, graduated trestle set, billboards, telephone poles.

1993 Toys-R-Us Midnight Flyer: Same as 1960, except 9365 instead of 9339.

1980
LIONEL CATALOGUE SETS

1050 NEW ENGLANDER: 8007 locomotive, 8007T, 9036, 9140, 9035, 9346, eight 5013s, four 5018s, telephone poles, manumatic uncoupler, 2905, 4060, DC power pack.

1052 CHESAPEAKE FLYER: 8008 locomotive, 8008T, 9037, 9036, 9017, 9038, 9381, 2717, 2180, eight 5013s, six 5018s, 4060, 2905.

1053 THE JAMES GANG: 8005 locomotive, 8005T, 9306, 9305, 9541, 2784, four plastic figures, six telephone poles, eight 5013s, four 5018s, DC power pack, 2905.

1070 THE ROYAL LIMITED: 8061 diesel, 9818, 9234, 9329, 9432, 9344, 9328.

1071 MID ATLANTIC LIMITED: 8063 diesel, 9370, 9369, 9433, 9233, 9371, 9372.

1072 CROSS COUNTRY EXPRESS: 8066 diesel, 9374, 9232, 9428, 9373, 9379, 9309, 2303, eight 5013s, six 5018s, 4060, 2905.

1960 MIDNIGHT FLYER: 8902 locomotive, 8902T, 9339, 9340, 9341, DC power pack, eight 5013s, two 5018s, 2905.

1963 BLACK RIVER FREIGHT: 8903 locomotive, 8903T, 9011, 9140, 9026, 9077, 2717, telephone poles, road signs, manumatic uncoupler, eight 5013s, six 5018s, DC power pack, 2905.

TEXAS & PACIFIC DIESEL: 8067 diesel, 9379, 9140, boxcar, flatcar with fences, 9039, four 5018s, eight 5013s, telephone poles, road signs 4-4060, 2905. Catalogued but never manufactured.

1981
LIONEL CATALOGUE SETS

1050 NEW ENGLANDER: 8007 locomotive, 8007T, 9036, 9140, 9035, 9346, eight 5013s, four 5018s, telephone poles, manumatic uncoupler, 2905, DC transformer.

1053 THE JAMES GANG: 8005 locomotive, 8005T, 9306, 9305, 9541, 2784, four plastic figures, six telephone poles, eight 5013s, four 5018s, DC power pack, 2905.

1072 CROSS COUNTRY EXPRESS: 8066 diesel, 9374, 9232, 9428, 9373, 9379, 9309, 2303, eight 5013s, six 5018s, 2905, DC transformer.

1150 L.A.S.E.R. TRAIN: 8161 diesel, 6504, 6505, 6507, 6506, L.A.SE.R. train play mat, eight 5013s, four 5018s, DC power pack, 2905.

1151 UNION PACIFIC THUNDER FREIGHT: 8102 locomotive, 8102T, 9017, 9018, 9035, 6432, eight 5013s, six 5018s, 2717, 2180, AC transformer, 2905, manumatic uncoupler.

1154 READING YARD KING: 8153 diesel, 9448, 6200, 6300, 9378, 6420, eight 5013s, four 5018s, AC transformer, 2905, manumatic uncoupler.

1158 MAPLE LEAF LIMITED: 8152 diesel, 6103, 9440, 9441, 6305, 6508, 6433.

1160 GREAT LAKES LIMITED: 8151 diesel, 9384, 9437, 9436, 9386, 9385, 9387.

1960 MIDNIGHT FLYER: 8902 locomotive, 8902T, 9339, 9340, 9341, DC power pack, eight 5013s, two 5018s, 2905.

1963 BLACK RIVER FREIGHT: 8903 locomotive, 8903T, 9011, 9140, 9026, 9077, 2717, telephone poles, road signs, manumatic uncoupler, eight 5013s, six 5018s, DC power pack, 2905.

OTHER 1981 SETS

1159 Toys-R-Us: 9388.

1982
LIONEL CATALOGUE SETS

1053 JAMES GANG: 8005 locomotive, 8005T, 9306, 9305, 9541, 2784, four plastic figures, six telephone poles, eight 5013s, four 5018s, DC power pack, 2905.

1150 L.A.S.E.R. TRAIN: 8161 diesel, 6504, 6505, 6506, 6509, L.A.S.E.R. train play mat, eight 5013s, four 5018s, DC power pack, 2905.

1151 UNION PACIFIC THUNDER FREIGHT: 8102 locomotive, 8102T, 9017, 9018, 9035, 6432, eight 5013s, four 5018s, DC power pack, 2905.

1154 READING YARD KING: 8153 diesel, 9448, 6200, 6300, 6509, 6420, eight 5013s, four 5018s, AC transformer, 2905, manumatic uncoupler.

1155 CANNONBALL FREIGHT: 8902 locomotive and tender, 9035, 9033, 9341, play mat, manual barrel loader, two 2710s, 2180, 2181, DC power pack, eight 5013s, four 5018s, 2905.

1252 HEAVY IRON: 8213 locomotive and tender, 9031, 9339, 9020, 9077, 2180, 2309, eight 5013s, four 5018s, AC transformer, 2905.

1253 QUICKSILVER EXPRESS: 8268-8269 Alco AA diesel pair, 7200, 7201, 7202, 2311, eight 5013s, four 5018s, AC transformer, 2905.

1254 BLACK CAVE FLYER: 8212 locomotive and tender, short gondola, boxcar, caboose, play mat, die-cut cave scene, DC power pack, 2905, eight 5013s, two 5018s.

1260 THE CONTINENTAL LIMITED: 8266 diesel, 9461, 9738, 6106, 7301, 6202, 6900.

OTHER 1982 SETS

1264 Nibco Express: 8182 diesel, 9033, 9035, 6482, two special billboards.

Number Unknown Toys 'R Us Heavy Iron: 8213 locomotive, 1130T, 9020, 9013, 7912, 9077.

1983
LIONEL CATALOGUE SETS

1252 HEAVY IRON: 8213 locomotive and tender, 9031, 9339, 9020, 9077, 2180, 2309, eight 5013s, four 5018s, AC transformer, 2905.

1253 QUICKSILVER EXPRESS: 8268 diesel, 8269 diesel, 7200, 7201, 7202, 2311, eight 5013s, four 5018s, AC transformer, 2905.

1351 BALTIMORE & OHIO: 8315 locomotive and tender, 7217, 7215, 7216, station platform, five telephone poles, eight 5013s, six 5018s, DC power pack, 2905.

1352 ROCKY MOUNTAIN FREIGHT: 8313 locomotive and tender, 9020, 7909, 6430, eight 5013s, four 5018s, playmat, DC power pack, 2905.

1353 SOUTHERN STREAK: 8314 locomotive and tender, 6207, 7902, 6104, 6434, five telephone poles, 2180, 2717, eight 5013s, six 5018s, DC power pack, manumatic uncoupler, 2905.

1354 NORTHERN FREIGHT FLYER: 8375 diesel, 6206, 6522, 9399, 9236, 6428, 2311, 2309, 2181, 2180, twelve 5013s, seven 5018s, 5020, AC transformer, 2905.

1355 COMMANDO ASSAULT TRAIN: 8377 diesel, 6561, 6562, 6564, 6435, play mat, eight 5013s, two 5018s, figures, operating supply depot kit, DC power pack, 2905.

1361 GOLD COAST LIMITED: 8376 diesel, 9290, 9468, 6357, 9888, 6114, 6904.

1984
LIONEL CATALOGUE SETS

1351 BALTIMORE & OHIO: 8315 locomotive and tender, 7217, 7215, 7216, passenger station platform, five telephone poles, eight 5013s, six 5018s, DC

power pack, 2905.

1352 ROCKY MOUNTAIN FREIGHT: 8313 locomotive and tender, 9020, 7909, 6430, eight 5013s, four 5018s, playmat, DC power pack, 2905.

1353 SOUTHERN STREAK: 8314 locomotive and tender, 6207, 7902, 6115, 6434, five telephone poles, 2180, 2717, eight 5013s, six 5018s, DC power pack, 2905, manumatic uncoupler.

1354 NORTHERN FREIGHT FLYER: 8375 diesel, 6206, 9236, C&NW coal dump car, C&NW searchlight car, Illinois Central hopper, 2311, 2309, 2181, 2180, twelve 5013s, seven 5018s, 5149, 5020, AC transformer, 2905.

1355 COMMANDO ASSAULT TRAIN: 8377 diesel, 6561, 6562, 6564, 6435, play mat, eight 5013s, two 5018s, figures, operating supply depot kit, DC power pack, 2905.

1402 CHESSIE SYSTEM: 8402 locomotive and tender, 6312, 7401, 6211, Chessie square window caboose, five telephone poles, 2180, eight 5013s, four 5018s, transformer, 2905, manumatic uncoupler.

1403 REDWOOD VALLEY EXPRESS: 1983 locomotive and tender, flatcar with fences, crane car, log dump car, square window caboose, barrel loader kit, five telephone poles, 2180, eight 5013s, four 5018s, DC power pack, 2905, manumatic uncoupler.

1451 ERIE LACKAWANNA LIMITED: 8458 diesel, 6210, 7303, 9474, 6118, 6524, 6906.

1985
LIONEL CATALOGUE SETS

1353 SOUTHERN STREAK: 8314 locomotive and tender, 6207, 7902, Southern hopper, 6434, five telephone poles, 2180, 2717, eight 5013s, six 5018s, DC power pack, 2905, manumatic uncoupler.

1354 NORTHERN FREIGHT FLYER: 8375 diesel, gondola, 6113, 6522, 9236, 9399, maintenance caboose, semaphore, crossing gate, 2180, twelve 5013s, seven 5018s, 5020, AC transformer, 2905.

1402 CHESSIE SYSTEM: 8403 locomotive and tender, stock car, tank car, gondola, 6485, five telephone poles, 2180, eight 5013s, four 5018s, transformer, 2905, manumatic uncoupler.

1403 REDWOOD VALLEY EXPRESS: 4-4-0 locomotive and tender, flatcar with fences, crane car, log dump car, square window caboose, barrel loader kit, five telephone poles, 2180, eight 5013s, four 5018s, DC power pack, 2905, manumatic uncoupler.

1501 MIDLAND FREIGHT: 8512 locomotive, 6258, 6576, 6150, AT&SF bobber caboose, eight 5013s, two 5018s, five telephone poles, DC power pack, 2905.

1502 YARD CHIEF: 8516 locomotive and tender, 6325, 9247, 6127, 6260, 6916.

1552 BURLINGTON NORTHERN LIMITED: 8585 diesel, 6234, 6235, 6236, 6237, 6238, 6913.

OTHER 1985 SETS

1594: Information Requested.

Number Unknown Sears Centennial: Identical to 1984-1985 Chessie System regular catalogue set, except Chessie short stock car is replaced by special edition Sears Centennial 027-style short boxcar. Sears catalogue number is 95339C.

NORTH OF THE BORDER
THE PARKER BROTHERS CONNECTION
By Glenn Halverson

When you are a new company just putting your wares out for sale, it is only natural for you to ask where your markets may be. It is even more true that if you have taken over a struggling concern, you seek to expand your horizons a bit. That is just what the new makers of Lionel Trains tried to do as the Fundimensions team first began its struggle to rebuild a market fallen into stagnation.

It is important to remember that the Lionel Corporation, despite its sale of trains the world over, was for most of its tenure a family-held firm. That meant a limitation of marketing to the abilities of the family itself, especially after the untimely death of Arthur Raphael, the Lionel Corporation's most skillful marketer, in the early 1950s. Inevitably, the lack of a firm marketing policy helped to drag the Lionel Corporation into poor decisions which meant its ultimate demise as a manufacturer of toy trains. Raphael would have gagged at the sight of the ill-advised Girls' Train of 1957 and 1958, just a few years after he had passed on.

For Fundimensions, the question was how to take advantage of the many resources of its parent company, General Mills, which has contacts and divisions all over the world. One place thought likely for marketing was Canada, and the Parker Brothers toy firm seemed a natural outlet for the new line of trains in that country.

According to Fran Mauti, the Director of Customer Relations at Parker Brothers in Canada, the firm distributed Fundimensions trains between 1970 and 1974. Fundimensions train products were packaged in bilingual boxes, French as well as English, because the trains were intended only for the Canadian market. These trains were not featured in the regular Parker Brothers toy catalogues; rather, Parker Brothers imported catalogues from the United States and listed the Fundimensions trains on its own price sheets for dealers.

Most of the trains marketed by parker Brothers were identical to contemporary Fundimensions American products, but a few items were not — and that is where the special interest in the Canadian distribution lies. Some of these trains, such as the 8031 Canadian National GP-9 with large metal or all-plastic railings, the maroon Canadian National gondola and the tuscan Grand Trunk caboose, were never marketed in the United States and are thus very hard to find here. Most of the Parker Brothers efforts were aimed at large department store accounts, such as Simpson-Sears, Ltd., the Canadian subsidiary of Sears, Roebuck & Co.

The trains distributed by Parker Brothers in Canada for separate sale come in boxes which are similar to the regular Fundimensions Type I boxes. However, as a rule the cellophane window in these boxes is much smaller, the "whirlpool" Parker Brothers logo is present and the boxes are bilingual. When compared to Fundimensions' success in the United States, the Canadian venture was not nearly as successful. The marketing efforts were not aggressive, so not very many sets and individual sale items were distributed in Canada, and as a result these trains are very difficult to find.

In 1971, Fundimensions put out a special train catalogue for the Parker Brothers distribution. This catalogue came in two forms: a regular 8 1/2" x 11" version somewhat similar to the American catalogue and a smaller size catalogue which represents real production more accurately. The Canadian sets and individual cars are preceded in number by a "T" prefix instead of the universally ignored "6" prefix Fundimensions uses for American distribution.

We have listed the following sets by set number and name. Reader comments, corrections and/or additions requested. Most of the individual rolling stock and accessory pieces found in the American catalogue were also sold as separate sale items in Canadian Parker Brothers-marked boxes. Clearly, the original box adds quite a bit of value to the car!

1971

T-1171 CANADIAN NATIONAL STEAM LOCOMOTIVE: 8040 locomotive, 9143, 9065, eight 5013s, two 5018s, CTC, T-4045, wires, instructions.

T-1172 YARDMASTER: 8010 diesel, 9141 or 9143, 9010 or 9011, 9061, eight 5013s, four 5018s, mechanical uncoupler, CTC, T-4045, wires, instructions.

T-1173 GRAND TRUNK AND WESTERN: 8041 or 8042 locomotive and tender, 9143, 9012, 9020 or 9022, 9062 or 9063, eight 5013s, six 5018s, CTC, T-4045, smoke fluid, wires, instructions.

T-1174 CANADIAN NATIONAL: 8031 diesel, 9012, 9120, 9040, 9143, 9065, twelve 5018s, eight 5013s, T-5020, CTC, T-4045, wires, instructions.

1972-1973

T-1173 GRAND TRUNK AND WESTERN: 8041 or 8042 locomotive and tender, 9143, 9012, 9020 or 9022, 9062 or 9063, eight 5013s, six 5018s, CTC, T-4045, smoke fluid, wires, instructions.

T-1174 CANADIAN NATIONAL: 8031 diesel, 9013, 9120, 9703, 9143, 9065, twelve 5018s, eight 5013s, T-5020, CTC, T-4045, wires, instructions.

T-1272 YARDMASTER: 8111 diesel, 9300, 9136, 9013, 9025 or 9061, eight 5013s, four 5018s, mechanical uncoupler, 25-watt Trainmaster transformer.

T-1273 SILVER STAR: 8203 locomotive and tender, 9136, 9013, 9020, 9062, twelve 5013s, four 5018s, 5020, mechanical uncoupler, 4150.

T-1280 KICKAPOO VALLEY & NORTHERN: 8200 locomotive, operating dump car, 9020, 9067, eight 5013s, two 5018s, 25-watt Trainmaster transformer. Colors of freight cars appear to differ from American production.

SERVICE STATION SETS
By Emil C. Vatter and Emil C. Vatter, Jr.

EDITOR'S NOTE: The authors have written extensively for the publication of the Lionel Collectors' Club of America, **The Lion Roars.** (This article first appeared in the October 1980 issue of that publication, and the authors have since sent us additional information and corrections to it.)

From 1971 to 1978 Lionel issued a yearly Service Station Set. The purpose of this set was to give authorized service stations a special set to sell. With the advent of uncatalogued collector sets in 1979, the practice was discontinued. Fundimensions apparently felt that dealers were splitting up the sets and that the larger dealers, who were not necessarily authorized service stations, were cornering the market on the sets.

Both the 1971 and the 1972 sets have aroused controversy because their existence has been questioned. In fact, service station sets were made in both years. I vaguely remember seeing a 1972 set, and I have a picture of this set and its set box from a fellow collector. All the items from these two sets were subsequently available on the open market, which has created the difficulty.

Most collectors agree that the 1973 Canadian Pacific set is the most prized, followed by (in my opinion) the 1977 Budd set and the 1974 Rio Grande set.

At the end of this article is a list of all Service Station Sets. The reader will notice that many cars were catalogued separately in later years. I have heard that there are differences between set cars and those available separately. (This has been confirmed by several collector observations — ed.)

Some interesting observations on Service Station Sets:

(a) Some cars were sold separately but never catalogued. Examples: 9113 Norfolk & Western gray hopper, 9626 Erie Lackawanna boxcar and 9138 Sunoco tank car. Since none of these are hard to find, Lionel must have produced them in large quantities.

(b) Some cars, though catalogued the next year, are hard to find: 9723, 9724 and 9166. Perhaps Lionel never ran them again, and those available came from broken sets.

(c) The 1972 set was the only one with a steam engine, the 8206, which was catalogued and available for four more years. The 1971 and 1972 sets were the only ones which came with track.

(d) The 1976 set came with a green and yellow caboose, which was true to the prototype. However, it didn't match the engine, so in response to collector demand, Fundimensions later introduced a black and gold caboose to match the locomotive. (This occurred again two years later, when the Santa Fe SD-18 blue and yellow locomotive was issued with a red and black 9274 ATSF caboose. Collector demand forced Fundimensions to issue a 9317 blue and yellow ATSF caboose. Thus, the 9274 is a scarce item — Ed.)

SERVICE STATION SETS

1971: No. 1187 - 8030 I.C. GP-9 diesel, 9200, 9215, 9211, 9214, 9230, 9160, 8-0 curve, 11-0 straight, 5502 remote control section; estimated production: 1,000.

1972: No. 1250 - 8206 NYC steamer, 9111, 9707, 9709, 9151, 9710, 9162; 8-0 curved, 12-0 straight; production not known.

1973: No. 1350 - 8365 and 8366 diesels, 9113 available separately, 9723, 9724, 9725, 9165; 8469 B unit available separately; estimated production: 2,500.

1974: No. 1450 - 8464 (powered) and 8465 (dummy) R.G. diesels, 9144, 9117, 9739, 9863, 9166; set production 3000; also available separately, 8474.

1975: No. 1579 - 8555 and 8557 F3-A diesel, 9119, 9132, 9754, 9758, 9169; 8575 available separately; estimated production: 6,000.

1976: No. 1672 - 8666 GP-9 diesel, 9267, 9775, 9776, 9869, 9177; 8668 available separately, 9268; estimated production: 6,000.

1977: No. 1766 - 8766, 8767 and 8768; 8764, 8765 available separately; estimated production 5,000.

1978: No. 1868 - 8866 diesel, 9138, 9213, 9408, 9726, 9271; 8867 diesel available separately; estimated production: 6,000.

OTHER SETS

1973: No. 1387 - 8305 locomotive and tender, 9500, 9501, 9502; 9505 and 9506 available separately.

1974-75: Broadway Limited No. 1487 - 8304 locomotive and tender, 9507, 9508, 9509.

1975: Coke Set - 8473 and 9073.

1975-76: 75th Anniversary Special No. 1585 - 7500 U36B diesel, 7501, 7502, 7503, 7505, 7506, 7507, 7508.

1975: Capital Limited - 8304, 9516, 9517, 9518; 9516 available separately.

1976-77: Amtrak Lake Shore Limited No. 1663 - 8864 Amtrak Alco A diesel, 6403, 6404, 6405, 6406.

1976: Spirit of '76 - Sold individually, not as a set; 1776, 7601, 7602, 7603, 7604, 7605, 7606, 7607, 7608, 7609, 7610, 7611, 7612, 7613, 7600.

1977-78: Southern Crescent - Sold individually, not as a set; 8702, 9530, 9531, 9532, 9533, 9534.

1977-78: Mickey Mouse Express - Sold individually, not as a set; 8773, 9660, 9661, 9662, 9663, 9664, 9665, 9667, 9668, 9669, 9671, 9672, 9183.

1978-79: Blue Comet - Sold individually, not as a set; 8801, 9536, 9537, 9538, 9539, 9540.

1978-79: The Historic General - Sold individually, not as a set; 8701, 9552, 9553, 9551.

1979: Quaker City Limited No. 1971 - 8962, 9331, 9334, 9882, 9333, 9734, 9231.

1979: Farr No. 1 - Sold individually, not as a set; 8900, 7712, 9880, 9332, 9321, 9323.

1979: Congressional Cars - Sold individually, not as a set; 9570, 9571, 9572, 9573.

1979: Southern Pacific Limited No. 1970 - 8960 and 8960 diesels, 6445, 9313, 9881, 9315, 9732, 9316.

1980: Chessie Steam Special - Sold individually, not as a set; 8003, 9581, 9582, 9583, 9584, 9585.

1980: Union Pacific FARR Series 2 - Sold individually, not as a set; 8002, 9811, 9419, 9367, 9366, 9368.

1980: Cowan 100th Anniversary - Sold individually except for 9433 which was sold as part of a set; 9429, 9430, 9431, 9432, 9433.

1980: Texas Zephyr - Sold individually, not as a set; 8066, 8067, 9576, 9577, 9578, 9579, 9580, 9588.

1981: The James Gang No. 1053 - 8005 General-style locomotive and tender, 9306, 9305, 9541.

1981: Maple Leaf Limited No. 1150 - 8152 Canadian Pacific SD-24, 6103, 9441, 6508, 6305, 9440, 6435.

1981: Great Lakes Limited No. 1160 - 8151 Burlington SD-28 diesel, 9384, 9305, 9436, 9437, 9386, 9307.

1981: FARR Series 3, Great Northern - Sold individually, not as a set; 3100, 9449, 6304, 9450, 9819, 6102, 6438.

1981: Norfolk and Western Passenger Set - Sold individually, not as a set; 8100 Norfolk & Western locomotive and tender, 9562, 9563, 9564, 9565, 9566.

1981: Chicago & Alton Passenger Set - Sold individually, not as a set; 8101 locomotive and tender, 9554, 9555, 9556, 9557, 9558.

1981: Rock Island & Peoria Passenger Set - Sold individually, not as a set; 8004 General-style locomotive and tender, 9559, 9560, 9561.

1981: Fast Food Freight - Sold individually, not as a set; 6160 Burger King GP-20 diesel, 7509, 7510, 7511, 9827, 9829, 9830, 6424; note that the 1982 numbers may change.

1981: Southern Pacific Daylight - Sold individually, not as a set; 8260 and 8262 diesels, 9589, 9590, 9591, 9592, 9593.

1981: Norfolk and Western - Sold individually, not as a set; 8100 locomotive and tender, 9562, 9563, 9564, 9565, 9566.

1981: Chicago & Alton - Sold individually, not as a set; 8101 locomotive and tender, 9554, 9555, 9556, 9557, 9558.

1980: Mid-Atlantic Limited Set No. 1071 - 8063 Seaboard diesel, 9233, 9369, 9371, 9370, 9433, 9372.

1980: Continental Limited Set - Sold separately, not as a set; 8260 diesel, 9461, 9738, 6106, 7301, 6202, 6900.

Chapter XV
TRUCKS AND BOXES

FUNDIMENSIONS CONSTRUCTION PRACTICES: SOME VARIATIONS

Throughout this book, the descriptions of the rolling stock issued by Fundimensions may include phrases such as "Type IX body" or "Standard 0 Trucks". In an effort to make clear what is meant by such classifications, we often preface the particular chapter with descriptions of body, railing or other variations which apply to the cars in those chapters alone. However, it is important to recognize construction variations which affect the whole range of Fundimensions' production, even though they may not have a dramatic effect upon value. The beginning collector will soon see that these universal variations have their own stories to tell.

One good example of the intricacies of the manufacturing process occurred rather early in Fundimensions' history. The couplers on rolling stock made by Fundimensions work by a snap-in plastic armature which, when pulled down by the magnet on a remote track, opens the coupler knuckle and uncouples the car. Postwar Lionel used several different assemblies which would be either ineffective or too costly in today's train world. Therefore, Fundimensions did considerable experimenting with its uncoupling armatures. We think that at first, the company tried to glue a flat metal disc onto the plastic surface of the armature shank where it was molded into a rounded end, although we have not been able to confirm this. Then, a metal bar was glued into a recess cut into the bottom of the armature shank. A short time later, someone at the factory came up with an idea which has no doubt saved thousands of dollars for the firm. Fundimensions changed the mold of the downward shaft of the armature so that there was a hole running down the shaft tube. Then, the workers placed a simple large, chrome-headed thumb tack into the hole! This solution has worked so well that it is standard practice on even the most expensive trains made by Fundimensions. Operationally, it is just as good as the reliable metal flap on the old postwar bar-end metal magnetic trucks - and it is a great deal cheaper!

In this introduction, we will try to classify four areas which cut across all of Fundimensions' production of rolling stock: the types of trucks, the types of coupler armatures, the types of wheelsets and the types of packing boxes. For areas particular to the type of car, see the introductions to the individual chapters.

TYPES OF TRUCKS

The plastic trucks used by Fundimensions are made of Delrin, a low-friction plastic patented by the DuPont Corporation. These trucks have a gloss and an oily feel to them; furthermore, they are much more flexible and far less brittle than the styrene plastic used in postwar production. These trucks have small holes drilled part way into the frames; these are the bearings for the wheel sets, which have their wheels fixed to the axles. The needle points of the axles fit into the holes and rotate within them as the car rolls. The wear characteristics of the bearings appear to be excellent. Since the rolling surfaces of the wheels are angled to allow for a differential action around curved track, Fundimensions trucks have been far better performers than their postwar equivalents. In addition, the knuckle springs are integral to the knuckle instead of a separate metal spring, which often became dislodged in postwar trucks.

The metal trucks used by Fundimensions also show advances over their postwar counterparts. In 1973 the firm produced a marvelously well detailed truck for its scale Standard 0 Series. This die-cast truck features a bolster bar suspended from the truck frame by functional springs, just like the prototype. It has been used on many other cars because of its high quality. Fundimensions has also produced a well-detailed six-wheel passenger truck in metal; it too has been used on steam locomotive tenders, crane cars and other pieces of rolling stock.

Type I AAR TRUCKS WITH TIMKEN BEARINGS: These trucks are carry-over pieces from later postwar production, except that they are made of Delrin plastic rather than styrene. The detail on these trucks tends to be grainy and rather blurred; apparently, the postwar die used to make them was worn badly. For that reason, these trucks are found only on stock issued in 1970 through early 1972, particularly some of the 9200 Series boxcars and the earlier large hopper cars. All of these trucks are of the later, open-axle style. (The ends of the axles are visible from the bottom.)

Type II: SYMINGTON-WAYNE TRUCKS (Formerly known as Bettendorf): These trucks are by far the most common ones on Fundimensions rolling stock. For all previous editions, we (along with the entire train fraternity) had been calling these trucks Bettendorf types. That is an error. In November 1964, an advertisement appeared in the trade magazine **Modern Railroads** for the Symington-Wayne Company of Chicago. This ad clearly shows that the truck Fundimensions used for its model is the Symington-Wayne high-speed XL-70 truck. The next issue of the magazine contains a feature article on these trucks. We are indebted to Mr. Thomas Hawley of Lansing, Michigan for sending us this information; our text has been changed to the new designation. There are several variations of these trucks. Most variations have to do with the rear projection of the truck as viewed from the underside, but there are other variations in coupler shank height to compensate for the differing fastening points on varying rolling stock. All variations may be found with either a coupler shank which angles downward or a coupler shank which comes straight out from the truck frame.

Type II A: The top of the truck frame is smooth when viewed from the side. There is a small, flat, square-shaped tab at the rear of the truck when viewed from the underside.

Type II B: Identical to Type II A, except that the top of the truck frame side is not smooth; it has a projection with five rivets.

Type II C: Large, round projection on the truck rear with a flat punched hole. Smooth truck frame side.

Type II D: Identical to Type II C, except that the truck frame has the five-rivet projection.

Type II B. R. Bartelt photograph.

Type II D. R. Bartelt photograph.

Type II E. R. Bartelt photograph.

Type II E: Rounded projection on the truck rear, but much smaller than Types II C or D. The hole at the rear of the projection is raised by a peg-like structure. Smooth-sided truck frame.

Type II F: Identical to Type II E, but has the five-rivet projection on the truck frame side.

Type II G. R. Bartelt photograph.

Type II G: Medium-sized block-like square projection on truck rear, much more massive than Types II A and B. Longer, self-centering couplers. Smooth truck sides. This truck can be found most often on bay window cabooses. There may be a version with the five-rivet projection, but confirmation is needed.

Type II H. R. Bartelt photograph.

Type II H: Identical to Types II A, C or E, but coupler is a non-operating solid plastic piece. Used on inexpensive production. There may be a version with the five-rivet projection, but confirmation is needed. Note that the top surfaces of the non-operating couplers are hollowed out, while the operating ones are solid.

Type III: STANDARD 0 SPRUNG TRUCKS: Many collectors regard these trucks as the finest ever made by Lionel, postwar or Fundimensions. Except for the Delrin armature, they are entirely die-cast; they fasten to their cars with a small screw and a fiber collar. The bolster bar running across the truck is suspended from the truck side frames by two tiny coil springs on each side; these springs actually are functional. The truck is close in design to the standard freight trucks used by the Association of American Railroads for many years; like the prototypes, the construction is open, with most of the wheel surfaces showing. There are no known variations. Fundimensions uses this truck on most of its Collector series freight cars.

Type IV: WOOD-BEAM PASSENGER TRUCKS: These plastic trucks have been used on the early 9500 Series passenger cars and the short 6400 Series Amtrak 027 passenger cars. Their latest use was on the 027 passenger cars from the Quicksilver Express set. They are modeled after the old wooden-beam trucks used in the 19th Century. It is curious that Fundimensions would use such an old-fashioned truck on relatively modern passenger cars, but so it goes.

Type V: ARCH BAR TRUCKS: These plastic trucks are a carry-over from the "General" style trucks used by postwar Lionel in the late 1950s for its Civil War locomotive and passenger coaches. They were also used on the Fundimensions revival of those cars, and lately they have been used for the new Bunk Car series and the Wood-sided Reefer series. They are more sturdy than their forebears, thanks to the Delrin plastic formula, but they are more fragile than other Fundimensions trucks.

Type VI: DIE-CAST 027 PASSENGER TRUCKS: These die-cast trucks are carry-overs from the original metal trucks used on the postwar 027 passenger cars, beginning with the 2400 Series in the late 1940s. Ironically, Fundimensions bypassed these trucks when it revived the 027 passenger cars, but the firm then reissued them for use on certain pieces such as the 9307 Animated Gondola, the four-truck depressed-center flatcar and certain bay window cabooses.

Type VII: DIE-CAST 0 GAUGE PASSENGER TRUCKS: When Fundimensions revived the extruded aluminum passenger cars with the Congressional Limited cars in 1979, the firm also revived the original trucks. These four-wheel die-cast trucks feature long coupler shanks which are made self-centering by a hairspring where they meet the truck frame. They have been used in all aluminum 0 Gauge passenger cars produced since then, but nowhere else.

Type VIII: DIE-CAST SIX-WHEEL PASSENGER TRUCKS: Fundimensions introduced an entirely new passenger truck when it issued its Blue Comet set in 1978. The truck frames are die-cast, as is the coupler and its shank. As with the 0 Gauge four-wheel trucks, the couplers are made self-centering by means of a hairspring. These trucks have been used on the Blue Comet, Chessie Steam Special and Chicago and Alton passenger cars, as well as the six-wheel tenders on most deluxe steam engines since then and most of the newer crane cars. It has one operating weakness; the axles are fastened to the trucks by slide-in plastic bearings which may come loose if not periodically checked.

TYPES OF COUPLER ARMATURES

Since the beginning, Fundimensions has used a detachable armature for all its trucks. This has operating advantages over the older postwar arrangement, since the operator can often cure a stubborn coupler which refuses to close properly by simply exchanging armatures. These armatures are made of Delrin plastic; they are made to plug into two holes in the coupler shanks and can be removed by simply prying them out with one's fingernail. They feature a small tab projection for manual uncoupling. Variations involve the uncoupling shaft protruding downward from the armature.

Type I: A small, flat metal disc is simply glued onto the flared bottom of the armature shaft. Confirmation of this is requested.

Type II: A metal bar is inserted into a recess cut into the flared bottom of the armature shaft. This variety is found most often on cars equipped with the AAR trucks with Timken bearings.

Type III: A flat-headed thumb tack with a blackened point is pressed into the armature shaft. This first appears in later 1970 production.

Type IV: A chrome-plated, large, round-headed thumb tack is pressed into the armature shaft. First appearing in late 1971 production, this variety is by far the most common.

TYPES OF WHEEL SETS

As has been mentioned, Fundimensions designed a new set of wheels for its rolling stock from the outset of its production. Regardless of type, these wheels feature angled rolling surfaces to provide for a differential action around curved track. This cuts drag and rolling resistance to a minimum. The wheels are integral with the axles, which have needlepoint bearings. Since Fundimensions has subcontracted for the production of these wheel sets (a much more common practice than one may think), there have been several different types of wheel sets used over the years. The differences are found for the most part in the

inside of the wheel surfaces. So far, we have identified seven varieties:

Type I: Blackened wheels and axles, deeply recessed inner wheel section with thick outer rim on inside surface stamped "LIONEL MPC". Four large round raised metal dots near junction of wheel with axle. This lettering is very hard to see on some examples because the die wore down with use. There is usually a casting mark between and just outside the circumference of two of the dots.

Type II: Same as Type I, except no "LIONEL MPC" lettering. These are clearly different from worn-die versions of Type I.

Type III: Blackened axles, shiny bronzed inner and outer surfaces, four less distinct (as opposed to Types I and II) flat metal dots near junction of wheel with axle. On some examples, there appears to be a manufacturer's mark which looks like a letter "F" extended to form a letter "C". The mark could also be a large "L" connected to a small "L" inside a slightly open rectangle.

Type III A: Same as Type III, but shiny chromed axles.

Type IV: Blackened wheels and axles, no lettering, three barely visible small flat round dots near junction of wheel and axle.

Type V: Same as Type IV, but shiny chromed axles, no dots on inside wheel surfaces. Except for axles, Types IV and V are very difficult to distinguish.

Type VI: Heavy light gray pressed powdered iron wheel (which can suffer chipped flanges with abuse), solid inner surface with one slight indentation, shiny chromed axles. Cars equipped with these wheels roll better because their center of gravity is lower. These wheels are the most common in current use.

Type VII: Black plastic wheel and axle, deep inner recess. Used exclusively for inexpensive production; will not operate track-activated accessories using insulated rails.

TYPES OF BOXES USED FOR ROLLING STOCK

Sometimes, especially with early production, it is important to know which type of box Fundimensions used for its rolling stock. A case in point is the rather limited distribution in early 1971 of the 6560 Bucyrus-Erie crane car. The Fundimensions box itself commands a substantial premium because it is critical to identifying the car. (For the full story of this mixed-up piece, see the main listings.) Sometimes Fundimensions simply packaged postwar leftover stock into the new firm's boxes, as with many accessories. Each type of box has several variations, and of course the boxes differ according to the product. Special boxes have been made for, among other items, the Walt Disney series and the Bicentennial products. However, there are only five basic types of Fundimensions boxes for rolling stock, as follows:

Type I: This box was used from the beginning until some time in early 1972. Its basic color is white; unlike its successors, it has no inner divider. It features a banner done in red and blue with the lettering, "A LIFETIME OF RAILROADING", in white. Larger boxes have a paste-on label across the right edge of the box front extending down the end flap; this label both pictures and describes the product. The product description is usually in red. The smaller boxes have no such label; instead, one or both ends may be rubber-stamped with the product description. One side of the box is blue, the other red. The

Type I, Type III, Type II, Type IV, and Type V boxes. G. Stern photograph.

back of the box has an elaborate banner with a central rectangle containing "LIONEL" in modern red typeface.

Type II: The production of this box began some time in early 1972. Much plainer than its predecessor, it has an inner divider and is thus larger and more rigid. The front of the box is red with "LIONEL" in white modern typeface. The product description on the ends may be rubber-stamped on a glued label or printed in black directly on the box. These descriptions have the prefix "6" in front of the number for the first time. Part of the sides and all of the back portray line drawings of various Lionel accessories and products in black.

Type III: This box, which was first produced some time in 1975, is still in use for rolling stock in the Traditional series. Its basic color is white; the front has "LIONEL 0 AND 027 GAUGE" in red modern typeface. The box ends follow the same pattern. The product description is either printed in black directly onto the box ends or printed onto a white label which is then glued to the box. Some of the front and all of the box sides and ends feature color photos of Lionel rolling stock, accessories and other equipment.

Type IV: This box was first used in 1978 for limited production sets; it was superseded by Type V in 1983. It is the most plain of all the rolling stock boxes. Its basic color is gold; the front has a black scrollwork logo and the wording "LIONEL LIMITED EDITION SERIES" within a black oval. There are no markings on the sides or back at all. The product description is either printed in black directly on the box or printed on a gold label affixed to the box ends.

Type V: First produced in 1983, this box is in current use for Collector Series products. It is a recreation of the older postwar box with some modern refinements. The basic color of the box is bright orange, as was postwar Lionel's basic box. Atop the front of the box is "LIONEL ELECTRIC TRAINS" in dark blue Art Deco typeface between two blue stripes on a cream background. The sides and ends of the box follow the same design, and the back of the box features a recreation of the old postwar Lionel rectangular logo in blue, orange and white. Collectors feel that this is an exceptionally handsome box, recalling as it does the glory days of the old Lionel Corporation. The product description is printed in black on a glossy orange sticker which is affixed to the box flap and matches the box color.

A NOTE ON BOX DATES

Mr. Thomas Rollo, a Milwaukee collector who has made many significant contributions to our books of late, has deciphered the dating process used on many Fundimensions boxes and, indeed, prewar and postwar boxes. This is important because it helps establish the date when a particular piece was issued. Sometimes variations in production occur which can be dated by the box dates. For example, it is quite possible to have two 9200 Illinois Central boxcars in the same style of box. Suppose one of them has the "I. C." spread apart in the black logo and the other has the "I. C." close together; this is a legitimate variation. Which one was produced first? The box dates may tell you the exact manufacturing sequence!

On many Type I and some Type II Fundimensions boxes, one of the small flaps has a symbol which looks like a clock face numbered from one to twelve. Two digits are inside the circle of numbers. To date these boxes, look at the circle of numbers; one of them will usually be missing. Then read the first of the two numbers inside the clock. The inside number designates the last digit of the year and the missing number of the clock numerals indicates the month. So, if the number "4" is missing from the clock face and the numerals inside the clock are "01", the box was made in April of 1970! The inside numerals of the Type I boxes will usually be "01" or "12". On some boxes, the die apparently broke, and there is only an indeterminate squiggle inside the clock. We believe that this represents 1972 production. The early Type II boxes may show the same type of clock face, usually with "23" or just "3".

Specific examples of this clock face dating from my own collection include a 9110 B&O Hopper in a Type I box from August of 1970, a 9161 Canadian National N5C Caboose in a Type I box with a smashed die, probably made in February, July or September of that year (three numbers are missing from the clock) and a 9214 Northern Pacific boxcar in a Type II box dated August 1972. This last example is revealing because the 9214 car was first made the year before; thus, my particular car is a late production model. Some of the later boxes can be dated in a similar fashion. There are some Type II and Type III boxes which just have two numbers on the flap — a single digit and a double digit. The single digit is the month and the double digit the year. Other boxes feature a variation of the clock face. There is a circle of numbers surrounding a company logo "P" with a dot in its middle. Below the clock face is the word "MENTOR" and a two-digit number corresponding to the year. Thus, I have a 9213 Minneapolis and Saint Louis hopper car whose box was made in January or February of 1977. This car was not produced until 1978, so it follows that you cannot always date the car by its box.

Unfortunately, not all boxes can be dated. The Type II, III and IV boxes marked "STURGIS DIVISION" have no discernible dating method. However, even some of the latest boxes have date marks. My 7522 New Orleans Mint Car shows evidence of an entirely new dating system. On the flap of this box, there is a row of numbers from "2" to "12" to the left of a corporate symbol. Below that are the numbers "85 86 87". This box must be read differently from the clock types. The missing number of the series "1" to "12" gives the month of manufacture, while the number immediately before the listed years gives the year. Thus, the box for the 7522 was made in January 1984, some time before the car came out in June 1985, but corresponding to the date stamp on the car! (All Fundimensions cars have a built date which shows the time of first production.) This raises an interesting question. Was the car made and then stored away for a year and a half before it was issued to dealers? My 5724 Pennsylvania bunk car has an entirely different dating system. Below the word "FEDERAL" are two small numbers. One is "83", which should be the year the box was made. Just below it in microscopic print is "10", which should be the month. There is also a part number: "705713200". The presence of "5713" in that part number indicates that this box was first designed for wood-sided reefer 5713, a Cotton Belt reefer first made in 1983. It was also designed to accommodate successive cars in that series. Apparently, only the later Type V boxes have been dated in this fashion.

As a point of interest, it should be noted that the brown corrugated boxes used to pack many prewar and postwar Lionel accessories and locomotives can be dated just as precisely. Every one of these boxes has a circular testing seal. Beneath this seal, you may find a single digit, a double digit or the entire year printed. (In the case of the single digit, it isn't too hard to deduce the decade of manufacture!) The month dating can be done in one of two ways. There may be a row of numbers from "1" to "12" printed around the disc. Let's assume that you see the numbers "5" through "12". In that case, the box was made in the month preceding the earliest digit; "4" would correspond to April. The other method uses a series of dots or stars around the circle on either side of the date. Count them up, and you will have the month. Eight dots would mean that the month of manufacture was August. I have seen transformer boxes dated in this way as early as 1921! Thanks to this information, I also know that my 1038 transformer was made in April 1940, my 2046 locomotive in August of 1950 and my ZW transformer in March of 1954.

Perhaps box dating is a relatively small matter for now. However, further research might uncover more information about the manufacturing process used by Lionel and Fundimensions, and even tell us about actual production figures. For that reason, we hope that many of you will add your own observations to this relatively new field for subsequent editions.

INDEX

Code	Pg	Code	Pg	Code	Pg	Code	Pg	Code	Pg	Code	Pg	Code	Pg	Code	Pg	Code	Pg	Code	Pg	Code	Pg	Code	Pg	Code	Pg
8304	60	8552	48	8771	51	9035	91	9143	152	9231	135	9327	159	9405-C	97	9466-C	105	9574	171	9712-C	108	9774-C	116	9834-C	118
8304	61	8553	48	8771-C	27	9036	157	9143-C	151	9231-C	125	9328	135	9406	97	9467	100	9574-C	166	9713	107	9775	115	9835	117
8305	61	8554	48	8772	51	9035-C	29	9144	152	9232	164	9328-C	127	9406-C	98	9467-C	105	9575	171	9713-C	108	9775-C	116	9835-C	118
8306	61	8555	48	8773	51	9035-C	90	9145	93	9233	164	9329	176	9407	97	9468	101	9576	171	9714	107	9776	115	9836	117
8307	61	8555-C	44	8773-C	103	9037	91	9145	177	9233-C	163	9329-C	175	9407-C	98	9468-C	105	9577	171	9714-C	108	9776-C	118	9836-C	118
8308	61	8556	48	8774	51	9037-C	90	9146	157	9234	164	9330	74	9408	97	9469	101	9578	171	9715	107	9777	115	9837	117
8309	61	8557	48	8774-C	22	9038	72	9147	157	9234-C	162	9331	159	9408-C	98	9470	101	9579	171	9715-C	108	9777-C	118	9837-C	118
8310	61	8557-C	44	8775	51	9039	157	9148	157	9235	176	9331-C	158	9411	98	9470-C	105	9580	171	9716	107	9778	115	9840	118
8311	61	8558	48	8775-C	22	9040	91	9149	164	9236	176	9332	176	9412	97	9471	101	9581	171	9716-C	108	9778-C	116	9841	118
8313	61	8558-C	34	8776	51	9040-C	90	9150	157	9237	95	9332-C	175	9412-C	98	9471-C	105	9582	171	9717	107	9779	115	9842	118
8314	61	8559	48	8777	51	9041	91	9150-C	155	9238	173	9333	164	9413	97	9472	101	9583	171	9717-C	109	9780	115	9843	118
8315	61	8560	48	8778	51	9041-C	90	9151	157	9239	135	9333-C	163	9413-C	98	9472-C	105	9584	171	9718	107	9780-C	116	9849	118
8315-C	54	8561	48	8779	51	9042	92	9152	158	9241	173	9334	159	9414	97	9473	101	9585	171	9718-C	109	9781	115	9850	119
8350	43	8562	48	8800	64	9042-C	90	9153	158	9245	176	9336	152	9414-C	98	9473-C	105	9588	171	9719	108	9781-C	116	9851	119
8351	43	8563	48	8801	64	9043	92	9154	158	9247	176	9336-C	151	9415	97	9474	101	9589	171	9719-C	109	9782	115	9852	119
8351-C	43	8563-C	41	8801-C	63	9043-C	90	9155	158	9250	159	9338	74	9415-C	98	9475	101	9590	171	9720	108	9782-C	117	9853	119
8352	43	8564	48	8803	64	9044	92	9156	158	9250-C	155	9338-C	71	9416	97	9476	101	9591	171	9721	108	9783	115	9854	119
8353	46	8564-C	25	8850	52	9045	92	9157	164	9259-C	125	9339	96	9416-C	99	9480	101	9592	171	9723	108	9783-C	117	9854-C	118
8353-C	19	8565	48	8850-C	36	9045-C	90	9158-C	155	9259X	135	9340	152	9416-C	99	9481	101	9593	171	9723-C	109	9784	115	9855	119
8354	46	8566	48	8851	52	9046	92	9158	164	9260	73	9341	135	9417	97	9482	101	9594	171	9724	108	9784-C	117	9856	119
8355	46	8566-C	45	8851-C	45	9046-C	91	9159	158	9260-C	71	9344	159	9417-C	99	9483	101	9595	171	9724-C	109	9785	115	9858	119
8356	46	8567	48	8852	52	9047	92	9160	130	9261	73	9344-C	158	9418	97	9484	101	9596	171	9725	108	9785-C	117	9859	120
8357	46	8567-C	45	8852-C	45	9048	92	9161	132	9262	73	9345	176	9418-C	99	9500	168	9598	171	9725-C	110	9786	116	9860	120
8357-C	19	8568	48	8854	52	9048-C	91	9162	132	9262-C	71	9346	135	9419	98	9501	168	9600	101	9726	108	9786-C	117	9861	120
8358	46	8568-C	45	8854-C	22	9049	92	9163	132	9263	73	9347	158	9419-C	99	9502	168	9601	101	9726-C	110	9787	116	9862	120
8359	46	8569	49	8855	52	9050	157	9165	132	9263-C	71	9348	176	9420	99	9503	168	9602	101	9727	108	9787-C	117	9863	120
8359-C	18	8570	49	8855-C	30	9050-C	154	9166	132	9264	73	9349	96	9420-C	99	9504	168	9603	101	9727-C	110	9788	116	9864	120
8360	46	8571	49	8857	52	9051	157	9167	132	9265	73	9349-C	75	9421	98	9505	168	9604	102	9728	108	9789	116	9866	120
8361	46	8571-C	26	8857-C	27	9051-C	154	9168	132	9265-C	71	9351	177	9421-C	99	9506	168	9605	102	9728-C	110	9801	116	9867	120
8361-C	41	8572	49	8858	52	9052	92	9169	132	9266	73	9352	164	9422	98	9507	168	9606	102	9729	108	9802	116	9868	120
8362	46	8573	49	8859	52	9053	92	9170	132	9267	73	9352-C	163	9422-C	99	9508	168	9607	102	9729-C	110	9803	116	9869	120
8362-C	41	8573	50	8859-C	35	9053-C	91	9171	132	9268	135	9353	158	9423	98	9509	168	9608	102	9730	109	9805	116	9870	120
8363	46	8573-C	25	8860	52	9054	92	9172	132	9268-C	125	9353-C	158	9423-C	99	9510	168	9610	102	9730-C	110	9806	116	9871	121
8363-C	44	8575	49	8861	52	9054-C	91	9173	132	9269	135	9354	158	9424	98	9511	168	9611	102	9731	109	9807	116	9872	121
8364	46	8576	49	8862	52	9055	151	9174	132	9269-C	125	9354-C	158	9424-C	100	9512	168	9620	102	9731-C	111	9808	116	9873	121
8364-C	44	8576-C	20	8864	52	9057	130	9174-C	125	9270	135	9355	135	9425	100	9513	168	9620-C	79	9732	109	9809	116	9874	121
8365	46	8578	49	8866	52	9058	130	9175	133	9271	135	9355-C	127	9425-C	100	9514	169	9621	102	9732-C	111	9811	116	9875	121
8365-C	44	8580	49	8866-C	23	9060	130	9176	133	9271-C	126	9356	159	9426	98	9515	169	9621-C	79	9733	109	9811-C	122	9876	121
8366	46	8581	49	8867	52	9061	131	9177	133	9272	135	9357	135	9426-C	100	9516	169	9622	102	9733-C	111	9812	116	9876-C	121
8366-C	44	8582	49	8868	52	9062	130	9177-C	125	9272-C	126	9358	74	9427	98	9517	169	9622-C	79	9734	109	9813	116	9877	121
8367	46	8585	49	8868-C	50	9063	130	9178	133	9273	135	9358-C	71	9427-C	100	9518	169	9623	102	9734-C	111	9813-C	118	9877-C	121
8368	46	8600	63	8869	52	9064	130	9179	133	9273-C	126	9359	96	9428	98	9519	169	9623-C	79	9735	109	9814	116	9878	121
8368-C	37	8601	63	8869-C	51	9065	130	9180	133	9274	135	9359-C	96	9428-C	100	9520	169	9624	102	9735-C	111	9814-C	118	9879	121
8369	46	8602	63	8870	52	9066	130	9181	133	9274-C	126	9360	96	9429	98	9521	169	9624-C	79	9737	109	9815	117	9879-C	121
8370	46	8603	63	8870-C	51	9067	130	9182	133	9276	73	9360-C	96	9429-C	100	9522	169	9625	102	9737-C	111	9816	117	9880	122
8371	46	8604	63	8871	52	9068	130	9183-C	103	9276	135	9361	96	9430	98	9523	169	9625-C	79	9738	109	9817	117	9880-C	122
8372	46	8650	49	8871-C	51	9069	130	9183	133	9276-C	71	9361	135	9430-C	100	9524	169	9626	102	9738-C	111	9818	117	9881	122
8374	46	8650-C	26	8872	52	9070	130	9184	133	9277	159	9361-C	127	9431	98	9525	169	9627	102	9739	109	9818-C	118	9881-C	122
8375	46	8651	49	8872-C	32	9071	130	9184-C	125	9277-C	158	9362	96	9431-C	100	9526	169	9628	102	9739-C	111	9819	117	9882	153
8375-C	19	8652	49	8873	52	9073	130	9185	133	9278	159	9362-C	96	9432	98	9527	169	9629	102	9740	110	9819-C	122	9882-C	121
8376	46	8652-C	45	8900	64	9075	130	9186	133	9279	159	9365	96	9432-C	101	9528	169	9660	102	9740-C	111	9820	152	9883	122
8376-C	33	8653	49	8902	64	9076	130	9187	133	9278-C	155	9365-C	91	9433	98	9529	169	9660-C	103	9742	110	9821	153	9883-C	121
8377	46	8653-C	45	8903	64	9077	130	9188	133	9280	96	9366	74	9433-C	101	9530	169	9661	102	9743	110	9822	153	9884	122
8378	46	8654	49	8904	64	9078	130	9188-C	125	9281	177	9366-C	71	9434	98	9530-C	170	9661-C	103	9743-C	112	9823	164	9884-C	121
8378-C	32	8654-C	20	8905	64	9079	72	9189	158	9282	164	9367	159	9434-C	101	9531	169	9662	102	9744	111	9824	153	9885	122
8379	47	8655	49	8950	52	9079	130	9193	158	9282-C	163	9367-C	158	9435	98	9531-C	170	9662-C	103	9744-C	112	9825	117	9885-C	121
8379-C	37	8656	49	8950-C	31	9080	130	9195	145	9283	152	9368	135	9435-C	101	9532	169	9663	104	9745	111	9826	117	9886	122
8380	47	8657	49	8951	52	9085	130	9200	93	9284	152	9368-C	127	9436	99	9532-C	170	9663-C	103	9745-C	112	9827	117	9886-C	122
8402	61	8658	49	8951-C	31	9090	93	9200-C	93	9285	164	9369	159	9436-C	101	9533	169	9664	104	9747	111	9828	117	9887	122
8403	61	8659	49	8952	52	9090-C	92	9201	93	9286	73	9369-C	158	9437	99	9533-C	170	9664-C	103	9747-C	112	9830	117	9887-C	122
8404	61	8659-C	35	8952-C	45	9106	157	9201-C	93	9287	135	9370	152	9437-C	101	9534	169	9665	104	9748	111	9831	117	9888	122
8406	61	8660	49	8953	52	9110	72	9202	93	9288	135	9371	74	9438	99	9534-C	170	9665-C	103	9748-C	113	9832	117	9888-C	122
8410	62	8661	49	8953-C	45	9110-C	70	9202-C	93	9289	135	9371-C	71	9438-C	101	9535	169	9666	104	9749	112	9833	117		
8410-C	55	8664	49	8955	52	9111	72	9203	94	9290	152	9372	135	9439	99	9536	169	9666-C	103	9749-C	113	9833-C	118		
8450-C	37	8665	49	8955-C	27	9111-C	70	9203 C	93	9290-C	151	9372-C	127	9439-C	101	9536-C	170	9667	104	9750	112	9834	117		
8452	47	8666	49	8956	52	9112	72	9204	94	9300	173	9373	158	9440	99	9537	169	9667-C	103	9750-C	113				
8453	47	8666-C	21	8957	53	9113	72	9204-C	93	9301	96	9373-C	158	9440-C	102	9537-C	170	9668	104	9751	112				
8454	47	8667	49	8958	53	9113-C	70	9205	94	9302	176	9374	74	9441	99	9538	169	9668-C	103	9751-C	113				
8454-C	20	8668	49	8960	53	9114	72	9205-C	93	9303	173	9374-C	71	9441-C	102	9538-C	170	9669	104	9752	112				
8455	47	8669	49	8960-C	28	9115	72	9206	94	9304	74	9376	96	9442	99	9539	169	9669-C	103	9752-C	113				
8458	47	8669-C	26	8961	53	9115-C	70	9206-C	93	9305	96	9376-C	91	9442-C	102	9539-C	170	9670	104	9753	112				
8459	47	8670	49	8962	53	9116	72	9207	94	9305	173	9378	176	9443	99	9540	169	9670-C	103	9753-C	113				
8460	47	8701	64	8962-C	27	9117	72	9207-C	93	9306	74	9379	152	9443-C	102	9540-C	170	9671	104	9754	113				
8463	47	8702	64	8970	53	9117-C	70	9208	94	9306	164	9379-C	151	9444	99	9541	169	9671-C	103	9754-C	113				
8464	47	8702-C	63	8971	53	9118	72	9208-C	94	9306	173	9379	164	9444-C	102	9544	169	9672	104	9755	113				
8464-C	44	8703	64	9010	69	9119	72	9209	94	9307	152	9380	135	9445	99	9545	169	9672-C	103	9755-C	113				
8465	47	8750	50	9011	69	9119-C	70	9209-C	94	9308	96	9381	135	9445-C	102	9546	169	9678	104	9757	113				
8465-C	44	8750-C	21	9011-C	67	9120	162	9210	95	9309	135	9382	135	9446	99	9547	169	9700	104	9757-C	114				
8466	47	8751	50	9012	69	9121	162	9210-C	93	9309-C	126	9382-C	127	9446-C	102	9548	169	9700-C	106	9758	113				
8466-C	44	8753	50	9012-C	67	9121-C	162	9211	95	9310	173	9383	164	9447	99	9549	169	9700-1976	104	9758-C	114				
8467	47	8753-C	36	9013	69	9122	162	9211-C	94	9311	74	9383-C	163	9447-C	102	9551	171	9700-1976-C	116	9759	113				
8467-C	44	8754	67	9013-C	67	9123	177	9212	95	9311	174	9384	74	9448	99	9552	171	9701	104	9759-C	114				
8468	47	8754-C	35	9014	161	9124	163	9212	164	9312	176	9384-C	67	9448-C	104	9553	164	9701-C	106	9760	113				
8469	47	8755	50	9015	69	9125	177	9212-C	162	9313	159	9385	152	9449	99	9554	171	9702	105	9760-C	114				
8470	47	8755-C	50	9015-C	67	9126	177	9213	73	9313-C	155	9385-C	151	9449-C	104	9555	171	9702-C	106	9761	113				
8470-C	25	8756	50	9016	69	9128	157	9213-C	71	9315	152	9386	159	9450	99	9556	171	9703	105	9761-C	114				
8471	47	8757	50	9017	151	9129	177	9214	95	9316	135	9386-C	158	9450-C	104	9557	171	9703-C	106	9762	114				
8473	48	8757-C	21	9018	69	9130	73	9214-C	95	9316-C	126	9387	135	9451	100	9558	171	9704	105	9763	114				
8474	48	8758	50	9019	161	9130-C	70	9215	95	9317	135	9387-C	127	9451-C	104	9559	171	9704-C	106	9763-C	114				
8475	48	8759	50	9020	161	9131	151	9215-C	94	9317-C	126	9388	96	9452	100	9560	171	9705	105	9764	114				
8477	48	8759-C	21	9021	130	9131-C	150	9216	177	9319	96	9388-C	91	9452-C	104	9561	171	9705-C	107	9764-C	115				
8480	48	8760	50	9022	161	9132	157	9217	94	9319-C	75	9389	164	9453	100	9562	171	9706	105	9767	114				
8481	48	8761	50	9023	161	9133	163	9217-C	94	9320	96	9389-C	162	9453-C	104	9563	171	9706-C	107	9767-C	115				
8482	48	8762	50	9024	161	9134	73	9218	95	9320-C	75	9398	174	9454	100	9564	171	9707	106	9768	114				
8485	48	8762-C	34	9025	72	9134-C	70	9218-C	94	9321	159	9399	174	9454-C	104	9565	171	9707-C	107	9768-C	115				
8500	62	8763	50	9025	130	9135	73	9219	95	9321-C	155	9400	96	9455	100	9566	171	9708	106	9769	114				
8502	62	8763-C	22	9025	162	9135-C	71	9220	95	9322	74	9400-C	97	9455-C	104	9567	171	9708-C	107	9769-C	115				
8506	62	8764	50	9026	162	9136	151	9221	95	9322-C	71	9401	97	9456	100	9569	171	9709	106	9770	114				
8507	62	8764-C	50	9027	130	9136-C	150	9222	164	9323	135	9401-C	97	9460	100	9570	171	9709-C	107	9770-C	115				
8510	62	8765	50	9028	72	9138	157	9223	95	9323-C	126	9402	97	9460-C	105	9570-C	166	9710	106	9771	114				
8512	62	8765-C	50	9030	151	9139	177	9224	95	9324	159	9402-C	97	9461	100	9571	171	9710-C	108	9771-C	115				
8516	63	8766	50	9031	151	9140	151	9225	152	9324-C	155	9403	97	9462	100	9571-C	166	9711	107	9772	114				
8550	48	8767	51	9032	151	9141	152	9226	164	9325	164	9403-C	97	9463	100	9572	171	9711-C	108	9772-C	115				
8550-C	20	8768	51	9033	151	9141-C	150	9229	95	9326	135	9404	97	9464	100	9572-C	166	9712	107	9773	114				
8551	48	8769	51	9034	72	9142	152	9230	95	9326-C	127	9404-C	97	9465	100	9573	171			9773-C	115				
8551-C	34	8770	51	9034-C	67	9142-C	150	9230-C	95			9405	97	9466	100	9573-C	166			9774	115				